PEACETIME PADRES

Vanwell Publishing Limited

St. Catharines, Ontario

Father of the Chaplain Branch, Bishop George Anderson Wells, CMG, VD.

PEACETIME PADRES

Canadian Protestant
Military Chaplains
1945-1995

❖

Major Albert G. Fowler, OMM, CD

For Greg
That the muse of
history might continue.

Al Fowler.

Vanwell Publishing Limited
St. Catharines, Ontario

For the
Protestant military chaplains
of Canada 1945-1995

First edition 1996
Printed in Canada
99 98 97 96   1 2 3 4

Canadian Cataloguing in Publication Data

Fowler, Albert G. (Albert George), 1942-
    Peacetime Padres: Protestant military chaplains,
1945-1990

Includes bibliographical references and index.
ISBN 1-55125-026-8

1. Chaplains, Military - Protestant churches.
2. Chaplains, Military - Canada. 3. Canada. Canadian
Armed Forces - Chaplains. I. Title
UH25.C2F68 1996   355.3'47'0971   C96-930779-9

CONTENTS

❖

Preface

"In the Cross of Christ I glory, Towering o'er the wrecks of time."
John Bowring, 1825

THIS IS THE STORY of the Protestant military chaplains who served in the Canadian Forces for fifty years following the Second World War and of the evolution of the Chaplain Service as a unit within the military during that time.

The activities of the clergy have always been a bit of a mystery to those outside the Church, but holy men have been in the company of armies since the beginning of time and the fundamental duties of the military chaplain have remained much the same since mediaeval times. You can read a chaplain's report from the army of General Wolfe during the attack on Quebec or from a United Nations operation in the former Yugoslavia and understand the padre who wrote it. After reading this book, you should even be able to tell if he was a good padre or if he or the organization in which he worked was missing the mark of the calling.

The relationship of the chaplain with soldiers and with their leaders was a distinctly British development which grew out of the relationship between the lord of the manor and his people. The lord was all-powerful and decided everything from what colour of clothing his people would wear to when they should form up and go to war. At home, the lord's chaplain would marry couples and baptize their children. He knew every family and each man personally. When the lord took up arms and went to war, the chaplain would go with him and his men. The chaplain did not need rank because he bore the authority of the Church, and he would address officers and men alike and in any manner he chose. He would be there when the soldiers were lonely, and he would comfort them when they were afraid. He would rejoice with them in victory, and he would console them in defeat. Should they die, he would pray for their souls and ensure that they received a proper Christian burial. Upon his return, it would be the chaplain who would tell the family, whom he knew so well, of the battle and of the fate of their loved one.

From the chaplain's perspective, the essence of his work has changed little over the centuries, save for the exigencies imposed by the times and their contemporaries' perceptions of the place of religion in their lives. During the Second World War, the chaplains who cared for the sailors, soldiers, and airmen were accepted as a worthy and necessary element of the Canadian military. Following the war, the chaplains at first worked in the reflected glory of those days, but as time passed and times changed, the credibility and the value of the chaplains were challenged both by their own civilian churches and by a changing military bureaucracy. The specific way in which the work of contemporary Canadian chaplains has evolved was rooted in the chaplaincy's wartime experiences but has been moulded by the political, economic, and cultural forces of the evolving Canadian ethos.

Under the dual demands of church and state, Canada's military chaplains nevertheless managed to survive during the fifty years since the Second World War in a country in which the average person exhibits growing indifference to both the military and the Church. The chaplaincy was integrated early on in the overall unification of the Canadian Forces, and so the chaplains were among the first to face the full implications of that process. Many traditions of the individual services, fashioned in the crucible of war, disappeared as rapidly as the stalwart men who had established them. Caught up as well in the waves of change that were washing through the civilian churches at the time—such as inter-church rivalries and the growing peace movement—the chaplains found it even more of a challenge than their civilian counterparts to establish a role for the 1970s but it was done. Then, with the demise of the Soviet empire and the West's growing realization of its own economic plight there came reductions in strength but additional peacekeeping duties. Nonetheless, the chaplains survived the pressures of the times. Those who know their contribution look upon them and their work as true symbols of Christian endeavour and as a valuable asset to the Canadian Forces.

While there is a considerable body of popular literature about the experiences of individual chaplains, there are only a few serious pieces of work on military chaplains and those relate to the experience in England and the United States. Canada's military and church historians have written very little about chaplains over the years. Official military histories give this particular group of clergy only cursory notice, and many times they fail even to mention that the chaplains were in the military at the time of the action, let alone that they were on or near the battlefield. *Strange Battleground*, the official history of the United Nations operations in Korea, offers a good example of such an oversight. And yet there has been no lack of heroes among serving chaplains as the stories in this book show. Perhaps the neglect of the chaplains is a consequence of their small numbers; perhaps it is because at the end of a war chaplains have usually returned with their parishioners to civilian life and slipped back into the national fabric. It was only after the Second World War that a core group of chaplains stayed on in Canada's armed forces to form a permanent service.

As the years passed, the chaplains of the postwar period realized that it was important to capture the history of the branch in some organized fashion before it was too late. Several books had been written on the wartime experience, but these had a limited circulation and were unknown to most chaplains. In the 1960s, there were two or three typed copies of an unpublished chaplains' manual which included several pages tracing the branch's history prior to integration. It had been written by Padre Howard Johnson with help from Padre C.H. Jensen. That manuscript was short and dated, but it was a respectable effort. The branch was in chaos around the time it was written, with Ottawa offices moving and Army, Navy, and Air Force chaplains being combined into one organization. In consequence, many important records were lost. Recognizing the danger of losing valuable materials, Lieutenant Colonel J. Cardy appealed for all concerned to forward significant files, letters, and other materials to the Directorate of History and to use the new Canadian Forces headquarters filing system to avoid confusion and delay. It was emphasized that letters should deal with only one subject, not several, and should be written according to service rules and not be personal. The response was far from overwhelming. By the mid-1970s, an even greater need was felt for a comprehensive branch history. The National War Museum was consulted when attempts were being made to include chaplain materials in the Royal Canadian Air Force Museum at Trenton, but the concern then was really with three-dimensional artifacts and nothing much happened.

The first mention of a formal attempt to write a historical narrative, with a view to publication, was in 1976. Brigadier General C.D. Nickerson, the chaplain general of the day, requested advice from the department's Directorate of History. The chaplains were not certain about what they wanted or how they would get it. They did believe that something had to be done in a hurry because fully 15 percent of the chaplains who had served during the Second World War had died between 1965 and 1975. Senior chaplains were concerned that the new generation of green-suited chaplains would soon be moving into positions of power without the benefit of wartime experience and with no written guidelines on how the job had been done in the past. The Directorate of History gave them a sympathetic hearing and advice but, as ever, was limited in manpower and funds. There was considerable discussion about the need, but no effective action.

By the 1980s, chaplains began to be worried about their image in and out of the military. Anti-military statements being made by prominent civilian churchmen led some military commanders to wonder where their chaplains stood on such questions as nuclear deterrence and the need for a traditional military. Chaplains had always believed that they were in the military to minister to the spiritual needs of the soldiers, sailors, and airmen —people who were prepared to risk all and, if necessary, to lay down their lives for their country and friends. Now, they were faced with criticism in the courts of the Church and sometimes with outright hostility. It became clear that the civilian churches really did not understand that the military chaplain was simply a civilian clergyman in uniform who ministered to the men, women, and children of the military community. It was time for the chaplains to tell their story–to capture their past.

In 1984 Brigadier General O. Hopkins, with the help of Major G.E. Peddle, rekindled the historical muse. Hopkins appealed to all serving and retired chaplains for artifacts, and Peddle constructed a new secure display case in which to keep them. A scrapbook was established to hold the many pictures that were around the Chaplain General's Office and serious discussions began about finding someone to write a history of the branch since the Second World War. Money would be required, and the Ottawa branch of the Chaplains' Association donated $50 to the cause. When the chaplains gathered at the Royal Military College in Kingston for their annual conference and retreat, they were prompted by Padres L.R. Coleman and A.E. Gans to donate $20 each, for two years, towards the establishment of a history project and the possible production of a book. The inevitable committee was formed and the chaplain general's history project was under way.

The history committee members in 1985 were Chaplains D.C. Estey, G.R. Ives, G.D. Prowse, A.E. Gans, and W.G. Shields. The committee acknowledged that a good deal of the historical paper trail was missing and perhaps gone forever. No one knew quite what they should be looking for, but letters were sent to all of the retired chaplains they could think of requesting information and support. Padre Ives consulted Professor G. Boutillier at Royal Roads Military College, who suggested that the committee begin by formulating specific questions to be asked of retirees. Requests were sent out to all serving chaplains to tape interviews with any retired men known to them and living close to their locations.

The historical pot had been stirred quite thoroughly, but results were still slow to surface. Only two chaplains responded with taped interviews of retirees, and very little other information or memorabilia was forthcoming. The committee recognized that military chaplains were busy with their normal duties and that a more focused approach would be required if the narrative was to be produced.

In 1988 it was decided that the only way to complete the project was to appoint a single individual to "do the history." Although a postgraduate student or a freelance writer was considered, who could understand a chaplain better than another chaplain? In 1989 I was tasked with preparing a book on the history of Protestant military chaplains in the Canadian Forces since the end of the Second World War. I began with studies at Carleton University which produced a master's thesis on the growth of the Chaplain Service up to 1968. After returning to my full-time job as a chaplain, I then began the long process of converting and expanding the thesis into a book.

As I have worked, the chaplains, both serving and retired, have been a major source of information–as well as inspiration and encouragement. This is their story, as they lived it and told it. Many have provided written reflections. Some thirty-seven chaplains–as well as the long-serving secretary to successive chaplains general–were interviewed under the Chaplain General's Oral History Project which I established while doing research for the book. Sincere thanks are due to all those who contributed and while all the material could not be included in the book, it is all secure in the Archives of the Chaplain General for future use.

Influential contributions were made by the late Brigadier General R.G.C. Cunningham, by Brigadier General J. Cardy, and by the chaplain general's secretary for forty-four years, Helen Bayne. Other significant contributors include K.D. Benner, G.F. Bickley, C.S. Black, G.G. Davidson, F.P. DeLong, R.H. Dobson, J. Dunn, T. Fenske, H.I. Hare, D.A. Hatfield, O.A. Hopkins, S.G. Horne, W.L. Howie, E.S. Light, C.E. MacCara, J. MacIntosh, C.H. Maclean, D.L. Martin, G.A. Milne, K.A. Minchin, C.D. Nickerson, R.C. Nunn, S.M. Parkhouse, H.R. Pike, L.R. Pocock, E.V. Porrior, G.D. Prowse, A.G. Reid, W. Rodger, P.D. Ross, D.R. Saunders, W.G. Shields, H. Todd, and A.I. Wakeling as well as others too numerous to mention. Of course, the book could never have been completed without the complete support of successive chaplains general and their staff. In particular, recognition is due to Padres D.C. Estey, S.H. Clarke, G.R. Ives, W.J. Fairlie, G.E. Peddle, F.W. Love, R. Ruggles, and, last but far from least, the successor to Helen Bayne, Barbara Zabchuk.

The other major source for this book has been archival material. This research has had some of the aspects of a treasure hunt as archives across the country were scoured for possible documents. A detailed description of these resources is to be found in the historiographical note accompanying the bibliography. A great host of people and organizations assisted in this search, and I offer them my thanks.

A considerable amount of information on the Second World War and the immediate postwar years was gleaned from the records at the National Archives of Canada. Dr. C. Christie of the Canadian Forces Directorate of History was especially helpful and encouraging as were his staff, S. Bourgeois and I. Campbell in particular. Initial academic guidance came from Dr. D. Crerar, whose excitement over the First World War chaplains was infectious, and from the church historian, Dr. G.E. MacDermid, of the Atlantic School of Theology, and continuing encouragement was provided by the principal and staff of the Department of History at Royal Roads Military College.

Thanks are due to the librarians and archivists of Queen's University, the United Church of Canada, the Presbyterian Church in Canada, and McMaster University Baptist Divinity College as well as to those of the British Columbia, Nova Scotia, and Ottawa Dioceses and the General Synod of the Anglican Church of Canada. All have dug deeply into their resources to find elusive references and have diligently sought to keep me going in the right direction.

This book is founded on my master's thesis in history, "The Growth of the Protestant Chaplain's Service in the Canadian Military 1945-1968: The Pursuit of Assumed Status," prepared at Carleton University under the supervision of Dr. B. McKillop. For the direction and wisdom gained from Dr. McKillop and his colleagues, in particular Dr. S. Mealing and Dr. R. Johnson, I will be eternally grateful.

Appreciation is also due to Vanwell Publishing of St. Catharines for taking on the publication of this project, and to editors Angela Dobler and Jocelyn Smyth and especially Marion Magee whose skill, patience, and persistence have made this humble manuscript a book. All royalties from the initial run of this book, which revert to the author, will be given to the missionary work of the churches from which the majority of the chaplains come.

Throughout the production of my thesis and this book I have been thankful for the support of my family: for the encouragement from my son John, for the patience of my wife Sheila, and for the dedication of my daughter Catherine who has checked every word of this manuscript and whose comments and questions have spurred me on to greater clarity and insight.

A.G.F. / July 1995

Chapter 1

GENESIS

❖

Every last Padre should be awarded a medal.

✝ *Brigadier C.G. Hepburn*[1]

"IT WAS NO SURPRISE," said his sister when asked to comment on Padre John Goforth's citation for bravery. "He is a quiet chap. He believes that what is to be will be. He would go on whatever happened."

Goforth was in Italy with a unit working its way north through constant rain and mud like plasticine that prevented the tanks from advancing to support the infantry. The enemy were out of food but had plenty of ammunition and were determined to hold their ground. After twenty-four hours of continuous mortar fire, a small group of Canadians found themselves up front and in trouble. All five had been wounded and were holed up in the shell of a building that was slowly being cut away by the gun fire.

Twice a stretcher party attempted to go to the rescue, and twice it was met with a solid wall of lead fired from six-barrel rocket mortars, machine guns, and rifles. In broad daylight and in full view of the enemy, Padre Goforth crossed the quarter-mile of open ground to the building. His only reason was to give first aid and spiritual support to the wounded men. For the next five hours he ministered to them physically and spiritually. At last, under the cover of darkness, relief was able to come forward.

John Goforth was indeed a brave chaplain and was rewarded for that day and others with a Military Cross. He was not alone. On all fronts during the Second World War, Canadian Army chaplains gave aid to the wounded and helped to identify and bury the dead. It was all too common to hear of a front-line padre who had crawled to where a soldier was lying wounded, dressed his wounds, helped to load him on a stretcher, and then crawled all the way back to unit lines. Overall, members of the Chaplain Service received an exceptionally high ratio of the accolades and decorations awarded during the war. By the end of the conflict over 800 Protestant chaplains had served in the Canadian military. Nine of them died, six as a result of enemy action.

GETTING THE CHAPLAIN SERVICE GOING AGAIN

To understand the position and role of the Protestant chaplaincy in Canada's armed forces in recent decades, one must begin with a brief look at the experiences of the service and its chaplains during the Second World War.

The early months of the war were a frustrating time to be a chaplain. The branch had been disbanded by the government after the First World War, and the churches had lost interest in the military. The few chaplains who had continued to serve were those associated with individual regiments or retired men who came out to preach on weekends. There was no central authority or coherence to their work. Many of the Air Force and Navy officers responding to the patriotic call of 1939 had therefore never known a real chaplain or experienced the help he could be in their unit. Even worse, there had been negative experiences with chaplains who were described as "incomprehensible on Sundays and invisible on weekdays."[2] This stereotype sometimes led to indifference and at other times to open hostility. Many officers looked upon chaplains as an unnecessary luxury.

The experience of reintroducing chaplains into the forces varied from one service to the another. Army chaplains had the best start. Padres who had served in the previous war, many of whom were decorated, were re-enrolled and placed in key positions. They were old friends who had a fair understanding of one another's capabilities. Even more important at the time, most had a solid rapport with the senior Army officers who remembered them from former battles. The Royal Canadian Navy was less welcoming. Indeed, chaplains did not receive permission to go to sea until 1942. Until then, they felt as though they were hiding ashore, where they knew that their ministry was not totally effective. Once they were at sea, their activities soon gained them a new respect, and they came to be accepted. In the Royal Canadian Air Force the senior officers wanted to do things in their own way and rejected the initial efforts from outside to establish a chaplaincy. They were allotted chaplains anyway, but it was only after a good deal of personal effort and pastoral skill that RCAF chaplains could be found wherever Canadian airmen were called to serve by the curse of war. Working solidly behind all the chaplains, but with a special interest in the Army, was the chaplain general, Bishop George Anderson Wells.

The outbreak of war in September 1939 created anxiety among some churchmen that steps be taken immediately to avoid some of the mistakes of the previous war. In the First World War a good many inexperienced clergymen had been imposed upon the military by the government, and senior appointments had sometimes been made largely on the basis of political or other connections rather than more substantive qualifications.

Immediately upon the declaration of war, therefore, the Anglican archbishop of Ottawa, the Most Reverend John Charles Roper, wrote to the minister of national defence on behalf of the Anglican primate, the Right Reverend Doctor D.T. Owen. The primate recommended that a principal chaplain be appointed for the Church of England chaplains and indicated that the church would be glad to nominate a bishop to do the job. The candidate should be a senior man with the necessary qualifications and experience.

The government responded favourably and an informal committee–which would develop into the official Inter-Church Advisory Committee on the Chaplaincy–was established. Bishop J.C. Roper joined with Dr. J.W. Woodside of the United Church, Dr. R. Johnson of the Presbyterian Church, and the Reverend J.W. Johnson, a Baptist clergyman from Montreal, to meet with the minister of national defence and the adjutant general. The group pledged the loyal support of the different branches of the Protestant Church and expressed the hope that one chaplain service would be established representing all of the Protestant groups. The committee agreed that the job of heading up the new organization should go to an experienced chaplain and senior churchman.

Meanwhile the Roman Catholic Church had been as active as their Protestant brethren. They, too, were determined that the unfortunate experience of the previous war would not be repeated. In the First World War, there had been a single chaplaincy service for all faiths, but poor leadership and a lack of sensitivity to other's practices had left a bitter legacy.[3] Indeed, in August 1939, the bishop of Quebec, J.M.R. Villeneuve, had taken advantage of a meeting with C.G. (Chubby) Power[4] to push for some say in the appointment of Roman Catholic clergy, should war be declared and a chaplain service be needed. Even before the Protestant committee had been organized, a group of Roman Catholic bishops from Ontario, speaking for their church in English Canada, had met and mapped out their plan. They insisted on their own separate organization, and they wanted Archbishop Charles L. Nelligan of Pembroke to lead it.[5]

In return for a French-Canadian vicar-general, the Roman Catholic bishops from Quebec agreed to collaborate with the efforts of their Ontario brothers and informed Prime Minister W.L. Mackenzie King of their decision on September 26, 1939.[6] On October 21, Archbishop Nelligan was appointed to lead the Roman Catholic service.[7]

This dual chaplaincy was not a surprising outcome in light of the country's cultural and religious diversity but it was unique to Canada. Elsewhere the state insisted on a single chaplain organization. The British Army had a chaplain general, who was Church of England, and under him were assistants representing the Roman Catholic, Presbyterian, and United Board Churches. In the United States the Protestant, Roman Catholic, and Jewish arms of the service also operated under one director, who was sometimes Protestant and sometimes Roman Catholic. Canada's dual organization was one of a kind.

WELLS, CHIEF OF CHAPLAINS

The Inter-Church Advisory Committee was not long in recommending that Bishop George Anderson Wells should be appointed to organize the new Protestant Chaplain Service. He had a proven record as a member of the Canadian Chaplain Service during the First World War and had been a member of the religious establishment in Canada between the wars. It would be an inspired choice. Indeed, some have said that the story of Bishop Wells is the story of the Chaplain Branch. Not everyone liked him—at times he seemed arrogant and his secretary was always fearful of him—but he was certainly the father of the revived chaplaincy.

The son of a Newfoundland fisherman, Wells first saw action as a trooper in the Boer War.[8] From those early days he remembered seeing only two chaplains, both of whom were British. One arrived late for worship and kept the soldiers sweating under the hot African sun as he preached a long and boring sermon. No one was impressed. The other chaplain galloped to join the soldiers at the front, leaped down from his horse, led some brief prayers, offered a few well-chosen words, and was gone. Everyone appreciated the message. Wells never forgot the experience or its lesson. On his return to Canada, Wells was ordained in the Church of England and, while serving in the parish of Minnedosa, joined the 12th Manitoba Dragoons.

When war was declared in 1914, Wells was among the first chaplains to go overseas with the 1st Canadian Division. Always ready for action, he was the first Canadian chaplain in France but was soon called back to England to be the senior chaplain at the large British training centre at Shorncliffe. When the 2nd Canadian Division arrived in England, Wells became the divisional chaplain. At the end of the war, he was awarded the Order of St. Michael and St. George (Companion), the 1914-1915 Star, the British War Medal, and the Mons Star.

Back in Canada, Wells served parishes in Victoria and Winnipeg and eventually was elected bishop of the diocese of Cariboo in south-central British Columbia. But his interest in the military did not diminish: he helped servicemen to adjust to civilian life, he established bursaries for their children to attend university, and when he completed a master's degree his thesis was entitled "The Effect of War on the Religious Life of Soldiers."

In September 1939 Wells's own experience as a chaplain and long-time interest in the welfare of the soldiery made him an obvious choice to create the new Protestant chaplaincy service. Once assured of the fullest co-operation of the heads of the Protestant churches and the military,[9] Wells rushed to Ottawa, reporting for duty on October 21, 1939.

Wells In Ottawa

Wells arrived in Ottawa with his files from the First World War. Making full use of his experience at war, he quickly pulled together a large corps of chaplains to serve the three branches of the forces. His first appointee and right-hand man was the Reverend Jacques Logan-Vencta, a Presbyterian who would serve as adjutant of the Canadian Army Chaplain Service. Private Charles Brownley was Wells's orderly, and a stenographer was appointed. In March of 1941 the office would add a corporal and another stenographer, Helen Bayne, who would serve successive chaplains general with great discretion until May 1985.

Wells's first job was to set up an establishment that would assure adequate coverage for all of the military groups in the field. The easy way would have been to send the serving militia chaplains overseas with their units, but these men were mostly Church of England. The branch would have to be opened up to include ministers of other denominations.

Ensuring that there would be a fair representation of the various denominations for the soldiers was, of course, a sensitive matter–one which Wells knew had not always been addressed during the First World War. From the very beginning therefore every effort was made to ensure that this issue was a constant consideration in administrative and staffing decisions and in the selection of individual chaplains. In general, Protestant chaplains were appointed at a ratio of one per 1000 soldiers of a particular denomination and Roman Catholics at a ratio of one per 500. In choosing this formula, the authorities kept in mind that many soldiers who had been listed as Anglicans were not necessarily members of the Church of England.[10] In the course of the war, chaplains were chosen from the Church of England, the United Church of Canada, the Presbyterians, the Baptists, the Standard Church of North America, the Lutherans, the Orthodox communion, and the Salvation Army. Most chaplains recognized that while they did represent a particular denomination both in themselves and in the forces, they were also acting for the wider Church in their services to the men. Thus, once they were in the service they served primarily as "Protestant" chaplains–all were of course considered to have equal status[11] and despite some doctrinal constraints,[12] they managed to do so with remarkable skill and harmony. At the end of the war Brigadier

Hepburn provided this assessment: "It is felt that on the whole the difficulties presented by the complex nature of the Protestant Communion have been happily overcome... The democratic right of every man to his own religion had been fully maintained by our service."[13] This sensitivity to the denominational issue would continue to be a hallmark of the Canadian Chaplain Service.

The constant supply of clergy with "the right stuff" and denominational sensitivity was assured by Wells through the newly constituted Inter-Church Advisory Committee on the Chaplaincy (ICAC).[14] Wells maintained a close liaison with the ICAC and sought its advice and assistance on the formation and conduct of the Chaplain Branch. The first members of the formal Inter-Church Advisory Committee were the Reverend H.H. Bingham, a Baptist; the Reverend Stuart Parker, a Presbyterian; the Reverend Harold Young from the United Church of Canada; and the Right Reverend J. Carlisle, the Anglican bishop of Montreal.

The committee felt that one of the most notable matters for its consideration was the selection of those for the highest positions, such as the principal chaplain (Protestant) in Canada and the principal chaplain (Protestant) overseas. The Army saw no problem with the senior chaplains seeking the advice of the committee, and Bishop Wells welcomed its support. He later wrote: "I feel quite sure that this committee will be of real value ... especially to the Principal Chaplain, whoever he may be, upon whose shoulders rests the responsibility of carrying on this work, as nearly as possible to the satisfaction of all concerned."[15] Once established, the system proved effective and continued through the war years.

The greatest and most immediate need for chaplains in 1939 was in the Army, and Wells dove into the work. He wanted all of his senior Army chaplains, at home and abroad, to be men with previous wartime experience. The Army, however, would not accept men under 30 or over 50 for duty overseas and would not compromise on the age limit.

ROYAL CANADIAN NAVY CHAPLAINS

Wells had only been in Ottawa for a short time when he ran into an old friend from the First World War, Admiral P.W. Nelles, who was busy trying to develop the Royal Canadian Navy. To Wells's offer of chaplains, Nelles replied that he was happy to have any and all help that Wells could give him. At the time there were 3000 sailors in Halifax and their numbers were growing. The archbishop of Nova Scotia insisted on having a full-time man to look after them, so J. Furlong, the rector of St. Mark's, the "Navy Church," was appointed. In Esquimalt the base commander indicated that the Reverend Arthur Bischlager of St. Paul's, the "Garrison Church," had been serving the base with "zeal and ability" for the three years. Wells concurred with the base commander's assessment and appointed Bischlager as its chaplain.

Wells planned for these Navy chaplains to be in the Army and hold the rank of honorary major but to come under naval control. The recommendation to give chaplains rank was actually approved by the Navy and then rescinded when the Roman Catholic chaplains objected. The new men were made members of the Canadian Active Service Force and were about to be given Army uniforms when they indicated that they would prefer to wear blazers and caps.

The first deep blue chaplains were appointed to the Royal Canadian Navy effective January 1, 1940. Right from the start, however, being required to report through both the Army and the Navy chains of command caused difficulties, and it soon became clear that the dual system simply would not work. Wells attempted to solve the problem by arranging for the chaplains to deal only with the chief of naval staff. Finally, in September 1940, the senior naval staff met with Wells to discuss the new chaplain organization.

From the very beginning, Canadian naval officers had maintained a close relationship with their British counterparts in the Royal Navy. They contended that Canadian chaplains should pattern themselves after those in the Royal Navy, especially in the areas of rank and training. Wells, however, considered the established British system to be ineffective. For example, he believed chaplains should have a rank. The Navy held firm, however, and Wells was forced to concede that the naval chaplains would not have rank. They would be classified as I, II, or III and would be accorded the respect due to a clergyman in the society of the day. As in the Royal Navy, a chaplain would wear a basic officer's uniform without rank insignia and he would live in the wardroom. However, he would have access to the mess decks and he would be considered equal in status with whomever he might meet. Like the chaplains of the Royal Navy, this would place Canadian chaplains on an equal footing with admirals and with seamen.

Promotions took place twice a year, and numbers meant that 20 percent of the chaplains could be promoted after three years of service. In theory, they would be promoted on the basis of length of service and ability. In practice, this would be a tricky matter for Wells because he had to consider denominational balance and an individual's seniority within the chaplain's denomination, as well as political and judicial naval concerns.

During the war years, the Navy chaplaincy was organized by command–Atlantic, Pacific, Overseas, Newfoundland, and Naval Divisions

–each with its own command chaplain. Most of the chaplains were appointed for duty on the east and west coasts, but some were stationed in Newfoundland and in Londonderry, Northern Ireland, to serve the men of the North Atlantic convoys. Another was located at HMCS *Niobe*, the RCN overseas command base.

While Royal Navy chaplains were busy at sea, the Canadian Navy chaplains were left ashore. There just wasn't the space on board the few small ships that Canada had in the early part of the war. With time on their hands, the chaplains volunteered to help out by censoring the mail. In September 1941 this amounted to processing 1600 pieces of mail a day, and by February 1942 that had increased to 2500 pieces a day. The average chaplain spent three hours a day, three days a week, censoring mail. Some resented this extra duty, but it was made easier by the realization that the chaplains' efforts spared the operational officers who were already working long hours of overtime. While a modern clergyman might question the ethics of censorship, it seemed appropriate given the times and the circumstances, and it did give the chaplains a personal glimpse into what the men were thinking and feeling about the war and their situation. All the same, when the fleet mail office was established in the spring of 1942, the chaplains breathed a sigh of relief. About the same time the number and size of Royal Canadian Navy ships increased and the chaplains were, at last, permitted to go to sea.

In 1942 the larger ships–cruisers and aircraft carriers–had their own chaplains. Among the first to go to sea were C.E. Hayard (HMCS *Prince Robert)*, F.H. Godfrey (HMCS *Prince Henry)*, G.L. Gillard (HMCS *Prince David)*, W. Hills (HMCS *Nabob)*, L.M. Outerbridge[16] (HMCS *Puncher)*. In addition there were three groups of destroyers, corvettes, and trawlers/frigates; each group was assigned a chaplain who moved from ship to ship. James Armstrong was the first chaplain assigned to a squadron (the North Atlantic). The squadrons of motor torpedo boats and minesweepers in the English Channel had their own chaplains. Whenever it was possible, chaplains sailed across the Atlantic with escort groups, but space for non-combatants was always at a premium.

Even after the Navy chaplains went to sea, there could never be a chaplain on every ship. Early on Wells had sought to ameliorate this problem by preparing audio recordings to assist with worship. A band would play hymns and then a confession of sin and absolution (short form) was read by Wells. Then would come the "Navy Psalm," the hymn "Eternal Father," a Bible lesson, "Abide With Me," and the blessing. The service would end with the band playing "Jesu Joy of Man's Desiring."

20

Chaplain Of The Fleet

On January 14, 1943, Bishop Wells was promoted to the rank of honorary brigadier and the chaplains had their first general–but not for long. In September 1943, an order came to remove all men from the Canadian Army who were over the age of sixty. Almost every district chaplain was a healthy and active First World War veteran, and over sixty. Wells himself was forced to retire. To replace him, the Army appointed another popular and slightly younger establishment man and First World War hero, Canon C.G. Hepburn.

Members of the Inter-Church Advisory Committee were pleased with the choice but annoyed that they had not been consulted. Quickly a conference was arranged with Chubby Power, minister of national defence for the Air. Power consulted with his colleagues for the Royal Canadian Navy and the Royal Canadian Army. Conscious of the political influence that the committee might have in the country and of the support they might draw in the civilian community around military bases, Power replied that the services were most happy to have the committee function. Nevertheless, "while advice may be solicited from the committee by any of the Ministers of National Defence, it should be understood that appointments to the Service are the responsibility of the Service affected, and are to be directed and administered through the normal Service channels."[17]

In response, H.H. Bingham wrote on behalf of the committee:

"The committee is quite conscious of the fact that there are limits to its scope, and that it has no right to interfere with the movements of Chaplains within the Services, but the committee does feel that in such an important change as that of Principal Chaplain, it might have been consulted, in order that we could give an intelligent account of our stewardship to the hundreds of thousands of communicants whom we have the honour to represent ... the function of this advisory committee ... is not to enter the field of providing for the forces when on leave or off duty ... Our function is to offer our service to the government in an advisory capacity, in assisting wherever possible to make the Chaplaincy service most efficient."[18]

On October 31, 1943, Bishop Wells, now unemployed, again ran into his old friend, Admiral Nelles, who suggested that he continue on with the Navy. "We have no such silly regulation about age affecting our officers," he commented.[19] The very next day, Wells took over the direction of the Naval Chaplain Service as chief of chaplains and as Canada's first "Chaplain of the Fleet."

In spite of objections from some naval chaplains (How could an Army chaplain ever understand the Navy?), Wells served in the Navy until the end of the war. The Inter-Church Advisory Committee believed that the place which religion and the chaplains held in the military were in no small measure due to the hard work of Bishop Wells. There were few people who knew him who did not respect him. He was the only chaplain entitled to wear the Mons Star, and he was the most decorated chaplain in the British Commonwealth when he retired on March 20, 1946.[20]

ROYAL CANADIAN AIR FORCE CHAPLAINS

In 1939, the Royal Canadian Air Force had no chaplains and no appreciation or understanding of the benefits a chaplain could bring to a unit. When Bishop Wells contacted the air member for personnel, Group Captain H. Edwards, and submitted an organizational plan, he was told that he was not needed as other arrangements were in train. Nonetheless, Wells began to appoint chaplains and placed a well-known Presbyterian churchman, John McNab, in charge of the fledgling organization.

It was decided that Wells and his Roman Catholic counterpart would continue to have overall charge of the chaplaincy but two senior chaplains, one Protestant and the other Roman Catholic, would be appointed for the RCAF and given the rank of honorary group captain. This meant that they would hold two commissions, one in the Army and one in the Air Force, but they would get only one salary. They would also get only one uniform and it would be Air Force. There would be two assistant senior chaplains who would hold the rank of acting honorary wing commander and be paid as squadron leaders. The Roman Catholic would be located in Trenton and the Protestant in Toronto. Command chaplains holding the rank of honorary squadron leader would be located with Western Air Command and at No. 1 Training Command in Trenton. Each RCAF station would have one Protestant and one Roman Catholic chaplain who would hold the rank of honorary flight lieutenant.

Wells went on to suggest that, as in the Army, there should be a Roman Catholic chaplain for every 500 personnel and a Protestant chaplain for every 1000. To qualify as chaplains, individuals had to be physically fit, have the official approval of the head of the church in which they served, and be between the ages of 30 and 50. Men who had served in the First World War would be given preference for appointments. He added that a fair distribution of religious denominations would be worked into the organization.

The RCAF continued to resent the "interference" of the Army's principal chaplain. Wells claimed that the rejection was due solely to the colour of his uniform and this was confirmed after the war by John McNab. As McNab put it: "It is doubtful that the angel Gabriel would have been successful as a Chaplain in the RCAF had he been in an Army uniform!"[21]

The first RCAF squadron to proceed overseas was 110 Army Co-operation (Toronto) Squadron, later renamed 401 Squadron. Wells recommended that the Reverend W.E Cockram, pastor of Sherbourne Street United Church in Toronto, be sent with the squadron to England as its chaplain. Cockram had served in the ranks of the infantry during the First World War and then as a pilot in the Royal Flying Corps, later the Royal Air Force. In February 1940, Cockram was commissioned and after a very brief tour at Trenton, St. Thomas, and Eastern Air Command, he sailed for the United Kingdom.

The squadron arrived in England ready to join the fray on the continent. In order to get there Cockram, now known as "Cockles," had already found a place in one of the aircraft as a rear gunner. Then it was announced that the continent had fallen into German hands and that 110 Squadron would remain in England. Because they did not have the right type of aircraft, they would spend the next few months sitting idly by while the Battle of Britain was being played out in the skies overhead–a very demoralizing experience for these eager young men.

Cockram was not about to sit down, however. His demoralized squadron needed a padre, but so did the many other Canadians who were serving in England with the RCAF at that time. A steady stream of young men was coming into the country and being integrated into the fighter squadrons of the RAF. These men were facing death on a daily basis. When one was killed or missing in action, it could take a considerable time for the British authorities to notify the Canadian government. With the permission of his commanding officer, Cockram began to travel the country, often by motorbike, seeking out the Canadians wherever they could be found and establishing a principle that later Canadian padres would work under throughout the war. His policy was to visit those places where the men faced the greatest danger and experienced the most desperate need. "Men who are facing death must be served before men who are merely lonely," he wrote. "The consolation, strength and faith of the Church must be given to those whose nerve and sinew are being tested and whose lives are daily endangered."[22] As well, hospitals had to be visited and wounded Canadians cheered. While dog fights continued in the skies over the cemetery, funeral services were conducted and the love and the power of God was declared.

At this point Bishops Wells and Nelligan made their first trip overseas. While they were out of the country, the air member for personnel directed McNab to go to Ottawa as acting principal chaplain (P). For several weeks

McNab travelled back and forth between Toronto, where he was command chaplain four days a week, and Ottawa where he worked for the other three days. When Wells returned to Canada, it was made official: McNab would be called the assistant principal chaplain (P) and would serve in Ottawa with the rank of honourary wing commander.

By the end of 1940 the first air training stations of the British Commonwealth Air Training Plan were being opened in Canada and numbers began to increase. In July 1940 there were 9440 men in No. 1 Training Command; by February 1941 there were 20,110. Chaplains were being appointed as soon as stations reached sufficient strength to justify having one. Eventually, 30 of these training stations would be staffed completely by RAF personnel, including RAF chaplains. The RAF chaplains reported to two senior RAF chaplains, one for the Church of England and one for other denominations. RCAF chaplains were also on loan to the RAF to help fill the need. The two RAF senior men came under the command and control of the principal chaplain of the RCAF.

As the year progressed, Wells discovered that personnel decisions were being made in the Air Force without any reference to himself as principal chaplain. On September 27, 1941, he refused to continue with the game that was so obviously being played and resigned from the RCAF part of his job. The Inter-Church Advisory Committee recommended that John McNab be appointed the first principal chaplain of the RCAF.

Wherever the chaplains worked, it was discovered that there was far more for them to do than just conduct the weekly church parade. There were opportunities to improve the morale of the men substantially which led, in turn, to a more efficient military force. The chaplains were proving their worth and more were required. It was decided that the Army ratio of one chaplain per 1000 men could not always apply to the Air Force. Where numbers at a station exceeded 1500, two would be appointed, and stations with over 500 personnel would be entitled to one. Part-time chaplains were appointed to smaller stations for a number of work-days proportional to the size of the station.

All the original RCAF chaplains were men of mature years and long experience in the ministry, but they knew nothing of how to be chaplains on Air Force bases. Some thought that the job would be comparable to that of an Army chaplain, but that was not the case. Army units were composed of large numbers of men nearly all of whom did the same thing at the same time. When the soldiers went into the field the chaplains could go with them. In the Air Force there were a great variety of tradesmen, all of whom were doing their own thing in separate locations and at the same time. The approach taken to ministry on one base would not work at another. RCAF chaplains soon learned to be flexible.

Chaplains overseas were given pastoral responsibility for small groups of Canadian airmen who were scattered on airfields across Britain. Some had up to 20 such locations to look after, and on good days, they could find a motorized bicycle for transportation. Roman Catholic and Protestant padres often travelled together. For a short period of time Squadron Leader R.B. Frayne had a staff car and driver which put him close to a frightening crash which he might otherwise have missed. Frayne's story–an experience he would never forget–is recounted in *The Happy Warrior*:

> The tiny slits allowed on automobile headlights in Britain during the war did no more than permit pedestrians to see the oncoming car. The glare from a flaming aircraft as it crashed earthward was by contrast a terrifying sight to Squadron Leader Frayne and his driver as they headed from one RCAF station to another.
>
> The crash took place only a few hundred feet from the airstrip and almost before it had hit Frayne was on his way to the burning spitfire. Ignoring the heat he fought his way to the unconscious pilot. With the safety belt untied the Padre was pulling the airman by the armpits out of the cockpit when the plane exploded. They found pieces of the pilot a hundred feet away; the Padre found himself several feet from the plane, stunned and badly shaken, but in one piece.[23]

In Canada, meanwhile, McNab had to deal with a senior officer who had demanded that only chaplains in their twenties should be hired for the Air Force. The officer reasoned that younger men could get more involved with the airmen on the sports field. McNab had to insist that the chaplains were being hired to give spiritual support, not to further the athletic ambitions of the stations.

A more important challenge came when another senior officer insisted on McNab hiring a particular member of the Christian Science organization and giving him the rank of honourary wing commander. When no action was taken, a fiery memo came to McNab demanding an explanation. McNab responded that the names of men recommended for the Chaplain Service normally came through their denominational headquarters to the Inter-Church Advisory Committee and not from serving members. He also noted that there were barely 200 Christian Scientists in the whole Air Force and that 500 had been set as a bare minimum for justifying the hiring of a chaplain.

Beginning in 1940 every RCAF chaplain was sent to manning school for two weeks. There, along with how to write letters acceptable to military authorities and the rules and regulations of the Air Force, he learned the basics of dress and the paying of compliments. Then he was unloosed on a station or base to sink or swim. He would be given no special privileges and his success or failure would determine whether the church was or was not accepted on that base. After June 1942, the training course was extended to one month in length and concentrated on administrative procedures. This included lectures from a senior chaplain on how to do the job. The new approach proved very effective and produced chaplains who were better prepared to go straight to work on their own bases.

Duties On The Home Front

Most of the early chaplains went straight from the introductory courses to a new station with other new officers who had no idea what the chaplain was supposed to do beyond the half-hour Sunday commitment. As a result the chaplains were not especially welcomed on the bases. They were looked upon as a kind of fifth wheel by the officers, although judgement was usually politely withheld by the men.

Very often the chaplain was made to feel most at home by the auxiliary services officer who was usually a member of the YMCA, the Canadian Legion, the Knights of Columbus, or the Salvation Army. Within a day or two he would be taken by an instructor for his first "flip" which usually consisted of as many aerobatics as the aircraft could perform. He was "given the works," and an hour later the airmen knew if he could handle it or not. The crucial test, however, would be his service of worship; it had to be brief and to seem brief. In the end it all came down to personality and character. This is what made or broke a chaplain.

Church attendance was usually voluntary at flying stations and compulsory at training bases. On many bases, church services were conducted in the recreation centre, which usually had a stage and seating for 500. At the rear was a projection booth and the office of the auxiliary services officer and a lounge for off-duty people. There would be a Gideon Bible and a piano. With any luck, there would even be someone who could play it. An order of service was laid out, but the chaplain was free to adapt it and to use the service with which he felt most comfortable. Army service books were used until March 1942 when the RCAF produced its own book with more hymns and more suitable prayers. All chaplains were required to wear clerical collars during worship, whether or not they had ever worn one before. In 1942, Air Force blue cassocks were provided for the Anglican clergy, and other clergy were issued Air Force blue academic gowns. All the chaplains were given a black scarf on which the chaplain crest was embroidered in gold: a Maltese Cross centred in a pair of wings.

The first Air Force chapel, a basement room that seated about 150, was opened in 1941 by Padre M.C. Davies at the huge and sprawling Technical Training School in St. Thomas, Ontario. The furniture was either made on the base or donated by local churches. The chapel was used for communion and other small services, and it provided a place for prayer and meditation for any who wished to use it. While the chaplains didn't lobby for chapels, the mothers of some of the trainees wrote innumerable letters to the Department of National Defence asking for suitable chapels. The defence minister for Air, Chubby Power, was annoyed to the point of responding to one complaint by asking if they realized that there was a war going on.[24] Eventually the government capitulated and 28 cheap but useful chapels were erected on RCAF bases in Canada and Newfoundland.

The other activities of the chaplain arose from his own initiatives. As he moved from workplace to workplace during the week, he got to know the men through casual conversations. If he was found to be a man of discretion, wisdom, and sympathy, he would have many men coming to him for advice and counselling. It was important for the chaplain to visit the unit lines and to be available to personnel at all hours. On many stations, the chaplain was required to speak to each new class of trainees. He had his place also in the fight against venereal disease, presenting the moral and spiritual side of the problem. Many became the president of the station library committee or editor of the station newspaper. Several stations had a daily flag-raising ceremony, where the chaplain was called upon to deliver a morning prayer. At other parades, the chaplain was in attendance and usually had some small part. For a number of years, it was the custom to hold a communion service on the morning of the Wing's parade for the graduating class. This was one service that the students really wanted to attend.

A chaplain's less pleasant duties arose from the inevitable casualties of war. When an aircraft crashed, the chaplain was called upon to break the news and usually to conduct the funeral. As casualties became more frequent in Europe, the chaplains in Canada were required to visit the next of kin and bring the sympathy of the RCAF and the consolation of the Gospel. Until 1944, Memorial Crosses awarded to the next of kin of those killed overseas were taken personally by the chaplain from the station located nearest to the family.

Three Principal Chaplains: H/Brigadier the Ven. Archdeacon C.G. Hepburn, CBE, MC, ED; H/Brigadier the Rt. Rev. G.A. Wells, CMG, VD; and H/Colonel the Rev. Dr. J. Logan-Vencta, OBE, ED.

Padres John Weir Foote, VC (left), and Ormond Hopkins (right), toast Helen Bayne, secretary to the chaplain general, 1941-85.

Padre John Goforth, MC, 1940-61: "He would go on whatever happened."

John Weir Foote, VC, visits fallen comrades on the beaches of France, 1948.

The War Front

After the Battle of Britain, the number of Canadian squadrons serving in England increased to 16 and in September 1941, Padre Cockram was brought back from England to serve in Ottawa as assistant principal chaplain (P) under John McNab. Cockram was replaced by G.O. Lightbourn who would develop and direct the work of RCAF chaplains overseas for the next four years. Much of the success of the overseas work of the RCAF chaplains was due to his wise planning and efficient supervision.

As the number of airmen, and chaplains, increased, the RCAF Chaplain Service was raised to the level of a directorate in August 1942 and Cockram was promoted to group captain and appointed director of the RCAF Chaplain Service. Group Captain McNab proceeded to the United Kingdom to become the principal chaplain of the RCAF overseas and there was thought of sending Lightbourn home. However, Lightbourn was so well respected by the chaplains and his organization was so securely in place that he was left to do the practical work which freed McNab to look after matters of policy. In December 1942, McNab was posted back to Canada and Lightbourn resumed the full scope of his overseas duties. While most of the wartime work of the Air Force chaplains was done in Canada, eventually the RCAF chaplain establishment in the United Kingdom would increase to 25.

As the number of Canadians increased in England, chaplains began to be assigned to specific stations and to bomber squadrons. The least desirable but most important of these postings was Bournemouth. It was far from the centre of action, but it was the manning depot where all Canadians spent their first few weeks in the United Kingdom. The biggest problems in Bournemouth were homesickness and the unrest that grew out of the idleness of young men waiting to get into action.

The most desirable and yet most challenging and difficult postings were those to the new bomber squadrons. These were on RAF bases and the RAF padres conducted the regular services of worship. The RCAF padres were thus free to spend more time with the men. As closer personal relationships developed, there was no question where the padre would be during a mission. He was there to see the men take off and there when they came home. He listened on the intercom as the aircraft circled and took their course for Germany, then counted the hours and the minutes until they came back. Afterwards there would be endless chatter and stories, then breakfast and sleep for all but the chaplain who would move on to other airmen who were preparing to go into battle the coming night.

Throughout it all, there were numerous opportunities for quiet one-on-one chats and encouragement. Friendship and sympathetic understanding were required far more than any talk of formal religion. In the words of one padre: "Perhaps that lesson was one of the most important of all to learn ... that religion is more than words, and can be expressed by a smile, a handclasp, a gift of chewing gum or a cup of coffee." Church services were held, but at odd times and in different places: "They were very informal and the language was often as colloquial as it was tuneless, but no cathedral ever seemed holier ground."[25]

In 1942, losses averaged 5 percent: one out of 20 aircraft did not return; five crew members out of every 125 were dead, captured, or missing in action. And there would be five more missing the next day, and five more the day after that ... The hardest part for the chaplain was to maintain a cheerful, confident, and companionable manner no matter how many ghosts haunted his mind.

In the fall of 1943, the Canadian bomber squadrons were concentrated in Yorkshire and Lincoln to form No. 6 Bomber Group. Canadian chaplains now had the station duties to do, but they felt that there was no more important or rewarding job in the whole RCAF. Following the lead of the Royal Air Force, the RCAF set up a school for Christian citizenship for airmen at Station Dishforth. The dean of the school was N.T. Chappel. Courses lasting one week included lectures on the Bible, religious psychology, and ethics and sought to promote religious co-operation and national unity.[26] It was hoped that airmen would return to their units more qualified to give spiritual direction and leadership.

As the war spread around the world, Canadian airmen followed it from the wastes of Greenland to the borders of Australia. They flew beyond the Arctic Circle, trained Russian airmen in the art of handling Hurricanes and Spitfires, roasted in the blazing heat of the Arabian Peninsula, were taken prisoner in Singapore, and in many an isolated place in between kept the radar equipment in working order on the stations that watched for the approach of enemy aircraft.

It was inevitable that as soon as chaplains were available they would follow their boys and serve them as best they could. To work his way around the Mediterranean, the chaplain had to hitch rides on airplanes to get from place to place. First came Padre E. Harston, then Padre H. Davidson, then Padre W.F. Butcher, following the war as it proceeded through Sicily to Italy. In the Far East, Padre J. Sargeant was the senior chaplain, and later Padres A.I. Higgins and W.P. Irving were sent to assist him. All of them carried out an itinerant ministry, catching the men where they could and offering whatever spiritual support was needed.

In May 1943, Padre Herb Ashford, a former missionary, deployed with squadrons in Algiers and Tunisia. His smattering of Arabic and French coupled with his knowledge of the ways of the local people and his skill and patience at bargaining with them made life a lot easier for the airmen. As the squadrons entered a period of operations with an intensity unequalled in the history of Bomber Command, Ashford worked tirelessly. He visited each aircraft before take-off and welcomed each aircraft and crew back. During the day he continued to scrounge luxuries from the locals at prices that no one else could even approach. Church services were held in a central area of the camp and the majority of personnel chose to attend them. Singing was helped by the YMCA supervisor, Ken MacAdam, who had an excellent voice. Together, these two men established rest camps on the shores of the Mediterranean where personnel went to recover from the nerve-wracking strain of operations. For his work in North Africa with the Canadian Bomber Wing and his previous outstanding work in the United Kingdom, Ashford was awarded the Order of the British Empire.

Action In Normandy

As preparations were made for the D-Day invasion, seven chaplains were assigned to the Tactical Air Force in the south of England. Padre Crawford Scott was the first to land in Normandy, going in with the invasion barges.

The work of the Tactical Command chaplains on the continent was very similar to their jobs as station chaplains except that the conditions were decidedly more difficult. Living under canvas, they were frequently under fire and plagued by German V-1 bombs. At times, they were surrounded by units of the German Army. Church services were held wherever and whenever the men could pause for the few necessary moments. Chaplains routinely held five to seven services per day in order to reach all of the men.

As unpleasant and dangerous as life was, it was the chaplain's greatest opportunity to live with the men, to share their discomforts and dangers, and to present the Gospel under conditions where it was sincerely appreciated. The only fatality among the RCAF chaplains was Squadron Leader Gordon Brown. On November 27, 1944, he had been travelling towards Antwerp in a truck with some sergeants. Around noon they stopped at an RAF station for lunch and Brown headed into the sergeants mess to eat with the men. Such fraternization was more than the RAF could handle, and Brown was politely but firmly directed towards the officers mess. While heading alone in the indicated direction, he was hit by a V-bomb and died within moments. Those who knew him said that Brown was one of the most successful and popular of all Canadian padres, and his death brought sorrow to all of his fellow chaplains.[27]

After the war was over, it was generally concluded that the chaplain was indispensable as a builder and maintainer of morale. At home and abroad he visited the sections where the men worked. He befriended them, saw their problems, and listened to their complaints, and he did his level best to come up with solutions to their problems. They had been suspicious of him at first, but in the end everyone agreed that the Air Force functioned more efficiently and did its job better when he was there.

CANADIAN ARMY CHAPLAINS

Canadian Army chaplains far outnumbered those who served in the other two services. Most of them served with units in the field and there were many tales of heroism and self-sacrifice. Of the many fine chaplains, several have been immortalized in Walter Stevens's book, In This Sign, and their stories will emerge as this peacetime narrative develops. However, the stories of John Goforth, with which this chapter began, of John Weir Foote, VC, and of the chaplains who were prisoners of war in Hong Kong had a profound influence on the expectation of how chaplains were to "do business" in peacetime.

The Padre Who Chose To Stay Behind

On August 19, 1942, the news of the ill-fated raid on Dieppe shocked the senior Canadian Army chaplain in London, Padre J. Logan-Vencta. As rumours spread of the tremendous loss of Canadian lives and the possible fate of one of his chaplains, John Weir Foote, Logan-Vencta headed for the coast and began a desperate search among the survivors.[28] Foote was nowhere to be found, but nearly everyone from his regiment, the Royal Hamilton Light Infantry (RHLI), had a story to tell about their padre. The rugged 37-year-old chaplain had appeared like a sturdy angel of mercy, walking calmly through the hell of the bullet-swept beach and inspiring everyone with his courage as he ministered to the wounded. No one knew if Foote was alive and a prisoner of war or if he had died on the beach. But as the days went on the legend of "Padre X" of Dieppe continued to grow. It was not until April 1943 that Mrs. Foote, living in Hamilton, received a message from her husband from a German POW camp and disclosed his identity. She had heard the story of Padre X from others, but had no idea that the stories were about her husband. While Padre Foote was a prisoner he was able to write letters to his wife but he never told her what he did or what had happened on the beaches until he was free at the end of the war.

A small-town Presbyterian parson with a shy, quiet voice, Foote volunteered for war duty and was sent directly to Hamilton, where he quickly earned the respect of the men and their families. While other chaplains were learning about military life, Foote made the best of the situation by visiting the families of nearly every man in his battalion. Should he have to write to these people later with bad news, he wanted the letters to be to friends, not to people he did not know.

Foote continued to impress his battalion during their long and often boring months of training in England. He always went with the men on exercises and did what they did. He played his trumpet and clarinet and took on the educational duties for the entire division. Somehow he acquired a library and then organized and sometimes even taught classes in subjects such as algebra and Greek. Describing him after the war in the *Globe and Mail*, Padre Foote's commanding officer, Colonel R.H. Labatt, reported that he "was a dynamo of energy and inspired energy where lethargy was the most feared enemy of morale."[29]

When it came time for his regiment to go into action the padre didn't have to go. In fact, the military were reluctant to take a non-combatant on a raid of this magnitude. According to the story often repeated by the members of the RHLI, Foote made it clear to Colonel Labatt that if permission were not given, he would go anyway and have to be arrested for disobeying orders when it was over. The colonel finally gave in and Foote went on the raid as a stretcher bearer.

During the night of August 18, 1942, the flotilla of eight Hunt class destroyers and over 250 ships and landing craft slipped across the English Channel. Inside them were 5000 Canadian soldiers, a few hundred British Commandos, 50 United States Rangers, and two dozen Free French Commandos. The specific purpose of Foote's unit, the RHLI, was to make a surprise attack on "White Beach." During the hours before dawn, Foote moved about his ship with words of encouragement and the occasional joke. He wanted the men to know that whatever dawn might bring he would be there to help them.

All too soon the orders for action were given and the battle was on. The Canadians raced up the beach under heavy fire. Foote attached himself to the regimental aid post which had been set up in a slight depression on the beach. He had no weapon and the location was barely sufficient to give cover to men lying down. As the citation for Foote's Victoria Cross notes, "thought for his own safety seemingly never crossed his mind." Time and time again through the next eight hours, Padre Foote left the shelter of the aid post to inject morphine, give first aid, and carry wounded from the open beach back to relative safety. As the tide went out, the medical officer was killed beside him, and it was decided to move the aid post to the shelter of an abandoned landing craft. Foote continued tirelessly and courageously to carry wounded men from the exposed beach to the cover of the landing craft until ammunition stored inside it was set on fire by enemy shells.

By 2:00 p.m. everyone realized that the attack was not going to be successful, and before long they heard the call to retreat. Small boats and landing craft began to edge in towards the beach. Still under heavy fire and with no consideration for his own safety, Padre Foote urged his fellows on to meet them with a cry, "Every man carry a man!"[30] Again and again, the padre turned down offers to board a vessel and save himself; others followed his lead. Many men were saved that day because of the actions and example of Padre Foote. Colonel Labatt reported that "his calmness and courage was an inspiration to all who were about him."[31]

Then came Foote's last opportunity to leave. At one point he was actually hauled aboard the last departing craft, only to jump back into the water and wade ashore. "I felt that the men left behind would be far more in need of me in the captivity that lay ahead than those who were going back to England,"[32] he later explained.

Foote's first few days as a prisoner of war were no less demanding than the battle had been. While carrying men to the landing craft, he had taken off his boots because they were too wet and heavy. Once captured, he had no chance to find them and was forced to march barefooted for two days over rocky roads and cindered railway tracks. Foote marched without a word of complaint. Eventually, Colonel Labatt, whom Foote had helped through the first couple of days, managed to get hold of a pair of French army boots, size 13. Bruised and bleeding, Padre Foote put on the large and unwieldy boots that were to be his only footwear for a considerable time. In spite of his discomfort it was said that the padre's "caring shone through like a beacon as he ministered to other prisoners giving them comfort and above all hope."[33]

Life in the camps was far from easy. There were many deprivations, but Foote spoke of Dieppe as his "mission". He said "it was the springboard that launched me on three of the most interesting years of my life."[34] He would serve in five different camps and with soldiers and chaplains from many different countries. Stevens's book, *In This Sign*, has Foote's own account of his work in the POW camps. Humble and true to character, Foote neglected to mention a few details. For example, he requested a transfer from an officers camp, to Stalag 383 because "the men needed him."[35] There "he preached from the latrines for want of a better place, and organized three prison camp bands with instruments received from Canada and an accordion given to him by a German guard."[36] By Foote's own admission, "It's hard to sing songs to Zion in a strange land,"[37] but he still did not find it impossible and so learned to play the French horn while he organized many choirs. Eventually, Canadian Engineers managed to build a church, including a pulpit, out of Red Cross boxes that was good enough to impress the Germans. Foote won the respect of his captors and by so doing won privileges for the men. He even started to learn German, with a view to gaining a better understanding and then to converting his captors.

Release finally came for Padre Foote on April 25, 1945, with the arrival of the British Grenadier Guards. Foote had been a POW for thirty-three months.

On February 12, 1946, while Padre Foote was serving as the senior chaplain at Camp Borden, the formal recognition of his heroism came. When informed of the award, his first statement was: "I would like to say only that I look upon the 1st VC award to a Canadian Chaplain not as a tribute to myself, but to the Chaplain Service and to the great regiment with which I served ... I simply did my job as I saw it and was glad I had a chance to be with the boys of the regiment and feel I was one of them."[38] In a typical gesture, Foote immediately donated the medal to the Royal Hamilton Light Infantry, saying that the cross could have been pinned on 50 people for action that day on the beach at Dieppe.

Padre Foote was demobilized in 1948 and soon became a member of parliament in his native Ontario. Later he served in various high-ranking civil service positions until retirement in 1964. He is the only chaplain to have a chapter of the Chaplains' Association named in his honour. Foote died on May 2, 1988, just before his eighty-fourth birthday. At the John Weir Foote VC Legion in Grafton, Ontario, they will never forget him "and they have stones from the Beaches of Dieppe that along with Ontario field stones form a Foote Memorial outside the branch to keep the meaning fresh." But, reported *Legion* magazine in 1988, "true valour is remembered by all generations."[39] Foote's valour has, indeed, been remembered by the Chaplain Branch. Even in the 1990s chaplains speak of their "unlimited liability contract" with the military and follow Foote's ideal of serving as, when, and where required.

Prisoners Of War In Hong Kong

When they left Vancouver heading for Hong Kong the soldiers of C Force, composed of the Winnipeg Grenadiers and the Royal Rifles of Canada, had no idea what the future would hold. With them were two Protestant chaplains, Uriah Laite and James Barnett, and one Roman Catholic chaplain, F.J. Deloughery.[40] The S.S. *Awatea* sailed out of

Vancouver on October 27, 1941. During the voyage across the Pacific Ocean, the chaplains conducted worship services and made regular visits to the crowded men's quarters and to the ship's hospital. Fortunately the weather was good and it was a smooth crossing.

The ships arrived in Hong Kong on Sunday, November 16. After a warm welcome from the governor of the colony and several senior military men, the soldiers were transported to quarters at Hankow Barracks in Shamshuipo. Some of the officers were put up at the Peninsular Hotel in Kowloon.

Over the next two weeks, C Force settled into their new home. The Protestant chaplains held weekly church parades and helped to get the mail and messages flowing between home and the men. They held counselling interviews related to home and personal problems, and they visited the detention barracks, the Bowen Road Military Hospital, and the men in unit lines. The three padres had lunch on November 23 with the welfare officer for the Hong Kong garrison. From his balcony you could see the airport and the many Japanese camps on the other side of the line.

Just as Deloughery was finishing mass on Monday morning, December 8, the sirens wailed and the bombs began to fall on the airport and on Shamshuipo Camp. It was not entirely a surprise: the previous day church parades had been cancelled as C Force deployed to its defensive lines. Under attack, Deloughery was assigned to Bowen Hospital and soon obtained a car with which he could visit soldiers in the line. Laite remained at Hankow Barracks until he could get a supply truck to take him to his battalion at Wan Choi Gap. Barnett took on the mail run and dodged air raids going back and forth to the post office in Hong Kong. The chaplains conducted short services when they could and filled sandbags when they couldn't. Barnett played cards with the men when they had time off, and all the chaplains visited with the men at their battle stations.

Things began to happen very quickly after the Japanese landed on Hong Kong island on Friday, December 19. C Force was ordered to evacuate to Stanley Peninsula, and Barnett headed down to his battalion headquarters at Stanley Prison to find out just what was going on. He didn't have to ask and spent the rest of the day helping out at the prison's casualty clearing station. That night Barnett heard that there were a large number of Canadian casualties at St. Stephen's Emergency Hospital and so he dropped every thing to go to their aid. The staff were short-handed and Barnett was able to help them prepare the wounded for the doctors. On Sunday, December 21, Padre Barnett celebrated Holy Communion in the main ward of the hospital and later that day conducted his first funeral service on the island.

Padre Laite had heard about the possible landing during the night of December 18 and was directed to go to the headquarters of D Company. He arrived about 5:30 a.m. and within 30 minutes D Company was engaging the enemy. As the battle went on sniper fire was constant. All telephone communications were cut off on the twentieth, and there were only 800 rounds of ammunition left. A small party was sent out that night to work their way through to friendly forces and request help. Although encouraged to go with them, Laite would not leave, insisting that it was his duty as chaplain to remain with the men. Everyone was tired and hungry. There had been neither food nor sleep since the battle started.

From the time the first wounded man was brought in to the kitchen that Laite used as a shelter, the padre realized what his job would be. He bandaged the wounded and tried to make them comfortable on the cement floor of the shelter. Often there was no water so he opened tins of vegetables to get pea and carrot juice for the wounded to drink. Laite tried to keep cheery and positive, talking to the wounded long into the night until sleep overcame their agony and fear. At dusk he would get a tin and do the bedpan round of the patients. These were the first wounded men that Laite had ever seen, but in the absence of any first aid men he did what he could.

During the night of the twenty-first, Laite rationed out the last cigarettes, one per man, and chatted with the wounded, trying to keep them cheerful as he did his best to comply with the many requests–"Padre, fix my leg ... fix my bandage ... lift my leg ... give me a drink." As dawn approached, the number of wounded in the small shelter had grown to 41 and the company's ammunition was exhausted. D Company surrendered to the overwhelmingly large enemy force at 7:00 a.m. on December 22.

Almost immediately Laite was moved out of the shelter and searched. He was thankful that he had managed to get all of the men's weapons out of the shelter before it was taken. What followed is best described in Laite's own words:

> Through their interpreter, to whom I believe we owe much, they learned that I was a Chaplain, or minister as he called me. I showed them my Bible and my field dressings and told them that my duties were to be with my men and to care for the wounded. I had made a complete list of our casualties but this was taken from me by a very arrogant Japanese officer. Water was asked for and was readily given, but they watched me closely as I gave each soldier a ration ... On my return to the shelter I saw a single stretcher being brought in ... I felt that the walking wounded would be given a chance so

my first words to the men were "Boys, if any of you can walk, for God's sake walk." I repeated these words and the men, realizing their significance, made every effort. I was then taken by armed guards along the paths and trenches calling to men to come out of the shelters with their hands up.[41]

Shortly after noon Laite was taken to the Japanese headquarters and was given a meagre lunch. When he had finished eating, a Japanese NCO and three private soldiers took him away. Three times during the trek that followed, Laite was sure he was about to be shot–first by his escorts, who simply didn't do it, and then by roving bands of enemy soldiers, who were stopped by sharp words from the Japanese NCO. At some point along the way, the padre realized, with a surge of hope, that the road they were taking led towards Hong Kong. This hope eventually proved justified when they reached the top of a knoll. The NCO pointed to distant hills and conveyed through sign language that there were British across the valley. Then he pointed down the hillside and indicated that Laite was free to go. Enormously relieved, Laite was now convinced that not only was he being given a chance, but that the men left behind would also be saved. Wanting to express his gratitude, he gave the NCO a big smile and a hearty handshake, and said a heartfelt "Thank You." The NCO seemed to understand: his handshake was firm and he smiled as if to say "The best of luck."

Laite, of course, was not yet out of danger. He hadn't gone far when he all but ran into a small detachment of the enemy. They shouted and waved their hands as if to signal that he should keep going. He needed no advice or encouragement.

More than once as he crossed the valley, Laite found it necessary to find shelter from shell fire and bombs. In one instance, he took refuge in a large culvert, or nullah, only to realize he was sharing this haven with upwards of one hundred Chinese citizens who were moving towards him. Badly in need of rest, he stretched out by the nullah wall and waited. The Chinese proved friendly, giving him water and some dry toast. After an hour's rest Laite asked if any soldiers had gone up the nullah and the younger Chinese who spoke English said that many Japanese soldiers had used the nullah on their way up Happy Valley.

Finally, Laite reached a built-up area. The sight of two European-style homes decided him to make contact in hopes someone could direct him to Bowen Road Hospital. As he neared the locked gate of one of the homes a Eurasian woman came to the door of the house and asked what he wanted. Laite replied "Rest for a few minutes, please."

The woman unlocked the gate, led Padre Laite into a spacious living room and gave him a cup of hot milk and biscuits. She told him that it would be impossible to reach Bowen Road, but that he could get to the temporary hospital at the grandstand of the racetrack. She then arranged to send her maid along as a guide and disguised Laite in a long Chinese gown. After passing through an area that had been badly damaged by shell fire, Laite heard voices saying "This way, down this way." A truck was standing by the roadside and in a trench nearby were three British soldiers. Thinking they were in need of assistance Laite ran across and asked if they were hurt. They replied "No Sir, but we were just machine gunned as we came across that open space ahead of you." It turned out that they were just three hundred yards from the hospital. Giving the girl the Chinese gown, he ran safely across the open space.

On arrival at the hospital Laite was met by Dr. Selwyn Clarke who took him on to Queen Mary Hospital. Laite would remain there until January 20, 1942, when, with 47 others, he was transferred first to Shamshuipo and then to North Point POW Camp.

Meanwhile, St. Stephen's Hospital had been shelled two days before Christmas, and later that day Padre Barnett had to dodge shell fragments at the cemetery. That night the severely wounded were transferred down to Stanley Prison Hospital. Barnett, three medical officers, and seven nursing sisters remained to man St. Stephen's. On Christmas Eve, Barnett conducted three burials and a carol service to the sound of exploding shells, breaking glass, and machine gun fire. The line had moved to the front door of the hospital. It was a night without sleep. The staff gathered in the main ward to reassure the patients, while soldiers gathered on the hospital verandah to regroup for a withdrawal. In Barnett's own words:

> About six o'clock this morning ... the Japanese troops entered the hospital from both the north and south doors. I saw them bayonet wounded soldiers in bed ... All patients who could walk and the staff were herded together, searched and put into the store room. We were left in the store room for about an hour and then we were moved to a smaller room. The nurses were separated from me. I saw one of the nurses hit on the head with a steel helmet, slapped in the face, and kicked by a Japanese soldier. About ninety men were placed in my room. We could not all sit down together. A Japanese soldier came in and made us put up our hands. He then stole our watches and rings from us. Later another Japanese came with a sack of .303 bullets and started to throw them in our faces. One Japanese soldier came in and took out a patient. We heard

screams which I believe came from him ... The men in the room asked me to tell the Christmas story and to say some prayers. We all thought it was the end. One Japanese soldier brought us a few cigarettes and a jug of water. About four o'clock in the afternoon a soldier came into the room all smiles and ordered us all out. We thought we were to be shot, but not so, he told us, through sign language, that the war was over and we could be friends now. We learned that the colony of Hong Kong had surrendered to the Japanese.[42]

The next morning the hospital staff were told that they could move around and Barnett immediately did a tour to see what damage had been done and to search for casualties. On that day, if not on any other, Barnett witnessed ugly sights about which he would testify at the war trials. He set out to bury the many broken and mutilated bodies but was ordered by the Japanese to cremate them instead. Building a huge fire out of bloody bed sheets, mattresses, and other debris, the survivors went about their grim task. Whenever they found dead bodies Barnett read a short funeral service and all who were able helped to carry them to the funeral pyre. Barnett listed the names of as many as he could, but the Japanese confiscated the lists and forbade him to make any more. When one wounded man asked for communion, Barnett complied using a tea cup and saucer as the chalice and paten, with water and hard tack for the elements.

The next few days were confusing at best as Barnett helped the staff to reorganize the hospital and the Canadians set out to find their wounded and bury the dead. Then Stanley Prison was evacuated, and its 2500 inhabitants were forced to walk twelve miles to Hong Kong. In the confusion that followed the move, Barnett struck up a relationship with a Japanese officer. The officer gave Barnett a pass and his staff car to take the sick to the hospital and to return with a doctor and medical supplies.

The Japanese permitted church services to be held, and Padre Barnett was rather proud of his innovative ways of finding an altar. On one occasion he had everyone gather around a long table set up in the corridor of the hospital. He placed the cross at one end and himself with the elements at the other. At Holy Communion on December 31, he used an old concrete block as an altar. (Later he would fashion purple and green altar frontals from bed sheets. He brought the green ones home with him.)[43]

On January 22, 1942, all of the Canadians were moved to North Point Camp, where they would stay until the following September. They lived in shacks that had been constructed for Chinese refugees before the colony fell. At first the buildings were filthy and there was no water. The next few months were not pleasant, but were at least a period of relative stability. British rations ran out in February, and the prisoners were then given rice and small quantities of meat or fish.

In April the Japanese started to pay the officers of the camp according to their rank. It was not a great deal of money, but it gave the officers the opportunity to supplement their diets from the canteen and to buy badly needed medicine and other supplies for the men. The officers shared about 60 percent of their pay with the men and the chaplains. It was a matter of great embarrassment for the Canadian chaplains that they did not receive any pay and so were an added burden to their superiors. All of the chaplains who were prisoners from other countries were paid, but the Japanese had observed that the Canadian chaplains were of honorary rank only and so not entitled to pay. (The Canadians petitioned the Japanese many times to rectify the situation but they went unheard until January 1944.)

In September 1942 the Canadians were moved back to Shamshuipo. For the next three years the chaplains spent their time conducting worship services, counselling, and encouraging the men to write home. The chaplains visited the sick on a daily basis, and if a man was too sick to write, they did it for him. Overall, morale was as high as could be expected, or higher, and the chaplains found only one or two cases of Canadian soldiers who could not take the strain.

Various places were used as chapels, but each time a group of the prisoners was sent to the work camps in Japan moves would take place and the chapel spaces would be lost. Evening talks on God in education, on history, and about postwar problems were all popular with the men. Deloughery, who by May 1943 had been transferred to a British officers camp, taught French and Latin.

All of the chaplains later paid tribute to the Red Cross. Delivery of a small parcel for each man and, in some cases, mail, did a great deal to boost health and morale. Cigarettes not only provide a good smoke but could be traded on the black market for food.

On many occasions, the fellowship of the Church not only encompassed the Canadians but reached out beyond nationalities and even the confines of the POW camps. Deloughery was in frequent communication with Roman Catholic civilian priests in Hong Kong, and he received a regular supply of wine for communion from Father Orlando, the pastor of St. Teresa's in Kowloon. At Shamshuipo, the Reverend H.L.O. Davie of the Royal Army Chaplain Corps and the Reverend C. Strong of the Royal Navy worked as a team with the Canadians. A roster was drawn up and the four chaplains took turns conducting worship just as they would on a multi-chaplain base at home. For a while the interpreter at Shamshuipo was a Japanese Lutheran minister, the Reverend Watensbe. Later Watensbe helped at Bowen Road Hospital, where he did a great deal to alleviate the suffering of our men. Dr. Harth, the bishop of Hong Kong, described this pastor as "one of the finest examples of Christian life" it had been his pleasure to know.

In August 1945 the first rumours of peace reached the POWs, brought into the camp by work parties returning from the city. Finally, on August 17, the Japanese withdrew their guards from the camp. Great celebrations followed and there were services of thanksgiving throughout the colony. The British fleet which included HMCS *Prince Robert* arrived at the end of the month.

The trip home through Manila, San Francisco, and Seattle was slow but joyous. After a short medical and administrative delay in Victoria, the chaplains were finally able to go home to their families.

After he returned to Canada, Padre Laite sent the following message to the next of kin of those who died in Hong Kong:

> Please accept my deepest sympathy as you face your tomorrow without him who sleeps in some quiet place in old Hong Kong–or Japan. The birds warble sweetly there and the flowers bloom profusely. Let the birds' song be the requiem of your own heart and the fragrance of the flowers be a reminder of the kindly influences of his life upon yours. In such a remembrance your loved one and my comrade will live while life shall last for us. Our memorial to him is a heartfelt gratitude for having had him as ours.
>
> With you in greatful remembrance of one who lived and lives for aye.[44]

RELIGIOUS RESULTS OF WORLD WAR II

The impact of war on the religious beliefs and later life of the armed forces is always difficult to calculate. During the six years of war there was no Revival and there were no miracles, but many a man who had not been to church in ten or more years began to attend worship. On the average, 75 percent of the men who could be spared from their duties went to the services. Over 70 young men indicated their intention to study for the ministry after the war.

Looking on from the outside, it seems more likely that any changes in a man's religious life were a consequence of the personal witness of individual chaplains. It was their courage, morality, friendliness, and assistance which brought the most effective spiritual results. Even in the church services the chaplains did not preach at the men, they talked to them. They talked about familiar things like the conditions under which they lived and the problems they faced in everyday life. The men listened to the chaplain and accepted what he said because he was there with them. He shared their difficulties and lived with their frustrations.

For the chaplains themselves, their experiences during the war offered them insights into minds and hearts that would serve them well in their future years as military and civilian pastors. Moreover they came home possessed of a great sense of the fellowship of the whole Christian Church.

During the war years, the chaplains worked alone or in small groups of two or three. On occasion, conferences were held to give them guidance and encouragement. The first such conference on record took place on February 10, 1941, when 16 RCAF chaplains from No. 1 Training Command got together to compare notes with Squadron Leader McNab. A similar RCAF conference was held in Montreal in April 1941. Bishop Wells knew the value of such conferences from his First World War experience and wanted to meet with all of his chaplains in Canada. Army chaplains were called to meet in the Windsor Hotel in Ottawa on March 24, 1941, and the senior chaplains were called together again for two days the following January. The first ever conference of Navy chaplains took place in Halifax on October 20, 1942, and in October 1944, an overseas Navy chaplains conference was held. Such gatherings were essential training vehicles and provided a fellowship which was unequalled anywhere else in the Christian Church.

The manner in which the chaplains–clergy of several different denominations–worked together had a great effect in making the men think more seriously and favourably about the church. Religious differences were not cast aside–no chaplain became less a man of his own denomination, but the various denominations found that they could co-operate without striving for unity on all details. Such co-operation was born of necessity, but after a short time was valued for itself: "In the Chaplaincy the immediate cause was the service itself and the enlistment to win the war against tyranny, but the great cause, highest of all, was never lost to sight, the Kingdom of God and the Service of Jesus Christ. It was a relief to be freed from the necessity of thinking always of one's own local church and of striving to increase the membership of one's denomination, and to rejoice in the larger challenges of relating to men in the kingdom, no matter which branch of it they might prefer."[45]

Similarly, in his final report before returning to the civilian ministry, an unknown RCAF chaplain wrote: "In the Chaplaincy I have seen a practical demonstration of the ecumenical spirit, and have discovered that it works. There has been a sense of comradeship with other Chaplains which was not dependent upon denominational loyalty. But the major aspect is the deepened understanding of life which this work has given. In civilian life, one has the feeling that a thin veneer of respectability hides the real problems of men. But in the Chaplaincy, the human problem can be viewed in closer perspective. We have seen unmasked the problems which confront society, and the need for spiritual undergirding has been the more firmly pressed upon us. It has been an experience that I shall never regret."[46]

In his annual report for 1945, the senior chaplain of the 3rd Division reported that "the chief value for the Chaplain of all his experiences has been that he has lived with, suffered with (to a degree), played with, talked with and known men, ordinary men. He was among them, without the respect due to position, simply as a man among men. That experience, from which the civilian clergymen are largely and, unfortunately, sheltered was his to a high degree. He knows what is in men and he knows how the gospel of Christ can reach men and make them braver, finer, stronger, better airmen of the RCAF and better citizens of Canada."[47]

Chapter 2

HOME AT LAST

❖

ADAPTING TO THE PEACETIME MILITARY

DURING THE WAR the chaplains had been left pretty much on their own. Now they were faced with the need to forge a place for themselves in peacetime military and ecclesiastical organizations. It did not take long for them to come to an understanding of the financial, political, and bureaucratic realities of being a full-time part of the Canadian military. As this happened the chaplains were genuinely surprised to find that they were being rejected as an organization by some quarters of the Church and that the military did not always seem to give them what they thought was their due. Chaplains, who had survived easily in the face of war, were now challenged to survive in peace.

Like everyone else, the chaplains were anxious to get home to their families. In readjusting to life in Canada, however, they faced a number of problems particular to their calling. Few knew if they would be asked to remain in the military or let go. At the same time, clerical appointments were normally made during the summer, and many of the chaplains arrived back in Canada in September 1945, too late to get a job with their denomination. Some continued to work in hospitals and in release centres until they found employment, while others just went on rehabilitation leave. No study has been done to determine if a number of chaplains left the ministry after the war, as had occurred in 1919,[1] but a cursory examination indicates that some did leave.

At the beginning of the Second World War an establishment[2] had been prepared and printed for the Protestant Chaplain Service, but no unit was ever called out on the basis of it. Certain districts and formations, such as the hospital ships, had shown Protestant and Roman Catholic chaplains on their own home war establishment, but the practice had been to post chaplains to "chaplains pools" in the various commands and districts from which they would be sent to work in specific areas. Strictly speaking, these pools were not units of the Canadian Army. This was not in order legally, but it served the needs of the day during the pressures of wartime. The administrative omission was discovered as it affected other services sometime during 1942, but it was only when a revision of the war establishment was undertaken in 1945 that the appropriate correction took place. Formally, the professional Chaplain Services in the Canadian Army, Navy, and Air Force came into being on August 9, 1945, and at a Treasury Board meeting on September 4, 1945, were made effective as of May 1, 1945.[3] To regularize the situation further, two Chaplain Units, one Protestant and one Roman Catholic, were called out based on a new establishment for the Canadian Chaplain Services.[4] This made very little difference as far as operations were concerned; the allotment of chaplains was still based on one Protestant chaplain for each 1000 Protestants and one Roman Catholic chaplain for each 500 Catholics. It did, however, put the chaplains on a sounder organizational footing for the postwar years.

Even before the war had ended, specific plans had been made concerning the size and leadership of a peacetime force. Having been caught off guard at the beginning of the war, the chaplains were determined to have a continuing organization. Starting at the top, peacetime replacements were chosen for the principal chaplains, subject to the approval of the civilian churches, which never seemed to disagree with the choices. After the senior men had been named, specific chaplains were invited to stay on in the postwar forces. These men would carry on as Canada's first permanent force military chaplains.

POSTWAR ARMY CHAPLAINS

The Army's quota of Protestant chaplains was set at twelve including its principal chaplain, Colonel C.G.F. (Cy) Stone. They were commonly called "The Twelve Apostles."

"THE TWELVE APOSTLES"		
C.G.F. Stone	J.R. Millar	J. Barnett
J.P. Browne	R.O. Wilkes	H.A. Merklinger
M.J.D. Carson	J.W. Foote	J. Cardy
J.F. Goforth	J.W. Forth	J.W.D. Duncan

Stone has been described as "the character of them all." He had served in the ranks in the First World War and as a chaplain in the Second, when he was awarded an OBE.[5] The citation for his award mentions his untiring devotion and service to the troops, and the well-defined influence of his high ideals, which won the respect, confidence, and admiration of the troops, their commanders, and the Chaplain Service. However, it was no doubt his capacity for sustained and relentless effort and his role in organizing a divisional cemetery with limited resources that were to make him such a formidable principal chaplain in the decade after the war when he had to fight for tents and jeeps and for just about everything that the chaplains needed to do their job. When he died of a heart attack on May 30, 1954, he was given a hero's funeral procession through the streets of Ottawa. In life, chaplains kept an eye out for "Stoney" because he always had somebody in the doghouse and no one wanted to be the one. In death, he was sorely missed and every chaplain agreed that no other padre could ever replace him.

POSTWAR NAVY CHAPLAINS

Towards the end of the war, Bishop Wells asked for a list of those chaplains who wanted to remain in the Navy. It was proposed that the peacetime Navy should feature a chaplain of the fleet, two command chaplains, and 20 other chaplains who would not wear rank but who, for internal purposes, would be known as chaplains "class III." Movement to a supervisory level known as "class II" would be based on suitability for the job as well as seniority. In fact, after the war the Navy was left with six Protestant chaplains and Wells's successor, E.G.B. Foote.

ROYAL CANADIAN NAVY CHAPLAINS		
	E.G.B. Foote	
C. De Wolfe White	I.R. Edwards	H.R. Pike
G.L. Gillard	B.A. Peglar	F.H. Godfrey

Chaplain Foote guided the Navy Chaplain Service through Korea and into the Cold War. In Foote's time, Royal Navy customs were retained. The chaplains were highly regarded, as were civilian clergy of that day. They enjoyed all the privileges of officers but, bearing no rank, were welcomed as equals throughout the ship. The Royal Canadian Navy was like a small old boys' club. Everyone knew the chaplains. According to Padre Bill Howie: "Chaplains were able to perform their ministry fully and rewardingly in a service that valued their efforts and returned their friendship. If a chaplain chose not to offer comradeship and friendship, he would be politely tolerated."[6] Foote served as chaplain of the fleet until 1962.

POSTWAR AIR FORCE CHAPLAINS

A decision was made to leave the RCAF with an establishment of twelve Protestant chaplains including its leader, Padre R.M. Frayne. Frayne was promoted to the rank of honorary group captain in the spring of 1951.

ROYAL CANADIAN AIR FORCE CHAPLAINS		
R.M. Frayne		
J.W.T. Van Gorder	W. Rodger	J. Dunn
B.G. Stibbards	A.T. Littlewood	R.P. Condon
W.K.R. Batty	L.C. Scott	G.B. Fee
E.W.S. Gilbert	F.W. MacLean	

Frayne died while serving, on the day after he was a principal participant in a service to mark the coronation of Queen Elizabeth II. In his funeral address, the Very Reverend John F. Woodside characterized Frayne as the "Happy Warrior": "The elements were so mixed in him that nature might stand up and say to all the world, 'This was a man.' No one came within the compass of his life but felt the virility and strength of his manhood. There was about him a crystal clear sincerity and forthrightness, tempered with an all embracing clarity of judgement, which belong only to those who are sound and true to the very core."[7]

THE CHURCH PARADE QUESTION

While the first Regular Force chaplains of the postwar era did their best to deal with the practical problems of demobilization and the establishment of new bases from one end of the country to the other, the civilian representatives of the churches who were on co-ordinating or advisory bodies dealt with the more political issues. One of the most persistent of these was the question of church parades.

There was an initial enthusiasm when the war was just over and 9000 Canadian servicemen paraded in front of the cenotaph in Ottawa on Sunday, November 11, 1945. It took two hours for the parade to pass the memorial. The parade then split into three sections, with the Roman Catholics heading to St. Patrick's Roman Catholic Church and the Protestants going to Lansdowne Park. Jewish personnel proceeded into a small building in the park.[8] From that time onward, local military representatives would plan special services of remembrance to be held in the churches on the Sunday closest to November 11. Then at 11 a.m. on November 11, a special parade would be organized by the Royal Canadian Legion at the local cenotaph.

On July 5, 1946, the three principal chaplains of the Protestant Service met and suggested that King's Regulations (RCN) published in 1945 and based on the Navy Act of 1944 should be used as the basis for a revised set of peacetime military regulations for chaplains in the three Canadian services. Brigadier W.H.S. MacKlin received the chaplains' request and noted that "the Naval Regulations are forthright and specific and in particular they require a church service for every ship or establishment every Sunday and compulsory attendance at same unless duties or weather prevents, or unless an individual has been granted permission to be absent." MacKlin recommended the use of the regulations but remarked prophetically: "The vexed question of compulsory Church parades will probably keep cropping up, but I am inclined to think that we would meet with severe opposition if these were abolished."[9] During the war, the Protestants tended to be overly open, and the Roman Catholics were determined to keep their parishioners free from Protestant spiritual influence. In particular, the Roman Catholics were annoyed with the cavalier way in which the Protestants had welcomed all servicemen, regardless of religion, to church parades.

The Army gave the matter due consideration but decided to go with British Army regulations which seemed to be more flexible. The British practice, recorded in the British Army's King's Regulation 1605, read: "So far as the exigencies of the service permit, Commanding Officers will afford facilities for the attendance of officers and soldiers and their families at public worship, including celebrations of Holy Communion. Except as provided in paragraphs 1606-08, officers and soldiers will not be ordered to attend a religious service or to parade before a service or on returning from it."[10] This meant that commanding officers could call compulsory church parades only on occasions of national or local importance when religious services were required. It also meant that no officer or man would be required to take part in the service of any religion other than his own. Boys under the age of seventeen-and-a-half at educational or training establishments would be required to attend divine service as a part of their curriculum. Bands might be ordered to play at services, and a suitable number of troops could be ordered to a funeral. The new order permitting this limited amount of religious freedom in the military came into effect in November 1946.[11]

In response to this Protestant initiative, the Roman Catholics agreed to permit their chaplains and personnel to participate in certain types of parades where prayers were said. Permission to worship together in any manner was seen as a real breakthrough. The type of joint parades permitted were those which were primarily and essentially military in character and at which prayers were non-denominational in nature and were offered only incidentally by a Protestant or Roman Catholic chaplain, or both, in uniform and without any distinctly religious insignia or vestment. If there was no chaplain available, a commanding officer might conduct the service.

This seemed to quiet the concerns surrounding church parades for the moment, but they continued to be a sensitive issue. Almost a year later, W.J. Gallagher, in his first official letter as general secretary of the new Canadian Council of Churches Chaplaincy Committee, commented on a rumour that regulations might be changed. In the opinion of the committee he wrote, "it is not compulsory Church Parades that are objectionable, but the exacting demands by which they are sometimes surrounded." The committee urged the minister of national defence to let commanding officers keep the discretionary power to order church parades when appropriate. The minister, Brooke Claxton, replied that "while consideration was at one time given to instituting voluntary parades ... it has now been decided that the present regulations should remain in effect."[12]

Within two years the issue arose again. At a joint meeting on May 17, 1949, the senior Roman Catholic chaplains convinced the senior Protestant chaplains that all orders referring to combined divine services should be cancelled. The Roman Catholic authorities felt that the spirit of the provisions had not been observed and that Roman Catholic personnel were still being required to take part in Protestant religious services. This was contrary to Roman Catholic Church doctrine and therefore unacceptable. At the next meeting of the military Personnel Members Committee, to whom the chaplains reported, it was agreed that the orders should be cancelled.[13] This left as the only regulation referring to the matter King's Regulation (Canada) 1149, which stated, in part, that "no officer or soldier will be obliged to attend the services of any religious body other than his own."

This new policy still created a problem for the military with respect to ceremonial occasions, and in 1950 an effort was made to introduce yet another order that would make it possible for personnel of the Protestant, Roman Catholic, and Jewish faiths to participate together in ceremonial parades, such as those held on Remembrance Day. This order said that joint parades could be held providing that the ceremony did not include prayer or hymns or other forms of religious expression of a denominational nature and that the parade was entirely military in character. On such occasions, however, it would be appropriate for the officer commanding the parade to order the observance of a period of silence in reverence for the dead.

As cancellation of the previous order for church parades had been initiated by the authorities of the Roman Catholic Church, they were first to be asked to comment on the order. They approved it. The Council of Churches Chaplaincy Committee declined to approve it, however, on the grounds that in any ceremony of this type, the religious element was essential to the service. They did not consider the period of silence to be worship.

This stalemate left the military unable to put a formed unit on a church parade unless separate arrangements had been made for each faith. To the military mind, this was not a workable solution to the problem. Chaplains on both sides of the issue were frustrated by the impasse and, as will be noted in a later chapter, even the Canadian Legion was prepared to write off military participation in Remembrance Day parades.

COMMAND AND CONTROL

By the end of the Second World War, Brigadier C.G. Hepburn, the senior Army chaplain, felt that chaplains had been treated fairly in the matter of rank, although not without some struggles from time to time. The Canadian chaplain's position in this respect compared favourably with that of chaplains in the United States Army and the British Army. Canadian chaplains were ordinarily given the rank of honorary captain and received full pay and allowances for that rank. In the main they were treated with the utmost respect and courtesy, usually being accorded a position beyond their rank in the mess and in the unit.[14]

Demobilization, however, meant reductions in rank for all servicemen, including the padres. Every chaplain had been warned about this, and some had decided to return to the civilian ministry because of it. The military, traditionally conservative in outlook, viewed the chaplains as above the issue of rank, but the chaplains had seen it as a real problem.

To the military, the rank awarded to an officer's position was simply that which was justified by the extent of the duties and responsibilities associated with that position. For many chaplains and their civilian ecclesiastical masters, however, military rank was a straightforward indicator of the respect and status that were their due. A chaplain's rank showed where he and the Church stood, or were seen to stand, in the military hierarchy. Canada's chaplains were not the only ones who seemed to be overly concerned with their military rank. In an attempt to explain the issue as it affected United States Army chaplains, Chester A. Pennington proclaimed that the excessive concern about rank was caused by the noble purposes which chaplains served. "A chaplain bears rank," he wrote, "not to exercise authority, but to serve people. He bears rank for others! It is an instrument by which he, not commands, but serves!"[15] To sort out the rank issue in Canada, the postwar Canadian chaplains had to deal with a new military organization: the Personnel Members Committee.

The Personnel Members Committee

When Mackenzie King appointed Brooke Claxton as minister of national defence in 1946, Claxton had been directed to create a single defence policy. The new minister brought together the chiefs of the respective services and the chairman of the Defence Research Board to form the Chiefs of Staff Committee. Under these men in the new National Defence headquarters organization was the Personnel Members Committee, composed of the chief of personnel for each of the services and a representative from the Principal Supply Officers Committee.

The Personnel Members Committee (PMC) had been created on April 28, 1944, "to deal with all matters of policy which may affect personnel with the objective of maintaining uniform practices throughout the three Armed Services."[16] As the military institution evolved and grew during the Cold War and as the Canadian military marched towards integration, the PMC became more of a decision-making body than a regulating body.

In the postwar forces the chaplains would report to the PMC, and all their major administrative decisions would require the approval of the PMC. This was a problem right away for the chaplains, who had always assumed that they worked for commanders and not for deputy commanders or for personnel officers. Knowing that the chaplains felt they should report directly to him, the adjutant general of the Army, E.G. Weeks, said that he was prepared to see them at any time, by appointment. However, he also made it clear that normally they would report to the PMC and to his deputy.[17]

The Canadian Council Of Churches

With the promise of peace before them, the individual churches soon disbanded their war committees and lost interest in the military, resulting in the dissolution of the Inter-Church Advisory Committee on the Chaplaincy. When this happened the logical move for the chaplains was to turn to the Canadian Council of Churches for support and assistance. They were warmly welcomed and the Chaplaincy Committee of the Canadian Council of Churches came into existence in 1947 as the umbrella organization of the military chaplains.

Even before the chaplains had turned to the council, Dr. W.J. Gallagher, the organization's general secretary, had been lobbying the government on behalf of the Canadian churches and clergy. Gallagher had written to the prime minister on behalf of the chairman of the Canadian

Council of Churches, Bishop Owen, to urge the prompt release of ministers and theological students who had served as chaplains and as combatants. They asked the prime minister: "to expedite their release from the service so that they could resume their theological training this autumn and not lose another year. The Churches have given generously of their ministerial personnel for the Chaplain Services, and many young men, candidates for the ministry, have delayed their training in order to serve in the Forces. The result is a great shortage of clergy."[18]

At this time and for the next twenty years James Gallagher was the chaplains' friend. He advised them on ecclesiastical matters, constantly spoke to the government on their behalf and even defended them against the occasional attacking church.

The chaplains were an organization ideally suited to Gallagher's character and aims. William James (Jim) Gallagher, M.A., D.D., was an ordained minister in the Presbyterian Church and had served pastorates in Harriston, Meaford, and Guelph. While in Guelph he began to express a deep concern for evangelism and social service, which led him to a unique ministry that became a consuming passion for the rest of his life. When he assumed the office of general secretary of the Canadian Council of Churches, Gallagher was confronted with a complex, challenging, and pioneering task. He was called upon to set up a co-ordinating organization for co-operation among the major Christian denominations in Canada. In addition, he was charged with promoting the new ecumenical movement. Gallagher laid the foundations of ecumenical work among the churches, in the armed services among the chaplains, and in all inter-church endeavour with skill and with scrupulous care. Until his death he was the mainspring of the ecumenical movement in Canada and a world leader in inter-church co-operation. In a very real sense Jim Gallagher was the architect of the Canadian Council of Churches and a major influence on the development of the Chaplain Service in the postwar Canadian armed forces.

The whole manner in which the chaplains were controlled left them in a precarious position straddled between church and state. They were required to be loyal to the military, with its growing bureaucracy, and loyal to their denominational leaders who held professional control over their every decision. When issues arose, letters and memos ricocheted like bullets off the inside walls of a box, with sparks flying at every hit. Always sensitive to political pressure and enquiry, the military, through the PMC, sought to accommodate the Chaplain Branch when bureaucratically possible. The Council of Churches Chaplaincy Committee, for its part, did not hesitate to speak directly to the minister of national defence and even, on occasion, to the prime minister. It never occurred to the churchmen that there should be any other way to make their point. Whether it was a simple request for the minister to support the annual chaplains' retreat or a nomination for the position of chaplain general, the churches went straight to the political top, and the chaplains seemed to be pleased to let them do it.

One might speculate that the problem, in the eyes of the chaplains, was that there was no-one left in the peacetime military who knew how to "play the game." Either operational commanders, with whom the chaplains had established a rapport during the war, were now civilians or they had been reduced in rank. From the senior chaplains' point of view, the men who had taken their place in the peacetime military seemed somewhat insensitive to the role of the Church and unresponsive to its needs. Nor were they always prepared to give the chaplains the respect to which they had been accustomed. In effect, the churches seemed to be fighting to recover the élite ecclesiastical status that they thought was their due, not realizing that the day of the ecclesiastical élite had passed.

Rank or Classification?

Inter-service discussion took place as early as January 1946 to arrive at some agreement as to the actual number of chaplains and the rank structure that would be appropriate for them. Considerable thought was given at the time to adopting the naval system, with chaplains having no formal rank and a classification for pay purposes only. But the military decision-makers could not agree on what to do. Finally, the decision was made by the minister of national defence: the ranks would remain as they had been during the war, although individually reduced. Chaplains in the Army and the RCAF would continue to have honorary rank and the Navy would retain its system of classification. This decision was based largely on representations from the Inter-Church Advisory Committee on the Chaplaincy and would have long-range effects on the number of chaplains in the military and on their status.

In July 1946 the new classification for chaplains was announced.[19] The navy's five classes were matched with the ranks of sub-lieutenant, lieutenant, lieutenant commander, commander and captain for pay purposes. These five classes were matched in the Army by the honorary ranks of lieutenant, captain, major, lieutenant colonel, and colonel, and in the RCAF by flying officer, flight lieutenant, squadron leader, wing commander, and group captain.

CHAPLAIN RANK		
NAVY	**ARMY**	**AIR FORCE**
Chaplain I/Sub-Lieutenant	Lieutenant	Flying Officer
Chaplain II/Lieutenant	Captain	Flight Lieutenant
Chaplain III/Lieutenant Commander	Major	Squadron Leader
Chaplain IV/Commander	Lieutenant Colonel	Wing Commander
Chaplain V/Captain	Colonel	Group Captain

The first shots of what would be a long battle were soon fired by the Council of Churches Chaplaincy Committee in an effort to correct what they thought was an oversight due to the rank structure of the different services at the time of demobilization and to rank reduction. The principal chaplain of the Army came to hold the rank of lieutenant colonel and the senior Air Force chaplain had become a wing commander. The principal chaplain of the Royal Canadian Navy, however, had ended up being classified as a chaplain V– one rank higher than the other principal chaplains. Of course, the Chaplaincy Committee pushed the government to give the Army and RCAF principals the appropriate higher rank that would put them on a par with the Navy.

In response to the request, Adjutant General Weeks was understanding but firm: notwithstanding the rank of the principal chaplain of the Navy, given the peacetime conditions, the rank of lieutenant colonel or equivalent should be sufficient for the other principal chaplains. He explained that the rank of colonel was more appropriate for the head of a directorate, where duties were "more exacting and onerous," and argued that a chaplain "should rely more on personality than rank for the successful execution of his appointment."[20]

Weeks was sensitive to the underlying concern of the chaplains with the question of their status; he was also aware of the government's push to eliminate duplication and to combine or civilianize services where possible. He was therefore quick to add, on the one hand, that in his opinion "the rank of Lieutenant Colonel for Principal Chaplains is in no sense any reflection on the authority and position of the various ecclesiastical authorities in Canada."[21] On the other, he suggested that if it were possible to amalgamate the three Chaplain Services, then there would be a case for giving the senior chaplain the rank of colonel or equivalent.

The idea of the possible amalgamation of various military services was an old one that had been revived by the prime minister's directive to the minister of national defence to make all necessary cuts in the military and to amalgamate as much as possible. In response, the Inter-Service Combined Functions Committee (ICFC), composed of senior officers from each of the services, was established to examine all the functions performed by the military with a view to effecting an economy of manpower by amalgamation or co-ordination. One specific task of the committee was to review the possibility of amalgamating the Chaplain Services.[22]

The ICFC report[23] was approved by the chiefs of defence staff and presented to the Defence Committee of Cabinet in April 1947. It recommended that the administrative services of the chaplaincy be combined and that the senior chaplain remain in Ottawa and be a civilian, "thus removing any feeling of discrimination that might be present in one service or another."[24]

When the Personnel Members Committee was asked to review the feasibility of such an amalgamation, it immediately requested the views of the senior chaplains of each service, who indicated that they did not like the idea of being under the control of a civilian. The PMC agreed with them on this point but supported the idea of a single senior chaplain. The chaplains were less than enthusiastic about that, but they were willing to support the idea of more co-operation between chaplains of the different services and on a geographical basis. In June 1947, before any firm decisions had been made, the chaplains of the three services began to co-ordinate their work on a geographical basis. Special attention was directed to Halifax, where naval chaplains were asked to look after army personnel.[25] The chaplains also insisted, and the PMC agreed, that if a single senior chaplain were appointed, then it should only happen in consultation with the Canadian Council of Churches Chaplaincy Committee, and the appointment should be made from the three services on a rotational basis.[26]

When the amalgamation plan returned to the military from the Defence Committee in May 1947, the PMC was directed to implement it. The chaplains were asked to give their views on the implementation, but things were moving too fast. They started to drag their feet, saying that the matter was one that must be referred for approval to the Council of Churches before any action was taken.

General Weeks was frustrated by the chaplains' objections to any and all proposals that would reduce the number of their senior officers. All that the chaplains really wanted to do, he said, was "maintain the status quo";[27] their proposals showed no sense of economy and allowed no possibility of amalgamation. Weeks was even willing to move the principal chaplains to other bases, from which they could maintain their ranks and control their chaplains while under the direction of a chaplain in Ottawa. This plan would at least reduce the number of senior men around National Defence Headquarters. But the chaplains then complained that these men would find themselves wearing two hats and being expected to do the job of the area chaplains as well as maintaining command of their service.[28]

After considering all arguments, the PMC asked the Defence Committee to approve several recommendations: "that there be a Chaplain to the Forces appointed on a three-year rotational basis and located at NDHQ" and that "he be granted the acting rank of Colonel or equivalent during the tenure of his appointment only."[29] The Defence Committee asked the PMC to reconsider the suggested rank,[30] but the PMC would not back down. The chairman of the Defence Committee agreed that any decision of this nature should be first discussed with the Council of Churches Chaplaincy Committee and took steps to start that process in the following September.

At first Dr. Gallagher attempted to find a bureaucratic solution to the problem. He wrote that the committee felt that the proposed plan to have one senior chaplain would be more costly and less efficient than the present organization.[31] In what Gallagher considered to be an arrogant tone, the minister of national defence replied to the effect that the policy of the department was one of consolidation, amalgamation, and co-operation between the services and therefore it had been decided to appoint one of the principal chaplains as chaplain to the forces.[32] It was as though Claxton had not even bothered to read Gallagher's carefully prepared letter and Gallagher was not impressed. He wrote again to point out that the practice of having one single head of the Chaplain Service was not working in a satisfactory manner in England or in the United States.[33] No further action seems to have been taken on the issue until the next year.

Already offended by the manner in which his original letter had been treated by the minister of national defence, Gallagher next complained that the principal chaplains of the Army and the RCAF were not being placed on the same level as the officers heading up other directorates and recommended that they be granted the rank of colonel and group captain respectively, to be on a par with the Navy. Gallagher claimed that it was the dignity of the senior representatives of the churches in the forces that was at stake. To give them the rank of colonel would only be "befitting the importance of the Chaplain Service."[34]

Responding on behalf of the Army, General Weeks again ran through the litany of his arguments: during the war the ranks were honorary brigadier at NDHQ Ottawa, honorary colonel at Canadian Military

They stayed in after the war, 1948.
L to R: M.G. Butler, J.F. Goforth, MC, D.R. Anderson, J. Cardy, MC, J.M. Anderson, MC; front: R.C.H. Durnford, DSO, C.G.F. Stone, MBE, J.W. Forth, MBE, and J. Barnett.

RCAF chaplains, 1951.
L to R: rear: L.W. Mould, J.S. Neff, C.H. Jensen, W.K.R. Batty;
centre: W.C. Hewitt, E. Eglisson, E. Martin, D.G. Madill, J.M.W. Beveridge;
front: E.W.S. Gilbert, R.M. Frayne, F.W. MacLean, B. Garrett

The Rev. W.J. Gallagher
General secretary of the Canadian
Council of Churches and the chaplains'
best friend, 1947-64

Col C.G.F. Stone, MBE
Principal chaplain of the Army, 1945-54

G/C R.M. Frayne
Principal chaplain of the Air Force,
1945-53

The Rev. E.G.B. Foote, OBE
Principal chaplain of the Navy, 1945-62
Third chaplain general, February 1962-
May 1965

Headquarters in the United Kingdom, honorary lieutenant colonel at Corps Headquarters in the field, and honorary major at Divisional Headquarters; with peacetime restrictions, the principal chaplain had rank sufficient to carry out his duties quite efficiently; a previous suggestion that the principal chaplains not hold rank but be classified for pay as in the case of the Navy had been turned down by the Council of Churches; the status of some naval chaplains was an exception to the norm, and it would be unfair to deprive them of the status they held, but when they retired, their replacements would be paid in line with their peers in the RCAF and the Army.[35] The PMC was requested to reconsider the senior rank question and, again, agreement could not be reached. Once again the Defence Committee was called upon to solve the problem. This time it supported General Weeks.[36]

At this point the Roman Catholic representative to the forces, Archbishop M.L. Roy, whose Roman Catholic chaplains fell under the same rules as the Protestants, threw his weight into the struggle. Roy wrote to the minister of national defence about the reported concern of the Roman Catholic ecclesiastical élite.[37] He urged the minister not to abolish the Army and RCAF directorates, but to consider upgrading the appointments and adding a sufficient quantity of sub-staff. Roy concluded: "I am prompted to make these suggestions, Sir, because of severe observations from some members of the hierarchy and because, as it stands now, the Chaplain Service has the appearance of a *parent pauvre* when compared with other services."[38]

An official reply was dispatched advising Archbishop Roy of the decision which had been reached in the Defence Committee. And at a meeting in May 1948, Claxton reassured the churchmen that while the principal chaplains were not directors, they certainly had access to the adjutant general on any matters they wished to discuss with him. He went on to say that he felt that the term "principal chaplain" was a much more appropriate designation than "director" and that everyone from the chiefs of staff through the Defence Committee thought that the rank of lieutenant colonel or equivalent was sufficient.[39]

Meanwhile in March 1948 the Soviet Union had decided to blockade the city of Berlin, just one month after a Communist coup in Czechoslovakia. In the midst of growing prosperity and having just reduced the size of the military, Canada was in no position to become involved in a military intervention. As the Americans flew endless planeloads of supplies into the besieged city, Canadians continued to believe that they should put their trust in the United Nations and in their imperialistic neighbour to the south which seemed to be replacing Great Britain as the power to which the free world must turn for defence.

While Canada gave no direct support to the Berlin airlift, international events pushed the government to show some concern for the state of the Canadian military. In early June, Claxton wrote to Gallagher to reassure him that no amalgamation of chaplain services would take place.

> It was thought some time ago that it would be for the best interests of the service to amalgamate the Chaplain's services, and considerable study was given to the problem of how this could be best implemented across Canada. It has been decided that rather than have a complete amalgamation, it would be more desirable to develop a plan of fuller co-operation on a geographical basis which would adequately provide for the spiritual welfare of the services, and at the same time eliminate duplication and retain the identity of the Chaplain Branch within each service.[40]

Instead of reducing the number of chaplains there would be establishment increases to correspond with the growing size of the military. The Army would now have nineteen Protestant chaplains, the Navy would have nine, and the Air Force seventeen. The principal chaplains, as Claxton had previously told Archbishop Roy, should have the rank of lieutenant colonel or equivalent. The senior Navy chaplains could remain paid as naval captains, the equivalent of colonel, until the present incumbents retired, and then they would come into line with the other services.

Again, the Council of Churches argued that the rank of the principal chaplains in the Army and the RCAF was not in keeping with their status. The minister responded in the usual way.[41] Finally, in December 1948, both the Canadian Council of Churches[42] and Archbishop Roy pressed the minister for reconsideration of the question of more senior rank for the principal chaplains, Protestant and Roman Catholic, of the Army and the Air Force. Roy's letter was a masterpiece. After praising Claxton for his support, he went on to write:

> In peace time, the Principal Chaplain has, in the normal discharge of his duties, to meet all the Bishops of the country. He is therefore one of the best ambassadors of the armed forces to the Hierarchy. The Bishops do not well understand why an officer with jurisdiction from one ocean to another is not of a higher rank than a Battalion Commander.
> It is almost useless to say that within the Army and the Air Force,

the authority of the principal chaplain of each Branch must needs be enforced by a rank proportionate to his trust.[43]

The matter was then considered by a committee of senior officers who re-examined the entire subject of chaplains' ranks. After careful reflection they observed that any chaplain who reached the level of principal chaplain probably would have reached the level of bishop in civilian life, which could be equated to the military rank of brigadier. However, in consideration of the rank of the heads of other corps in the Army, other directors in the RCAF, and the heads of the military legal and dental organizations, and notwithstanding the chaplains' lengthy education and experience in the Church prior to joining the military and the extended responsibility for dependents, the senior officers recommended that the principal chaplains of the Army and Air Force be granted the rank of colonel and group captain respectively. They further recommended that the Army and the RCAF conform to the Navy and "provide a similar proportion of lieutenant colonels and wing commanders in support of the proposed structure and in light of the strength and geographic distribution of the particular service."[44] The chaplains were encouraged but not pleased with the report.

Then, in what appeared to be a dramatic change of heart, the minister gave in to the pressure. The senior Protestant and Roman Catholic chaplains would be appointed "on a rotational basis from each service for a tour of three years, on completion of which they would retire."[45] Subject to the approval of the Defence Committee of the Cabinet, the rank of the new senior men would be brigadier general or equivalent. Persistence and working together with the Roman Catholics, with the help of the growth of the Cold War, had won the day and some of the status which the clergy sought.

The minister of national defence then asked the Council of Churches Committee and the archbishop if the appointments should be made immediately or if they should wait until 1953. Immediate appointments would mean that the first Protestant chaplain general would remain in that position until his retirement in 1957, a full seven years. The minister suggested that the churches might wish to hold off making the appointment until 1953, when he would only be able to serve for three years. In any case, the minister indicated that nominations were open for the job.

The Chaplaincy Committee was delighted, but having achieved one goal in the quest for appropriate status, it was not about to give up. Even with a chaplain general there was still the question of the rank of the principal chaplains serving under him. On May 17, Gallagher wrote to Claxton to present the views of the Council of Churches at length.

> Our committee appreciates greatly the consideration you have given our representations from time to time, and especially the desire that there should be no ground for any suggestion that the armed services are not fully conscious of their responsibility for the spiritual and moral welfare of their personnel.
>
> In our discussion of this question of the rank and status of the Principal Chaplains, the members of our committee have expressed a strong feeling that the standing of these officers in each force should parallel that of the senior officers of other professional services, and that the lack of such status (1) hindered the full effectiveness of the Chaplain Services and (2) suggested a lack of appreciation of the significance of religion and the Church.[46]

Gallagher went on to reiterate the old arguments: that the idea of having only one principal chaplain had not worked in Great Britain or in the United States and the fear that waiting four years for a chaplain of the forces and then the problem of choosing the man for the job would create more problems than it would solve. His committee, he said, was aware of the recommendations of the senior officers, and if these were accepted, they "would offer a career in the Chaplain Services that would provide encouragement and incentive to all chaplains in the service and it would give an added inducement to prospective chaplains."

Gallagher stressed that the "fact that there is a dual Chaplain Service in each Force is a matter of policy based upon certain well-known factors of the Canadian situation for which, in our judgement, neither the Protestant nor the Roman Catholic Chaplain Service should be penalized." Moreover, he continued: "It is our view that the 'cure of souls' is of the highest value and importance, and that the Chaplain Services should be given whatever facilities are necessary to enable them to render the most effective ministry. We believe that both the military authorities and the people of Canada would support that view."

Gallagher then added one more argument from a former letter:

"The rank and status of the Principal Chaplain is not merely a matter of his personal standing, but has an important bearing upon the estimation in which his work is held, the staff and facilities provided for it, and the priorities that go with rank in any military establishment. These in turn bear upon the opportunity for effective service."

When still no change took place, Archbishop Roy wrote once more to the minister of national defence:

But there is one point on which I feel that I must insist, namely: that a minimum rank is required in order that a senior staff officer be enabled to do his work efficiently. This I have learned through my own experience during the war, and I have seen more than confirmed by all that I know of the peace time force. In that respect I must say that the present set up does not give the Principal Chaplains a full opportunity of discharging their duties ... Whether there be a Chaplain General of the three services or not, the Principal Chaplain of each Service will always have difficulty in efficiently acting and being properly recognized as the Director of a service that functions all over Canada, unless he be at least a Colonel. This is not only felt among the members of the Forces: it is also very obvious to the civilians, who often wonder why the head of an important service should come after so many others when he attends a ceremony."[47]

The chaplains, Protestant and Roman Catholic, were not about to accept anything less than what they thought was their due. They had regained the wartime status for their most senior chaplain and now sought to make the rest of the Chaplain Service "right."

Joint Services Chaplaincy Committee

As the concerns of the chaplains increased, the PMC, realizing that it had neither the time nor the expertise to deal with some of the more mundane matters of the Chaplain Branch, brought into being the Joint Services Chaplaincy Committee (JSCC). The JSCC gathered for its first meeting on May 17, 1949. Under the interim chairmanship of the principal chaplain (RC) Army and the interim secretaryship of the principal chaplain (RC) Air Force, it was agreed that the appointment of the chairman and secretary of the committee should be by seniority of service and change every four months. Accordingly the Protestant and Roman Catholic chaplains of the fleet were appointed secretary and chairman respectively. It was further agreed that there would be two subcommittees which would reflect the current basic organizational division of the branch. The Protestant subcommittee was very active and has left a considerable trail of records, but the Roman Catholic subcommittee was more private concerning its affairs.[48]

Officer or Clergyman?

When the Income Tax Act was amended in 1950 to allow clergymen to be exempt from paying income tax on the rental value of their

65

residences, military chaplains found that the new rule did not apply to them. In the opinion of Dr. Gallagher, however, the language of the act was inclusive of all clergymen, including chaplains, and on July 3, 1950, he wrote to the minister of national revenue, James J. McCann, to clarify the status of chaplains.[49] The chaplains, said Gallagher, are ministers in full status in their church. They come under the jurisdiction of the appropriate church authority and serve only with the consent and the approval of their respective churches. Because they are recognized by the churches as having all of the rights and the responsibilities of ministers, they should have the same tax exemptions. When the minister of revenue finally replied in December, he insisted that chaplains did not fall within the meaning of the act: "It is our understanding that notwithstanding their calling and the religious duties required of them, all chaplains are Commissioned Officers entitled to the pay and all allowances of their rank, to which all other officers of that rank are entitled."[50]

Undaunted, Gallagher decided that the minister and his advisers could not have properly understood the position of the chaplains. He wrote again and at length explaining that chaplains care for the spiritual welfare of military personnel, use their residence in their work just as civilian clergymen do, and should not be penalized for their willingness to exercise ministry among the armed forces. The chaplain is primarily a minister of religion, Gallagher insisted, noting that King's Regulations stated: "A chaplain is given a commission in order to establish his status in the service." "Any suggestion that his military status over-rides his position as a minister of religion," Gallagher concluded, "can not be accepted." This time, the minister of revenue responded promptly, reiterating his position that "it is not the legislative intent that the deduction should extend to chaplains nor does a correct interpretation of the law warrant such conclusions."[51]

Gallagher, however, was not about to stop here. On February 8, he wrote to Prime Minister St. Laurent complaining of "improper discrimination against clergymen serving in the Armed Forces."[52] He quoted *Hansard* of November 10, 1949: "So long as the clergyman's full time occupation is the ministry and he is engaged in full time religious work, he is allowed this deduction from taxable income." "Chaplains," proclaimed Gallagher, "are engaged in full time ministry." The last word, for the time being, fell to the minister of national defence, who seemed to be somewhat annoyed that Gallagher had gone outside the department to solve an internal problem. Claxton wrote, with the backing of the Personnel Members Committee,[53] that no one was going to deny that chaplains were full-time ministers of religion engaged in a full-time ministry.

The problem was that it was never the intention of the government to include chaplains in the income tax exemption. Moreover, he added, having the tax break would "give chaplains an advantage over other officers of similar rank and would not help the chaplain in establishing the relationship of trust and understanding they should be first to want to have with their comrades at arms."

On May 22, 1952, in a brief to the minister on matters relating to Korea, Gallagher raised the tax topic once again.[54] This time he tied the whole question to the difficulty in getting chaplains for the forces. Chaplains were finding themselves at a disadvantage compared with the clergy in the civilian parishes. The chaplain "has very little opportunity for promotion or advancement. He has been denied the income tax exemption on the rental value of his house which is allowed other ministers. He must retire from the Chaplain Service at a much earlier age than the Church requires." Some chaplains were at a disadvantage in comparison with others who might have the good fortune to live in less expensive married quarters where even the income taxes were lower.[55] Chaplains were also at a disadvantage compared to other officers who, entering at the rank of second lieutenant through the last year of their college course, had often had books and tuition paid by the government, had more opportunities for promotion and at a younger age, and could usually retire with a higher pension because of more years in the service. Some were even given professional allowances in addition to their regular pay. The prospective chaplain, however, could not be subsidized during his college course, had few opportunities for promotion, and received no professional allowance. Because of the length of training and the required three years' experience he had little opportunity to serve long enough to receive as high a pension. Some of the conditions of service should be changed, Gallagher concluded, but "in particular, we think that adjustment should be made with regard to the income tax exemption on the rental value of the chaplain's residence and/or in the matter of professional allowances."

Gallagher's formidable presentation and persistence at last caused the government to wonder if chaplains were getting fair treatment. Eventually, in 1953, the government capitulated and the chaplains were allowed to have their tax break as clergymen.

THE MOVE BACK TO EUROPE

Postwar euphoria did not last long. The Communist coup in Czechoslovakia and the East-West disagreement over Berlin were followed in 1949 by the explosion of the first Soviet atomic bomb. Later that year, the United States, Canada, and ten European countries met to form the

North Atlantic Treaty Organization (NATO). In response, various countries in the Soviet bloc joined together under the Warsaw Treaty Organization. The Cold War had begun. In 1951, as its contribution to the NATO forces, Canada sent the 27th Infantry Brigade to Europe and 1 Fighter Wing of the Royal Canadian Air Force to North Luffenham, England.

The first RCAF chaplain on the ground in England was Flight Lieutenant A.T. Littlewood. With a background of service in England during the Second World War and a British wife, he was the ideal man for the job. In the beginning he was located with 421 Squadron at RAF Station Odiham.

As had been the case during the war, the accommodations and food that the RAF national service airmen took for granted were unacceptable to the Canadians. Littlewood wrote to his principal chaplain, R.M. Frayne:

> The "beefs" we heard over here during the war are still being heard; indifferent hygiene conditions prevail that border on the really bad, particularly in the Airmen's Mess. Slight temporary improvement takes place after general complaining only to be lost shortly thereafter. Revision of longstanding RAF methods would be necessary to remedy matters and one RCAF Squadron can hardly assume the responsibility for so comprehensive a task. Airmen eat quite a few meals in local cafes, usually the evening meals.
>
> On the station, there is not a great deal, if anything, by way of entertainment; in Odiham village there is a picture theatre, and it is believed that station authorities agreed not to enter into competition with the same, so that here on the station there are no films shown. When squadrons are not flying on weekends, there is a general exodus."[56]

Littlewood encountered one problem that had not existed during wartime: the presence of dependent wives and children. Although the RCAF had made it abundantly clear that wives and children were not to be brought to England, approximately twenty families arrived at their own expense. They found places to live in the surrounding hamlets, but for some it was very difficult. Eventually, the RCAF, while not condoning the situation, began to pay subsistence allowance to those servicemen with dependents living off the base.

Littlewood seemed to communicate well with the RAF chaplain at Odiham, but he was not given any real opportunity to conduct worship services. The station chaplain, with the backing of his command chaplain, made it clear that the Canadian would only conduct worship "on rare and unavoidable occasions."[57] No one was happier than Littlewood, therefore, when changes were announced. The officers and men of 421 Squadron would be shipped home, with their families, and Littlewood would be moved to wing headquarters at North Luffenham. Here, the RCAF was in charge and both the Protestant and Roman Catholic padres would have their own chapels.

The Nissen hut allotted to the Protestants was soon outfitted with furniture from the officers' mess. Littlewood discovered that the RAF's principal chaplain was Group Captain Murdock McLeod, with whom he had been stationed at Edinburgh at the end of the war. Littlewood visited McLeod at the Air Ministry and from that point on described his work as "fascinating, demanding, and interesting, with never the barest possibility of boredom."[58]

The RCAF, which had dropped to 14,821 men in 1949, grew to 38,351 by December 1952 in order to provide a complete air division for NATO. In 1952, 2 Fighter Wing was established at Grostenquin,[59] France, and RCAF overseas headquarters moved from Paris to Metz. An air supply base was established in the United Kingdom at Langar, near Nottingham. In the spring of 1953, 3 Fighter Wing was formed at Zweibrüchen and 4 Wing at Baden-Soellingen. Canadian aircraft flew practice missions at Rabat in Morocco and later at Decimomannu in Sardinia.

In its heyday, the RCAF had twelve squadrons of F-86 Sabre jets, four squadrons of CF-100s, and the best pilots in Europe. When Padre Parkhouse went to Zweibrüchen in 1954, he reported that there was still a kind of wartime "it takes a tiger to do this" approach to flying. "They hadn't got around to thinking about safety and there were a lot of crashes and a lot of good pilots were lost."[60] Very few chaplain records exist from those days but, because of the hazards of flying, there was a real need for chaplains to serve with the squadrons.

The first 6000 Canadian soldiers in postwar Europe were temporarily assigned to serve with the British Army of the Rhine at Reinschlen, near Hanover, in northern Germany. With them were nine chaplains, four Roman Catholic and five Protestant. In this area of Germany there were several thousand refugees, often young mothers with children and no husbands. It was only a matter of time before young Canadian manhood was investigating the situation.

Very little was said about the moral problems of such a situation, and no chaplain reports have been found for those early days. The earliest document available is an article written by a Canadian war correspondent, Lionel Shapiro, in 1953. Shapiro declared that the Canadian soldiers were the most immoral group in NATO and backed up his arguments with alleged statements by chaplains who believed that the soldiers were living in an "abyss of immorality." The report didn't cause a great deal of concern among senior officers because some of them agreed with Shapiro's opinions. The men, however, were outraged. It was an especially sensitive matter for those who were starting to receive worried letters from their wives back in Canada.

The senior chaplain overseas was Major John Rand and he was livid about the report. "This Brigade is not a failure," Rand reported to Ottawa. "We have bad lads in it, but we have a lot of good ones in all ranks, and I personally don't feel that this Brigade has let Canada or Canada's reputation down one jot."[61] Rand had investigated the source of the alleged chaplain statements and concluded that the chaplains in question were misquoted. He charged that various phrases had been taken out of context and some may even have been fabricated.

In response to the allegations, Rand went on to write his own article on the 27th Brigade.[62] He had witnessed how much Canadian soldiers could put up with in time of war, he reported, but "in 'peace,' no matter how precarious the times may be or how 'vital' the individual job, the problems of those concerned with the physical, mental and spiritual well-being of a soldier are naturally much greater."

The chaplains found much to be critical about, but they decided that their approach would not be that of moral policemen or welfare critics. Rand reported that there was a faithful nucleus of men who never missed a chapel service. These were men of good character whose life style made them a good morale factor and a good moral influence on all who were around them. Some chaplains worked very hard to build up a congregation at the unit level, but then the unit would go out on spring manoeuvres and nothing would take place for two Sundays running. Very often the men would get back to their barracks from an exercise on Saturday and sleep in on Sunday morning. Alternatively, they might be going out on Monday and be away from the base for one last day of relaxation before leaving. Chaplains found it hard to maintain any sense of chapel ministry. Their efforts were also frustrated by the fact of the soldiers being in a foreign country, different from anything they had known before, and on duty so close to one of the world's "hot spots." There was little opportunity for the men to let off steam after hours without getting themselves into trouble. Rand observed that virtues that are "fugitive and cloistered at home" often broke down overseas. This affected church-going habits, but it also applied to education, self-discipline, motivation, democratic conviction, and so on.

One opportunity for chaplains to talk with the men was the padre's hour.[63] The chaplains insisted that padre's hours be the "real thing" and not just "beef sessions." Topics popular with the men were Communism and the Church, the nature of the German people whom they had so recently fought, and the relation of the German churches to such dreaded names as Belsen and Dachau. Questions were often asked about the form and history of German Christianity.

On Padre Rand's team were A.J. Alfred, G.A. Hatton, E.J. Dossett, and J.A. (Jock) Davidson. Just prior to this first team handing over to J.W.D. Duncan, A.F. Otke, J.A. Munroe, J.D.L. Howson, and J.B. Adams and returning to Canada, Davidson wrote an article intended for publication in the Toronto *Star Weekly*. The article, which took the form of a letter from an Army chaplain serving in Germany to one of his friends in Canada, gives us an insight into the life of an Army chaplain in 27th Brigade (see Appendix I).

The chaplain's concerns during this time in Germany were reflected in "Padre's Patter," the weekly column in the newspaper of the 1st Canadian Highland Battalion, *The Kilt and Sporran*. Between February and July 1953, Padre Davidson wrote on subjects such as the need for self-examination, the need for moral integrity, and the problem of alcohol abuse. Davidson reminded married soldiers of their marriage vows and told single soldiers that in matters of love their head was as important as their heart. On the subject "Going Home," he wrote:

> All of us will have to watch ourselves when we get home. Perhaps a special course should be laid on for us, as there are some things we may have forgotten. For example, the standard procedure in the dining room is, "Pass the butter, please," not "Sling me the ... grease, you ..." and some of the hi-jinks which are apparently quite acceptable in such emporiums of joy as Brinkman's and the Mittelpunkt may not be appreciated in your places of recreation back home.[64]

Chapter 3

UNITED NATIONS OPERATIONS IN KOREA, 1950-1953

❖

JUST LIKE OTHER CLERGY, Canadian military chaplains have always sought to minister to the spiritual needs of God's people. They have attempted to do this during times of war and during times of peace, often putting their own lives on the line as they carried the message of eternal life to their parishioners.

The war in Korea began when forces from North Korea crossed the 38th parallel on June 25, 1950. On August 7, 1950, Prime Minister Louis St. Laurent announced that a Canadian Army Special Service Force would be recruited for service in Korea.

Immediately, the military informed Lieutenant Colonel C.G.F. Stone, principal chaplain of the Canadian Army, that he could hire four additional chaplains to go to Korea. Just as Bishop Wells had done at the beginning of the Second World War, Stone went looking for clergy with wartime experience. Here was an opportunity for the boys to serve together again, and Stone was certain that they would jump at the chance. There being no doubt in his mind that this was just the beginning of something big, eleven messages went out from Ottawa inviting experienced men from across the nation to join the battle. Some of the messages went to former chaplains, while one or two went to soldiers who had gone back to school after the war to be ordained as clergymen. The demands for service and for a sacrificial life style are roughly the same for the wartime soldier and the Christian, and Stone knew that there were many good soldiers who had joined the ranks of the clergy. He also knew that the experience of former soldiers like R.G.C. Cunningham would be invaluable in the early stages of this new conflict. Experienced wartime chaplains such as Roy Durnford and Joe Cardy were still serving and would be needed when the new force expanded or if the going got rough. For now they would have to remain at their posts in Canada.

The Reverend Ray Cunningham was working with the militia and was away ministering to the artillery in Picton, Ontario, when the message arrived at his home in Sydney. It said that only four chaplains, two Anglicans and two United Church, were needed to serve in Korea. By the time the message caught up with him, Cunningham was afraid he would be left out and sent off a positive reply as quickly as he could.

In fact, Padre Cunningham needn't have worried. The clergy, like most people throughout the country, were sick and tired of the separation and the hazards of war. A goodly number of those approached by Stone volunteered to join the Army but would only serve in Canada. This, they surmised, would free some serving chaplains to go to Korea. They did not have the will to go themselves. Only Cunningham and R.C. Nunn said yes to the call to serve. Nunn had been a missionary in Korea before the war. He spoke the language and wanted to go back to the land and the people he knew so well. Both Cunningham and Nunn were ministers of the United Church of Canada.

All too soon the first soldiers of the Special Service Force were leaving Ottawa, and to the principal chaplain's great embarrassment, no Anglican clergyman had been found to go with them. It was the first time in history that Canadian soldiers were being sent out of the country on active duty without an Anglican chaplain to support them.

Stone felt that the problem of manpower "was only part of the general picture of the lack of appreciation of the real work of the whole Church." He described a large service held in Ottawa to say goodbye to two battalions of the Royal Canadian Regiment as they left for Korea: "I felt very sad because here is a regiment which all through its history has had none other than a Church of England Chaplain whenever it went on active service. It seems a pity both for the Regiment and the Church if we have to break that tradition."[1]

Before this time Church of England clergy had always played a key role in the Army Chaplain Service and the branch had always been extra sensitive about denominational balance. Stone, an Anglican himself, was a hard-working and determined man and he continued the struggle to recruit experienced chaplains even as his health began to fail. Additional ministers were asked to go and appeals went out to specific churches for clergy with wartime experience. Eventually twenty-four Army chaplains would serve in Korea, but some of them arrived there with no real knowledge of the Army or of their role.

NAVY CHAPLAINS – FIRST IN KOREA

While Padre Stone continued his search for volunteers, the Royal Canadian Navy was steaming towards Korea. Within three days of the notification of Canadian involvement in the war, four destroyers had sailed from Esquimalt. Soon after they arrived on station, a Roman Catholic and a Protestant chaplain joined them.

Throughout the action the Navy kept ships in the Far East, each staying roughly eighteen months. Duties were generally coastal patrols and shore bombardments. Fortunately, there was no naval challenger, but life on the high seas could, in itself, be a challenge. Chaplains joined the ships and served with the men during those years. They conducted services of worship, calmed anxious thoughts, and did a fair amount of social work.

NAVAL CHAPLAINS, KOREA		
H. Todd	J. Wilson	A.G. Faraday

The only chaplain injured during the Korean War was in the Navy. Chaplain Horatio Todd was washed back into a bulkhead by a large wave in the North China Sea. Later, he reported that he was just standing by the rail and the next thing he was in the water. When recovered, Todd had a large gash in his leg and a cut on his head. Todd was sent home, but there was no one to replace him.

Eventually, the chaplain of the fleet, E.G.B. Foote, came up with a young Presbyterian, J. Wilson. From their first meeting, Foote was deeply impressed by this keen young clergyman. With Foote's blessing, Wilson was recruited, indoctrinated, and on his way to Korea. The whole process took under two months. Throughout it all and throughout the Korean tour, Foote kept a supportive eye on Mrs. Wilson and wrote long, paternal letters to her husband.

Chaplain Wilson joined HMCS *Cayuga* in Sasebo, Japan, on April 5, 1952, and sailed three days later. Soon afterwards, he switched to HMCS *Athabaskan* and then to HMCS *Nootka*. Basically, he arrived in port on one ship and immediately switched to the next departing vessel. On June 22, Wilson could report that he had not spent one night ashore. He had conducted services on the ships and once on the American destroyer *Munro*, having been transferred there by a helicopter from HMS *Glory*, and on May 25, he had gone ashore to conduct a service for American soldiers on the Korean island of Paengnyong Do. Later, he would visit some Canadian sailors awaiting court martial in Kure. On August 9, he conducted a funeral in Yokohama for a young sailor who had died during an emergency appendectomy. The death was a shock for the whole ship's company, and Wilson wrote a letter to the boy's father, as did the medical officer and the commanding officer.

During his tour in Korea the main problem for Wilson was the immorality of the sailors. The venereal disease rate was exceptionally high on all the ships except *Athabaskan*. (Wilson attributed this exception to what he described as the "extreme propaganda campaign" which Captain W.M. Landymore had waged since the ship left Halifax.) In his frequent letters Foote was always asking if he could be of any help, and Wilson finally had a tasking for his mentor: to provide appropriate anti-venereal disease posters and mottoes to wage a moral propaganda war.[2]

THE RCAF IN KOREA

A small number of RCAF Sabre pilots served with the American forces in Korea while the North Stars of 426 (Transport) Squadron RCAF served as the Canadian rear link from the war zone to McChord Air Force Base in Washington and neighbouring Fort Lewis where the Army trained for Korea. Padre Bill Rodger, the command chaplain of Air Transport Command for part of the war, made several trips to Japan on the North Stars. Normally there would just be Rodger and the Roman Catholic chaplain in the back of the aircraft, making themselves as comfortable as possible on the cargo, be it mail or munitions. The long trip to Japan (normally via the Aleutians) required fuel stops along the way, and the chaplains would slip out to hold a service or otherwise minister to the Canadian ground crew. Once, when Rodger was returning to McChord, a piston went through the cowling of one engine. Soon after, another engine started to leak oil and had to be turned off. With only two engines left the mandatory Mayday signal was sent out and a USAF B-25 bomber, specially equipped with a boat in its bomb bay for sea rescues, was sent to accompany the Canadian aircraft "home." About four hours out of McChord the aircraft came into visual sight, but that was it. Even on two engines, the North Star managed to limp back to McChord and arrive fifty minutes ahead of the B-25.

ARMY CHAPLAINS IN KOREA

Padre R.C. Nunn would be the first Canadian chaplain on the ground in Korea with the 2nd Battalion of the Princess Patricia's Canadian Light Infantry. After only two months at the Canadian training area at Miryang, however, he had a severe recurrence of pneumonia, an ailment which had plagued him since training in Wainwright, and he was forced to withdraw to the hospital in Seoul and then return to Canada. Immediately, Durnford and Cunningham were dispatched to Korea, and the latter was sent forward to carry on in Nunn's place.[3] These men were soon followed by Padres G.F. Bickley and H.A. Doig. Eventually, Nunn was able to return to Korea and fulfil his year's commitment. Roger Nunn was a quiet man who, while gentle, could be a real strength for the men because he was a good listener. When the going got rough Roger Nunn could sometimes be seen setting up his easel to paint on the hills of Korea. Later in 1951, R.E.M. Yerburgh, J.D.L. Howson, J.F.S. Ford and, for a short time, G.A.W. Lark arrived in Korea.

ARMY CHAPLAINS, KOREA		
R.C. Nunn	R.W. Pierce	M.K. Roberts
R.G.C. Cunningham	R.E.M. Yerburgh	E.W. MacQuarrie
R.C.H. Durnford	K.G. Docksey	G.G. Mercer
J. Cardy	W.W. Buxton	J.D.L. Howson
J.A. Filshie	G.F. Bickley	J.F.S. Ford
R.H. Dobson	H.A. Doig	G.A.W. Lark
J.F. Moorhead	H.W. Johnson	H.H. Vines
L.A. Dignan	O.A. Hopkins	J.A. Davidson

The Army trained for Korea at Wainwright, Alberta, and at Fort Lewis, located south of Seattle in the United States. The senior brigade chaplain, Major Roy Durnford, and his team soon moved to Fort Lewis, and Wainwright was taken over by a reinforcement brigade which would be cared for by a team under Major Joe Cardy. Durnford had served during the Second World War as regimental chaplain of the Seaforth Highlanders. Soldiers from the Seaforths remembered Durnford from Christmas Day at Ortona when he had led carol singing in a shell-battered church. Durnford had received his DSO for evacuating the wounded under heavy shell fire north of Bagnacavallo. The official citation told of the padre taking D Company's casualties back to the regimental aid post under machine gun and mortar fire. He then set off on foot to aid the men of A Company although advised that the ground might not be cleared of enemy. Major Durnford organized a shuttle service and remained in the open at a crossroads, completely disregarding occasional mortar fire until all were taken care of.[4]

In Korea, the Durnford legend continued to grow. On one occasion, following an ambush, Brigadier J.M. Rockingham, commander of the 25th Brigade, issued an order that no one was to drive around unaccompanied. It was not long before Rockingham and his escort chanced to meet Durnford driving around, as always, by himself. "Roy, didn't I issue an order that no one was to travel around unprotected?" Durnford replied: "Sir, you have only the 25th Brigade to protect you but I have the whole host of heaven! Good day, Sir." And Durnford drove off leaving Rockingham speechless.[5]

Padre Cunningham was the first chaplain to be recruited who was never given an honorary rank.[6] The plight of the Canadian chaplains held prisoner in Japan had created such embarrassment that a decision had finally been made to give all future chaplains substantive rank. In Cunningham's case the process was easy because he had held a commission while serving as an infantry officer during the Second World War. From this point in October 1950, all serving chaplains and all newly hired chaplains in the Army and the Air Force were commissioned as officers. This was an important change and yet it slipped through, perhaps because of Korea, without controversy or dissent.

Recruited on the streets of Calgary, the Princess Patricia's Canadian Light Infantry (PPCLI) left Canada to train in the United States in November 1950 and then spent ten more weeks training just south of Seoul. Many Canadians remembered what had happened in Hong Kong less than ten years before and would not tolerate the same mistakes. It was not until March 1951 that their commanding officer, Colonel James R. Stone, decided that his soldiers were fit to fight. The Canadian battalion would go into action as a part of a Commonwealth Division.[7] The Patricias served with the Royal Australian Infantry and the New Zealand Artillery. They were supported by the Indian Field Ambulance. These were excellent units whose commanders all had Second World War experience. According to Cunningham, the Chinese, while being a formidable enemy, were not in the same league as the Germans had been in World War II. Unlike the situation in the previous war, he described the ground and the weather in Korea as absolutely terrible.

It was for its part in the battle of Kapyong that the 2nd PPCLI was awarded a United States presidential citation, an award that Cunningham would wear proudly for years to come. The actual fighting line was ten miles north of Kapyong and was held by the 6th Korean Division. On April 23, 1951, the Koreans were routed by the advancing Chinese and the 25th Brigade was ordered to hold the valley at Kapyong. An Australian regiment was assigned to the east side of the valley on Hill 504 and the PPCLI was sent to the west side of the valley on Hill 677. Two British regiments were positioned slightly to the rear to give depth to the defence. On the night of April 23-24, the Australians were severely infiltrated and engaged and were forced to pull back to the British position. This left the PPCLI on Hill 677 with no friendly troops on either flank. On the night of April 24, B Company, which had been moved from its dug-in position to protect the flank, was attacked. One platoon was overrun but the company held while a strong enemy force moved against battalion headquarters. When the enemy broke through the trees within 200 yards of the Canadian position, every available support weapon opened fire. Nonetheless, D Company was soon overrun, and the company commander called down artillery fire on his own position in order to drive off the enemy. By the morning of April 25, things were relatively quiet. The PPCLI had lost ten men and twenty-seven had been wounded, but morale was never higher.[8]

In Korea Cunningham normally worked closely with the medical officer. He knew that it was important to be in the field with the men and at the position where casualties would be dealt with. "Fellows don't want to die," he said, "and the chaplain can give them assurance just by being there.[9] Cunningham also spent time with the men in the front trenches as often as was possible. One thing for certain, he was not going to get the reputation of one chaplain he had encountered in the Second World War who had earned the nickname "Burying Sam" by turning up to ask "Anyone to be buried today?" and moving on immediately if the reply was negative.[10] The men were not impressed. In the early days of the war, Cunningham's habit of visiting the trenches held its dangers, but he would never carry a weapon. He could see no justification for a padre to carry a weapon at any time. His favourite saying on the subject was: "The time that I have to carry a weapon is the day the war is over."[11]

In Korea the men were scattered all over the place and worship services were held wherever they happened to be. Cunningham found himself climbing hills and going from place to place, sometimes not even knowing what day was Sunday. "Grab'em where you get'em" was his motto. Cunningham observed that in situations such as Korea "soldiers were not as indifferent to religion as you might think."[12]

In April 1951, the United Nations opened a new cemetery in Pusan. Chaplains from each of the twenty-five nations involved came together for the dedication. Because most of the casualties had been Protestant, Cunningham was selected to take a couple of soldiers and represent Canada. During the rehearsal, chaplains from various countries wandered out onto the field to lay their wreaths. Their lack of soldierly conduct disturbed Cunningham, and when Canada's turn came he instructed his soldiers to look smart. Together they marched up to the monument, saluted smartly, and placed the wreath. Later, the officer in charge of the operation asked them to repeat their performance and held their efforts up as an example to the other nations of the proper way to behave at such a ceremony.

Meanwhile, back in Canada, Padre Stone was still struggling to find men who would go to Korea. Second World War chaplains remained reluctant to go overseas and to complicate matters, the decision to send families to Germany with the occupation forces meant that a constant supply of clergy would soon be needed for that tasking. When Howard Johnson, who had served in the Second World War, was approached about rejoining and going to Germany he and his wife were delighted. They would be one of the first Canadian military families to move to Europe. There was some confusion about how the move would be paid for, but in good faith the Johnsons began to pack. Within two weeks, probably unknown to them, the posting was changed to Korea. Johnson felt that he had been duped and protested, but, good soldier that he was, within three weeks he was on Hill 355 facing the Chinese with the Royal Canadian Regiment (RCR).[13]

Johnson's home away from home was a dugout in the side of a hill. Each day he was on the hill at 5:00 a.m. Services were held in the men's bunkers, perhaps with a flag spread over a box of ammunition and candles and a cross on top. Sometimes under fire, men of all denominations came to these services. When there was a break in the fighting, Johnson would push for a church parade. On one occasion, his jeep was hit by a mortar round. Fortunately, he was away from it at the time. During a big push when the Chinese overran the hill, Padre Johnson located himself at the regimental aid post. Afterwards, he conducted a large memorial service for those whose lives were lost in the battle. Johnson then moved to the 25th Canadian Field Dressing Station for the rest of his year of duty and continued to serve in the same outstanding manner.

After his tour, Padre Howard Johnson was awarded an MBE. The citation[14] related how he had "devoted himself wholeheartedly to the welfare of the men in the units under his care, to the point of endangering his own health." On many occasions he "visited forward positions" and "was always on hand to encourage the wounded and to minister to the dying, giving comfort and encouragement wherever his presence was required." Padre Johnson "conducted services of worship frequently in company areas under shellfire and during periods of enemy assaults against our positions he moved continually among the men, by his presence providing a steadying influence which contributed in great measure to the high morale of the battalion."

Police Action

When Padre Joe Cardy finally arrived in Korea to replace Durnford, the war had been reduced pretty much to the level of a police action. Earlier, the two sides had spent much of their time chasing each other up and down the country. Now the positions had been stabilized and would stay that way, dug in for the rest of the war. There were still casualties and a fair amount of danger as both sides were actively involved in probing and patrolling. On Cardy's team were J.A. Filshie, J.D.L. Howson, J.F. Moorhead, J.F.S. Ford, M.K. Roberts, and R.H. Dobson.

The team had trained with the reinforcement brigade in Wainwright for eight months and during this time Cardy, who had come to be known as a rather tough or severe chaplain, received wonderful support from all of the local churches and especially from Bishop W.F. Barfoot, the Anglican archbishop of Edmonton. Although the men were training, they could be relieved from their duties to attend church membership classes, and Cardy was able to prepare one hundred and twenty young men of all denominations for confirmation.[15]

On one cold, wet, and windy Saturday night Bishop Barfoot arrived at Wainwright with plans to confirm the Anglican candidates the next day. He found Cardy waiting for him in the officers' mess with a problem: some of the young men who were to be confirmed the next morning were being shipped out in the early hours before any service could take place. At that very moment, Cardy had them standing by in a tent down the road from the main camp, waiting to see what could happen. The bishop graciously agreed to confirm them that night. While Padre Cardy held up a gas lamp, Bishop Barfoot conducted a memorable confirmation service, which Cardy described as "personal, warm and loving."[16] The young soldiers never forgot the bishop's concern for them.

R.H. Dobson received his orders to go to Korea in March 1952. In a paper describing his experiences, Bob Dobson gave the following account of his trip across the Pacific on the USS *Marine Phoenix*:

> I went with 1000 RCR and 3000 Americans aboard an old Kaiser built boat that had a reputation for breaking apart in the middle of a storm. We had storms: enroute there were many soldiers who wanted to go home. I was the only chaplain on board. The captain gave me his cabin for interviews. I became sick. His response, "Chaplain, that cabin in the bow goes up and down 14 feet with every seventh wave." On deck, in a warm sun, I administered Holy Communion to several thousand soldiers until my back ached with the bending over. Otherwise, it was a heady experience.[17]

During the trip, Dobson had to deal with a Spanish-speaking soldier who tried to commit suicide by jumping overboard and whom Dobson described as a manic depressive. Then there was an interview with a "religious depressive": a young man secured in a straitjacket and a padded cell. On top of it all was the challenge of his own occasional feelings of homesickness and two days of extreme seasickness.[18]

The relative stability of these later times gave the chaplains in the rear lines an opportunity to fashion a more permanent set-up. At the front they lived in underground bunkers, but those in the rear enjoyed the luxury of a canvas camp. Eventually wooden floors were installed in the tents, and there was even a floor in the chapel. A Korean carpenter cut up bingo balls and used them for edging around the altar. There was lots of brass available and some of it was put to use for the cross and for flower vases.

The quieter time gave men the opportunity to think more about home and the problems they had left behind. In Korea they were halfway around the globe and even minor problems that would have been easily solved in Canada took on a major significance. Since there was no way for them to get home, a good part of the chaplains' time was spent helping them deal with those personal problems.

Not long after he had arrived, Durnford had acquired his own compound and a Quonset hut in which he set up a Christian leadership school. Soldiers in need of a break from the front lines could go back to the compound for two weeks of moral and spiritual training. Soon after arriving, Joe Cardy had confirmation classes going and the school was full of soldiers.

Cardy's course included a one-day trip to Seoul, which was thirty miles to the south of their location.[19] Cardy would take the men to visit a hospital run by a Canadian United Church medical missionary, Dr. Florence Murray, who was assisted by Ada Bourns, RN. The hospital and medical school was located in a decrepit old building and it was a beehive of activity. Knowing the kind feelings that all soldiers have for little children, Cardy would take the soldiers first to the children's ward of the hospital, and then to a nearby orphanage. While being shown around, the visitors would come across a room full of cleaning supplies and paint and they were always happy to clean up the place. Cardy reported: "Florence Murray did a wonderful job in Korea."[20] The chaplains' school was a good idea: the courses and the visit to the hospital gave the soldiers something positive that they could carry back home.

Another project that received a tremendous amount of support from Canadian soldiers was Bowha Orphanage. Writing home shortly after his arrival in Seoul, Padre Dobson[21] reported: "They are gradually building and their story is pathetic. They need money. They need drugs. They need clothes. They need food. Tell your friends to send me parcels. Send me your cast off clothes. The lads in the 27th Bde. have donated over $10,000.00 of their own pay already."[22] The orphanage, run by a Buddhist society, housed two hundred and fifty children. Every room was crowded with children who ate, slept, and took their schooling all in that one room. Their clothes were cast-offs and their food was leftover Army rations.

Eventually, when Padre Alex Filshie had to be pulled back because of medical problems, Dobson made it to the front lines. Following Filshie would not be easy because he had been very well-liked by the battalion, as was the battalion's Roman Catholic padre, Father John H. MacGregor. MacGregor was probably the best-liked chaplain in all of Korea and was one who would "pop up anywhere and everywhere. He held the respect and the trust of the men."[23] Dobson, saxophone in hand,[24] moved quickly to meet the challenge of the position and expressed his delight in a letter written to Colonel Stone, the director of Chaplain Services in Ottawa:

> This note is to inform you that I am in the field, cosily situated in my own dug-out, built this week by the loving hands of a dozen Korean labourers. I'm situated on the side of the hill and the mortars in the valley seem intent on lifting the sand-bags off my roof. Father MacGregor (RC) is right next door and we've tramped around the hills together this week, introducing ourselves to the companies in their positions and holding services at the same hour everywhere in order to provide the maximum coverage with the minimum confusion to the lads. This is the opportunity I've sought ever since I joined the Army in 1942 and I'm enjoying every minute of it. The men here are more warmly disposed, and respond to the chaplain more readily than the men in static units farther back, or amid the dissipations and immorality of Seoul.[25]

The front line in Korea would be an experience that Dobson would never forget. There were hair-raising moments such as the time when Dobson was helping the stretcher bearers through the barbed wire on the perimeter of the camp. The team was on bare rock when mortar rounds started to explode around them. Later they measured and discovered that the shells had landed in a triangle pattern about fifteen yards around them. It was Dobson's first real appreciation of what it was like to face death and, after that, he was no longer afraid of enemy fire.[26]

In an interview with Padre Gordon Shields, years later, Dobson reported:

> I remember a communion service that I had arranged for my troops up the line, and that day they were badly clobbered by the enemy. Six of our lads got killed. I had the communion service that night. And when it came to the place "my blood shed for you," I broke and there happened to be another chaplain there—Padre Pelletier

was with me. He carried on. You know it was years after that before I could do the communion service without pausing and getting my composure straightened out. That's what I cherish about the experience in Korea, the new understanding I had of death and the new understanding I had of the blood of Jesus that was shed for me - for all of us. It was a great understanding.[27]

Most of the chaplains developed good relationships with the men in Korea, and some, such as Padre George Bickley, had equally good relationships with their officers. Bickley's commanding officer referred to his chaplain as his "spiritual staff officer" and expected a daily visit from him. Speaking of Bickley's work in Korea, Brigadier General Rockingham said: "George's name will be remembered with the RCR where every man loved him. Every man who was wounded or killed tore at the heartstrings of Bickley. No one could have done more than he did in the total giving of himself."[28]

Just out of seminary, Padre Ormond Hopkins[29] got along especially well with the adjutant of his regiment. Back in Canada the adjutant's wife was very active in her church and he wanted to take confirmation classes. A few nights later he was confirmed and his example was soon followed by the second in command of the unit and then by fouteen other unit officers.

The chaplains gave spiritual support to the soldiers, but they were concerned about every phase of their unit's life. Padre Alex Filshie, a recipient of an MBE for his service in Korea, was one of these men. Filshie, who had been a tank commander in the Second World War, served with the 2nd Battalion of the PPCLI from October 23, 1951, and then with the 1st Battalion of the same unit until moving back to the hospital[30] in Hero, Japan, in May 1952.

In Korea, Filshie was popular and his services were well attended. He visited all the unit positions on a regular basis, especially those in the front lines. He would never take a jeep anywhere that he could walk, a fact that was not overlooked by the soldiers. Lieutenant Colonel Jim MacIntosh, then a private in the infantry, recalled that you would see Filshie coming with a big bag on his back, full of books and other physical comforts, and he always found the time to sit down and talk with you for hours.[31] Filshie conducted padre's hours and bunker services whenever and wherever he could. Always, he exhibited a quiet and contagious confidence. When patrols went forward he waited with the regimental medical officer where his presence brought comfort to the wounded. He was well known for his ability with the plasma bottle. According to the citation for his award, Filshie's greatest contribution was in the quality of his example: "His absolute sincerity, his sense of vocation, his complete dedication to the sacred office to which he had been ordained was an inspiration to all who knew him."[32]

For the chaplains, a lot of training had to be done on the ground when they got to Korea. As the senior chaplain, Padre Cardy gave people an opportunity to serve in the quiet rear areas at first and then, when they had gained some experience and confidence, he let them go forward with the infantry. This was a sensible scheme but it didn't always work out as planned.

A Sense Of Survival

When Padre M.K. Roberts arrived in Korea, Cardy said that he was looking up a hill and there was a fat little guy standing there. "Come down and let me get to know you," shouted Cardy, who went on to report that: "It was just great because Matt was a terrific person and the soldiers just loved him."[33] Matt Roberts had been recruited in Newfoundland. He trained for three months at Longue Point and Ipperwash. Then after two weeks' training on a reserve chaplains' course at Petawawa, he was sent to Fort Lewis and then to Korea.

Padre Cardy took Roberts on a swing around to familiarize him with the area. They came across a tank that had been winched up a hill into a better shooting position. "You should know some of those boys around that tank," said Cardy, "because you came out on the same boat with them. Would you like to go up there and visit them?" "I should like that very much sir." Just as the two chaplains started up the hill, the enemy started to range in with some mortars. Being new to Korea, Roberts probably didn't know what was about to happen. All there was to see were some white puffs on the ground.

Cardy's adrenalin started to flow, and he knew that they had better get up to the tank pretty fast. Back in Canada Cy Stone would never forgive him if he got this brand new chaplain killed on his first day on the job in Korea. "I want to see what kind of shape you're in Matt," shouted Cardy. "See how quickly you can get up under that tank!" Roberts took off up the hill as another round came in and wounded a British soldier just below their location. Like a flash, Cardy, who had been known in the Second Wold War as a man with courage to burn, was down the hill to give what aid he could to the soldier. Later, on the way back to camp, Cardy apologized to Roberts: "I wasn't trying to be smart with you. The last thing I expected today was to get you into a dangerous situation like that and I do apologize. It's not fair to a new guy to throw him in when mortars are falling all around." Of course, the tank had fired back and there had been quite a bit of noise. Roberts said: "Oh, sir, after I get a little experience it will be quite

Archbishop W.F. Barfoot confirms a Korean interpreter working with the Canadian Army in Korea, 1951.

Padre R.C. Nunn

Chapel made of ammunition boxes: "A Korean carpenter cut up bingo balls and used them for edging around the altar."

Padre J.D.L. Howson conducts field service, Korea, 1952.

all right—when you learn how to tell the difference between the ones coming in and the ones going out."

The more experienced of the wartime padres already enjoyed that sense of survival that Matt Roberts was learning. The story has been told about Roy Durnford who was travelling in his jeep when he met up with another padre. They stopped on the road to chat and all of a sudden Durnford shouted "Get out of here!" Seconds later the chaplains looked back at the shell hole where they had been parked. "Roy had that sense of survival."[34]

Once every week Cardy held a meeting for all of his chaplains at the headquarters building. One day he asked Matt Roberts how he could manage so well and never be afraid. Roberts responded; "I get up in the morning and I commit myself to God. After that it doesn't matter what happens to me."

Roberts served in Korea with the 1st Battalion of the Royal Canadian Regiment. The battalion had taken over from the 2nd RCR and had inherited the responsibility for a young Korean orphan named Noo Nong-Joo but ever after to be known as Willy Royal. When the 1st Battalion neared the end of its tour, Matt was given the task of getting Willy into one of the many overcrowded Korean orphanages. Roberts appealed to a bishop in the civilian church in Seoul and a place was found for the boy. The years passed and Roberts kept in touch. Eventually the two were reunited in 1987 when Willy Royal came to visit Canada and the padre who had helped him survive.[35]

MORALITY, IDEOLOGY, AND WELFARE

When the Americans first arrived in Korea they had been pulverized. The first soldiers in the fray had been occupation troops in Japan. These men had been used to the living "good life." They were out of shape and lazy, and many were accused of being morally corrupt. There were a lot of deaths and a lot of prisoners, many of whom were won over to the other side. Once captured, the enemy found that the Americans could easily be converted to the Communist way of thinking. Back in the United States, this fuelled the idea that the conflict was really an ideological battle for the minds of men. Steps would have to be taken to strengthen the moral resolve of the American serviceman. In training camps, the Americans started to toughen up their men. They tried to treat them just as they would be treated if they were captured by the enemy. This did not work. Men were still being captured and they were still being brainwashed.

As time went on, the Americans found the solution to the ideological problem in the resolve of the Gloucestershire Regiment. Early in the battle, the British Gloucestershire Regiment[36] had been overrun and captured by the Communists. Their lives as POWs had not been easy, but not one of them went over to the Communist side. The British Army attributed the moral strength of their soldiers first of all to their strong religious faith. The next strongest bond that could not be broken was the soldiers' ties to their regimental family. The British knew that wars were not won by tough men but by ordinary citizens with strong family ties and a moral resolve to fight. It was not long before chaplains in the American Army were seriously involved in creating and conducting a program of moral training and character building.

While Canadians did not move in this direction with the same degree of fervour as the Americans, some influence was inevitable. Early in 1950, even before Korea, Dr. Gallagher of the Canadian Council of Churches suggested to the Canadian government that it would have to do something to counter the ideological deterioration of Canadian soldiers and that a training program might be appropriate.[37] About this time the Moral Rearmament Movement had started to exert its influence on the civilian churches in Canada. Individual Christians, some of whom would be senior soldiers in Korea, were being challenged to exert political pressure whenever possible. To clarify the chaplains' own thinking on Moral Rearmament, the Joint Services Chaplaincy Committee decided that current affairs and spiritual direction were two different things and reaffirmed the decision of the Canadian Council of Churches that the chaplaincy was the only recognized channel for the spiritual direction of armed forces personnel.[38]

The year passed without any response from the government to Gallagher's request for a training program, and the chaplains attempted to raise the issue again in January 1952. At a regular meeting, the JSCC considered the need for missions as a response to the alcohol problem and to the moral laxity of the soldiers in Korea. They discussed "the need for some positive action to counteract the ever increasing apathy towards the value of things spiritual." As an example, they referred to "materialism and communism from without and a general deterioration of morals from within."[39] Later that month the chaplains received a very reserved approval for such missions from the Personnel Members Committee.[40]

The JSCC decided that at least one mission per base per year would be necessary to accomplish their ends. A typical mission would last for one week.[41] Senior chaplains from Command and Ottawa would be brought in along with special speakers. Members of the chapel congregations and all personnel on the base would be encouraged to attend. A request was made to the PMC to pay for the special speakers.

In light of the PMC's lack of enthusiasm for the project, Dr. Gallagher outlined the plan in a letter to the minister of national defence, Brooke Claxton, noting that the American military had initiated monthly compulsory padre's hours for every soldier. Gallagher hoped that the Canadian government would be persuaded to follow the American lead and get on the moral bandwagon. Claxton responded to Gallagher in the same reserved manner as the PMC had, saying that it was not his intention to curtail padre's hours in any way, but he would make no commitments. Two weeks later the PMC again turned down the chaplains' request for money, explaining that the cost of missions should be borne by the people to whom the chaplains ministered and not by the public.[42]

Back in Canada, a few missions were held as base-wide chapel activities, but these never amounted to the ideological missions that were first envisioned. This may be contrasted with the situation in the United States where the chaplains became a regular part of an ideological training program. Since Korea, all United States servicemen have been required to attend at least one highly structured padre's hour a month as a part of the Character Guidance Program.[43]

While this discussion was taking place, the moderator of the United Church of Canada, Dr. C.M. Nicholson, and other Canadian church leaders[44] were visiting Canadian soldiers in Korea during the summer of 1951. While he was there Nicholson received a message from his church headquarters in Toronto, saying that concern was being expressed in Canada about the welfare of the soldiers in the Special Service Force.[45]

In contrast to the situation during the previous two wars, Canadians were not self-contained in Korea and so had taken no auxiliary services, such as the Salvation Army or the YMCA, to care for the needs of the soldiers. Welfare needs were the responsibility of the Americans and the British. The Americans provided all the comforts such as ice cream, steaks, and vegetables to soldiers in the rear echelons. Closer to the front, the Canadian soldiers used their own ingenuity.

On his return to Canada, Nicholson first sought to reassure the public that their sons and husbands were being cared for spiritually. In notes for a speech, Nicholson wrote: "For those whose own kin are in Korea, there can be the assurance that their spiritual needs are constantly remembered. Our Churches have carefully chosen men for the office of Chaplain,—men who have an easy approach to other men, and above all, men who have mature experiences of people's troubles and hopes and trials. When I think of Padres like Roy Durnford, Chief Chaplain in Korea, and Padres like Roger Nunn or Alex Filshie, I can tell you that in war and the shadow of death, the promise of life more abundant in Christ receives its great witness. And the men I have mentioned are only three of an excellent company of men of all Churches who are with our troops every day every week."[46]

Behind the scenes, however, Nicholson pushed for more adequate welfare facilities and for something to be done about the misuse of alcohol. The minister of national defence reacted strongly to the suggestions of inadequate care. Writing to the Canadian Council of Churches Chaplaincy Committee, he assured Dr. Gallagher that canteens did exist to serve non-alcoholic drinks. Indeed, the minister had been there and had enjoyed them. Also, Gallagher was assured that qualified and carefully selected welfare officers were attached to units serving abroad and all possible facilities and equipment had been provided for their work.

In response to the minister, the Council of Churches Chaplaincy Committee joined forces with the Roman Catholic bishop of Ottawa and paid Mr. Claxton a visit. In their brief they wrote that they were glad to hear about the welfare officers appointed for Korea but would now like to know more about their qualifications, equipment, and facilities. Reports reaching the Canadian churches alleged "that an oversupply of hard liquor is finding its way into illicit traffic in Korea,"[47] and the churches therefore renewed their requests for an appropriate educational program, that might be conducted under the direction of chaplains, on the effects of alcohol.

The minister of national defence responded to the churches by having a detailed report, dated June 11, 1952,[48] prepared on the welfare of the 25th Brigade in Korea. It noted that each battalion in Korea had a welfare officer, accountant, and projectionist. At the brigade level was a captain, a driver, a storeman, and an accountant for a total complement of six officers and twelve men. They had projectors, a jeep, and seven three-quarter-ton trucks. Most of the films used by the welfare team in Korea were obtained through American and British sources. Field units always had their own supply of sports equipment. The Canadian Legion had provided thirty pocket books per month. In addition it provided forty different magazines and newspapers, and so on. The newspaper *Japan News* was provided free at the rate of one copy for every three men. Stationery, in addition to that supplied with rations, amounted to three envelopes and six sheets per man per week. Canteen supplies including beer and soft drinks were purchased from British, Australian, and American sources and were sold at minimum price. CBC radio shows were broadcast and live shows were supplied in the form of American and British concert parties. There were twenty free cigarettes per day per man and an additional eight hundred per month could be obtained through the paymaster.

British and American leave centres were available in Japan for the Canadians. The Commonwealth Division leave camp at Inchon accommodated seven hundred and fifty at a time. The division's entertainment group was at Inchon, and Canadians could have seventy two hours leave there every one hundred days. After four months in Korea a soldier was entitled to transportation by air to Japan for five clear days at Ebeau Camp, Tokyo. This camp was run by the Australians and accommodated a maximum of one hundred and fifty Canadians at any one time. It provided reading rooms and an information service, arranged tours, and helped soldiers to purchase gifts to be sent home. Games such as cribbage and dart boards could be purchased through military stores at very little cost. Special low rates were in effect for telegraph and cable services, and the Legion's educational service was available.

Nothing more was heard from the churches on the matter of welfare. They seemed prepared to accept what had been done and, in any case, the Korean War had settled down to being little more than a political confrontation along the 38th parallel.

The exchanges with the government over the issues of morality and welfare provide an example of where the Church stood in the eyes of the Canadian government. The clergy felt that they were entitled to speak on the welfare of the soldiers and that it was their responsibility to uphold the important function of character guidance. The Canadian government accepted the churches' concerns but suggested that everything that was necessary for the men's welfare was being done. Any missions or character guidance would be the responsibility of the churches, not the government.

CEASEFIRE

The official ceasefire of the Korean War was signed on July 27, 1953. Terms included the withdrawal of forces from the declared demilitarized zone within seventy-two hours, the construction and occupation of new positions, and the exchange of POWs. All of the combatants, save for a South African fighter squadron, remained to ensure that the peace would hold. India agreed to chair the Neutral Nations Repatriation Commission and withdrew its field medical unit. During those last days of that phase of the conflict, Padre Gordon Mercer was there to witness the exchange of prisoners: a total of thirty-two Canadians were returned between April and September 1954. He noted that a group of fifty Koreans came across the line carrying a huge banner of the cross of St. Andrew, a reminder of the many Presbyterians in that country. The Gloucestershire Regiment marched across as a unit.

THE CHAPLAIN IN THE THEATRE OF ACTIVE OPERATIONS

On his return to Canada, Padre Ray Cunningham was posted to Eastern Command headquarters and was asked to speak at Camp Aldershot about his experiences. Coming from a padre of his stature so soon after World War II and Kapyong, his talk on the role of the chaplain in a theatre of operations was a classic. (A written version of this talk is to be found in Appendix II)

Another report on the role of the chaplain in Korea was presented to a group of Army chaplains at Camp Borden by Padre Roger Nunn on his return to Canada. Nunn wrote:

> Two weeks ago, I decided to devote most of the afternoon to this paper. Of course there was the regular Thursday afternoon visit to the Guard Room; but from the experience of the past few weeks that would not take long. Then one pastoral call must be made on a woman who was having husband trouble. Still the larger portion of the afternoon should be mine. But five men saw me at the Guard house—all with troubles, some very real and some fancied, but everyone demanding attention; even the lad who asked if I would put in a word for him because he had been AWOL for 45 days for what was originally his grandmother's funeral. I had to spend time explaining that nothing I could say would help and that he could trust the fairness of the Commanding Officer. The troubled wife had a long story of distress, which it would have been cruel to cut short. And by the time I had given what help I could, the afternoon was gone. Everyone here has had the same experience. At all hours people are seeking us out and we as pastors must not fail them.
>
> What a responsibility! Heavy enough if it were social welfare only, but almost crushing when we are charged with the care of souls. We are charged before God with the souls of our people. Jesus asked Peter to furnish only one proof of his love: "Feed my sheep." We are no different from Peter. And if we fail to feed Christ's sheep and Christ's lambs, we fail all along the line.
>
> During the brief period I spent with the 2nd Patricias at their training area in Miryang, Korea, I conducted a Padre's Hour with members of Support Company. Later I discussed that padre's hour with my tent mate, the Roman Catholic chaplain, Jim Valley. I had been dealing with the number one Korea problem, venereal disease. In the Padre's Hour considerable time had been spent discussing various factors tending to lower morale and open the

way for Venereal Disease. Jim, with his Irish up, exploded, "It's their souls, it's their immortal souls we must talk about." He was right. Only by getting to grips with their immortal souls and awakening within those lads their need for God was there hope of shaking them from moral lethargy into moral purity. Jim's explosion was a timely reminder that we must look on men as souls for whom Christ died and for whose eternal welfare He rose again from the grave.

Now in order to meet the needs of a man's soul we may possibly have to see the Commanding Officer about securing 14 days compassionate leave to be with his dying child or to prevail upon the powers that be to secure him better housing or credit at the camp store to provide his family with essential groceries in time of emergency or it may mean first aid on the battlefield. These good works may be done as the expression of our love, the cup of cold water was given in Christ's name. In them we do what we do because we are interested in the man as a child of God. We are trying to follow the footsteps of our lord as he moved about the villages and cities of Galilee, doing good."[49]

Chapter 4

BUILDING THE PLANT

FAMILIES AND CHAPELS

IN THE DECADE after the war Canadian society underwent an extraordinary transformation as the servicemen came back from overseas. Those who returned to civilian life were eager to plunge into new jobs, to establish families, and to enjoy the many new experiences that were open to them. Among the many changes that occurred was the flowering of suburban communities on the edges of towns and cities to accommodate and service growing populations. The churches were quick to realize the opportunity thus offered, and they were soon vying for the best locations for their buildings in the new communities. The many programs these churches offered to the newcomers helped to create a true sense of community in these suburbs.

These developments in the wider world were paralleled in the armed forces. Despite the overall reduction in the number of personnel after the war, the Canadian military establishment remained substantially higher than it had been in 1939. Moreover, now that the war was over, the servicemen who remained were no longer prepared to endure separation from their families or accommodation in the substandard or temporary buildings. Just as the suburbs had blossomed in civilian life, so living accommodation for military families—Permanent Married Quarters (PMQs)—were created close to the various bases. These new planned communities were largely in place by 1950, but it was to be some time before they acquired all of the amenities that their civilian counterparts possessed.

Life in a PMQ was a novel experience for most of those who occupied them. The number of families who had been part of military life before the war were few and scattered, and in any case the established way of doing things was not always suitable to this new era. During this unsettled period, the churches and chapels provided a centre for socializing and many other activities. The chaplains found that ministering to servicemen and their families in peacetime was not confined to conducting services and offering spiritual guidance. Just as they had been during the war, they were soon involved with—and often the initiators of—many other endeavours and organizations as the bases developed into communities that encompassed not just the servicemen but their families as well.

The ability to take the initiative and to innovate that had marked the best wartime chaplains was evident in the activities of Padres Rodger, Light, and, especially, Cardy in the early years of peacetime. In Trenton Padre Bill Rodger spent most of 1947 locating apartments, rooms, and other housing for the families of the airmen. Towards Christmas he was feeling quite good about having everyone under some kind of roof, when he remembered that his own wife and children were still with relatives in Ottawa! The base commander offered Rodger the unused annex to the base hospital, along with tools, wood, and gyprock. Rodger immediately created a lovely three-bedroom apartment for his family permitting them to be together for Christmas.[1] The following summer they were posted to Rockcliffe.

At Borden, an Army base, the large numbers of men and their families made the accommodation situation more difficult. When Padre Joe Cardy[2] arrived there was no official accommodation for married people on the base, and there certainly wasn't enough housing available in the surrounding villages or in the town of Barrie. Cardy soon found himself on a committee to build emergency housing. Two or three young families would be given materials and part of a temporary wartime building known as an H hut. They would be told to go and build their own houses. Some of the apartments were splendid productions while in others the rooms might only be separated by bed sheets or partial walls that didn't reach the ceiling. Hundreds of young families were thereby established in crude but comfortable housing. Like the early pioneers, soldiers who had fought side by side in the war now helped each other to build suitable accommodations.

Joe Cardy had been on his own at Camp Borden for about a year when the adjutant general of the Army visited the camp. Cardy was called into an office and asked how he spent his day. A typical day for this postwar Army padre started at 6:00 a.m. at the office where he spent two hours getting his staff work ready for his secretary's arrival at 8:00 a.m. Cardy then returned home for breakfast before starting to make the rounds of the camp's training schools. He might attend a graduation parade at the school of armour and then stop for coffee at the school of infantry prior to delivering a padre's hour at one of the schools training soldiers under the apprentice system or at the detention barracks. After lunch was time for interviews with troubled soldiers and confirmation classes for teenagers. And once the Army had started a public school for dependent children on the base, the padre had to fit religious education for each grade into his schedule. For three hours in the evenings, Monday to Thursday, he visited PMQs, because that was the only time that he could see husbands and wives together. In every visit he included a prayer for the individuals, their family, and the home. At 10:00 p.m., a tired padre would meet his wife, and they would go to a friend's home, usually the commanding officer's residence, for coffee and bridge. It made for a long day, but after the war Cardy was glad just to be alive, to be able to work hard, and to do what he loved to do. The adjutant general was impressed with the volume of work and arranged for Cardy to have a chaplain to assist him.

At first, the only chapel at Camp Borden was one that had been used for prisoners within the detention barracks. Getting a chapel in the new accommodation area became one of Cardy's prime goals. The commanding officer of the base told him and his Roman Catholic compatriot, Father Dillon, that they could make a chapel out of the first building that they found empty.

Cardy and Dillon set their minds to it, and before long they found a suitable hall that had been used by the YMCA during the war. However, it was now being used to store refrigerator motors. Then, one morning the chaplains saw a large line-up of trucks outside the building. The men in charge had been given orders to move the motors out and to return with seven- to eight hundred pot-bellied stoves. As soon as the motors left Cardy shouted to Dillon: "Bar the doors ... don't let anybody in!" He then raced to the commanding officer: "We found a building for the chapel. Get in the car and come to see the building." Immediately the CO agreed and said: "It's yours!" When the trucks returned the padres told them that they would have to find somewhere else for their stoves.

The engineers were called upon to build the holy tables and other furnishings because there was no money to buy them. The badly worn floor was fixed by armoured corps apprentices. The wife of Cardy's new assistant, Padre M.J.D. Carson, was organist. She was a "real smasher," according to Cardy, and at padre's hours he would tell the apprentices where the church was and that they could join the choir. Then Mrs. Carson would come out and Cardy would "almost be trampled in the rush to sign up!"

Eventually the building had a main hall that could sit three- to four hundred people and an impressive lounge with nice furniture that could accommodate eighty or ninety teens for a Friday night dance. A second hall was set up as a small chapel for eighty to ninety people, and there was everything that the chaplains needed for office space and equipment.

This building soon became a centre of many community services which were badly needed. Many of the young wives were having babies, and the chaplains established a Red Cross unit with classes on child care and cooking. Cardy's wife, Maureen, talked to the Singer sewing machine company and they sent out an agent to conduct sewing classes. No one had very much money, and the chaplains made arrangements to provide a layette for each new baby. A chapel ladies' group was formed, which organized a swap shop and then went in with the Roman Catholic ladies to run a bazaar. The soldiers came to the bazaar and bought Christmas presents for their wives. There were no Scouts or Guides, so the Cardys started groups and remember having some lovely camping trips.

The deep commitment of Padre Cardy to the servicemen and their families was also evident in more personal ways. While visiting the big detention barracks at Camp Borden, Padre Cardy took a special interest in one of the prisoners. This man had been running a transport company scam sending convoys of cigarettes and alcohol to illegal destinations. After the fellow had served his time, Cardy helped him get a job in South America. Cardy was also in the habit of co-signing for bank loans because pay was quite low in the Army and very few personnel had any savings. One day he got a call from a bank to say that a soldier had defaulted and that the co-signer would have to pay a considerable sum. The camp commander found out and told Cardy it was wrong that he should get stuck like this: "The chaplain shouldn't be the font of all blessings," said the commander. The solution was to establish the Camp Borden Community Chest, the first of its kind on a military base. Units would compete to raise funds and then money would be available to loan those who really needed it.

Many of the soldiers in Borden had served in the war and they welcomed and responded to the dynamic ministry that Joe Cardy provided. Indeed many of them were a big help to the padre. Eventually Cardy organized a four-day conference for lay people which was held in North Bay with Arnold Edinborough as the guest speaker.

Ted Light had returned to the University of Saskatchewan in 1946 and served in the Air Force Reserve. When, in 1948, the final decision was made to have a permanent chaplain service in the RCAF, Light was invited to join it, and he found himself on a roving mission along the Alaska Highway. Light's responsibilities included Fort Nelson, where there were seventy-eighty Americans, Fort St. John, Whitehorse, and places in between such as Snagg, Watson Lake, and Asiac. The highway was under the control of the Army and most of the men were stationed in Whitehorse, so Light took services there.

In 1949 Padre Light was posted to Rivers, Manitoba, replacing Padre George Fee. The station commander was from the RCAF but the personnel were about half Army and there were even a few sailors. Among its other functions, Rivers was a parachute school, and as the initial accommodation problems had been resolved, Light sought to develop his role in other ways. To that end, he took the jump course during his tour of duty at Rivers, because "it seemed like the right thing to do."[3] During his time at Rivers, Padre Light also opened a new chapel. It was the second chapel in the RCAF, the first having been opened by Padre Bill Rodger at Rockcliffe. Suitable chapels might seem an obvious component of the new base communities but the construction of permanent chapels would soon become a vexatious and contentious issue.

WARTIME EXIGENCY OR PEACETIME REALITY

Although the chaplains knew that their role within a peacetime military would be different from that in war, they hardly expected that their work—indeed their very existence—would be challenged. Nor did they expect that such a challenge would come from the Church of England which had always had a somewhat privileged position vis-à-vis the military.

In fact, there had been a critical element within the Church of England for many years,[4] but it had been mostly silenced by the exigencies of the war. As peace came and the Chaplain Service expanded, old chains were rattled, and questions which the chaplains thought had been long since put to rest rose again.

The main question was one of ecclesiastical jurisdiction. The Chaplain Service was seen by many to be a wartime exigency that had undermined the jurisdiction of the individual churches over both clergy and doctrine. The distinctiveness of the denominations was endangered. After all, even when the churches co-operated with each other in the postwar years, there was always a sense of competition.[5] Moreover, the chaplains were presumed by some clergymen to have come to be too close to the government. Most of the major Protestant churches in Canada have sought to stand apart from the state and exercise their own authority over their adherents. The Church of England had managed to have the best of both worlds. It had been disestablished in Canada for many decades and thus controlled its own affairs, but it had nevertheless managed to retain a privileged position in society and hence a certain influence in government. During the war the numbers of Anglicans in the forces, the constraints on co-operation arising from certain rules of the denomination, and the residual effect of its position in society had meant that the Church of England and its chaplains had enjoyed a rather special position in the Chaplain Service. There were those to whom it never seemed to occur that things should be otherwise, and even after the Second World War their self-assurance had continued.

More specifically, in their dealings with military chaplains and with the government, it never occurred to some élitist elements, especially those of the Church of England, that their church should be given anything less than preferential treatment. The government and the military tried to respect the position of all of the churches but had insisted during reorganization that the Chaplain Service should be integrated into existing military structures. The Church of England soon learned that it would be tied, roughly, into the same bureaucratic organization as the other churches. Once the Church of England became aware of this decision and of its implications for jurisdiction over and service to the large peacetime military forces, the issue was joined. It was the Reverend Harold Luxton, bishop of Huron, who brought it into the open.

Before and during the war, Bishop Luxton had been a staunch supporter of chaplains. He had encouraged several men to join the military, not the least of whom was the Reverend Harold Appleyard, who would become, much later, the Anglican bishop ordinary to the forces. But, after the war, this support seemed to stop. It appears that Luxton looked upon the Chaplain Service as a simple, military, wartime exigency that had no role or purpose in peacetime.[6]

In December 1949, Luxton wrote to the minister of national defence, Brooke Claxton.[7] Noting the growth of the two new Air Force communities of Centralia and Clinton, he requested a site in each of the communities for construction of a Church of England, which would be staffed by his own clergy. He felt that a grant from public funds to help to build a parish hall would also be reasonable. Luxton noted that he was asking for no more than had been given to the Roman Catholic Church, which already had building plans in progress. He realized the difficulty in dealing with the many divisions of the Protestant Church but protested against "the war-time expedient in interdenominationalism being continued through the years of peace." He described the religion being offered by chaplains as "a vague conglomerate thing beaten up by the Air Force Chaplaincy authorities."[8] These authorities had decided that all Protestant enlisted men should be tossed together in one group and now they would go one step farther and apply the same program to the families. Bishop Luxton sought the same opportunity to minister to his people as had been granted to the Roman Catholics.

The minister received Luxton's letter and referred it back to the Personnel Members Committee (PMC) who passed it on to the Protestant Joint Services Chaplaincy Committee (JSCC(P)) to draft a reply. With the draft came a confidential note to the PMC pointing out that Luxton was a newly appointed bishop and was probably not aware of the development of the Chaplain Service and of the committee's ecclesiastical authority. The Church of England had been kept informed of the service in the peacetime forces, had its own representative on the Council of Churches Chaplaincy Committee, and even had its own chaplaincy committee to deal with particular Church of England problems. The JSCC(P), composed of the three principal Protestant chaplains of the Army, Navy, and Air Force, believed that once Bishop Luxton was acquainted with the facts, his assessment would be altered in both tone and content, and it went on to speak highly of the chaplains who were serving on the two bases concerned. Clearly, the JSCC(P) thought that this challenge was no more than a case of an uninformed new bishop.

The reply from the minister of national defence was dated January 9, 1950, and Bishop Luxton was quick to respond.[9] Luxton acknowledged the courteous reply but complained that it only defended the chaplain set-up that he had criticized. He repeated his demand for sites in Centralia and in Clinton on which to build churches. Luxton's basic message was that the chaplains could minister to the men, but that he would be responsible for the families. If this was not acceptable to the chaplains, Luxton was prepared to raise the matter at General Synod.

Meeting on January 26, the Anglican chaplaincy committee was very concerned about Luxton's drastic proposal. There was a serious shortage of clergymen and of money in the Anglican communion. The Church of England could not afford to supply additional clergymen to service military families, nor did it want to upset the other non-Catholic denominations of the Chaplain Service. The committee decided to write to Bishop Luxton and bring to his attention that the present policies and their committee had been established by the House of Bishops to deal with military matters. If Luxton wanted to change things, he should have been communicating with the bishop of Ottawa who had been designated by the House of Bishops to look after the Chaplain Service, and not directly with the minister of national defence.

Then, on April 18, the minister received a petition from the secretary of the House of Bishops of the Anglican Church in the province of Ontario. It basically requested "the authorities of the Department of National Defence to delay further action in the matter of building 'Protestant' Chapels for the two Air Force communities adjoining R.C.A.F. stations at Centralia and Clinton until the matter of Ministration to Anglican families in these new communities be reviewed by the House of Bishops in September."[10] This was the last of the matter, as far as military files are concerned; but turning to the diocesan archives in Ottawa and to the papers of Canon C.G. Hepburn (the wartime chaplain general) the story continued.

In May, Bishop Luxton received a long letter from Dr. W.J. Gallagher, chairman of the Council of Churches Chaplaincy Committee. Gallagher explained the chaplaincy arrangement with the government and the churches in some detail. He noted the great sensitivity of the chaplains to the wishes of the Anglican General Synod that had met in Winnipeg in 1946 and to the wishes of all denominations. Gallagher wrote that the chaplains "greatly resented" Luxton's suggestion that in their teaching they omitted almost half of the New Testament. He noted that chaplains had been advised to make every effort to encourage the service families to preserve their denominational affiliations and to provide the opportunity for them to receive the ministrations of their own church.[11]

In his June 5 reply to Gallagher,[12] Luxton wrote: "If you, as members of different Christian Communions, do not see the inadequacy of our present approach to the men of the forces, when compared to the complete adequacy of the Roman Catholic approach, then I have little hope of arousing you to seek something better than the present watered-down 'Protestant' ministrations. For my part, I shall keep on pressing until we find a better system than the present one." Luxton went on to revive what he considered to be his main issue. He accused the committee of having "overstepped its rights" and of having "gone far beyond any terms of reference granted ... by the Church of England." His immediate concern was "to discover who holds pastoral authority over the Anglican families in these two new communities of Centralia and Clinton" in his diocese. He said that he did not question the good intentions and the good will of the chaplains, but he regretted "that they have accepted limitations that they view as being necessitated by 'practical politics'." Luxton's conviction was that "these communities should partake of the normal Church life of a Canadian community and not have imposed upon them a Governmental 'Church union' that was a wartime expedient, limited solely to the chaplaincy work in the Armed Forces." Finally, he advised the chaplains to prepare a brief to justify their position to the House of Bishops at the next meeting in September 1950.

What happened over the summer one can only surmise, but no such brief was prepared by the chaplains. Instead, a paper was presented to the House of Bishops requesting that a priest be appointed as Anglican bishop ordinary to the forces. This, they argued, would maintain the proper church government and was a system currently in effect in the Church of England in Britain and in the Roman Catholic Church in Canada. The bishop so designated would be the Anglican representative on the Council of Churches Chaplaincy Committee, would offer the proper ecclesiastical supervision to young chaplains, and would mean that the work of the Anglican Church in the military would receive proper and fitting recognition throughout the church.[13] Nothing was said about the potential utility of having their own bishop to represent their needs at Synod or in the House of Bishops! This action seemed to ease the situation and permit the chaplains time to deal with more pressing issues such as the coming conflict in Korea.

October 1950 found Colonel Stone devoting most of his time to finding suitable Anglican priests for the chaplain sevice in Korea. Having their own bishop would certainly improve the chaplains image in the wider Anglican Church and, eventually, make his recruiting task easier.[14]

NEW CHAPELS AT LAST

The presence of a permanent chaplains' organization in the Canadian forces called for the development of permanent chapels on military bases. The chapels would be visible symbols of the presence of the Church. They would indicate that the Church and the military cared for the serviceman, his work, and his family. Neither the chaplains nor the churches were prepared for the struggle that ensued as the government worked to cut back the costs of construction.

During the war, many rooms and temporary buildings at bases across the country had been put to use as chapels.[15] In late 1941 makeshift chapels had been set up on bases and although Bishop Wells did not approve of them, he dedicated them anyway. (Because he saw the chaplains' task in Canada as one of training men for going to war, Wells had never tried to get government money to build chapels. Overseas, the new chaplains would have to do what they could to hold services in the field.) Some chaplains, however, had used their initiative to get excellent chapels built on various bases and at little cost.[16] By New Year's Day 1943, there were thirty-eight chapels in use in Canada, and the total would rise to fifty-two before the government was finally convinced that it should build them. As Bishop Wells described it: "After much effort and considerable friction, a policy was approved and authority given for chapels to be built in specific centres. Each was to be used ecumenically, by Roman Catholics and Protestants, with a partition which could be moved so that half or the whole of the building could be utilized by any denomination if that were found necessary. There was a vestry in each which served as an office for the chaplain, where he could meet at any time, day or night, anyone who wished to talk with him privately." He went on to comment that "nothing in our work in the Chaplain Service during the war caused as much friction and criticism in the Army and out of it, as the building of these Chapels."[17]

After the war as communities of military personnel and their families developed on or near the forces' bases in Canada, the need for new and larger chapels became ever more apparent. On the larger bases after the war, the chaplains used their initiative and took over what buildings they could for chapel activities. Nevertheless, the few permanent chapels that existed in 1950 were far too small and, with the exception of HMCS Cornwallis,[18] in poor repair. Many local churches enjoyed having the military in attendance and the extra money that was brought in by the military. However, they could not always drop their own programs at a moment's notice to take in a special service for 1000 military men, and so they too realized the need for some other arrangement. If the Church was to display a caring presence in the military for all to see, then at the very least it would need purpose-built permanent chapels.

During the summer of 1950, the three principal chaplains submitted plans for proposed new chapels to the military. These plans were tentatively approved, and in November the requirements were passed to architects Marani and Morris of Toronto for preliminary sketches. The construction engineers of the RCAF were put in charge of the actual building, and they received the first sketches in January 1951. The chapels would come in Roman Catholic and Protestant models and in several sizes. Roman Catholic chapels would come in four sizes, ranging from one hundred and fifty to four hundred seats and having one to four classrooms depending on the chapel size. They would also have suitable living accommodation for the priest with kitchen, bathroom, living room, bedroom, and a small office. Protestant chapels would also come in four sizes and would include a Sunday School hall and office space as well as a club room and a kitchenette.

These plans were approved with minor modifications, but the director of construction engineering then decided that the costs of construction were going to be far too high. A "hold up" design order was sent to the architects, and the principal chaplains were asked to cut the chapels down to what was "absolutely necessary."[19]

After considerable discussion, a letter was sent to Marani and Morris in June 1951 asking for a new set of plans.[20] The basic chapel was to accommodate two hundred and fifty people, with a chancel twenty-five feet deep and forty feet wide, and a nave that could be expanded to seat four hundred. Behind the chancel there should be a vestry, a sacristy, one office, and, for the Roman Catholics, living quarters consisting of bedroom, living room, kitchenette, and bathroom. In Protestant chapels, because there was no need for living quarters, the same space would be used for three twenty-by-thirty foot classrooms. In addition there would be a large thirty-by-forty foot meeting room. These chapels could be planned with a basement if that was more practical.

In August the architects submitted a revised set of designs to the RCAF.[21] After minor changes and many consultations, the Joint Services

Accommodations Committee (JSAC) approved the new designs in October.[22] Estimates ranged from \$118,000 to \$189,000 per chapel, and the architects were advised to proceed. Further sketches were produced in late November 1951, along with a schedule of completion dates.

Satisfactory progress with the construction project seemed to be reaffirmed during February and March 1952 when the Roman Catholics received the draft specifications and working drawings for their chapels, but final government approval was still to come. It was at this point that the office of the deputy minister of national defence intimated to the engineers that unless requirements and costs were drastically reduced the whole chapel programme would be scrapped.[23] The architects were again asked to stop work and to await further government approval.

The situation did not look good. Very shortly thereafter a survey of the available chapel space done by the chaplains found its way, by unrecorded means, into the hands of the minister of national defence.[24] The survey reported that in the Navy there was a good chapel at Cornwallis, although it was small and had to be shared by Roman Catholics and Protestants. At Naden, Shearwater, Stadacona, and Dockyard the chapels were all converted parts of old buildings. The Army reported a number of fairly good reconstructed huts but McGivney Junction did not have a chapel and was thirty miles from the nearest civilian church. The Roman Catholics were using an old powder magazine in Quebec City, and the Protestants used a dental clinic in Ladner. There were no chapels at Ipperwash, Picton, Sunnybrook, Shilo, Dundurn, Carpiequet, Greisbach, Gordon Head, Work Point, or Vernon. But in Fort Churchill there was a permanent church which had opened on February 24, 1952. At the time there was a large American military and scientific presence at Churchill. Camp Wainwright, which had been a training and staging base for Korea, reported a nicely reconstructed building. For its part, the Air Force had converted canteens into chapels at Gimli and Winnipeg and was using a former link-trainer building in Aylmer. Every base with married quarters complained of overcrowding and of inadequate space for Sunday School. The best complaint came from Chilliwack where the Sunday School met in a theatre. The reporter noted: "A wet canteen abuts the end of the Chapel— Sunday School accommodation grim, classes have to be held in washrooms."[25] Clearly, from the chaplains' point of view, something had to be done about the chapel situation.

At this point the minister of national defence seemed to be quite in sympathy with the chaplains. Claxton confided to the defence secretary that even the buildings described as adequate by the chaplains were not always suitable for worship. Of the particular design of chapel that had a

Standard chapel under construction, Base Gagetown, Oromocto, New Brunswick.

Interior of a standard military chapel, Camp Borden, Ontario.

105

Standard military chapel, RCAF Uplands, Ottawa, Ontario.

Interior of standard chapel, Base Kingston, Ontario.

Circular stained glass window seen by many recruits in the chapel at HMCS Cornwallis, Nova Scotia

Interior of HMCS Naden chapel at Esquimalt, British Columbia

107

Chapel of St. Mark, Fort York, Soest, Germany.

The PPCLI window from chapel,
Deilinghofen/Hemer, Germany.

Protestant altar at one end and a Roman Catholic altar at the other, with pews whose backs could move so that parishioners could sit in the direction of their choice, he wrote: "The old wartime chapels were designed as a temporary measure but the experiment has proved unsatisfactory from both the Roman Catholic and the Protestant standpoint. Where this type of chapel is used by Protestants and Roman Catholics, it necessarily means considerable limitations in the services of both denominations. On units where there is a large number of dependants, this type is totally inadequate."[26] The memo went on to note that Sunday School accommodation was severely overcrowded.

Meanwhile, the military bureaucratic wheels continued to turn as the director of construction engineering attempted to cut the costs below $100,000. Several schemes were prepared and revised until a design estimated to cost $85,000 was considered suitable and sent to the JSAC for final approval.

When the principal chaplains saw the revised plans, they were furious. They complained that "the attached plan which was submitted appears to be mischievous in that it provides one type of Chapel for the Roman Catholics and another type for the Protestants which is totally inadequate, and completely ignored the recommendations that were forwarded to the JSAC by a full meeting of the JSCC(P)." The chaplains, both Protestant and Roman Catholic, felt that the matter had gone beyond the discussion stage and called for action by the services concerned. They suggested that the Personnel Members Committee "might wish to discuss this with the Deputy Minister concerned with a view to expediting the acceptance of a satisfactory plan and the expediting of the construction program in this fiscal year."[27] Reporting to the PMC on the complaint, the director of construction engineering claimed that the plans had not actually been sent to the chaplains until July 2, 1952, and that they had been returned to him with the signed approval of the respective chairmen of the Protestant and Roman Catholic Joint Service Chaplaincy Committees: Chaplains Foote and Bergeron. This explanation covered the director but contributed very little towards the fellowship of the chaplains. The others felt that because Foote was chaplain of the fleet, he did not have the same interest in chapel construction as did the principal chaplains of the Army and Air Force. E.G.B. Foote was an outstanding chaplain, and the full explanation for this incident has been lost in time.

Now it was decided that the architects would have to have all of the final drawings done within one month. Marani and Morris could not do it because their people were on vacation and they lost the contract. A new contract was negotiated with Duncan N. MacIntosh of Hamilton,[28] who agreed to produce working drawings in three weeks if he could make use of the work already done for the Roman Catholic chapel. Plans were produced and received by the military in mid-August 1952. Later, the drawings revealed some discrepancies, and these were corrected. MacIntosh was specifically told to keep the cost under $85,000, and he did.

The chaplains drew back, and chapel construction began. A complicated formula had been worked out to determine the size of chapel a base should get. Some believed that there should be a joint service formula, but it was necessary to judge every case on its own. Factors to be considered were: the size of the basic congregation, based on 2.5 dependents per serviceman; whether potential members lived on or off base and whether they were Roman Catholic or Protestant; the assumption that at any one time ten percent of the personnel and dependents were on leave, five percent on duty, and three percent sick; the distribution of faith and the attendance at isolated posts where twwenty-five percent of the total population attended church. (At semi-isolated locations, thirteen percent attended, but adjacent to larger churches you could expect nine percent.) The proximity of PMQs and barracks to the chapel was another consideration.

The chapels would come in three sizes: two hundred and fifty, three hundred and fifty, and four hundred and fifty seats, and they would not have basements. The churches were delighted with the progress that had been made but wondered about the cold and unthinking decisions to cut out parts of the buildings, especially the basements, that seemed necessary to chapel operations. The Protestants were happy to see the Roman Catholics being treated in a fair and reasonable manner but wondered why the plans for the Roman Catholic chapels were well presented while the Protestant plans were no more than four lines on a paper.

It appeared that chapel construction was finally about to begin on Army and Air Force bases across the country. In the Navy it would not be so straightforward. A certain lack of care for the welfare of the dependents of Navy personnel was reflected in the struggle to construct chapels at the new Navy town sites in Halifax and Victoria. In 1950, when homes were being built for the families of sailors at Shannon Park near Halifax and at Belmont Park near Victoria, it was suddenly discovered that no space had been allocated for chapels. This meant that no funds had been allocated for them either and that all costs, should chapels be built, would have to come from the Navy's operational funds.

This pleased some senior people in the government who noted that Navy chapels had always been and should remain in operational areas and be, primarily, for the sailors. C.M. Drury, deputy minister, wrote to the chaplain of the fleet: "While the minister is willing to facilitate and agree to the construction of Chapels at locations where we have a deficiency in this regard, he does not feel that it is within departmental policy to extend these projects for the provision of Chapels for dependents."[29] He does not feel, therefore, that he can approve the recommendation for construction at Shannon Park and at Belmont Park as these are locations removed from service establishments and devoted entirely to dependents." The Navy chaplains, however, noted that the Navy recognized chaplains' duties to dependents and they urged that, even if operational money had to be used, chapels be built in the PMQs.[30] But when the new houses began to be occupied there were still no plans for chapels, and the chaplains took the initiative. There were no civilian churches nearby and so chapels and Sunday Schools began to meet in the public schools.[31] The first service of worship in Shannon Park was held on Easter Sunday 1952 in the Shannon Junior School. The chaplain at the time was the Reverend Tom L. Jackson, and later that year the Reverend Gordon Faraday was appointed.

In a private interview with the minister of national defence on October 14, 1952, the chairman of the Canadian Council of Churches Chaplaincy Committee noted that in the case of Belmont Park the local school was co-operative but was not happy with this arrangement. Gallagher said that someone outside the military was also objecting because provincial law forbade the use of schools for such purposes. In any case the whole situation was only possible at Belmont Park because it was taking place on federal property and it had the support of the school teachers, many of whom returned to teach their classes Christian education on Sundays. Adding fuel to the chairman's fire was the letter from C.M. Drury, indicating that the minister of national defence would not build chapels for any dependents.

Gallagher stated that such a statement was contrary to Queen's Regulations, which read: "A station shall ... provide the opportunity for an officer or man or his family to attend religious services" and the chaplain "shall promote the moral and spiritual welfare of all persons on the station or unit."[32] In fact, Gallagher argued, the government has and did look after dependents with housing, schools, hospitals where necessary, and even chapels.[33] He urged that chapels be built quickly at Belmont and Shannon Parks.

By now some chapels were actually being built. In a letter to the minister, Gallagher noted that there were seventeen chapels under construction on November 8. He went on to wonder, however, why sixteen of them were RCAF chapels.[34] (It might be of passing interest to note, although there is probably no connection, that it was the RCAF engineers who had been given the construction task.) Chapels for places like Shilo had appeared in the estimates for years but had never been approved. In fact, the Army had only one permanent chapel.[35] By December 31, 1952, the JSCC(P) noted that many contracts had been awarded, but that most chapels were still inadequate temporary buildings.

In the end it was not the chaplains but the resident servicemen and their families who pushed for and got a chapel for Belmont Park.[36] They signed a petition and sent it to their member of parliament who happened to be the retired general, George R. Pearkes. An anonymous source claimed that they had seen the padre driving around the park in his little red sports car, handing out leaflets and petitions, but there is absolutely no proof that this ever happened. The parents of over five hundred and fifty children of all denominations signed the statement saying that the facilities at John Stubbs Memorial School were far from satisfactory for religious uses. In addition, British Columbia law prevented religious groups from using the schools. While this legality had been overlooked so far, strong objections were being prepared by various groups. If Belmont Park were a civilian community, the residents would arrange for churches. Pearkes accepted the petition and commented that the sailors were often away and that the government had provided other facilities for the families: housing and schools. "May I strongly urge," wrote a supportive Pearkes to the minister of national defence, "that a Church be constructed in Belmont Park because I am sure that if the spiritual needs of their families are provided for, such action would do much to help maintain the morale of the servicemen themselves."[37]

The first hint of success in the campaign finally came on April 14, 1953, when the chief of personnel for the Navy presented the case for chapels at Belmont and Shannon Parks to the PMC.[38] The PMC noted that at this time the minister of national defence wanted chapels at units, not at housing sites, and therefore the request for any chapels had to be integrated into overall service construction requirements. But the Navy argued that these two places were not comparable to other bases. Both were clearly too far from any operational part of the base where a chapel might be placed and too far from civilian churches for the people to use them. The issue was put aside until the next meeting of the PMC when the decision was made to give the RCN first priority for chapel construction and to request that a review be made of all the chapel construction projects. The subsequent study confirmed to the PMC on May 28, 1953, that while Air Force plans were well under way, nothing had happened in the Army or the Navy. The PMC suggested that the work on chapels for these two groups should be brought up to speed and that special emphasis be placed on Belmont and Shannon Parks.[39]

The battle was basically won in that the two Navy town sites would get their chapels. It was not until April 30, 1956, however, that the sod was turned officially for the building of a chapel at Shannon Park. According to a vestry book, the first service was held on January 1, 1958, and the dedication of the Church of the Redeemer took place on January 15, 1958. HMCS *Bonaventure* donated $3,000 towards a stained glass window. The remaining funds for the window were canvassed from PMQs and other ships' personnel. Chimes were made possible through a donation from the crew of HMCS *Magnificent*.[40]

The new buildings were strategically located in the living areas and served as visible proof that the Navy was concerned about the spiritual care of the servicemen and their families. In the process of getting them built, Dr. Gallagher and the chaplains had learned the value of persistence and the usefulness of outside political pressure. They had come to realize that they would have to deal with a growing and seemingly unfeeling bureaucracy. The Navy chapel issue had taught the chaplains that it was necessary to fight for their rights. The time had passed when the clergy could make things happen simply because of their special ecclesiastical status.

A NEW BRIGADE TO GERMANY

At this time changes were starting to take place in Europe. In 1953 it was announced that the 27th Infantry Brigade would move to more permanent quarters in the area around Soest, Germany, and, in essence, become the 1st Canadian Infantry Brigade. Soest was located in Westphalia between the Rhine and the Weser rivers.

The brigade would be stationed in four main camps; the camps formed the general design of a rectangle. Fort Chambly and Fort York were each about five miles from Soest. Fort Chambly had all the logistic services and Fort York had the 2nd Battalion of the Royal Canadian Regiment and contained Fort Henry with the brigade headquarters and the detention barracks. A housing site for these camps would be located on the opposite side of Soest. The third camp, located near Werl, would really be three "forts" occupied by the Royal 22nd Regiment, 2nd Field Squadron of the Royal Canadian Engineers, and D Squadron of the Lord Strathcona's Horse. The fourth camp was located much farther away from Soest and contained two forts: Fort Prince of Wales, occupied by 2nd Royal Canadian Horse Artillery and Fort McLeod, occupied by 2nd Battalion of the Princess Patricia's Canadian Light Infantry.

Rumours soon leaked out to the men that official plans were being made to bring their families to Europe. The padres were greatly disturbed by the rumours because at that time there were no facilities of any kind in the Soest area—no housing, no schools, no family shops, no medical facilities. Meetings were being held at the highest levels to determine questions such as what banking arrangements could be made by dependents and what school system might be acceptable. Military housing sites were tentatively planned for the edges of Soest, Werl, and Iserlohn. The senior chaplains were tasked to investigate the possibility of using German churches in the three towns or in neighbouring rural areas and determined that the Canadians would be better off with their own buildings.

There followed long debates, first over the need for chapels in Europe, and then over their condition and their size. As senior Army chaplain in Europe, John Rand took a firm and consistent stand. He wanted chapels built on or near the housing sites rather than on the bases. Because there had been no club rooms or amenities of any kind planned for the housing sites, Rand hoped to have good basements or halls attached to the chapels for dependent organizations such as Scouts, Guides, and women's groups.

While the Army was arguing over whether there would or would not be chapels in Soest, the Air Force was already using their new chapels at Baden and Zweibrüchen. The basic design of these identical chapels was simple. They had a small change room just inside the entrance and a small office at the other end. They were spartan but had a lot of atmosphere. The communion tables and the reading desk were stone, and the stone pulpit was six or eight steps up from the congregation. The Protestant chapels in Europe were mostly constructed of a kind of red sandstone, and they looked like churches. By December 1953, another new chapel had been built at Baden. In the United Kingdom there was a temporary chapel at 1 Wing, North Luffenham, until 1955, and another at 1 Wing, Grostenquin, France, until 1953. There was no chapel at Metz, and none was authorized until 1958. There, the congregation met in the theatre for services. When the authority to build came, it was just as quickly withdrawn as plans were made to downsize and move the base to Germany.

Around Easter weekend, 1954, the Canadian Army in Europe was in the field and on the move during NATO exercises. Each chaplain conducted services "out under the trees"[41] With movie cameras rolling, for later release on Canadian television, the commander read a lesson and Padre Jim Duncan celebrated Holy Communion. A Mother's Day service had also been recorded in the field for release in Canadian movie theatres. Padre Duncan had conducted that service using his jeep hood as an altar. There were about three hundred and fifty men in coveralls on parade. Lieutenant

Colonel K. Corbould read the lesson and Padre Fred Otke "officiated" at the organ.

During the following summer the Canadian Army appeared to be getting a solid grip on family activities in Europe. It was officially reported that in addition to their service duties, every effort was being made by chaplains to encourage family worship. There were Sunday Schools at all military establishments, and many bases had young people's groups, Scouts, Guides, ladies' auxiliaries, and missionary societies. In addition, plans were being made to give religious instruction in the schools. The new Army military community in Europe seemed to be progressing on schedule and in an exemplary manner. However, when Dr. Gallagher requested permission from the minister of national defence to go and visit Soest, permission was denied and it was suggested that it would be better for him to wait a year—until the summer of 1955.

The reason for the delay was clear from a letter (marked personal and confidential) from Padre Jim Duncan to National Defence Headquarters.[42] Duncan presented a slightly different picture of the European scene and hoped that the principal chaplain had not been taken in by the "political propaganda of the press and the policy to play to the gallery and put on a wonderful show."

Duncan reported that there were about one hundred and sixty families living in the United Kingdom and about nine hundred families in the brigade area in Germany. The latter were living in pensions, hotels, leave centres, farms, villages, rooms, and houses spread over an area of seventy by thirty miles. The married quarters, anticipated the year before and promised for the summer posting rotation, would not be completed until September in Soest and October in Hamer. Some of the accompanying services, like the schools, would not be finished until January 1955. The shopping centres had not even been started. There was a "church house" in Fort Chambly and another in Fort York, but no place for church services in Fort Henry except when something was improvised on Sunday afternoon in the canteen. The chaplains were of the opinion that no dependents should have been allowed to come to Europe until the 1955 rotation. Despite these deplorable living conditions, Duncan was able to report that "the morale of the Brigade has been surprisingly high, and the serious problems few."

In anticipation of some 12,000 Canadian soldiers and family members, the British and German governments had given money for construction and buildings for religious uses. Two fine chapels were being built, one in Fort Chambly and one in Fort York, but there would be no church in the married quarters area. Families would have to travel five to six miles to church and there were no Sunday School facilities. A two-hundred-seat chapel was being constructed in Werl, but again it was on the base; families would have to travel about two miles to get there, and no Sunday School was provided. Padre Otke was already holding church services in the church house at Fort Prince of Wales. The PMQ area was about three miles away. Otke held church parades in a nearby Lutheran Church.

Additional base areas and service personnel were scattered from north of Hanover down through Antwerp, a distance of four hundred miles. There were units at Wihmegan near Hanover, Hertford, Wetter on the Rühr, München-Gladbach and Viersen near Holland, Wulfen, and Antwerp. Some of these had as few as seven servicemen. Attempts were made to visit these units once per month and a padre's hour was held on each visit. At Antwerp a church service was also held for the soldiers and their families.

There were no Canadian Army clubs or canteens at Soest or Werl, and the chaplains felt that some were needed. In the meantime, as Duncan reported, "the Salvation Army has been doing valiant service in a small canteen in Soest, and deserves full marks, and even more credit than they have been getting."

Another issue on which Duncan reported was the rate of venereal disease. It was, he said, "still a problem" although the rate was "not as high now as it was." The arrival of families had made "a big difference."[43]

By 1956, the whole Canadian Army community in Europe was better organized. When not in the field, the chaplains could concern themselves with annual meetings and Sunday School materials. A limited number of buses had been made available to transport dependents from the living areas to the chapels, and Padre R.C. Nunn's choir was presenting Stainer's *Crucifixion* as an Easter special. The biggest issue during February 1956 was the amount of time allotted to the chaplains for daily devotions on the brigade radio station. The chaplains, both Protestant and Roman Catholic, had been allotted five minutes to share and felt that all interests would be better served with a total of fifteen minutes. A solid chapel community was developing that would lead Padre Ormond Hopkins, years later, to say that "the best expression of chaplaincy ministry was that which was found in Germany."[44]

Chapter 5

INTEGRATION AND ITS IMPACT

FIRST TO INTEGRATE

THE CHAPLAINS were one of the first of the branches of the Canadian military to be integrated in the move towards unification of the forces which occupied the government's attention throughout the 1960s. In many ways they were an ideal group for early integration. From their very beginnings they had worked together in war and in peace. Moreover, the natural collegiality of all clergy and the ties between the civilian churches bound the chaplains together in formal and informal ways that their military masters rarely comprehended. Nonetheless, traditions in the military and in the chaplaincy ran deep, and there was bound to be some distress not so much over the original decision as over the fairly sweeping changes which its implementation brought.

The idea of integration/unification of Canada's military forces—in the interests of efficiency and economy—was not new. There had been two serious attempts to deal with the question: one in the early 1920s and another in the later 1930s which had been pre-empted by the outbreak of war.[1] Instead of amalgamation the war had lead to a much expanded military—both in personnel and in bureaucracy. At the end of the war, the issue of manpower economy came to the fore again. When Prime Minister King appointed Brooke Claxton as minister of national defence in 1946, his task was to create a single defence policy. At the organizational level Claxton did bring together the chiefs of the three services and the chief of the Defence Research Board to form the Chiefs of Staff Committee and the new national headquarters included tri-service committees such as the Personnel Members Committee.

At the moment when integration ceased to be a persistent rumour and began to take shape, the Chaplain Service had evolved into three independent elements for the Army, the Navy, and the Air Force, but they had much in common. The Joint Services Chaplaincy Committee, composed of the Protestant and Roman Catholic principal chaplains of the Army, the Navy, and the Air Force, provided a forum through which to co-ordinate combined activities in the military sphere. As clergy the Protestant chaplains were united under the umbrella of the Canadian

Council of Churches Chaplaincy Committee. On religious matters they worked in a common direction while maintaining their denominational distinctiveness. In this way it had been possible to create a single *Divine Service Book* and a unified Sunday School curriculum. This mutual co-operation was enhanced by an annual conference and retreat that brought together the chaplains from all three services. Despite all the things they held in common, the chaplains did approach their work differently in each of the services and these differences would have to be overcome if integration was to succeed. Moreover, most of the chaplains were no more able than any other member of the military to set aside their long-standing loyalties and emotional ties to a particular service or unit without a backward glance.

THE BASIC PLAN

On August 8, 1957, the Personnel Members Committee was directed to prepare a plan for the integration of the Chaplain Service and an Ad Hoc Committee was established under Commander J. Plomer of the RCN.[2] The members of the committee were the Protestant and Roman Catholic principal chaplains: the Rev. E.G.B. Foote, Colonel J.W. Forth, Group Captain F.W. MacLean, the Rev. R. MacLean, Colonel C.H.R. Charlebois, and Group Captain A. Costello. Mr. C.B. Smith was the secretary. For terms of reference it was given that the goal would be a single chaplain service with two principal chaplains: one Roman Catholic and one Protestant. All chaplains on the integrated list could be employed at any place and in any of the three services. The RCN system of grading would become the method of classification for all chaplains, but it was stressed that there was no intention to cause a reduction in rank for serving chaplains. Overall control of the Chaplain Service would be an RCN responsibility, but the administrative organization would be along the lines of the Royal Canadian Dental Corps, which had been under Army control from its wartime beginning. The Ad Hoc Committee was also tasked to consider command and control in the field and matters of dress. The new service was to be in operation by April 1, 1958.

The Conservative government of John Diefenbaker had just replaced St. Laurent's Liberals in June 1957 and it seemed as if they wanted to effect changes in the military quickly. The report of the Ad Hoc Committee was pushed through in less than three weeks and presented to the PMC on August 27, 1957.[3] Although the principal chaplains signed the report, they felt they had been pressured into doing so. They were embarrassed to have to sign without first being able to consult with the Council of Churches Chaplaincy Committee. They believed that the changes recommended would have a tremendous adverse impact on the morale of those now serving, and on future recruitment, and that they would undermine the long-established confidence between the chaplains and the men and thus reduce the service's effectiveness.[4]

In their study of the report the principal chaplains compared the proposed system with the present one. They noted that the manner in which they had functioned was generally acceptable to serving personnel and had proven effective. They were satisfied that Canada's servicemen were receiving adequate spiritual assistance. They noted that the present system afforded the opportunity for the identification of the chaplains with the troops they were serving and set out their belief that wearing the same uniform and having the knowledge of the traditions and organization of their particular service was often a significant factor in a chaplain's success.

On the matter of rank, they noted: "The Geneva Convention protects chaplains who presently carry rank in the event they become prisoners of war. If rank is lost, chaplains might not be recognized as such, or if they appeared to have no rank they might be considered as other ranks—that is to say, they might be forced to work at physical labour instead of being free to minister to the spiritual needs of their fellow prisoners of war of all ranks."[5] Moreover the existing system, with three principal chaplains, had made it possible to preserve denominational balance at the top of the Chaplain Service and had permitted adequate discussion of any theological points raised. The new system, with a single Protestant chaplain general, would be more efficient bureaucratically but less sensitive theologically.

However, the existing system was not without its problems. It had encouraged chaplains to develop particular loyalties and interests in their service as opposed to the corps. The rank structure curtailed career possibilities and duplicated and handicapped the efficiency of the administration. Having six members on the JSCC slowed down administration. Service control had sometimes conflicted with the chaplain's functioning in his spiritual work and some commanding officers in the RCAF and the RCN had tried to employ chaplains as unit officers. This had never happened in the Army where the chaplains were a separate corps. It was obvious that some increased bureaucratic efficiency could further the chaplains' goals.

The new plan would have some advantages. The proposed structure would increase the prestige and efficiency of the Chaplain Service. Integration would make for better denominational coverage in the field, improved administration and organization with fewer chaplains employed on purely administrative duties, and better leadership, as all directives would come from one source. It should result in a common policy

119

governing the implementation of all ecclesiastical directives and, therefore, the equivalent treatment of chaplains regardless of their service affiliation. Loss of rank would silence those who felt that chaplains should not be mistaken for being regular military officers. All servicemen would recognize the common uniform of the chaplain and the autonomy inherent in the plan could add to the prestige of the chaplains. It could offer better career prospects and would stop competition for recruitment among the various branches.

The disadvantages of unification would be the lack of close identity and relationship with a particular service. Service loyalty might be lost, although the same sense of identity would be hoped for in the larger service. Some Army and Air Force chaplains would feel keenly about the loss of rank. Unless the services recognized the prestige of the Church, the loss of rank could be significant because of the rank consciousness of the armed forces and because of the Geneva Convention's clause on prisoners of war.[6] The chaplains' "old boy" net would disappear and administration would become less personal but this might be an advantage. Loss of uniform may separate the chaplain from his flock although this may in part be compensated for by the use of "working uniforms" in the field. There may be the danger of the chaplains being regarded as "outsiders" to the service, as was the case with the commissionaires or, during the war, with the Auxiliary Service. If economy resulted in a reduction in the rank structure, morale would suffer and recruiting would be more difficult. The balance of denominational power would be lost at the top but this might be resolved by a term limit for the chaplain general with an opportunity for rotation according to denomination.

On September 6, 1957, the Chiefs of Staff Committee met and accepted the Ad Hoc Committee's report, subject to review of some matters which were referred back to the committee: the command structure of the service, the integrated gradation list, the manning of staff positions by civilians, uniform, and the requirement for setting up a school for chaplains in Ontario.[7]

THE CHURCHES' RESPONSE TO THE PLAN

As soon as the Ad Hoc Committee had been given its task, the new minister of national defence wrote to advise the Canadian Council of Churches of the study. Pearkes promised that the integrated service would not lead to any decrease in facilities for spiritual care. Rather, "it is considered that the efficiency of the Chaplaincy Service would be increased and economy of administration would be realized by the proposed integration."[8]

Immediately following the PMC's acceptance of the report, the chairman of the Joint Services Chaplaincy Committee wrote to each member of the Council of Churches Chaplaincy Committee. Colonel Forth offered to have the three principal chaplains, who were now sometimes referred to as "directors," meet with the council for discussions on the Ad Hoc Committee's report which he noted was very long. Forth "emphasized that the plan is only in the study phase at present, and there has been no final decision."[9] The Council of Churches Chaplaincy Committee moved swiftly, but it was not until September 24 that they were able to meet with the minister of national defence to present a memorandum setting out their views on the proposed plan.[10]

The committee declared that they held the Chaplain Service in high esteem and would be opposed to anything "which might appear to be a depreciation or demotion of them." In the light of its relationship with the chaplains, the committee felt that it should have been consulted from the very beginning. "Even now," it reported, "the Committees in the various Churches, not just the Council of Churches Committee, were meeting to consider the documents."

The church committees would be considering at least three matters. First, they would assess the wisdom of any form of integration. It appeared that this basic question never had been put; it had not even been in the terms of reference of the Ad Hoc Committee. Second, there was the question of effectiveness. Administrative efficiency and economy were obviously necessary, but the Churches Chaplaincy Committee had always felt that a chaplain should be able to identify with the congregation to whom he ministered: "He should share their life and be an integral part of the Force to which they belong." The committee argued that the number of chaplains could not be reduced by very much because they were already under strength for doing their job. Finally, the rights and privileges of all the denominations must be recognized. "With the present system the three directors have been drawn from three denominations and this has led to considerable harmony. Provision for such denominational harmony must be included in any new proposals." It was clearly difficult for the churches to conceive of the integration of the chaplains apart from the integration of the forces as a whole because each of the services was so different: "The proposed plan would seem to hinder Force identification. Rank should be retained because to take it away would have an adverse effect on Army and Air Force Chaplains. We fear that in these forces the abolition of the Chaplain's rank would be regarded as a demotion and with his rank might go status, prestige, and facilities the lack of which would handicap his ministry." In summary, the churches felt that more study should be given to the basic question of whether or not any integration should take place.

Shortly thereafter, Chaplain Forth wrote to thank the chairman of the Council of Churches Chaplaincy Committee for the committee's presentation and support. In his letter,[11] Forth agreed that an improvement in the rank structure was needed to attract acceptable recruits and to keep pace with the other professions. He stressed that the biggest concern of the chaplains about integration was their identification with a unit, arguing that "the efficiency of a Chaplain is dependent in direct ratio to his identification with his congregation." The principal chaplains were therefore recommending that "the present policy in respect to recruiting, Service affiliation, and place of Service in the field be continued; and that integration, where required, be introduced only for purpose of administration and supervision." These proposals "were compatible with the Minister's expressed desire for integration, and would, at the same time, preserve the well known values and loyalties and traditions which helped to identify the Chaplain with his service congregation."

PUSHING AHEAD REGARDLESS

On November 14, the completed plan for integration was presented to the PMC by the Ad Hoc Committee. The committee's chairman believed that the main problem with the plan would be "the basic difference of organization requirements of the services."[12]Without regard for the concerns of the churches, the PMC pushed forward. The Chiefs of Staff were informed[13] that the command structure for the chaplains would combine geographical and functional elements. An integrated gradation list would be prepared and no sub-staff manning plans would be made until a command structure had been approved and put into operation. The wearing of insignia and uniform would remain on a voluntary basis for five years. The only apparent problem was "that it was virtually impossible to make an organization such as the Chaplain Service, responsible for the spiritual and moral welfare of the officers and men, fit in with [the style of] an organization which is purely a technical corps, like the dental corps." And, the PMC concluded: "Every effort was made reflect to economy in the proposed integration ... The results may be considered disappointing, however, this must be weighed against the fact that the Chaplain Service has always been economically staffed and that in presenting this new establishment it was not possible to reduce the number of Chaplains required and still maintain the present standards attributed to the Chaplain Service."

It was only in December that the PMC considered the points raised in the Council of Churches' memorandum of the previous month.[14] By this time the concerns of the individual services about integration were also beginning to be heard. The PMC therefore wrote to the Chiefs of Staff Committee stating the view that "it is essential to have complete co-operation between the Church and the Military authorities if a proposal of this nature is to be successful." They recommended that, "in view of the unfavourable reaction of the Church authorities," "it would be inadvisable to proceed with integration of the Chaplain Service at this time."[15]

The government nevertheless seemed determined to pursue at least partial integration. In a memo to the chief of staff in January, the minister of national defence set out the future quite firmly:

> The following action would be taken. In the first step, a Chaplain General with the rank of Brigadier General would be appointed to supervise all three services. There would be an assistant Chaplain General for each service. The three positions for directors of Religious and Moral Training would cease to be and would be replaced by one man. In the second step, Command Chaplains would be appointed on the basis of the army commands, not functional commands. The Command Chaplains would be given Chaplains from the three services to serve within their commands."[16]

This partial integration was to take place by April 1, 1958. In a letter to the chairman of the Council of Churches Chaplain Committee,[17] Pearkes wrote:

> I have carefully considered your comments and have decided not to proceed with a single Chaplain Service at this time but to provide for certain integration at National Defence Headquarters and in Commands. Accordingly, no changes will be made in the uniforms worn by chaplains nor in the rank procedure or rank badges worn ... the integration at National Defence Headquarters will provide for the appointment of two Chaplains General, possibly in the rank of Brigadier.

The PMC's final plan to integrate the Chaplain Service was made public on January 30, 1958. It had been decided that steps toward integration would proceed only with the concurrence of the Council of Churches Chaplaincy Committee and the Roman Catholic bishop ordinary. Each would be asked to nominate its respective chaplain general. Authority was granted for the implementation of the new headquarters organization in February, and the terms of reference for the chaplains general were approved. At this time no one questioned the continuance of separate Protestant and Roman Catholic services. There would be two chaplains general at the brigadier level, two directors of religious and moral training who would be colonels, and several command chaplains at the rank of lieutenant colonel. The headquarters would be integrated first and then the commands. By this time rumours were everywhere among servicemen and in the press, and so it was time for a press release. As well, a letter was sent to all chaplains stressing that no one would lose his rank or his job because of integration.[18] At this stage, General Foulkes, the chief of defence staff, cautioned everyone against moving too fast. Before the church authorities nominated the chaplain general, he urged that the nomination should have the approval of the rank structure committee and the minister of finance.[19]

The integration of the Chaplain Service was announced to the House of Commons on September 2, 1958, and it met with some public scepticism. An editorial in the *Ottawa Journal* asked: "Is This Integration? Or is this the creation of two new senior posts and no reductions in administration and personnel?" From Winnipeg, a Mr. Tonkin wrote to the minister urging him to make some real savings by cutting the Chaplain Service. In response to this letter, it was reported that the Chaplain Service had gained two generals, lost four lieutenant colonels, and freed eight command chaplains for other duties.[21] Partial integration appeared to result in a better disposition of manpower.

On September 23, a day after integration officially took place at NDHQ, a letter went out to all chaplains from the new chaplain general, Brigadier J.W. Forth. He explained that the chaplain general would be responsible for the overall policy, organization, supervision, and administration of the newly integrated Chaplain Service. There would be three assistants—one for each branch of the forces—to be called deputy chaplains general. Filling these new positions would be the former RCN and RCAF principal chaplains, E.G.B. Foote and F.W. MacLean, and J.P. Browne of the Army. There would be five tri-service commands and one overseas command. They would follow "the Army system of geographical areas, but would incorporate the functional aspects of the RCAF in so far as that Service is concerned. Area and unit chaplains would not change. Rank and uniforms would not be abandoned and no one would lose their rank or be released."[22]

On September 24, the chairman of the Chiefs of Staff wrote to the chief of naval staff, the chief of air staff, and the chaplains general. All recommendations for future appointments and promotions would now be made by the chaplain general, after consultation with the appropriate church authorities, to the chief of staff concerned. "For appointments to the rank of Colonel and above, which required ministerial approval, the recommendation should be forwarded through the chairman of the Chiefs of Staff."[23]

Many practical matters remained to be worked out. At the PMC meeting on September 25 it was declared that the RCN would assume housekeeping duties for the new chaplains general. The chaplains general would brief the PMC at the regular Tuesday meetings. They would prepare a letter for the new command chaplains outlining the new organization and they would prepare a joint organization order for the PMC. They would evolve the new orders necessary for the reorganization. After some consultation with church authorities, they would submit recommendations for directors of religious and moral training and they would consider the future status of the JSCC.[24]

Almost immediately it was decided to replace the Joint Services Chaplaincy Committee with two new Chaplain General's Committees, one for the Roman Catholics and the other for the Protestants. At the last JSCC(P) meeting on September 30, the imminent integration was hotly discussed. The PMC had proposed that the new organization would come into being on November 1 and had directed the chaplains general to meet alone with the PMC to work out a joint organization order. On October 1, the JSCC was replaced by the Chaplain General's Committees. By November the new command chaplains had been named: Chaplain B.A. Peglar, Eastern Command; Wing Commander W. Rodger, Quebec; Lieutenant Colonel Rusty Wilkes, Central Command; Wing Commander A.R. MacIver, Prairie Command; Lieutenant Colonel M.J.D. Carson, Western Command; Padre E.S. Light, Europe. The three most important functions of the command chaplains were: to provide spiritual leadership, to ensure that chaplains were placed to the best advantage, and to co-ordinate the work of the chaplains in accordance with the policies of the chaplain general. Integration became official at the command level in December 1958.

Not surprisingly, it was soon clear that there was a need for some fine tuning in the implementation of command and control of the new structure, particularly the powers of the chaplain general. The former principal chaplains (now deputy chaplains general without the rank) were functioning as if integration had never taken place. Transfers mandated by the chaplain general were not made, and the chaplain general found that his travel budget had been depleted by his deputies. The Ad Hoc Committee was reactivated to review the apparent inconsistencies in Joint

Organization Order 24. It would be necessary to change the designators for positions, to establish clearly the channels of communication on administrative and ecclesiastical matters, and to recognize the need for command chaplains' conferences and for the Chaplain General's Committees to include representation from the three services.

Nevertheless, it was the consensus at a command chaplains conference, held on October 29 and 30, 1959, that while no particularly beneficial results were apparent to date, the work of the chaplaincy had not been adversely affected. Personal relationships between command chaplains and chaplains from other services had generally been good. The chief problems encountered had to do with senior staff officers who did not understand the function of the command chaplain in the new organization. For effective man management, the command chaplains would require personal information regarding the postings and promotions of chaplains from services other than their own. The duplication of function and responsibility as between command chaplains and assistant command chaplains was another mystery for the military. The overall feeling was that partial integration seemed to be working within the limits imposed by its partial nature.

As 1960 began, rank and status once again became an issue. In a letter to the minister of national defence,[25] the Roman Catholic bishop ordinary spoke of the "universal consciousness" of rank in the military: "The thinking and attitude of the serving man is influenced by the emphasis given to rank; and the relative importance many men attribute to a department is usually measured by the rank and status held by the head of the department." Archbishop Roy went on the state that this perception was "especially true in the Chaplain department where the cause, benefits and effects are so intangible," and that therefore "the *status* given the head of the Chaplain Department of the Canadian Armed Forces is of the utmost importance." He concluded with an appeal to elevate the chaplain general to the rank of major general, just like the surgeon general.

In July 1960 the chaplain general wrote to the PMC with his concerns about command and control:

> Organization Order No. 24 does not provide the Chaplains General with sufficient authority to function effectively. While the Order in question makes the Chaplain General responsible for policy, the existence of the Chaplain's Committee implies that it is this Committee, rather than the Chaplain General, who carry the ultimate responsibility. Repeated requests from deputations for definition of the authority of the Committee seem to affirm this

view as prevalent among the Deputies in general. When decisions were made by voting in Committee the Deputies were in a position to negate the opinions and recommendations of the Chaplains General, placing the latter in a position that was most awkward and embarrassing.

The chaplain general felt that the same precepts of command should apply for the chaplains as for the rest of the forces. His recommendation was: "That the present Chaplain Committee should be dissolved. Each Chaplain General has access to his respective Deputies. Co-ordination or rank structure, staff visits, leave, recruiting, releases, transfers, postings and appointments, would be effected at the Chaplains General level."[26]

In response, the PMC clearly established that the chaplains general were the only advisers to the PMC and that the deputy chaplains general were both under their own services for certain administration and under the chaplain general for other matters. To clarify things, the name of the Chaplain General's Committee should be changed to "The Chaplain General's Advisory Committee." This committee would advise the chaplain general on all matters pertaining to spiritual and moral welfare of the military and would offer advice on policy affecting the organization, supervision, and administration of the Chaplain Service. It would meet only when required to do so by the Chaplain General.[27]

Because the original joint organization order declared that the intention was "to effect a partial integration of the Chaplain Service at NDHQ and at Commands while leaving the three branches of the Chaplaincy to function within each of the services much as heretofore,"[28] it was necessary for the PMC to spell out the senior chaplains' areas of responsibility in more detail. Staff visits to bases would be the responsibility of the deputy chaplains general, but the chaplain general would be permitted comment on local situations. When they wished to go on leave, the deputies would be required to seek the permission of their respective chaplain general. Postings to integrated positions would be made on the recommendation of the chaplain general to the PMC. Postings to non-integrated positions would be made by the deputies in consultation with their own service and without necessarily having to obtain the permission of the chaplain general. It would be the responsibility of the deputy chaplains general to nominate suitable men for appointment. Releases from the forces would be permitted only with the permission of the chaplain general.

In December 1962, the chaplains general reported that NDHQ had been integrated as requested, although there were still problems. In the commands the scheme had proven to be premature, unworkable, and the source of much confusion. In spite of early optimism, the new scheme existed more on paper than in reality. Over the four years the integrated tri-service command chaplains' structure had been largely ignored, and the individual service command chaplains had continued to function as before partial integration. Throughout the process, the chaplains' work had been competently supervised and effectively carried out.[29] Based on this report the senior chaplains suggested that the effort to make integration work at the command chaplains level cease until the armed forces reached a stage of greater overall integration.

In a parliamentary return, dated January 24, 1963, in response to a question about the Chaplain Service, it was observed that while integration had not led to substantial savings of dollars and personnel, it had achieved the primary purpose of promoting a complete unification of policy as well as an effective and efficient co-ordination in the organization and administration of the Chaplain Service. There had been a substantial reduction in the number of civilian officiating clergymen employed by the services, but the loss of two senior positions had not resulted in any financial saving. Prior to integration, the Chaplain Service had cost the taxpayer $1,999,805.36. After integration it cost $1,967,997.20, but the efficiency had been greater.[30]

The march towards the complete unification of the forces continued, and in September 1964 plans were announced for phasing out the PMC. The reins of responsibility for the chaplains and other personnel matters were handed over to a new integrated division, the Personnel Branch.

Unification of the armed forces formally took effect on February 1, 1968. During the process of unification the Chaplain Service had become a more integral and regular branch of the Canadian Forces. The collegial control of the JSCC had been replaced by a chaplain general with executive powers. The service would function now without the massive input from the civilian churches that had been the norm from 1939 onwards. The Council of Churches Chaplaincy Committee continued to exist and the contribution of the church representatives still seemed to be accepted by the government—but more out of respect for past tradition than out of necessity. Before 1946, the chaplain general had been under the close control of senior Canadian ecclesiastics. After 1968, the churches retained their right to appoint the chaplains general, but they always chose their new man from a list of those who had progressed through the bureaucratic system.[31]

CHAPLAIN TO THE QUEEN

Some of the chaplains did not seem to understand the bureaucratic growth that was taking place around them. As every hint of the old ecclesiastical élitism was being replaced by modern bureaucratic military efficiency, the chaplains began to pursue the appointment of an honorary chaplain to the Queen. While it seemed an odd request for the times, perhaps it was the uncertainty provoked by so much change which led the chaplains to attempt to acquire this tangible recognition of their rightful place in Canadian society.

It all started in 1957 when Dr. Harold Young of the United Church of Canada and chairman of the Council of Churches Chaplaincy Committee asked the military to appoint one or more of the three principal chaplains to the honorary position of chaplain to the Queen.[32] The head medical doctor in the military and the head nurse had already received this honour, and to some in the military it seemed a reasonable suggestion.

At the request of the defence secretary, the Personnel Members Committee considered the possibility and requested more information from the Army member of the Joint Staffs Committee in London, England. London reported that, with the exception of Canada, the Commonwealth countries had no regular chaplain establishments and no honorary chaplains to the Queen had ever been appointed. However, in Britain, a number of service chaplains from the major denominations had held the appointment of honorary chaplain to the Queen and the British chaplain general could see no objection to the Canadian proposal.[33] The PMC accepted the report but expressed concern about limiting the appointment to one religious group—not that any such limitation had ever been proposed. The PMC decided, there being no established church in Canada, "to stay in line with other Commonwealth countries and thus avoid embarrassment to both Church and state."[34] On July 3, 1957, the PMC wrote to the minister of national defence explaining its negative response.

Informal and unrecorded discussions at the time must have indicated that the real problem was a fear of offending the Roman Catholics and so the senior Protestant chaplains checked with the Roman Catholics. On October 24, the JSCC, which of course included both Protestants and Roman Catholics, wrote to the PMC indicating that while the Roman Catholic chaplains were not in a position to accept such an appointment, they had no objections to the Protestants doing so. The PMC meeting in November considered this additional endorsement but felt that, while the senior Roman Catholic chaplains might not object, there were junior chaplains throughout the service who certainly would be upset. The PMC reiterated that no recommendation would be made at this time because there was no established church in Canada and such an honorary appointment would necessarily be limited to one religious group at a time.[35]

The issue returned in 1960. At the PMC meeting in July, a memo from the Council of Churches Chaplaincy Committee to the minister of national defence, suggesting the appointment of the chaplain general as an honorary chaplain to the Queen, was discussed. Air Force and Navy members of the PMC recognized that there was no state religion but noted that there were state-supported chaplains! If a chaplain was appointed, they felt the embarrassment to other religious groups would be slight. In their opinion, "such an appointment would strengthen the Canadian Council of Churches in somewhat the same way that an honour recently conferred on the Chaplain General(RC) had done for those of the Catholic faith."[36] Following this meeting the minister of national defence was informed that due to divergent views the PMC was still not able to make a recommendation. The minister then informed the Churches Chaplaincy Committee that such an appointment would not be appropriate to recommend at this time because, since there was no established church in Canada, it might be construed as showing favouritism to one religious group.

The issue would not go away, however. In response to yet another letter from the Council of Churches Committee, the issue was reconsidered at a PMC meeting in March 1961 with the same results.[37] One last effort was made to appoint a chaplain to the Queen in February 1964. The acting Air member personnel wrote a memorandum recommending that the chaplain general(P) be made honorary chaplain to the Queen. He made four points. Presbyterian, Methodist, and Congregational chaplains had all held the position even though the Church of England was the established church in that part of the United Kingdom. In Canada, the Roman Catholic Church had for many years been able to recognize the contributions of its chaplains to the forces by elevating several of the senior men to the position of monsignor, a title and office conferred by the Holy See. The Protestant section of the chaplaincy had not been able to give similar recognition because of its varied denominational groups. The position of honorary chaplain to the Queen would be one avenue of recognition. The senior medical officers and nursing sisters had held honorary appointments to the Queen for a number of years which provided a precedent for the Council of Churches' request. Her Majesty was queen of Canada, and it seemed only fitting that she have an honorary chaplain who represented this country.

The Navy member expressed considerable general sympathy for the proposal but had reservations on several points. The Army member said that his concern was that no cause be given for denominational friction or for the minister to be open to possible criticism. He recognized the arguments and went on to note that over the years the Anglican Church had, on occasion, recognized their chaplains' contributions by granting the ecclesiastical rank of canon or archdeacon. He did not believe that it would be sound to support a course of action which excluded a major religious denomination. When the Air member pointed out that the Roman Catholic Church had just appointed a Roman Catholic chaplain, Wing Commander Gallagher, as auxiliary bishop, the Army member replied that the inability of the Protestant chaplaincy to grant similar titles was inherent in the nature of some Protestant denominations. He wondered whether honorary chaplain to the Queen should be regarded as a Protestant equivalent.

The final decision returned to the previous argument: "The members of the PMC were of the opinion that an appointment of this nature to the Chaplain General(P) would imply a favoured position for one religious group, a situation that should not obtain in Canada where there is no established Church, and under the circumstances therefore, it would be inappropriate to recommend such an appointment."[38]

In so far as the PMC was concerned the chaplains had their place in the military structure and, by implication, a status in Canadian society. The Protestant chaplains' circumstances were such that they would not be granted the possibly equivalent honorary status to the Roman Catholic chaplains and they would not have the status of the senior officers of the medical and nursing branches of the Canadian military. But as Brigadier Cardy said: "It never really struck me as necessary."[39]

PERSONNEL EVALUATION REPORTS

Before integration, promotions in the Chaplain Service had been automatic. Confidential reports were written on chaplains, but no one worried too much about them. In the Navy, for example, it took about eight years of service before a man would receive his first, and probably only, promotion. If a chaplain was not promoted, it meant that he had simply run out of time due to his age or else had done something that had severely upset his superiors.

In 1965, despite integration, the three services were still using different forms of confidential or performance reports to determine promotions. The minister's manpower study of May 1965 stated that a sound basis for promotion required a system of reporting which accurately reflected the performance and the potential of the officer in question. The study recommended the development of a reporting form common to all military classifications, and a new personnel evaluation report (PER) was brought into use.

In 1967 promotion boards for chaplains were held under the new system for the first time. Input was restricted to the military and the chaplain general. The comments of civilians, including those of military dependents who attended the chapels, were not invited. Early in the following year the first integrated captain to major promotion board was held. This new style of board consisted of five people: a chairman and four members, of whom only one came from the chaplain(P) classification. It was said that they were as fair and unbiased as possible, and that no one member could seek to sway or influence the board without bringing his own integrity into question. The boards worked from PERs and from course reports and for the most part did not know the people they were considering. No attention was to be paid to the denomination of the chaplain or to his element. When the first results of the new system appeared there was considerable upset. Of the first four chaplains to be promoted to the rank of major, all were Army men and three of the four were Anglicans. Moreover, one of these four had been a captain for only four years.[40]

Because of the unique nature of a chaplain's work, it proved difficult to obtain proper evaluations using the standard reporting form. Chaplains and medical officers received "inadequate, bland, inconsequential confidential reports completed by either or both professional and line officers. One of the more glaring deficiencies was a tendency to confine the reporting channels exclusively to either the line channel or professional net."[41] Neither one alone could adequately describe the military attributes and the professional capabilities or talents of the chaplains. Reporting officers were encouraged to ensure that both line and professional input was received on chaplain and medical PERs.

On the chaplain's part there was the equally strong feeling that the base chaplain should have an input into the PERs. Some base chaplains went so far as to prepare PERs on their assistants so as to be adequately prepared to discuss the evaluations of their men. The results were varied and met with mixed responses in the newly integrated force. On one large Army base when a new "Navy" base chaplain made his rounds to discuss the PERs of his "Army" chaplains with their "Army" commanding officers, he felt like he was intruding on sacred territory that was not his own. One commanding officer simply tossed the base chaplain's PER into the garbage pail. Two others incorporated his work into their own. For one very junior chaplain this meant that he received two PERs that year. The first was from his unit and it was so impressive that it would have made Moses blush. The second was from his unit after the visit of the "Navy" base chaplain. It was presented with apologies from the unit and with the explanation that the base chaplain quite obviously did not like him and that all this didn't really matter because as a first-year chaplain he wasn't in the promotion zone. More needed to be decided, understood, and said about the base chaplain's input on PERs.

Writing to his command chaplains in 1969, Chaplain General Cardy brought to their attention that "a directive would soon be issued to all commands to the effect that all Chaplains'(P) Confidential Reports must be initiated by the military, that meant by non-Chaplains. The Command Chaplain(P) could be the reviewing officer or have special input on the Chaplain(P) Annex Form."[42] In response to the command chaplains' meeting in 1970, Padre R.G.C. Cunningham, then director of chaplain administration, further refined the reporting procedures.[43] He reminded the command chaplains that some chaplains' PERs had not arrived in Ottawa in time for the promotion board meetings. While that was not their responsibility, he asked them to monitor the progress of the PERs through the system to safeguard the career possibilities of each chaplain.

Cunningham went on to note that the job description and level of responsibility was not adequately covered on the PER. He anticipated that the evaluation form would soon be revised. It was hoped that it would include a section for job description and an indication of the level of responsibility at which the chaplain functioned. Until that time, command chaplains were to make certain that all chaplains used the sections on primary and secondary duties to describe their jobs and areas of responsibility.

On a large number of chaplain PERs, the sections concerning the chaplain's relationship with his subordinates was being checked off as not applicable. While not every chaplain had supervisory responsibilities for other chaplains, every chaplain did have some involvement with a group or groups within the chapel framework. In any and all of these areas the chaplain had a real responsibility for the guidance and development of leadership within the group. The assessment of the chaplain's leadership abilities thus was extremely relevant. All sections of the PER were applicable to chaplains.

Finally, Cunningham pointed out that the command chaplains alone were responsible for specialist input into the PERs of the chaplains in the command. He directed the command chaplains to ensure that "if a base chaplain acts temporarily as command chaplain, the base chaplain, in his acting capacity, will neither have access to nor comment on any chaplain PER referred to the Command Chaplain(P)."[44]

In general, as the PER system came into use, chaplains rated very highly in the eyes of reporting officers and very close to one another. Typically, in 1975, eighty percent of all chaplains were rated "better than most." Such results tended to make selection very difficult when promotion opportunities were limited, such as they had been after the military forces had begun to reduce in 1967. Nevertheless, a survey of promotions made between integration and the mid-1970s[45] indicates that each element and each denomination had received its fair share.

By 1976, the chaplains had become used to the military performance evaluation report but recognized that it had obvious shortcomings when it was prepared without adequate input from the base chaplains. An attempt was made to overcome this problem by using a narrative insert which allowed the command chaplain and the chaplain general to have some professional input into the reports. Appropriate numerical assessments on the form were red-circled and initialled by them to indicate where the professional assessment was at variance with the assessment of military performance made by the reporting officer. Following the basic assumption that there was a requirement for some kind of "specialist" assessment and that the specialist reporting and reviewing officers should be chaplains, a committee was struck to recommend a more effective method of evaluating the professional performance of chaplains.

A study of the methods used to assess chaplain performance in the United States Army, the Royal Navy, and the Royal Air Force convinced the committee that the current Canadian method was as useful as any other. The British Army, however, had developed a new evaluation form for chaplains which offered a marked improvement. Using this form and other British literature as the basis of the study,[46] the committee decided that a Canadian Forces Specialist Chaplain(P) Performance Evaluation Report should be created which would assess the various aspects of Christian ministry and provide an opportunity for a numerical rating of that performance. The narrative assessment, made by a specialist reporting officer, should be consistent with and substantiate the numerical ratings. The specialist reviewing officer could red-circle and initial any changes which he made in the specialist numerical ratings and support his evaluation of the professional performance with a narrative assessment. The chaplain general would continue to be the final reviewing officer of both the military and the professional assessments made on Protestant chaplains in the Canadian Forces.

This procedure would eliminate many of the problems with the general form. Chaplains would continue to be available as advisers to military reporting and reviewing officers and the professional assessment could be inserted in the PER at the command level whether it was initiated by the base chaplain and forwarded to the command chaplain for his input as the professional reviewing officer, or initiated by the command chaplain. The committee enclosed a sample form with their report along with a list of performance objectives and recommended that the new format be introduced on a user-trial basis for a three-year period beginning January 1, 1977.

The new PER insert would assess chaplains(P) in six areas of ministry: chapel ministry, pastoral ministry, teaching ministry, response to military role, leadership, and administration. The committee defined each of the requirements in an illustrative rather than all-inclusive way, counselling that the specialist reporting officers would have to use their judgement in applying them, given the nature and scope of each chaplain's assignment. The committee's definitions give an invaluable overview of chaplaincy work in the 1970s and will therefore be set out in some detail.

Chapel Ministry

"Carried out those aspects of ministry which were centred in or grew out of chapel(P) services and programs." The relevant concerns were: leadership appropriate to the role assigned to the chaplain in the total programme; professional competence in preparation and delivery of sermons and in preparation and conduct of worship; the provision of a sacramental ministry appropriate to local needs; sensitivity to the denominational requirements of the churches represented in the congregation; development and maintenance of a meaningful and challenging stewardship program; development and maintenance of both evangelistic outreach programs and of programs designed to serve the local community; development of lay participation and leadership in chapel worship, programs, organizations, and activities; and professional competence in any other aspects of ministry relevant to chapel ministry.

Pastoral Ministry

"Demonstrated a concern for people and took positive action to meet their needs." Relevant concerns were: the provision of a pastoral visitation programme; competence and flexibility in counselling; the provision of programmes to meet the special needs and to respond to special interests in the community; support and encouragement for all organizations and activities devoted to improving the quality of life in the community.

Teaching Ministry

"Effectively taught the Christian faith." Relevant concerns were: operation of a Sunday School; provision of a Sunday School teacher training program; provision of confirmation and church membership classes which meet the denominational requirements of the churches represented in the congregation; development and support of activities designed to foster Christian growth and nurture; support for the Religion-in-Life program of the Scout/Guide movement; appropriate preparation and follow-up for parents bringing infants for Baptism; support for Christian education programs within the DND schools; development of effective padre's hours programs; demonstration of a concern and enthusiasm to provide a specifically Christian input into other community activities; to be sensitive to and to respond promptly, creatively, and imaginatively to all opportunities to teach the Christian faith.

Response To Military Role

"Performed effectively as a clergyman in the military environment." Relevant concerns were: "Awareness that, like all other service personnel, he has accepted an unlimited liability contract to serve anywhere at any time; awareness of the specifically military role of the Chaplaincy in the context of both his assigned position and the Canadian Forces as a whole; flexibility and adaptability during field training and operational deployments, availability during both duty and silent hours; physical fitness; military deportment; and the ability to relate the faith to, and have rapport with, all ranks."

Leadership

"Effectively demonstrated his capabilities as a spiritual leader." Relevant concerns were: evidence of a life style and moral character consistent with his role as clergyman; demonstration of loyalty, support, and pastoral concern for both his subordinates and his superiors; demonstration of the ability to identify goals and objectives, to assign priorities, to plan, to recruit resources, to support and to supervise as appropriate, to engender and to sustain enthusiasm, to ensure continuity, to demonstrate the ability to think creatively, to communicate his ideas; to inspire respect and trust, and to work successfully with others.

Administration

"Effectively demonstrated a knowledge of and the capability to carry out the administrative functions of his assigned role." Some relevant concerns were: ability to carry out and/or supervise normal office

136

procedures; demonstration of a knowledge of military writing and of current regulations and procedures dealing with staff duties; demonstration of capability to manage effectively his time and resources and to plan and organize the work of subordinates.

In 1977, it was recommended that the reporting officer responsible for the evaluation would be the appropriate command chaplain and that, beginning in 1978, command chaplains would report on all majors and on those captains who were on single bases/units within their commands, but that base chaplains would report on all captains serving under their supervision.[47]

The question of revealing to individual chaplains their rating by the Promotion Selection Board was the subject of a letter from the chaplain general in 1976.[48] The arguments in favour of disclosure centred around a "need to know" by those who were uncertain and puzzled that the many excellent reports they had received did not lead to promotion and whose service might soon be terminated because of lack of promotion. Traditionally, an individual was told only where they had placed on the merit list: top, middle, or bottom third. It had been found that more harm than good resulted from a more detailed accounting. The example used was of a chaplain who ranked first on the Promotion Selection Board list. He would have every expectation of promotion and yet might never be promoted because of the lack of a vacancy. Then, when a promotional opportunity did arise, it might be that the board had met again and he was no longer in the number one position. Such an experience could entail considerable heartache. The chaplain general reported: "This, and the fact that comparisons are insidious, makes it imperative that standings not be disclosed."

The chaplain general went on to make other points. The command chaplains' input was in the form of reporting from the professional point of view and not as a reviewer of the reporting officer. The command chaplains' remarks were subject to the same kind of review as those of the reporting officer in that anything detrimental must have been discussed and an opportunity must have been given to correct the fault. All exceptional performance had to be substantiated. The chaplain general's comment was partly an attempt, from his knowledge, to determine the chaplain's capacity to undertake the responsibilities of higher rank as well as acting as reviewing officer for the command chaplains. Finally, the chaplain general noted that, in the opinion of the promotion boards and the PER monitoring organization, the chaplains' PERs were considered to be the most carefully and best prepared of all submitted.

WITH NATO IN THE SIXTIES

Parkhouse Returns To Germany

While chaplains in Canada were worried about promotions and the redefinition of their role, some really interesting work was being done in Europe. In 1964 S.M. Parkhouse, who had served as a navigator in the Second World War, returned to Europe: this time as a padre at the air base in Marville, France. Again there were too many trips to the cemetery, this time because of the CF-104 Starfighter aircraft, alias "the widow maker." There was a small chapel on the base but regular services of worship were held in the recreation hall in the PMQ patch because there were very few French churches in the neighbourhood. When the wing got a second Protestant padre, they started to have church services in the afternoon in a small Protestant church just across the border in Belgium. On Christmas Eve they held services at all three church sites. Sunday Schools were popular and well attended.

Army Operations

In the spring of 1955 Jim Browne was in Germany as the senior chaplain of the 4th Canadian Infantry Brigade Group. In the 1960s, he was followed by G.E. Darrach, W.W. Buxton, and then A.G. Reid. During this decade there were 10,000 Canadian soldiers on the ground in Europe. Some sixty percent of them were married and the average family had 3.5 dependents.

The chaplains had their work cut out for them—not just in providing spiritual leadership but as general problem solvers. For example, the families were scattered in German towns all around the bases as well as in the military town sites, but there were very few telephones in Germany. As a mission project, the chapel at Werl had a telephone installed in their chaplain's house. This was passed on from chaplain to chaplain over the years and was looked upon as a great asset. A chaplain always tried to meet the families when they first arrived to help them adjust to the different cultural setting. If there were any social problems during their posting the chaplain was almost certainly involved. And, as always, it was usually the chaplains who informed families of bad news—whether of deaths that had occurred in Canada or of serious accidents or deaths during training exercises in Germany. There were many stories of chaplains searching through the night in obscure German towns, trying to find a particular family.

The Army chaplains in Europe were particularly busy because any time of day or night the brigade could be "bugged out." If it was at night, trucks would come into the living areas and blow their air horns until all of the soldiers were aboard. The families never knew if it was just another exercise or if it was the real thing and they were at war. The chaplains would move tactically with their units. A chaplain might go with a company or a platoon and do whatever it did on the exercise. In action, he would co-locate with the unit aid station. Always there would be a chaplain that the unit padres could count on serving with the field ambulance. In Germany the brigade and the chaplains spent a lot of time in the field.

When exercises were on, five chaplains would deploy and three would remain behind to deal with the family problems and to conduct worship services. Annual leave was taken in three sections to ensure adequate coverage. It was also arranged that the chaplains would be rotated home on a separate slate and not with their units to avoid a complete turnover of chaplains in any one summer. As well, the padres would sometimes be sent to visit Canadian Forces serving in the Middle East. In 1966, for example, Padre Kels Minchin was in the Middle East in January and March of 1966 and the RCAF chaplains were there in May and July. The purpose was to provide the sacrament for soldiers who were not the same denomination as the incumbent chaplain.

Christian Education In The Schools

This was a more burning issue for the Roman Catholics than it was for the Protestants, and the Protestants tended to follow along in their wake.

In Canada, when the dependents of servicemen moved to accommodation on military bases it was expected that many of the services that they might find in civilian communities would be provided. This was especially true in the field of education where some of the servicemen demanded separate schools. As early as the summer of 1949 it had been decided that religious instruction in the schools would be arranged to conform with the requirements of the province in which the base was located and that these services would be supplemented as thought desirable by the chaplains. In Germany, where base schools were guided by the rules of the province of Ontario, this meant that Christian education was normally provided by the teachers. Not surprisingly, there was some variation in the quality and the quantity of what was taught.

The discussion became a debate in 1958 when the adjutant general issued an order directing that "pupils will receive religious instruction in accordance with the established curriculum" and that "no pupil will be required to read or to study in or from any religious book, or to join in any exercises or devotion or religion objected to by his parent or guardian."[49] In response, the Roman Catholic chaplains did a survey of their families and

BGen J.W. Forth, MBE
First chaplain general
September 1958 - December 1959

A/C F.W. MacLean
Second chaplain general
January 1960 - February 1962

BGen J.R. Millar
Fourth chaplain general
May 1965 - July 1966

BGen E.S. Light
Fifth chaplain general
July 1966 - October 1968

The Rev. (Cl.5) C.H. Maclean
Chaplain of the fleet, 1964-1967

Col. J.P. Browne, MC
Principal chaplain of the army,
1959 - 1963

Anglican padres K.A. Minchin, L. Coleman, and J. Farmer entertain the archbishop of
Canterbury, Michael Ramsey, Germany, 1964.

"Catch the men when and where you can..."

Service in the pines, Sennelager, Germany, 1963.

Padre A.G. Reid and his team in Soest, 1970, entertain a distinguished visitor.
L to R: standing: S.H. Clarke, R.S. Woods, R.B. Cope, J.I. Mills, G.G. Davidson, D.R. Blair, J.A. Klingbeil; seated: A.G. Reid and the visitor, Rev. Dr. J. Logan-Vencta, OBE, ED.

"Just like the suburbs": Canadian PMQs, Soest, Germany.

in April 1958 reported that the Ontario system did not provide sufficient time for the proper Christian education of Roman Catholic children. The DND school system responded with its own survey a month later, but the chaplains argued that this survey was out of tune with the real situation.[50] Then in June the chaplains approached the Personnel Members Committee with a request for one hour per week of religious instruction in the schools. The PMC tabled the proposal because it was felt that it infringed upon human rights.[51]

At its meeting of December 15, 1958, the Chaplain General's Advisory Committee decided that overseas the Ontario curriculum would apply for students in grades one to eight. Grades nine and ten would use the books, *Jesus and His Teachings* and *Myself and My Creed*. There would be no instruction in grades eleven to thirteen. The chaplains were annoyed that the senior students were being missed and let it be known. The deputy minister informed the chaplains general that the decision not to teach religion at the secondary level had been made strictly on the basis of a lack of competent teachers of religion. In response, the chaplains reasoned that if the schools had a time for recreation activities and if the Ontario high schools could work religion into their busy schedules, then so could the schools in Europe. In fact, Padre Light reported to Forth that in 4 Wing there was no religion being taught. In 3 Wing, grades nine to twelve got two half-hours per week. In 2 Wing, grades eight to eleven got two half-hours per week. In 1 Wing, students in grades six to nine got half an hour per week from the teacher and half an hour per week from the padre.

In February 1959, it was decided that there was a need for a clear policy on religious education in DND schools in Germany.

In the 1960s in Europe there was a desire amongst the servicemen and their families to make the Christian education in the schools an ecumenical endeavour. This was rooted in the manner in which living in such a socially tight community brought together Protestants of all denominations and leanings. Some even asked: "Why can't we include the Roman Catholics?" Administratively, the schools wanted it too: "Both on idealistic and practical grounds there was a ground swell of interest."[52] The Roman Catholics had an impressive tradition of teaching catechism and their programs were very well developed and easily presented. The Protestants didn't have material that was anywhere nearly as good and were always searching for something appropriate. It was decided that the Protestants would have no great difficulty in adapting the Roman Catholic curriculum to Protestant ends but the Roman Catholic chaplain general said no!

The Salvation Army

Captain and Mrs. Hopkinson of the Salvation Army moved to Germany in 1952 to work with their British Salvation Army counterparts to serve the Canadian Army in Europe. When the soldiers went on manoeuvres, the Hopkinsons borrowed a Red Shield mobile canteen from the British and went along with them. They served hot coffee, milk shakes, hamburgers, and cold soft drinks from the truck and had newspapers from home.

When the Canadians moved to Soest, the Hopkinsons rented a small building near by and served coffee and donuts. Their first meeting in Soest was a watch night service held on December 31, 1953.

At the height of the Canadian presence in Germany the Salvation Army operated up to four Red Shield Clubs and a youth centre. This included a French-language club for the families of soldiers of the Royal 22nd Regiment when they were stationed at Fort Werl, a small operation at Hemer, and a youth centre at Deilinghofen. They operated a reception centre at Fort Anne.

In 1970 when the Canadian Forces in Europe were reduced in number and relocated, the Salvationists followed the soldiers to Lahr and then to Baden. The operations at Werl and Hemer were closed and later reopened by the British Salvation Army.

In the early days at Lahr, while accommodation was still a problem, the Salvation Army set up two large tents: one for use as a snack bar and the other for the use of mothers and their babies. Eventually a Red Shield Centre was established near the base. In it was a non-alcoholic single men's lounge, a gift shop, and a seventy-five-seat cafeteria. The objective was to provide a home away from home for all ranks of military personnel and their dependents.

Consolidation Of Bases

In the summer of 1967 the government of France requested that Canadian airmen be moved from Marville and Metz. The decision was made to relocate the 3000 airmen and their families in Germany: 1, 2, and 3 Wings would join 4 Wing at Baden. Then, because Lahr in Germany had the longest runway in the area, it was decided that the Canadians would take over from the French who were at that location. The move soon became a nightmare for the families and for the chaplains who were attempting to support them. The French were in no hurry to move out of Lahr and seemed to be taking advantage of the situation. The move from Marville was planned to take place just when the lease on the married quarters there ran out and there could be no extensions. Many of the

145

Canadian families thus found themselves living in tent and trailer parks around Lahr waiting for French military families to vacate the Lahr married quarters.

The 1969 decision to reduce Canada's commitment to the NATO force in Europe by fifty percent led to another exodus as the Canadian Army also moved south to Baden and Lahr. Soest and its ten satellites were closed, and 5000 men and their families were sent home to Canada while another 3000 moved to Lahr and 2000 to Baden. Zweibrücken closed in 1970 which meant even more airmen moved to Baden. Accommodation and other problems were acute and the chaplains were very busy.

The departure of the troops meant that some of the chapels, conceived and constructed in the midst of so much debate, were now closed. These chapels contained some fine stained glass and memorial windows such as those of 3 and 4 Wings. Fortunately many of these windows were removed and now grace chapels at various Canadian Forces bases,[53] providing a continuing reminder of the role of chapel life and chaplains for servicemen and their families who are posted overseas.

Chapter 6

PEACEKEEPING AND AID TO THE CIVIL POWER

ALTHOUGH THE WORLD has been spared the horrors of global war since 1945, war and the threat of war have remained omnipresent. At first this threat seemed most obvious in central Europe where East faced West and Canadian soldiers maintained a presence in Europe all through the Cold War. One of the most fearful moments in this confrontation was the Cuban missile crisis of October 1962. On October 25 Chaplain G.R. (George) Bell, serving on HMCS *Bonaventure*, had just come ashore from a tour when he was recalled to prepare to go to sea. Every naval vessel on the Atlantic coast was put on alert as the United States and the Soviet Union confronted one another. Over a weekend, the aircraft carrier was restocked and slipped out to sea with 1200 men and two Protestant chaplains. Bell reported that he did most of his work at night. He would wander down to have coffee in the mess around 10:00 p.m. and would visit with the crew coming on at midnight. Then for the next two hours he would catch those who were finishing their shift. Fortunately, the crisis was soon resolved, and the Navy resumed its more normal daily war with the sea.

However, Canada's internationalist role in the postwar world meant that the country was involved in many of the attempts to find resolutions to the hundreds of smaller conflicts that have occurred during the past half-century. The use of peacekeeping forces under United Nations auspices was one of the ways in which the world's leaders sought to defuse or even end some of these conflicts. From the very earliest days, Canadian personnel have served overseas in blue berets under the United Nations flag—mainly in the Middle East, Cyprus, and the Congo. They were perceived as ideal candidates for peacekeeping duties because of their professionalism, their special skills, their rapid deployment capability, and, as time passed, their experience. Canadian troops also participated in a similar but non-UN operation at the end of the war in Vietnam. Because United Nations peacekeeping operations are authorized for six-month periods, soldiers (including their accompanying chaplains) are rotated on that basis as well and Canada's chaplains have had many interesting experiences.[1]

At home Canada's forces were closely involved in two major national events—the FLQ crisis of 1970 and the Olympics in the summer of 1976.

THE CONGO

When Canadians became involved in the United Nations operation in the Belgian Congo in 1960, many of the chaplains knew little about this huge territory of over 900,000 square miles straddling the equator. Padre Bill Buxton described the country as "unexplored rain forest ... steaming hot jungle, huge lakes, prairie lands and beautiful highlands as you gradually move up toward the mountains. Throughout all of this, moving in almost a complete circle, flowing in every direction as it makes its way from the rain forest to the sea, is the mighty Congo River. Together with its tributaries it covers at least three quarters of the country ... and with the exception of a few disjointed railway lines was the main means of travel, communication and commerce."[2]

In the late 1950s, world opinion and nationalist agitation in the colony forced Belgium to grant the Congo its independence. Immediately after the formal declaration of independence on June 30 1960, the country erupted into violence leading to extreme social disorder as the many tribal and political factions fought for control of their particular turf. Eastern and Western bloc countries took sides, and the possibility of a more widespread conflict emerged. At this juncture the United Nations responded to an appeal from the Congo's elected leaders to step in and in July authorized an international military force to restore law and order, Opération des Nations Unies au Congo (ONUC).

CHAPLAINS, ONUC, 1960 - 1964		
D.L. Martin	W.W. Buxton	G. Youmatoff
D.C. Johnstone	A.J. Fralick	J.H. Jackson
A.G. Reid		

The Canadian contingent in the force, based in Léopoldville, was chiefly responsible for communications throughout the country and for air traffic control at all airports. The task was extraordinarily difficult both because of the country's poor infrastructure and because the soldiers in the United Nations contingent were from twenty-three different countries. To do the job, bilingual soldiers were sent from the Royal Canadian Corps of Signals accompanied by infantry personnel to provide housekeeping services and additional security. A small group of Air Force traffic control officers manned the major airports.

148

Small Canadian detachments were scattered all over the country: at Matadi in the Congo delta; at Coquilhatville on the east bank of the Congo River, some four hundred miles northeast of Léopoldville; at Stanleyville, about six hundred miles farther on by air; at Bukuvu on the border with Rwanda; at Urundi, between Lake Kiver and Tanganyika; at Albertville, three hundred miles south of Bukuvu on the shores of Lake Tanganyika; at Elizabethville, another four hundred miles south of Albertville; at Kamina, thre hundred miles northwest of Elizabethville; and at Luluaburg about three hundred miles farther on in a northwesterly direction. With a parish of this size, it was a real challenge for a chaplain to reach his parishioners. Buxton remembers the Congo for "the heat, the snakes and the rickety old planes."[3]

Chaplains are employed with the understanding that they might be called upon to serve anywhere and at any time. When Captain D.L. (Don) Martin heard, on November 7, 1960, that he would be the first chaplain going to the Congo, he was advised by Deputy Chaplain General Browne that conditions were most unsettled. Even the role that the UN soldiers were to play was not yet clear. Martin was advised to "play it" according to his own judgement, guided by his own sense of vocation and ministry. Browne told Martin to get to know people as well as he could, to be co-operative, and to be keen and zealous for the spiritual welfare of his people. Browne wrote:

> Expect some hardship, Don. Separation in itself is a hardship—remember that all the others are as lonely and as "fed up" as you will sometimes be. But, because commitment is part of your way of life, you can accept it and minister out of it. Others will complain and criticize and cry, but I know you won't. Only criticize when by constructive and reasonable suggestion situations can be changed and improved. When things are just tough—you will remember that the Christian Gospel never promises that life will be easy or comfortable or devoid of tragedy—it only promises that the grace and presence of God will enable men to face it and keep their faith and confidence.[4]

Martin had many experiences in the Congo, some of which he will never forget. One day he was being driven in a jeep just outside the United Nations compound. The vehicle was stopped by a mob, but when they saw that he was a padre and was unarmed, they permitted him to pass. Later, a jeep with two young Canadian officers was stopped; the soldiers were severely beaten, and their weapons were taken. On another occasion, the story is told that Padre Martin and his driver strayed off the main route between two locations. Eventually, Martin realized that he was lost and stopped to ask directions. He was told how to get back to the UN lines and that, if he hurried, he might not be killed.

Padre W.W. Buxton arrived in the Congo in October 1961 after an arduous week-long journey from Victoria in an RCAF North Star. By that time the Canadian chaplains had been given the use of a house that had been rented from a Belgian business executive. It was just a few blocks from the river and across the street from a former church college. The college had ceased to operate, but its large swimming pool was kept functioning by the United Nations for the use of its personnel. The two-level house had two bedrooms, a kitchen, and a large room which would hold forty to fifty people. Buxton acquired some folding chairs and the room soon doubled as the Protestant chapel and a lounge. A sideboard was used as an altar, and there was a portable field organ. The Roman Catholic chaplain, Father Fourcier, shared the house, but he was able to hold worship services in a lovely convent chapel that was nearby.

The UN had established a schedule for cargo planes—old DC-3s and C-46s—to supply the soldiers disbursed throughout the country. The padres decided that every week one of them would be in the country while the other stayed in Léopoldville. In this way three detachments could be covered each week, but the two padres were always in Léopoldville on Sunday to hold services for the main detachment. Every Monday morning, therefore, the chaplains would get up at 4:00 a.m. and drive the twenty miles to the airport.

Sometimes this trip could be quite dangerous, and it helped to know a number of alternate routes to avoid the riots and mobs which seemed to erupt at a moment's notice. At the airport one of them would board the transport and the other would drive the jeep back.

The chaplain who went up country would spend two days at a detachment and then fly on to the next detachment. At each location a church service would be held, reading material exchanged, and sometimes a movie shown. Because the detachments were small there was time to visit with each man and a family feeling soon grew up. Information on events and friends was exchanged. These visits were perhaps the most important part of the chaplain's job because the situation in the field was always explosive and soldiers were often under fire. They appreciated the chaplains' visits, and there was always full attendance at services.

The work of the chaplain in Léopoldville was just as varied and interesting. To restore order in Léopoldville, the UN brought in large numbers of British-trained Nigerian military police. The UN appointed the Canadian padres as chaplains to these police. The Nigerian Christians

150

insisted on weekly Bible study courses, confirmation studies, and Sunday services. These were covered by Buxton with the assistance of Fred Drake, the general field secretary of the British Baptist Mission Society, who had a community church in Léopoldville. Because their different traditions complemented each other, Buxton and Drake exchanged for the sacraments, announced each other's notices, and did as much together as time permitted. Padre Buxton also held Sunday services with a small American advisory group at the air base because their Lutheran chaplain was only able to come down from Libya once every two months. The Queen's Own Nigerian Rifles were stationed on the outskirts of Léopoldville and after their chaplain left because of illness, Buxton also tried to fill in for him.

Directly across the river from Léopoldville was the city of Brazzaville in the Republic of the Congo. The main European language in this former colony of France was French and the main religion Roman Catholicism. When the English-speaking community in Brazzaville heard that there was an English-speaking Protestant chaplain with the Canadian contingent, they arranged to have services in the British embassy every second week. Some of them also came to the services in Léopoldville on the alternate weeks. Although these services were for the soldiers, they were attended by the public and developed into a kind of international family service. Parishioners were largely diplomatic folk and included Americans, British, Indians, Nigerians, and a Japanese family. By the end of his tour Buxton had accumulated thousands of francs from all these services. Congolese currency had to remain in the country and this money was presented to Mr. Drake for the work of his mission amongst the Congolese.

The family atmosphere prevailing at these services provided social and religious contact for those soldiers who were interested. Films and other mid-week activities were available at the Baptist Mission Centre. And for those who could adapt to the climate, there were opportunities for golf, swimming, and tennis.

The North Star from Canada arrived in the Congo once each week to drop off a small group of Canadians and to take another small group home. A chaplain met each flight to say farewell and to welcome the newcomers and help them to adapt to the new environment. Everyone who came to the Congo seemed to suffer a couple of days' confusion because of the long trip, the noise of flying in a North Star cargo plane, and the intense heat and humidity into which they were plunged.

Because of the climate the UN worked from 7:00 in the morning until noon or 1:00 p.m., and then took a break for three hours before returning to work. During the break people would try to sleep or to swim. With

151

nightfall safety became the primary concern. It was necessary not only to lock up the building, but to lock even your bedroom door. At times the situation was so tense that when darkness came you could not move about but had to stay wherever you were until the next morning. Unsettled conditions meant that robbery was rife.

There were some good buys to be found in the Congo and everyone collected souvenirs and goodies from the military store to take home. Unfortunately, two out of every three soldiers were robbed before they could get their purchases out of the country. Early each Sunday morning, a one-armed man arrived at the chaplains' door asking for alms and every Sunday morning they had a small stack of francs waiting for him. Buxton came to believe that somehow the man was linked to the padres' good fortune. Indeed, Buxton and Fourcier were the only officers in their contingent who were never robbed and, in retrospect, he has come to think that they had not been giving alms but paying protection money.

Buxton's successor, A.J. Fralick, did not give "alms" to the weekly visitor, and one night he awoke to find a thief in his room. The padres had been offered pistols because of the dangers of the situation but, as always, the chaplains were reluctant to carry arms and Fralick had opted for a baseball bat. Quickly he leapt out of bed, grabbed the bat, and swung hard at the thief. The thief was scared off empty-handed, and Al was never bothered again.

During the truce between the breakaway province of Katanga and the central government, Moise Tshombe came to Léopoldville for negotiations. Katanga's leader came as head of state with a large entourage and was under the protection of the UN. While in Léopoldville he insisted that all the food he ate be prepared by the Canadians. Tshombe was one of the few Congolese leaders who was a Protestant, and he always came to church with a UN bodyguard and others. This meant that Buxton had to do a French transcript of the service and sermon for Tshombe spoke no English. Once again, Father Fourcier was a great help.

The actual work of the chaplains in the Congo was much the same as it was anywhere. They ministered to the sick, the troubled, and the anxious, and they even dealt with some deaths. They tried to teach and to preach the Word, and they administered the sacraments. They went wherever the men were required to go and tried to be a friend under all conditions. Although they were always aware that peaceful scenes could become violent within a moment, they felt very secure in their ability to cope. Their greatest concern was about the impact of press reports of atrocities in the Congo on their families back in Canada. They sought to keep their own personal channels of communication open so that their wives and children would know that they were safe. Nevertheless, working conditions in the Congo were more unstable and dangerous than in the usual peacekeeping operations of this time. The stress, coupled with the extreme climate, meant that chaplains tended to return home from a tour of duty run down and in need of a time for rest and readjustment.

CYPRUS

The beautiful island of Cyprus in the eastern Mediterranean was granted its independence from Britain in 1960. Tension soon developed between the Greek-speaking, largely Christian, majority of the country's population and the Turkish-speaking, largely Muslim, minority. Late in 1963 the Turks withdrew from the central government and intercommunal fighting broke out. In March 1964 the United Nations Force in Cyprus (UNFICYP) was established to keep the peace until some acceptable constitutional arrangement could be negotiated. Canada agreed to participate and later that month the aircraft carrier, HMCS *Bonaventure*, delivered four hundred and eighty Canadian peacekeepers to the island. It would be their job to maintain a United Nations presence in the northern part of the island. In time the number rose to nine hundred and fifty and then began to drop. With the Canadians in UNFICYP were soldiers from Austria, Denmark, Finland, Ireland, Sweden, and the United Kingdom.

CHAPLAINS, UNFICYP, 1964-			
K.A. Minchin	G.W. Lanctôt	R.S. Wood	W.N.C. Fry
C.E. MacCara	J.E. Craig	A.I. Wakeling	J.C.E.K. Massey
F.B. Jenkins	D.V. Funnell	R.H. White	D.I. Cosman
L.R. Coleman	K.J. Garrity	C.S. Black	J.E.R. Wiley
G.A. Milne	R.E. Gilbert	R.R. Murray	T.W. Blizzard
W.G. Shields	C. Mury	W.R. MacLennan	R.K. Deobold
A.G. Fowler	N. Shaw	W.G. Schurman	P.G. Day
W.C. MacLellan	W.D. Raths	A.E. Gans	D.C. Hansen
G.N. Ward	B.C.A. Hicks	T.P.R. Needham	J.D. Vaillancourt
B.E Sweet	G.G. Davidson		R.M. Durrett

Padre K.A. (Kels) Minchin has reported that as the Canadians were establishing their presence on the island, some military action was deemed necessary as a response to provocation. There are stories that when Canadian telephone land lines became impossible to use because of the number of telephone taps on them, an electric charge would be sent over the line. The telephones would then be clear for a number of days. Sometimes responses were, by necessity, more violent.

In 1968, Padre G.G. Davidson wrote an article on his recently completed tour of duty as a Canadian chaplain in Cyprus.[5] George Davidson's duties were typical of chaplain's work on peacekeeping tours over the years. While fun-loving tourists enjoyed Cyprus, which is sometimes called the Isle of Aphrodite, Davidson dealt with the soldiers' experiences of anxiety, tension, separation, and extreme loneliness. Because Greek and Turkish Cypriots lived in little enclaves all around the island, the soldiers of the 1st Battalion of the Black Watch and a reconnaissance squadron from the Fort Garry Horse were scattered throughout the northern district near Kyrenia. Davidson's job was to visit the nineteen observation posts, one of which was 1800 feet up in the mountains and reachable only by scaling a cliff with the help of a rope. He visited the posts in a low-key manner and with regularity, three days per week, so as to build rapport with the soldiers.

During this time Davidson was assisted by his driver, then Private A. (Willi) Williams, whom he had inherited from Padre Minchin. Later, Corporal Williams would work for Padre Lyman Coleman and then return to the chapel at Base Gagetown to work as the batman/driver for the Royal Canadian Regiment's padre there. Williams was always an infantryman but remained with the chaplains for many years. Long after batmen ceased to exist in the Canadian Forces, Williams could be counted on to keep the Gagetown chaplains in rations and vehicles—and out of harm's way.

When he was not visiting posts, the padre had lots of other work. Thursday was spent visiting the hospital at Camp Maple Leaf and the British military hospitals at Dhekelia and Akrotiri, and the Austrian field hospital in Nicosia. On Fridays he would go on a patrol with the reconnaissance squadron. On Sundays Davidson conducted worship at a remote company location and later at a chapel at Camp Maple Leaf. He also held worship services in Kyrenia at the Coeur de Lion Hotel and, on alternate Sundays, at the Church of England in Kyrenia.

The readiness to serve in the wider community would bring serendipitous awards as Padre Lyman Coleman discovered in 1972. The Anglican Church in Kyrenia was the centre of the English-speaking community in that part of Cyprus and during Coleman's tour it was without a priest. Coleman therefore volunteered to preach on Sundays at the church. Appreciative of his efforts, and worried about the growing tensions on the island, one British family asked Coleman if he would look after their Mercedes and their house while they went on an extended vacation to

England. Padre Coleman was happy to help out and made good use of the house, sometimes as a kind of retreat centre for visitors from Germany.

Coleman and the Canadians also provided considerable support to the staff and thirty children of the Red Cross Children's Hospital in Kyrenia. Both Greek and Turkish Cypriot children were cared for there. Many of the children were horribly crippled, others suffered from neglect and malnutrition, "yet all of them were full of a love and affection that could tug the heartstrings of even the toughest soldier."[6] Coleman organized frequent visits by his soldiers to cheer up the children. The 2nd Battalion, Queen's Own Rifles, gave $1200 to the hospital as well as cartons of clothing sent over by their wives. In later years, the Canadians moved their charitable work to the Theotokos Institute for mentally retarded children in Limassol and to the Red Crescent School for Special Children in Kyrenia. When Padre Eldon MacCara was in Cyprus he took prayers every second Sunday at the Red Cross orphanage.

MacCara lived in the low metal-roofed huts just up the street from Maple Leaf Camp at Blue Beret Camp, as did many of the chaplains over the years. There was a constant threat from poisonous snakes, and MacCara reported that he was always happy to wake up and see lizards on the walls and ceiling. If they were around he knew that there were no snakes in the room.

Not all chaplains lived in Kyrenia or even in Blue Beret Camp. For one period of time chaplains were given an office and room in a former five-star hotel located on the Green Line in Nicosia, the Ledra Palace. The Ledra still had circulating air, which passed for air conditioning in the 110-degree Fahrenheit summer heat. But all was not luxury: one padre reported that the carpet of his room was soiled by a large blood stain, a reminder of a terrorist gun battle in the hallway years before. At night, the hotel's wooden window shutters were always closed to discourage snipers, and the padre could not miss the many bullet holes in his shutter. The Ledra Palace boasted a lovely pool for those off-hours moments, but swimmers and sunbathers were always aware of the watchful eyes of Turkish soldiers whose observation posts overlooked the location.

In 1974, when there were seven hundred and ninety Canadian soldiers on the island, political developments in Cyprus culminated in an invitation from the leader of the Turkish Cypriots for the Turkish army to intervene to protect his community. A British dentist and his wife, Dr. and Mrs. French, sat in their living room in Kyrenia and watched as 6000 Turkish soldiers with forty tanks landed on Snake Island. The Greek population quickly fled in the face of such overwhelming firepower and the size of the Turkish force soon swelled to 40,000 men and four hundred tanks. When

155

the Turkish advance stopped, they held the northern third of the island. After this intervention the basic role of the Canadian soldiers changed. The commanding officer of the Strathconas, Lieutenant Colonel J.A. Fox, reported: "We are here as a Regiment to stand behind the men, who at this moment are standing between the opposing forces on the 'Green Line'."[7] The Green Line was the demarcation line which cut across the island creating a buffer zone between the positions of the Turks and the Greeks.

From time to time a senior chaplain would visit Cyprus. There was a story told about such a visit from Lieutenant Colonel Bill Buxton who was now a command chaplain. A young infantry officer, Captain "Hap" Stutt, was tasked to escort him at all times and to keep him "out of trouble" by guarding his every move. This did not prove difficult until Buxton announced that he was going to tour the Green Line and visit soldiers at the observation posts. At each location, Buxton would get out of the jeep and would not permit Stutt to go with him into the post. Stutt complied, figuring that Buxton simply wanted to have a quiet moment with the men without an officer present. On his return to Canada, Padre Buxton contacted the relatives of every young soldier with whom he had visited. To these parents, wives, and children Buxton passed intimate greetings and announced that he had personally witnessed the fine and outstanding job that the particular soldier was doing in Cyprus, serving God, Queen, and country. Relatives responded with a flood of positive letters to the military and to their members of parliament. All chaplains benefited from actions such as this done by men such as Bill Buxton.

Padre Roland Murray was in Cyprus over Christmas 1976 at a time of reasonable stability and he provided a vivid picture of the impending celebrations:

> We are now getting ready for our Christmas celebrations which will begin with a Christmas eve ecumenical service just before midnight. This will be held at Holy Cross Church, Paphos gate, which is situated in the demilitarized zone. Following the service, the RC padre and I will be visiting the men manning the observation posts (OPs) and the next day we will be taking in several Christmas dinners at different locations. On Christmas day the officers and senior NCOs will be manning the OPs so that the men can partake of the Christmas dinner and other festivities. The Christmas spirit has started to hit the men over here and it is quite the sight to see men returning from night duty on the OPs with helmets, flak jackets, and rifles singing "Silent Night." In a way it contrasts the peace of Christ offered to us with the violence

towards one another which we often choose, necessitating our being here on Cyprus in a peacekeeping role.[8]

Christmas was a special time when acts of thoughtfulness were always appreciated

Many of the Canadian chaplains who served in Cyprus developed a close working relationship with their British counterparts, one of whom was located in Nicosia, and with some of the British parishioners. Occasionally, Canadians would take the services at the Garrison Church at Blue Beret Camp. One Canadian chaplain visited a British family after their eighteen-year-old daughter had been injured at a party sponsored by the younger Canadian and British officers. The girl's back had been burned, and there would, no doubt, be scars. The parents, true "international military Brits," appreciated the visit but explained that the injury was nothing compared with the time when a python had grabbed the girl while she had been playing in the backyard of their married quarters in Burma.

During most tours of duty, Canadian chaplains conducted memorial services at the British military cemetery in Dhekelia. During the early Canadian tours of Cyprus soldiers who died were buried there, and Dhekelia holds the graves of nine Canadian soldiers.

During his retirement speech at the annual chaplains retreat, Bill MacLennan spoke of an incident that occurred when he had just arrived in Cyprus. The outgoing padre, skin bronzed and blue beret faded from the tropical sun, was taking MacLennan and his driver on a tour of the Green Line. At some places the route was little more than an alley with only a few yards separating the two sides. As the jeep rounded a corner the padre ordered the driver to halt. About fifty yards in front of them was a small Greek girl who had chased a ball out into no man's land. There, to their left and on a low roof top, was a young Turkish soldier, rifle raised and about to shoot. "MARHIBAH!" shouted the padre to the young soldier: "How are you doing?" The young soldier lowered his rifle and returned a big smile and the greeting "Marhibah." The padre directed the newcomer to remain there with the jeep as he walked forward to the child and carried her in his loving arms to a terrified mother. For MacLennan, this act of kindness was what peacekeeping was all about.

MIDDLE EAST

The United Nations established the United Nations Truce Supervision Organization (UNTSO) in 1948 to supervise the ceasefire and other agreements between Israel and its Arab neighbours following the first Arab-Israeli conflict. By 1949 the number of observers along the borders had reached 600, but Canada was not involved until 1954 when four officers were sent to Egypt. One of the four was Major General E.L.M. Burns who was placed in charge of the entire operation. Over the next two years tension mounted, and there were repeated flare-ups between the Israelis and the Egyptians. In July 1956, President Nasser of Egypt nationalized the Suez Canal, which was operated as an independent company backed by French shareholders. The action should not have been a surprise in light of growing Arab nationalism; nonetheless the Western world was shocked.

After several months of diplomatic manoeuvring, Israel's fears of Nasser's possibly expansionist designs led it to take the initiative on October 29. Moving swiftly, it had soon occupied much of the Sinai Peninsula and was close to the Canal. Britain and France reacted by issuing an ultimatum to both sides on October 30 to leave a ten-mile buffer zone on either side of the Canal and stating that British and French forces would be sent to protect vital national interests at Port Said, Ismailia, and Suez. Nasser rejected the ultimatum outright, and the next day French and British aircraft attacked. On November 5 and 6 the promised soldiers arrived. The situation was already under discussion at the United Nations which was taken aback by the British and French aggression and demanded a ceasefire. The ceasefire took place on November 6 and on the following day the United Nations Emergency Force (UNEF) was established under the leadership of General Burns to monitor the ceasefire and the subsequent agreements.

UNEF 1, 1956-1966

CHAPLAINS, UNEF I, 1955-1966		
O.A. Hopkins	D.C. Johnstone	H.R. Coleman
L.A. Dignan	E.V. Porrior	D.D. Davidson
R.H. Dobson	P.L. Sams	

Burns wanted a powerful force for the task and had the Queen's Own Rifles dispatched to Halifax for transport to the Middle East. But Egypt objected on the grounds that Egyptians would perceive these particular soldiers to be too closely aligned, in name and uniforms, to the British. Immediately, Burns changed his own uniform to look more "Canadian" and came to terms with the reality of the situation. UNEF would be a lightly armed buffer force between the two sides. The Canadian contribution would consist of a signals squadron, a transport company, a field hospital, and an RCAF communications squadron.

The Queen's Own Rifles were sent home and an advance party of support personnel began to assemble at Longue Pointe Barracks near Montreal. The first one hundred and twenty three men and sixteen officers flew to Naples and on to Abu Suweir, twelve miles west of Ismailia, on November 24. They were followed by four hundred men, one hundred tons of stores, two hundred and thirty vehicles, and four light aircraft on HMCS *Magnificent*. By the end of the 1957 there were 1000 Canadian soldiers in the Middle East, and a reconnaissance squadron with fifty-six Ferret scout cars was on its way.

At first the living conditions at Abu Suweir were deplorable. Idealistic young Canadians who thought that they were coming to serve the cause of peace in this new way felt they were treated like prisoners in a concentration camp. They were not allowed to go anywhere outside the camp without an Egyptian army escort and there was a 10:00 p.m. curfew. Eventually, they were given more control over their own activities and were allowed to patrol the Canal zone.

At the same time the UNTSO observers moved their centre of operations to Israel's borders with Jordan and Syria. UNEF established a second station on the west side of the canal at El Ballah. There was also a Royal Canadian Air Force station at Abu Zenima, near Ismailia. Later it was moved to Rafah in the Gaza Strip. Early on, there were lots of casualties from accidents and mines, and these men were buried in the Commonwealth cemetery just outside Ismailia. One Canadian died of a heart attack when he ran out into a minefield to deter children from playing there.

By the end of 1957 small groups of Canadians were scattered throughout the theatre of operations, and life settled into a routine that would continue for several years. Classes were started, and hobby clubs formed. Gifts were given to Palestinian and Bedouin refugees.

Captain H.R. Coleman was with UNEF in 1962-3. He conducted regular services at the Chapel of the Good Samaritan at Rafah, which he described as "very nice," in the Signals canteen in Gaza, and at Marina at El Arish, which included the Air Force. He had Canadian, Indian, and Scandinavian parishioners. During his tour Coleman prepared soldiers for confirmation, and the archbishop of Jerusalem confirmed six Canadians in the chapel at Rafah.

In June of 1963 as he prepared to hand over to Captain D.D. Davidson, Coleman described the Middle East experience[9] as "a most rewarding year": "The attendance in the Chapels has been steadily increasing, along with the collections which have been surprisingly high. We have given to the

Near East Council of Churches approximately $700 in the past ten months and have about an equal amount on hand."[10]

Many chaplains took advantage of their tour of duty to visit the Holy Land. Harold Coleman, who took movies and photographs of his entire trip, described his visit to Jerusalem as "the climax of a chaplain's tour to the Middle East": "We spent from Friday noon to Tuesday noon on a complete and comprehensive tour of the Holy Land and sang our Christmas carols in Shepherd's Field, for the Christmas broadcast which will be on radio and TV in Canada."

During the mid-sixties tensions in the Middle East began to rise again. In 1964 Palestinian guerrilla groups began their attacks on Israel and each attack brought a reprisal. Syria began to shell Israel intermittently from the Golan Heights. In 1966, Israeli tanks moved to confront guerrilla bases in Jordan. In 1966 Canada announced that its reconnaissance squadron attached to UNEF would be withdrawn as a cost-cutting measure and after the withdrawal Nasser ordered the United Nations out of Egyptian territory. Egypt's Russian-built T-34 and T-54 tanks started to move into the international zone in May 1967 and on the twenty-seventh Nasser ordered a complete withdrawal of the Canadians whom he accused of being friends of the United States and Israel. On May 29 and 30, 1967, 18 flights of RCAF C-130 Hercules aircraft moved a record seven hundred men and their equipment out of the zone.

On June 5, 1967, in retaliation for Egypt's blockade of the Canal and other actions, Israel launched a pre-emptive strike on its Arab neighbours. In short order the Sinai Peninsula, the west bank of the Jordan River, the Gaza Strip, East Jerusalem, and the Golan Heights were in Israeli hands. The United Nations ordered a ceasefire and UNTSO was brought in to establish new ceasefire lines.

During the next few years regional and international tension increased. Sporadic fighting occurred across the Canal (the so-called War of Attrition) and the power of the Arab members of the Organization of the Petroleum-Exporting Countries was enhanced through the control of oil prices. Then, on October 6, 1973, the Syrian Air Force attacked Israel in the sky and the Egyptian army attacked on the ground. After suffering initial losses, Israel regrouped and brought a quick end to the October War. During these full-scale hostilities, UNTSO observers on the east bank of the Canal had no problems but those on the west bank came under fire.

UNEF II and UNDOF

CHAPLAINS, UNEF II, 1973-9, and UNDOF, 1974-91		
J.W. von Schmeling	K.D. Benner	J.H. MacIntosh
M.M. Holobow	S.D. Self	R.A.B. MacLean
D.A. Hatfield	S.G. Horne	L.T. Barclay
K.A. Minchin		
	Resident chaplains in the Golan	
L.T. Barclay	F.W. Love	J.W. von Schmeling
R.A. Jones	G.E. Tonks	G.A. Milne
S.D. Self	F.L. Tassinari	G.E. Tonks
J.M. Cook	J.A. Klingbeil	C. Mury
J.A. Alexander		

By October 25, 1973, new ceasefire agreements were in place and UNEF II had been created to monitor them. Once again, a Canadian logistical support unit was established. In a matter of three days, four hundred and eighty-one soldiers and one hundred and fifteen tons of equipment were moved into place at the Heliopolis racetrack in Cairo, to be known as Camp Sham. This time the Canadians shared the logistics functions. The Poles provided medical, engineering, and transport facilities while the Canadians provided signals, postal, military police, maintenance, and air transport support.

In July 1974, the Canadians moved to El Gala Camp on the outskirts of Ismailia (OP Danaca). Eventually a small Canadian hospital and a dental unit were added for the use of the Canadian contingent. Soon these resources came to be used by all the soldiers in UNEF II. Soldiers became comfortable at OP Danaca with ATCO trailers replacing the temporary wooden structures supplied by Turkey. Air conditioners and a closed circuit television network appeared. In 1975, women soldiers were employed on peacekeeping for the first time.

Very early on August 9, 1974, a Buffalo aircraft was shot down by a Syrian missile. All nine Canadians on board were killed. This tragedy confronted every Canadian airman and soldier in the Middle East with the realization that the area was a war zone.

The United Nations Disengagement Observer Force (UNDOF) was formed some six months after UNEF II when Israel withdrew its forces from the Golan Heights and a force was required to monitor the disengagement and the "area of separation" between Syria and Israel. Once again Canada

Padre R.S. Woods climbs to UN outpost, "Hill Top", in the Kyrenia pass.

Christmas at the orphanage in Jerusalem - even the sisters join in the fun.

Padre George Davidson with some children from the Kyrenia children's hospital, Cyprus.

The cross says it all. Padre R.H. White constructs a cross in the field.

Following an epic trip from Germany, Padre K.A. Minchin hands over the keys of a Volkswagen Passat to Sheik Lewis Massoud Saleeb, elder of the Coptic Evangelical Church, Ismailia, April 20, 1976.

163

Home away from home:entrance to the Canadian UN base on the Golan Heights, from an original painting by Padre G.E. Tonks.

The medical inspection room and padre's bunker on the Golan Heights.

United Nations chaplains from seven countries gather to worship in an ancient amphitheatre near Limmasol, Cyprus, Whitsunday, 1968.

shared logistics duties with Poland. At first, as Padre von Schmeling noted, it was a challenge to survive with the soldiers housed in roofless buildings. However, they were eventually replaced by ATCO trailers and Camp Ziouani was soon well organized. On a second tour of duty fifteen years later, von Schmeling described life on the Golan Heights as pretty routine.

When Padre K.D. Benner was in the Middle East in 1976-7 he worked hard to keep the off-duty hours of the soldiers filled with positive activities. Benner organized a weekly personal growth/development group which offered an opportunity to increase one's spiritual awareness and discover a faith for the day. Another night each week was devoted to Benner's service club which was dedicated to leaving the world a little better than the participants might have found it. To all of this was added a glee club which enticed young men to meet and learn to sing on the steps of the female soldiers' quarters.

During their earlier stay in Ismailia with UNEF I, the Canadian chaplains had developed a relationship with the Coptic Evangelical Church, whose members were extremely poor and war ravaged. On June 5, 1975, four chaplains who knew of these problems met at the annual retreat in Kingston, Ontario, and they decided upon a plan to purchase a suitable vehicle for the church. Within five months, twenty-four Canadian chapels had raised $5000 in addition to their regular offerings and a Volkswagen Passat station wagon was purchased by the Christian Men's Club at Lahr, Germany, under the guidance of Padre Ormond Hopkins. Padre Kels Minchin, who was in Ismailia at the time, co-ordinated his United Nations leave in order to transport the vehicle by road from Germany through France and Monte Carlo to Italy and by ferry from Venice to Alexandria. After customs problems on the Italian border, a ship strike in Venice, and Muslim religious holidays in Alexandria, Minchin (who had developed a kidney stone on board a doctorless ship) and the vehicle arrived in Alexandria on March 10, 1976. The Coptic Church put the vehicle to immediate use, ministering to 300,000 inhabitants in Ismailia and to nine Christian communities outside the city. The church also served as a distribution centre for used clothing sent from Canadian Forces bases.

Another favourite project of the chaplains and the soldiers was the Home of Peace Orphanage. The orphanage, founded after the 1967 war to look after Palestinian children, was operated by the Polish Sisters of St. Elizabeth, under Sister Raphaela. It was located in a building in East Jerusalem beside the Mount of Olives and not far from the Garden of Gethsemane and offered a panoramic view of the Holy City. In 1977, there were thirty-five girls in the orphanage (aged five to twenty) from a variety of racial backgrounds. That year, one hundred and twenty soldiers raised $1500 for the orphanage. The sisters used the funds to establish a library.

In 1979, there were one hundred and seventy Canadian servicemen on the Golan Heights, and thirty-two children at the orphanage. On Christmas Day a busload of children arrived at Camp Ziouani at 7:00 a.m. The chaplains reported:

> Upon arrival the children attended Mass with the Canadians. During the service the children sang several Christmas carols, in English with a mixture of Arab and Polish accents. Following the service it was on to the mess hall for a traditional Canadian lunch of hamburgers, french fries, cake and ice cream. They were entertained by the Golan all male voice choir singing a selection of Christmas music. As the choir was singing "Here Comes Santa Claus" the old gent, in the person of Sergeant Pete Lawe, appeared with two elves carrying sacks of presents which Santa then distributed to the children. The fierce-looking ex-paratrooper was turned into a lump of jelly as a wide-eyed four year old Arab girl hugged him and thanked him for his present.[11]

The link with the orphanage continued, and in 1985 Padre F.W. (Fred) Love spent a lot of time trying to reconstruct the building's roof. However, by 1988 circumstances had changed and the PLO did not want any Christmas parties at the orphanage. This made Christmas a little harder to get through for the peacekeepers, but the chaplain's secret weapon, Corporal Max Peddle, came to the rescue. A popular and very dedicated layman in the chapels over the years, Peddle had left his family behind at CFB Uplands. The Uplands chapel community decided that they would send Max a Christmas stocking. The stocking, made by the padre's wife, Sheila Fowler, was eight feet high and at least two feet in diameter. The chapel filled it with presents for Max and the orphans. Somehow, Peddle managed to get the presents delivered to the orphans but there were some left over. On Christmas morning, each peacekeeper woke up to find a surprise Christmas gift left by some mysterious Santa on his pillow. Later that year, Padre von Schmeling convinced the Canadian embassy to give $27,000 in support of the orphanage.

The Christmas season was always a lonely time for the peacekeepers, and the chaplains made a special effort to help organize activities. Padre S.D. (Stan) Self's report of Christmas 1977 is typical. On Christmas Eve over three hundred people gathered outside the chapel at El Gala and sang Christmas carols. The carollers then walked into the Polish camp next door and sang for them while bags of Christmas candy were passed out. On

Christmas Day, Self reported that almost six hundred men gathered for Christmas dinner served by the officers and senior NCOs. This was followed by a stage show called "The Western Canada Review" and a gala reception. The next day Self drove with his Roman Catholic counterpart to the Indonesian battalion where seventy Christians attended a very meaningful communion service that had been arranged by their Muslim staff officer. The group gathered around six-foot-long tables set up in the form of a cross, and each man passed the elements to his neighbour with the appropriate words. Finally, on New Year's Eve, Self joined with the Coptic Evangelical Church for a pageant and communion service. The service, with an attendance of about 1000 people, started at 7:00 p.m. and ended at 1:00 a.m. Self commented: "They are dear Christian people and are so very kind to Canadians."[12]

Padre G.A. Milne spent a year on the Golan Heights. Milne had an air-conditioned trailer to himself, including a shower, office, and fridge. The chapel section of the trailer seated about twenty-five people. It was open all the time and services were held at 6:00 p.m. on Sundays. About half of those attending were Roman Catholic. The food was good, and Milne obtained a coffee maker and a portable stereo. He looked after the Canadian Logistics Support Battalion, Ausbatt (the Austrian guards), Finbatt, PolLog (on the Syrian side), UNDOF headquarters in Damascus, and the military police.

In the 1980s the padres found that many of the young servicemen were not very regular church attenders. In 1985, Fred Love had even changed the time of worship to Wednesday at 7:00 p.m., just before a daily movie, and this had helped for a while. However, many of the soldiers were interested in the life of Jesus and in visiting the places where he taught and ministered.

Over the years the chaplains loved to do "church" runs to the local sights. Buses would take the soldiers to Tabagha, on the shores of Galilee, to Nazareth, Tiberias, and Mount Tabour, and to Jerusalem. The applicable Gospel story would be read and the padre would be able to say: "This story occurred right here!" In 1987, it was the great pleasure of Padre von Schmeling to celebrate midnight mass at Tabagha.

When Milne arrived he thought that this interest in the sights might mean that servicemen had questions and were looking for some answers.[13] To meet this challenge, Milne brought in a Canadian Roman Catholic priest, Father John Domotor,[14] from Tiberias every month and this gave Milne a chance to take a busload on a tour to worship at some historical sight.

Over the years the chaplains on the Golan Heights took on a variety of tasks beyond their primary mandate. They visited UNTSO groups in Jerusalem, Tiberias, Nahariyah, and Damascus and Canadians in hospitals at Zefat and Tel Aviv. At times they were key encouragers of various social services such as the Alcoholics Anonymous groups, helping AA members to get on trips to meetings in Haifa and Tel Aviv. Milne assisted with the *Golan Journal* and organized a Terry Fox fun run for the benefit of cancer research in Canada. At other times the chaplain served as information officer, preparing news briefs from Canada for the men and contributing the Canadian portion of the Golan peacekeepers' quarterly, *Golan Journal*. Canadian chaplains stopped going to the Middle East in March 1992.

OPERATION GINGER: THE FLQ CRISIS

In 1970, a decade of activism by the Front de Libération du Quebec (FLQ) escalated when one of its cells kidnapped the British trade minister in Montreal on October 5 and another kidnapped Quebec's labour minister, Pierre Laporte, on October 10. In response, soldiers were ordered to guard public buildings and prominent politicians in Ottawa. On October 15 the government of Quebec requested assistance from the Canadian Forces to supplement local police, and the following day, at 4:00 a.m., the federal government invoked the War Measures Act.

Padre Eldon MacCara, who was base chaplain at the Combat Training Centre in Gagetown, New Brunswick, said that the FLQ crisis was an unsettling experience for the whole community and "a time of some stress." There was no warning. Soldiers at Gagetown were sent home from work that morning to pack their kit. Instructions were that they would be going to an undetermined destination for an extended period of time. The men and their families were used to exercises of this sort but, normally, there was more warning. Some soldiers didn't even get time to pick up things from home. Some went straight from the field. Padre J.M. Cook's unit was called to leave and within a couple of hours he had departed from the Fredericton airport.

The most complete report on the role of the chaplain during the FLQ crisis was presented by Padre G.A. Milne. His unit, 3 Royal Canadian Horse Artillery, had just moved into CFB Shilo a month earlier. That morning, while Milne was in church, they had been given twelve hours to get on the road. One of the battery commanders lived across the road from the padre and gave him the news. The regiment really didn't have its own chaplain at that time, thanks to the vagaries of unification which had placed all chaplains under base command, so Milne phoned the commanding officer, Lieutenant Colonel Charlie Simonds, and asked him if he intended taking a padre to Montreal. His answer: "Of course, we're not going down there without a chaplain!" Milne conferred quickly with his base chaplain whose answer was: "Get on your horse and get going!" First, however, Milne undertook to find housekeepers for six members of the regiment whose wives were either away or in hospital and whose children could not be left alone. Milne managed to find five, and the remaining soldier, disappointed, was left behind with the rear party.

Just before midnight, Padre Milne was on a Yukon aircraft leaving Rivers for Montreal. The regiment arrived at Mobile Command (St. Hubert) early the next morning to discover a huge concentration of troops on the ground. It was the day of the discovery of Laporte's body. Hartley Johnston, the assistant command chaplain of Mobile Command, gave the chaplains a briefing. Shortly after that Milne was informed by the unit's adjutant that they were going to the base at Longue Pointe on the island of Montreal. The other units were staying in St. Hubert. That was the last Milne saw of the other chaplains except for David Davidson who was the resident chaplain of Longue Pointe and Hartley Johnston who checked in on him regularly. After a couple of weeks, the Princess Patricia's Canadian Light Infantry from Winnipeg arrived and A.D. Turnbull accompanied them.

Padres A.M. Flath and C.G. Curties from Petawawa had arrived at St. Hubert prior to Milne. Reporting on his experience, Colin Curties said that worship services were provided as required but that the individual contact with the soldiers was more important. The chaplains visited the men at stations and outposts, in quarters, and at their places of work. Eight-hour shifts of guard duty gave the men time to think of new and old difficulties. Sometimes the soldiers felt lonely. Often they were bored. At times they were harassed. On occasion they were scared. The chaplains comforted the hurting and reassured the soldiers of their role and worth and of the interest of their superiors in their individual problems and legitimate complaints. Rumours were dispelled as the chaplains were able to keep themselves and the soldiers informed. In co-operation with the adjutant and the deputy commanding officer, Curties was able to supply the recreational needs of the soldiers: movies, dart boards, playing cards, reading material, and cribbage boards. He also kept an eye on the living and working conditions of the soldiers—their food, comforts, pay, and rum rations. When the crisis erupted the men had departed in a hurry and a few had left problems at home. The chaplains were able to liaise with the families and help to sort out many of the difficulties.

On Greg Milne's third day in Montreal the word came that the situation was very serious. All jeeps on the streets of Montreal were to have their canvas tops up and sides in place so that no one could lob a grenade into them. Of greater consequence to the padre was the order that no one would be permitted to leave the garrison unless they were armed. Everyone was to report to stores and pick up their five rounds of ammunition and their respirators. Milne's first response was that this did not apply to him because Canadian chaplains did not bear arms. The regimental sergeant major informed him that the order was clear: everyone leaving the compound would be armed and there were no exceptions.

The next morning Milne had to line up to get a respirator. When his turn came, he took the respirator, and then was asked which weapon he would be using. He answered: "none." The storesman simply responded by putting on the desk a holstered 9-mm pistol with five rounds of ammunition and a loan card with the serial number for his signature. "Sign here!" said the corporal, and the padre signed. Milne put the ammunition in his pocket and immediately hid the pistol inside the respirator carrier. He didn't want anyone to see him actually carrying a pistol. He had been given some arms training during his basic indoctrination course and so he knew how to handle the weapon, but he did not think that a chaplain should be carrying it. He took the pistol back to his room and hid it in his barrack box.

That evening, Milne discussed his dilemma with senior officers in the regiment and asked about getting out to visit his troops who were spread out in about twenty locations in the greater Montreal area. They were guarding private homes, power towers, and power sub-stations, and there was a fairly large contingent at the CIL ammunition factory at Sorel. He found there would be no problem with transportation as he was to share a jeep and driver with the maintenance officer.[15] That was a good deal because the maintenance officer rarely required a vehicle. However, everyone seemed adamant that no one would be allowed out of the garrison unarmed.

The next day, before setting out on his visits, Milne took the pistol and loaded it, being careful that there were no rounds in the breech. Then, instead of putting it on his combat web belt, he put it on his trouser belt, with the bottom of the holster in his hip pocket. No one would be able to see it. It was, of course, completely illegal to carry such a concealed weapon, but it would serve his purpose. When he got to the gate, and the guards asked him to produce his weapons, he showed them his pistol, and once out of sight of the guards, immediately hid it again. Much later, Milne heard that Padre George Davidson had replaced the pistol with a Bible in the holster. He had no idea whether or not it actually happened, but knowing George it would not have surprised him. The scheme would not have worked at Longue Point, however, because the guards there insisted upon seeing the weapon in the hand. The more famous "holster-packin" padre of Operation Ginger was Ken Benner. He always wore a self-designed shoulder holster when in the field. It contained his Bible and paper and pencil.

When Milne's commanding officer eventually asked him how he was managing over the issue of weapons, the padre confessed and stated that he did not want the soldiers to know he was armed and that he had been doing this because there was no other way of carrying out his duties. The commanding officer decided that there was a better solution. By the next morning chaplains had permission to proceed on duty unarmed, providing that the driver and one other person in the vehicle were armed. There was no shortage of gunners and bombardiers who were more than willing to mount up with the padre and carry a sub-machine-gun to protect him and so Milne no longer had a problem. The pistol went back into Milne's barrack box and stayed there until the crisis had passed.

Morale was always a concern of the chaplains, and during this crisis, Milne made an interesting discovery. He noticed that morale was high in some of the units in the field while in others it was poor, although all had roughly the same duties and the same amenities. One group were positively grumpy, far beyond the normal "healthy bitching" state. They also seemed exhausted, and their lieutenant couldn't figure it out. Everyone had to do eight hours of duty a day seven days a week. Some units were using a four on, eight off shift, but this troop and a couple of others had gone to two hours on and four off. It didn't take long to figure out the problem. The men may have been uncomfortable with four hours of straight duty in rotten weather, but if they only stood a two-hour watch there was no way they could get a decent sleep in their four hours off, let alone travel, feed, and clean themselves. Over some opposition Milne persuaded the troop commanders to change their tack, and an improvement in morale was soon apparent.

The biggest issue of the FLQ crisis was the problem of the possibility of violence between Canadian citizens. No one felt very good about that prospect. The longer the soldiers stayed in Montreal, the more they experienced the wonderful hospitality of the Quebec people. Restaurateurs put up with poor French and were always gracious. Many people let soldiers stay in their garages rather than having to live under canvas in that very wet October. The general feeling was that Quebec was a nice place to be and these were wonderful people: therefore this trouble must have been caused by a few "hotheads."

VIETNAM

During a conference on the role of the chaplain, held during the summer of 1967, General Wilson-Smith compared his days as an infantry commander in Korea with the very different type of battle going on in Vietnam. As a result, Padre E.S. Light contacted the executive secretary of the General Commission of Chaplains and Armed Forces Personnel in the United Sates, the Reverend Ray Appelquist, to explore the idea of a Canadian chaplain or chaplains going to Vietnam to consult with the American chaplains in that theatre. Light felt that it would be a valuable experience for the Canadian chaplains to know at first hand what their role would be like in that kind of warfare. Applequist forwarded the idea to the American Army chief of chaplains, Frank Sampson. Sampson replied to Applequist that he would prefer to withhold comment until a request reached him through the proper diplomatic channels. It appears that no formal request was ever made.

By the end of 1972 negotiations to bring the war in Vietnam to an end were under way, and, with a great deal of persuasion from the Americans, Canada was making plans to send a contingent of 1000 soldiers to participate in the International Commission of Control and Supervision (ICCS) whose job was to oversee the accords which were reached. This was not a United Nations operation, and the government's concern about the commission's ability to function was clear from its decision to commit for only sixty days initially.

The commission was composed of soldiers, for the most part officers, from Canada, Hungary, Indonesia, and Poland. Padres Eric Porrior and D.R. Blair were named to go but when it was decided that only two hundred and sixty-four soldiers would be sent, that meant only one chaplain would go. The commander of the force, Duncan McAlpine, wanted a young major to go with him and, depending on one's point of view, Padre D.C. Estey's name was at the bottom or the top of the list. Dave Estey received the tasking message on a Thursday, and he was to report to Montreal for one week of indoctrination training on the following Monday.

Before he left Montreal, on January 27, 1973, Estey received advice from Padres R.C.G. Cunningham and W.W. Buxton, both of whom had previous experience in a war zone. The trip to Vietnam was not without incident. En route, the Canadian contingent received a bomb threat at Trenton and were delayed while the aircraft was searched, but nothing was found. The Trenton padres, H.T. Cox and D.D. Davidson, were a great support to Padre Estey at the time. The aircraft then made the twenty-five and-a-half hour flight from Canada to Saigon via Alaska and Toyko.

ICCS headquarters was at Tan Son Nhut Air Base in Saigon. One-half of the commission's forces remained there while the others were dispersed in teams throughout the country. Each team had one soldier from each country. Padre Estey and his Roman Catholic counterpart, Major Maurice Labrie, took turns visiting the sites with the alternate week spent in Saigon.

The countryside was under the control of the North Vietnamese forces and the biggest difficulty for the padres was to get to the sites. When they did get through to an observation post, a service would be held. Estey remembers that one of the most moving services for him was that which was held with Colonel Harky Smith, a long-time chapel supporter and Anglican lay reader, and a good friend.

Estey visited team sites at Danang, Hoi An, Tam Ky, and Chu Lai. At Hue, he ran into Colonel Bill MacLeod, a solid churchman and brother of Chaplain Hinson MacLeod. MacLeod took Estey to the devastated city of Quang Tri to give him a first-hand look at the utter devastation of war. In a letter to the chaplain general, Estey reported: "The city is in ruins, and for miles along the road to it, vehicles destroyed in battle are strewn everywhere. I now have some idea of what the devastation must have been like in previous wars."[16] Later, MacLeod took Estey on a trip across the Thach Han River into territory controlled by the Provisional Revolutionary Government (PRG, of which the Vietcong was a part) for a discussion between the ICCS and the PRG. The group took a boat to the middle of the river but then they had to slip over the side and wade ashore: "It was an occasion for lots of tea and North Vietnamese candies," Estey recorded.[17]

The training in Montreal, prior to departure, had included weapons training as everyone had to qualify on a weapon in order to go with the contingent. In Vietnam there were weapons allocated for the chaplains, but they left them in the contingent stores. Estey remembered that when Padre Bill Buxton had found himself in a scrape in the Congo, it was observed that he didn't have a weapon. "If I had," reported Buxton, "they would have brought us all back in body bags!"

In the Middle East Eric Porrior had not been allowed to go out in a jeep unless there was a weapon on board to protect the jeep. At night the vehicles would form a circle and the padres had to take their turn guarding the vehicles. Porrior felt that to carry a weapon was to lose something essential of the image of being a chaplain and was just asking for trouble. While Estey was in Vietnam, concerns were raised in the House of Commons about this rather "cavalier and unnecessarily valiant" attitude towards weapons because the war was still on. The matter was raised as a safety concern. Once again, the chaplains held firm to their non-combatant belief and to the Geneva Convention.

174

In Saigon an effort was made to hold regular services in an American chapel every Sunday. American chaplains ran the chapel until they finally lowered the flag for the last time and prepared to leave.

Originally the Canadians were committed to stay in Vietnam for sixty days, and that was planned to stretch into one year, but they were limited in what they could do because the fighting was not really over. They had enough experience from other peacekeeping operations to know that the circumstances for effective operations were not in place. After two hundred and ten days and one death, Canada's contingent came home. Canada was replaced by Iran, but then everything fell apart and the ICCS left Vietnam.

OLYMPICS

During the summer of 1976, considerable effort was undertaken to ensure the security of participants in the Montreal Olympic Games. No one wanted a repeat of the hostage-taking incident that had marred the Munich Olympics in 1972. That year the chaplains' annual retreat was cancelled because so many padres were employed at sites around Montreal and Kingston. Several naval vessels were also in the area with their chaplains aboard. The focus of operations was in Montreal where chaplains lived with the soldiers in local schools and visited them as they provided security services at the athletes' living and training sites, the airports, and the competition sites.

A typical operation was that of Task Force II which covered all aspects of the security of the airports and the western end of Montreal. Four to five thousand soldiers, mostly from the brigade group at Petawawa, were spread out at five accommodation sites throughout the area. The one Protestant chaplain assigned to this task force was located with 2nd Service Battalion at Honoré Mercier School in Verdun. When the chaplain was not racing back and forth between schools delivering compassionate messages and counselling soldiers, he was visiting the men on guard duty at the airports or training sites. He reported that there was nothing so exhilarating as driving a jeep across the runway at Mirabel airport while being shadowed by jumbo aircraft.

It was during the Olympics that electronic pagers made their first major appearance among the chaplains. The senior Olympic chaplain, Eric Porrior, remembers them well. On one occasion a chaplain on board a ship paged Porrior simply to see if the pager worked from inside a ship. Another time Porrior was taking a shower at the end of the day when his pager went off. He quickly jumped into the first thing he could find—a new pair of trousers–and rushed down the hall to his office. As he rounded the corner at top speed he realized, too late, that the cleaners had just soaped down the floor. Away went Porrior, new trousers and little more, skidding, sliding, then head over heels down the hallway. Recovering his now dampened composure he made it into the office and returned the call. A chaplain was just checking in at the end of the day to say that all was quiet and nothing much was happening!

Chapter 7

MORE THAN A PASTOR IN UNIFORM

❖

May your reward be in heaven and I hope you don't get it too SOON!
✝ *Padre R.C.H. Durnford*

BETWEEN THE MID-1960s and 1990 the adaptation of the Chaplain Service to military bureaucracy evolved at the same time as secular humanism seemed to be sweeping Christianity into the background of Western culture. As integration jelled, plans were implemented that would shape the administration of the Chaplain Service for many years to come. The director of chaplaincy administration (DCA), Colonel Ray Cunningham, established a solid team around him and policies that would bring the chaplains more into line with the current military way of thinking. "In the trenches," on land, at sea, and on air bases, the chaplains soldiered on, increasing their more secular counselling and military qualifications and sometimes wondering more about how they could get promoted than how they could improve their Christian education program. As the authority of God continued to be replaced in the popular mind by the authority of the individual and the power of government, the chaplains had to come to terms with issues such as the Access to Information Act, common-law marriage, and the peace movement. Reflecting the growing societal sensitivity to gender roles, the first woman chaplain was hired in 1981.

In the front lines of the new generation of chaplains, and the father of what some would come to call the "Pine Hill Mafia," was Padre R.G.C. Cunningham. The advantage of being the leader of the new wave is that innovation is welcome and you are free to establish the direction that the organization will follow for succeeding years. Many of the themes of the Cunningham years remained issues of greater or lesser importance for the next twenty years. Successive Protestant chaplains general each worked diligently on their own particular challenges, but these were often new variations of the Cunningham themes.

RAY CUNNINGHAM: GENERAL PRACTITIONER

Raymond George Chesley Cunningham was born in Springhill, Nova Scotia, and was a graduate of Mount Allison University and Pine Hill Divinity Hall. At Mount Allison Cunningham had been recognized as one of the university's best all-round athletes. Cunningham, who served in the Second World War as an army officer,[1] returned to the military as a chaplain to go to Korea. There he served with the Princess Patricia's Canadian Light Infantry and was with them when they were awarded the Presidential Citation.

Writing of his classmate in *Dialogue*[2] magazine at the time of his retirement in 1976, Colin Nickerson reported that Cunningham "adopted a common sense approach that education consisted not of knowing but of knowing how. His approach to theology was equally direct. He had no use for dense, theological dissertations, stuffiness or pretentiousness. His faith was uncomplicated, straightforward and clearly expressed." Cunningham was a talented leader and a man with a great ability to organize and to delegate. He also brought to the job "a military knowledge, unparalleled by any other chaplain, which has engendered the deep respect of senior commanders."

As early as the mid-1960s, when he was the area chaplain for western Canada, Cunningham realized that the successful chaplain of the future would be the one with experience in all three environments: land, air, and sea. Together with the base chaplain from Calgary, Eldon MacCara, Cunningham set out to find a promising young chaplain who might be trained as a prototype for the chaplain of the future. Just up the road in Penhold, they found the ideal candidate in D.C. Estey. David Estey, an RCAF chaplain, was a graduate of Mount Allison and Pine Hill. He was the son of Norman Estey, a well-known Maritime United Church clergyman who had been an RCAF wartime chaplain. When Cunningham and MacCara dropped in on Estey, he may have thought that they were just stopping by for coffee, but they soon convinced their prey that it would be a wise thing for him to broaden his experience and come and work with them in the Army. During the next posting season, and after some quick explanations to his RCAF seniors, Estey was sent to serve with the Army in Calgary.

Cunningham went on to be the first command chaplain of Mobile Command. On his arrival in Montreal to take up the duty he attempted to find out just what this job entailed. He was shocked, but not surprised, to find out that there was no job description and no guidelines. In 1968 Cunningham became DCA, and one of his first tasks was to establish job descriptions for the command chaplains. He then went on to write a proper job description for the DCA and to deal, as best he could, with some other major administrative concerns.

In the field and on the bases, the average chaplain knew very little about the way in which the headquarters of the branch worked. There were formal communications through the chain of command and there was the annual retreat but more was required. Cunningham decided that more could be provided in the form of a chaplains' newsletter which eventually evolved into a monthly publication, *Dialogue*.

As the DCA was in charge of postings, Cunningham developed specific policies in that area as well. It was decided that each command chaplain would bring his recommendations for postings in and out of his command to the DCA. After everyone had their say, Cunningham would integrate the suggestions with the branch philosophy on postings that he had developed earlier: namely, that postings be arranged so the young chaplain would gain experience in at least two of the three environments and do his share of "hardship" postings at sea, on the radar chain, and with an active army unit prior to promotion. Cunningham would then invite the command chaplains back into his office and show them the year's posting plot. Prior to 1971, promotion from the rank of captain to major was promised within twelve to fifteen years. If a padre was not promoted by then, he was deemed to have the right to raise the topic and receive some kind of explanation for his situation. Cunningham's intention was to arrange at least one promotion for every chaplain who was deemed worthy, although it was not always possible to do so because of other constraints.

By the summer of 1972 various postings had taken place as a result of the full unification of the forces which resulted in chaplains with a background in one branch of the service, such as the Navy, being in charge of a team of chaplains from another branch of the service, such as the Army. Because each individual branch had developed its own approach to the pastoral care of its airmen, soldiers, or sailors, there was bound to be a period of adjustment. When disagreements arose individual chaplains tended to fall back to the basic tenets of their denomination. Long-established policy permitted complaints of a denominational nature to be taken directly to the senior chaplain of that denomination, which meant that the Chaplain General's Office was immediately involved in the problem.

To counter this situation Cunningham dusted off a policy statement that had first appeared in 1962 and presented it to the January 1973 meeting of the Canadian Council of Churches Chaplaincy Committee.[3] With the committee's endorsement he could straighten out most of the denominational complaints. The accepted policy stated that base or unit chaplains were required to provide the denominational sacramental ministrations required by all persons under their care. The 1962 policy had pointed out that there should, however, be no coercion of chaplains, choirs, or other worshippers, collectively or individually, either for or against minor variations in liturgical practices. Full liberty should be allowed in these matters.

With respect to Holy Communion, this meant that the base chaplain was required to arrange, as necessary, for ministers of churches other than his own to conduct appropriate services. The acceptability of the communicant in his own church would be the sole condition of acceptability for Holy Communion within the Chaplain Service. Prior to the service the minister should announce: "This service of Holy Communion will be according to the usage of the (denomination). Communicant members of all denominations are invited to particpate."

When it came to baptism, the chaplain was required to conduct the service according to the order of his own denomination. Every effort would be made to use the services of a clergyman of the same tradition as the family, but in any event, the clergyman must use the rite of his own denomination. When a chaplain baptized an infant not of his own denomination, he was required to say: "(Name) has now been received as a member of the Church of God, which is the Body of Christ. Therefore receive (him/her) in the Lord as Christ also received us. It is the duty of all who have participated in this holy act to take care that this child be brought up in the nurture and admonition of the Lord to lead a Godly and Christian life. It is your solemn obligation to teach (him/her) the truths and duties of the Christian faith proclaimed this day in (his/her) name."

The 1962 policy had also spelled out the chaplain's responsibilities with respect to confirmation: "The chaplain is responsible for the seeking out and the training and preparing for confirmation of full Church membership of all under his pastoral care. In the case of those of his own Church, it is his duty to arrange for their instruction by Clergymen or other qualified instructors of their own Church."

Even in the case of a funeral, every effort was to be made to use a minister of the denomination of the deceased. If requested, the chaplain could perform the service but again was required to use the rite of his own denomination. For general services, chaplains were to use the order of service contained in the *Divine Service Book for the Armed Forces* and "none other." Ordinarily the prayers used were to be selected from those in this book. Nevertheless, chaplains were encouraged to use contemporary or experimental forms of worship occasionally as a means of enriching the devotional life of their people.

While doing their jobs, chaplains were reminded that their full-time service would be devoted to their chaplaincy. There was no objection to a chaplain giving assistance to other ministers and existing congregations, but the propriety of their participation in such activities outside the chaplaincy would be determined by their senior chaplains. In other areas, such as Christian education and stewardship, chaplains were directed to be responsible for the operation of Sunday Schools, with a chaplain-general-approved curriculum, leadership training for teachers, training in worship, and lay training. All chaplains were encouraged to remember that stewardship—the offering of one's self and one's possessions—was part of the Christian life and an integral part of worship and of their leadership.

First and foremost, the statement clarified that the chaplain had to understand his dual status as an officer and as a clergyman: "While we are first and last clergymen, we volunteer to exercise our ministry setting which imposes a particular organizational structure and a less easily defined but nevertheless identifiable, social climate. In effect, we can't slight the implications of either our ecclesiastical status or our military status, and be viable and credible as members of the military body. The same dual status sets the stage for team ministries and internal relationships one to another in the Chaplaincy." After outlining the qualities and attributes of officers as set out in *Leadership for the Professional Officer*, the statement continued: "The authoritative approach to leadership can, in the short term, effect an impressive standard of performance but, in the long term, will debilitate morale and enthusiasm. The free-rein approach keeps everybody happy but the goals of the work are slighted. The optimum state of affairs, which combines popular leadership and top performance, is most likely to result in the participative approach to leadership."

Turning to the chaplain's role as the upholder of moral and spiritual values, the statement spoke first of the chaplain as a "presence": "When we're in the field with the troops ... when we bring bad news which plunges those who receive it into darkest despair and sharpest pain ... when we stand beside the bed in intensive care and the thread of life etches its path unevenly across the scan screen ... what is our role? So often the answer is just to be there." Then, there is the chaplain's role as prophet: "There are times when it is mandatory for the Chaplain to be heard. He stands in the tradition of Isaiah, Amos, Hosea, John the Baptist and Jesus. 'Now here this!' There are three considerations in this regard: Having the facts, timing and confidentiality." A chaplain must be reminded to schedule monthly appointments with his commander.

For Cunningham, however the main duty of the chaplain was to get out among his people.

The work of many caring officers and agencies is characterized by the client "coming in" to them. The person who needs help either knows that they are a resource and comes in to them or ... someone ... refers him. Traditionally, the work of Chaplains has been our motivation but a preventative caring-type ministry has been a by-product which the Forces have come to value and to rely upon ... Chaplains, consciously or unconsciously, intentionally or unintentionally, bring us into the "come in" category when they are almost always found at the chapel; when they can not see the point of going out into the field on exercises; when they want to work almost exclusively as counsellors. Jesus told us to go out into all the world. As long as we obey the spirit of his command there will be military chaplains because, very literally, there is no one else who can and does go, as we are allowed to go and are expected to go.

Standing in during the summer of 1973, because of the sickness of General Cardy, and in anticipation of his own promotion to chaplain general on Cardy's retirement, Cunningham's attention turned to the activities of the Chaplaincy Committee of the Canadian Council of Churches. Cardy had encouraged the committee to bring their wives to the meetings of the committee in Ottawa. The members liked the idea, and the meetings had become occasions on which the "military brass" and federal politicians could be impressed with lots of alcohol and fine food—all paid for from the chapel offerings. For Cunningham, a solid United Churchman who was not a teetotaller but of whom it was said that "he knew every tea house in the south of England," this was an intolerable misuse of offering money and a hangover from previous, inefficient organizations. In the name of common sense and efficiency Cunningham tightened his grip on the committee and declared that "some members had to learn that the military was not made just to support them in their pursuits."[4]

In the fall of 1973 the branch was officially taken over by the "new regime" led by Ray Cunningham as chaplain general and his old friend, Colin Nickerson, as DCA. Cunningham brought his headquarters team together and told them that they were his board of directors. They would be consulted on all major decisions and on all postings.

Cunningham and Nickerson had sensed that there was dissatisfaction among the ranks of the ordinary chaplains and a lack of confidence in the leadership of the branch. They therefore set out to visit all the bases and all the chaplains. Within six months they had visited some twenty bases and had sat through many zone conferences. Assessing the outcome of these visits, Cunningham wrote: "Hopefully we are achieving stability and will be able to operate from a broad base of understanding and trust." "What I learned from these conferences and visits," he noted, "coupled with my observations of the way in which the business of the Chaplaincy is being transacted, makes it abundantly clear that there are still areas which require clarification regarding the proper attitude and reaction of chaplains."[5]

Cunningham believed that the chaplains needed to stop and re-think their role. If a chaplain was going to fulfil his mission—no matter what level he might be serving at—he must understand exactly what the mission of the formation was and how it functioned. Only then would he be able to understand what his job must be and how best he could do it. Should the chaplain be one member of a team of chaplains, he must know his particular areas of responsibility and the limits of his authority: which decisions were his to make and which belonged to his senior chaplain. If a chaplain was in any doubt about his duties, he should be able to request and receive from his senior chaplain a clear delineation of his areas of responsibility and decision-making authority. On occasion, it might even be necessary for a base chaplain to seek this same sort of information from his command chaplain. Once the limits were established, each chaplain would be expected to avail himself of his freedom of action and to assume full responsibility for each of his self-generated activities.

Cunningham considered that the proper use of the chain of command was essential to the successful functioning of the branch. If a chaplain must seek a decision at a higher level, his request must go, together with a fully substantiated recommendation and supportive data, to his immediately senior chaplain. In normal situations, if the chaplain had done his homework and put his case together well, approval would almost be automatic. If the recommendation had to be turned down, then the one who made that decision must provide a full explanation of the reason so that there be no misunderstanding. Use of the chain of command would also avoid matters which could be settled at a lower level being referred without full information to the chaplain general's desk.

Responsible action and decision-making meant that the individual chaplain would have to familiarize himself with all Canadian Forces administrative orders and instructions relating to chaplain activity and pay particular attention to information disseminated verbally at conferences. Needless to say Cunningham was jubilant when it was announced that all junior officers, including chaplains, would have to take officer professional development examinations. Cunningham's theory was that good decisions made at the lowest possible level would produce a more efficient and less bureaucratic organization.

One of Cunningham's biggest concerns was the way in which some chaplains were beginning to look upon themselves as specialists in some particular aspect of ministry instead of general practitioners. There had been a long history of chaplains developing specific military skills in support of their jobs: army chaplains who were parachutists and navy chaplains who obtained watch-keeping certificates. One RCN chaplain, Dave Peebles, had even qualified as a ship's diver. But all of these men had recognized that their first duty was to be a pastor. By the early 1970s, however, reflecting a growing trend in the civilian churches, many chaplains had developed skills in a variety of activities as a result of attending secular counselling training programs and new pre-enrolment theological qualifications. There were chaplains with special training in Christian education, addiction counselling, marriage and family counselling, staff procedures, techniques of instruction, and clinical pastoral education. Occasionally, there was evidence that a chaplain had become so intrigued by a particular aspect of his work that it had come to dominate his thinking to the detriment of his overall ministry.

While Cunningham believed that a chaplain's specialty should be effectively exploited, he did not think that it was acceptable to do this at the expense of his ministry as a whole. Cunningham told his chaplains not to undermine their ministry by using their entitlements, training, and postings to gratify their self-interest at the expense of the whole job and to the detriment of the chaplain's image. Cunningham recognized that it was sometimes difficult for a chaplain to maintain enthusiasm for all aspects of his work. Nevertheless, he always stressed that a chaplain must be a well-qualified "general practitioner" and not a "specialist."

Once a chaplain knew his general area of responsibility then it was just a matter of establishing priorities among the various tasks involved. Some—worship, funerals, counselling, emergency calls, responses to crisis—were commitments that had simply to be done because they were the core of the job. Other activities were to be prioritized. Cunningham warned his chaplains:

> Development of a good set of priorities is essential in the area of activities which can be carried out only at the expense of other activities. Then one must decide if the cost is too great. A good example of this is that of chaplains teaching religion in DND schools. While this activity is good in itself, can it be justified if it is done by trespassing on time that rightly belongs to the servicemen, or if it entices a chaplain away from time and effort required to build a viable chapel community life? I do not think so.
>
> In other areas the choice is more clear cut. No chaplain should complain of overwork or shout for assistance who can indulge in

time consuming activities connected with community offices such as mayor and counsellor or who is over-committed to non-chapel oriented community or recreational activities. If a chaplain is on a Base where he can handle all of these extra-curricular activities and still fulfil his primary function as a chaplain, this is quite acceptable. But if he is having problems with priorities, the non-chapel oriented activities must go first.[6]

As Cunningham neared the end of his tenure as chaplain general, two more specific issues drew his attention: bearing arms and the alarming increase in the disintegration of chaplains' marriages. As on other matters, he sought clarity for the chaplain's role.

Beginning in 1971 all new chaplains had been required to take the Direct Entry Officers basic training course in Chilliwack, with all other officers joining the Canadian Forces. This meant that the chaplains would have to bear arms throughout the course. If such soldierly training was necessary, some new chaplains wondered if they should not carry weapons on other occasions, such as on exercise or in battle. Others revolted at any idea of bearing arms, even on basic training, and wondered if the senior chaplains really knew what was going on in the fields of Chilliwack. Cunningham was quick and firm in his response. He pointed out that under the Geneva Convention chaplains were classified as non-combatants and were not allowed to carry arms. Even though they were ministering to people whose profession at times involved them in violence, chaplains did not and would not contribute to that violence. Becoming a chaplain involved the willingness to accept the risks of war without becoming a combatant. Cunningham advised all the chaplains that if they were not prepared to accept such a risk, then they had better re-think their vocation. No matter what the provocation, with the exception of basic training, chaplains would not carry arms.

Cunningham's words would stand firm on the bearing of arms, but he could not control the break up of chaplains' marriages. Although it could be seen as a reflection of the times, Cunningham was truly shaken by the number of chaplains who had separated from their wives or who, from his perspective, had allowed their marriages to disintegrate without too much resistance. A chaplain's ministry involved the strengthening and shoring up of family life as well as the salvaging of broken or fragile marriages, leading Cunningham to comment: "Since our ministry is not the do as I say not as I do approach, inevitably the continued service of a separated Chaplain is brought into question. A broken marriage can not fail to have an impact on his effectiveness and the total credibility of Chaplaincy." While continuing to point out that help was available at all levels, Cunningham stated that "it is necessary to decide if the Chaplaincy can continue to employ a chaplain in this category," meaning one who is separated or divorced.[7] However, the message was clear to all chaplains. If your marriage is in trouble, don't let any other chaplain know. A marriage problem will have an adverse effect on your career and a final break-up will probably lead to a request to resign from the military.

Throughout the last years of his career Cunningham had worked hard to increase the effectiveness of the Chaplain Service and to bring it more into line with modern military requirements and practice. During integration and unification he had watched the chaplains of the Army, Navy, and Air Force come together. He had observed that "some of the chaplains were a little childish ... and tried to hang onto things that didn't really matter."[8] He had observed how integration combined with the new promotion system to place chaplains with limited experience in a particular environment as senior over chaplains with extensive experience in that environment. The resulting tension broke out into embarrassing and totally unacceptable public arguments between chaplains. To counter such incidents and situations required personal attention from the chaplain general's office and often that meant from Cunningham himself. Cunningham fought for the production of a new hat badge and proclaimed:

> When we put up the new cap badge, let it mark the final cementing of the bonds of a great fellowship we entered into nine years ago. Our ministry is not to one group, either operational or support, but to all servicemen ... Our love affair with the old Navy, Army and Air Force is a personal treasure which will always be in our hearts. Now let us give our loyalty and devotion unreservedly to our present Chaplain Service that not only we be seen to be one but we will in fact be one in all aspects of our ministry and service.[9]

Ray Cunningham was a kindly but firm individual. He had become a chaplain because he wanted to look after people and that is what he looked for in a chaplain: "I looked for someone who tried to do the best he could, was safe and didn't let the Chaplaincy down."[10] "The ingredients I see for the effective chaplain are simple—a strong faith, a concern for people, a large portion of common sense and a capacity for hard work. This constitutes the kind of person that has made our Chaplaincy—not the faddist. Knowledge in many fields is admirable but should be kept in the proper perspective and used as a tool. The Chaplain is not a "specialist"—he is a "general practitioner."[11]

186

COLIN NICKERSON: HUMILITY AND DEDICATION

Cunningham was succeeded in 1976 by his lifelong friend, fellow bridge player, and classmate from Mount Allison, C.D. Nickerson. Colin Nickerson had been a member of the COTC at university and, later, an officer in the Princess Louise Fusiliers. Originally he had served as a signals officer but then became the mortar officer of that unit. During his active service in Italy, he was wounded three times and awarded the Military Cross for gallantry. His final wound was grievous and it cost him an arm. It is a mark of the man that he accepted his loss without complaint and never lost his sense of humour or his sense of dedication.

Nickerson was ordained by the time the Korean War broke out and volunteered to go into that battle as a chaplain. Because of his medical category he was at first turned down, but the Army soon recognized that he had a great deal to offer to the services and in 1951 he was accepted into the chaplaincy. During his years of service Nickerson, a humble man,[12] became one of the most respected chaplains of all time and numbered a wide variety of military personnel and civilians as his friends. Cunningham reported that Nickerson brought to the service "the courage of his convictions, an understanding of people and a compassion which is all too rare."[13]

As chaplain general, Nickerson carried on much of the work which he and Cunningham had begun. He encouraged the development of professionalism among the chaplains, sought to hold the line on common-law relationships among the servicemen, counselled the chaplains on the matter of confidentiality in the light of the Access to Information Act, and took a special interest in the relationship of the chaplaincy to the civilian churches.

On the latter issue, Nickerson believed that as the Church in the Canadian Forces, both congregations and chaplains had something to say to their parent churches in civilian society. He urged chaplains to make the church courts aware that the chaplaincy was and remained a real, active, and valid ministry: "Let us make the civilian churches aware that we are a caring people, and worshipping people, that stewardship has meaning for us, that the church is alive and well and part of the life of the forces. We have good news to tell: 'O thou that tellest good news to Zion'."[14]

On retirement, Nickerson reported: "I think as chaplains we have a God-given opportunity to demonstrate practical ecumenicity. Thrown together willy-nilly one denomination with another, we are able to learn from each other and gain insight of the riches each has to offer. Sensitivity, respect and consideration are the watch words as understanding frequently is of slow growth. Let us not flaunt our denomination, but remain true to it.

Let us remember our ministry to all and our call to bring people in—not shut them out."

The question of confidentiality of information came to the fore with the introduction of bill C-72 which would, if adopted, allow the release of much information heretofore unavailable to the general public. The chief Forces documents that would be affected were performance evaluation reports, promotion merit lists, and personal confidential files. Chaplains, of course, had always faced the difficulty of being asked to reveal information received in confidence. Would a chaplain be able to maintain a confidence if he was challenged in court under the proposed legislation? At first, the NDHQ chaplains adopted a "wait and see" attitude and decided that they would only respond to specific proposed changes when it was clear that they would become law.

It had always been the case that every once in a while a chaplain would be involved in a court action that "required" him to release "confidential" information. This placed the chaplain in the impossible situation of being damned if he did and in danger of contempt of court if he didn't. Regrettably, there was no legal recourse or protection for a chaplain in this circumstance. Fortunately, most judges and lawyers were sympathetic to the vulnerable position in which chaplains could be placed and exercised considerable discretion in questioning or cross-examination, accepting oblique replies or "the soft answer that turneth away wrath."

In writing to his chaplains, however, Nickerson cautioned that they should exercise extreme care in these matters and seek professional advice from their supervising chaplain(s) as well as military legal aid, should the problem arise. Despite every precaution Nickerson recognized that a chaplain might have no alternative but to "face the music" and be found guilty of contempt of court. If this should happen, Nickerson promised that he would do all within his power to support that chaplain and protect his military and professional career. He assured the chaplains that in taking this position, he had the support of the Canadian Council of Churches Committee on Chaplaincy.[15] All of this had to be laid out, but in the end only a few chaplains have been called to court as witnesses and no one has found it necessary to take a stand and risk being charged with contempt of court.

CHAPLAINS AND MILITARY PROTOCOL

Following up on Cunningham's grave concerns about the life styles of some of the younger chaplains, and based on their own personal observations and biases, the NDHQ team under Nickerson felt that it was appropriate and necessary to comment, for better or for worse, on certain aspects of military etiquette. Guidelines, reflecting a philosophy of military etiquette, were presented to the chaplains' indoctrination course at National Defence Headquarters (September 24-28, 1977) and then to the command chaplains conference in October 1977.

In introducing these guidelines, it was noted that officer training in the Forces always had courses designed to bring along the young officer so that he could take his place as confidently at the dining table and in the drawing room as on the parade square or out in the training area. Military etiquette began to lapse when the Forces began to focus on "what an officer does" to the exclusion of "what he is." Because character and leadership are inextricably meshed, any such regression had a far-reaching implication. It was Socrates who first said that manners make the man, and, ultimately, our manners reflect our character. In a very real way the senior chaplains believed that good etiquette guaranteed that the moral insights received and lessons learned down through the years would be preserved and observed.

The senior chaplains pointed out that it was inexcusable for an officer to be socially gauche when the word "officer" is equated with the word "gentleman." The chaplains were therefore directed to know "Emily Post." They must know what is correct. The times in which they were living and local conditions might obviate the need to use the knowledge, but they should have it anyway. Even if the ramifications of etiquette were sometimes trivial, it was rooted in great principles. Etiquette had a threefold value. It was practical because it offered time-and-thought saving decisions concerning technicalities such as the wording and forms of invitations. It had an aesthetic value, in that many of its rules and customs were designed to create courtliness and graciousness. Finally, it had great social value because etiquette inculcates, and, to an extent, ensures consideration for others.

Military etiquette was described in basic terms as ordinary good manners coupled with any quirks which might be peculiar to one or another military formation or unit. Military etiquette ensured that the appropriate respect and deference would be paid to superiors, women, and elders and, of equal importance, that officers would entertain a proper respect for subordinates. Military etiquette ensured graciousness, courtesy, and decorum. Knowledge of it inspired confidence. It guided officers in effecting introductions, going through receiving lines, extending invitations, answering invitations, writing "thank you" letters, making official calls, and recognizing and extending hospitality to visitors and strangers in the mess. It delineated the officer's duties as both guest and host.

The guidelines also directed that chaplains were to be immaculately turned out, whether in uniform or in mufti. One of their first duties as officers was to acquire a good tailor. They were counselled to purchase the items of conservative haberdashery appropriate for wear at mess functions, even if they preferred a more casual style of dress. They were reminded that good grooming went beyond military hair cuts to include all aspects of personal hygiene and that the importance of being well groomed could not be overstated. It was stressed that good grooming took on a special significance in the military community and that any omission, oversight, or neglect was bound to be tacitly noted within a community where so many had been schooled to inspect and assess others.

Punctuality was another military "must." As Nickerson put in a 1976 letter to his chaplains:

> I expect that because the success of military tactics so often depends on precision timing, an emphasis on punctuality carries over into military life generally. Being late is not a peccadillo but can be the unforgivable sin. Think of being late as almost an obscenity. It will never go unnoticed, and should be avoided both in our work-a-day world and in attending military functions. Of course, when you shift to home entertainment, it is almost equally important to avoid being ahead of time. If you arrive at the door ten minutes ahead of time for dinner at the CO's home, and find the CO vacuuming the living room and a child dusting, and you catch a fleeting glimpse of her ladyship disappearing up the stairs still in curlers, it gets the evening off to a doubtful start.[16]

The senior chaplains noted that enrolment in the Canadian Forces ushered the newly minted chaplain into a world with very different social norms and mores from those which prevailed in a parish setting and on a contemporary campus. The chaplain would simply have to accept that the military was a stratified society. Such an arrangement was believed to be necessary for operational effectiveness. Even though there was a process of democratization going on in the Forces in the mid-1970s—which had been variously assessed within the military leadership—the senior chaplains insisted that all chaplains would have to comply with the prevailing guidelines governing social intercourse within the military community and certainly would not be permitted to exploit their status as clergymen. The chaplains were told that:

> Pastoring in a stratified society has its challenges, but they are not insurmountable. You are an officer. This status lays certain

obligations and certain restraints on you. It gives you certain privileges and opportunities as well.

The Officers' Mess is your home. You have host responsibilities there. It should be as unthinkable to be aloof or inhospitable there as it would be in your own home. Neither the Sergeants' Mess nor the Corporals' Club is your home. They are someone else's homes. If you come, you are a guest. Whether you come to those messes by specific invitation or by a standing invitation, you are still a guest. Privileges achieved at one Base aren't portable to another. You will be aware that there are proliferating opportunities today to relate to all ranks through community activities and sports such as curling, bowling and golf which have social facilities associated with them.

Camaraderie and friendships don't require familiarity. The French have their "vous" and their "tu". For many clergy, and, indeed, in some circles of Christian community, I sense that there is a hang-up on first names. Personally, I make it a rule to never call an officer of a higher rank (other than a Chaplain) by his first name outside of such obviously special situations as dealing with grief and related crises. I have the same rule for the CO's wife.[17]

The senior chaplains knew that their emphasis on matters of etiquette would not commend itself to all chaplains. However, whatever a chaplain's personal style might be in one-to-one and private encounters, it was strongly felt that they should observe the traditional military conventions for showing respect both to subordinates and to superiors in public, meaning in the presence of others. As an aside on this point it was noted that while keeping his proper distance, the friendship of a chaplain might be well received by a commanding officer who may find himself somewhat isolated and lonely. The chaplain could be an intimate friend in a way that is precluded to other unit officers, but the chaplain should never be seen by others to take advantage of such a circumstance.

On the question of rank, it was felt that while no one should be ashamed of his rank, neither should anyone try to use his rank around the chapel. This would be not just misuse but abuse of rank. It was recognized that this could be a sensitive subject to all concerned, so tact and patience were indicated. (The device of replacing rank titles by "Mr." for chapel notice and announcement purposes was considered to be unnecessary.) Chaplains could set the tone by observing a certain standard of formality among themselves during divine service and at chapel meetings. They were always expected to address colleagues as "padre" in these contexts and to set the tone by addressing all others by their proper titles. The young chaplains were assured that many of the people around the chapel were sticklers for correctness. They were reminded that disaffected members of chapels didn't complain or explode but, like old soldiers, just faded away.

The senior chaplains realized that they were always in danger of creating a backlash by placing so much stress on these details but they seriously contended that military manners were at least as important as civic manners. The chaplain who slighted or neglected good manners would be undermining the effectiveness of something very vital to his ministry. Padre Nickerson's epistle on the subject led to this exhortation: "Have you experienced the problems of moving in a funeral cortege through a busy city centre against the tide of rude pedestrians and even crasser motorists? How one's heart swells with pride when one sees a young serviceman standing smartly at the salute as the bier passes. We do not need to look far to realize that good behaviour is everybody's business, and that good taste is a companion of good behaviour."[18]

Mess Dinners

The rules which govern mess dinners in general and the customs of some units in particular were discussed at a meeting of the command chaplains in 1977.[19] Feeling varied on the degree of decorum which was appropriate during the playing of the March Pasts. The chaplain general requested that all chaplains should stand during the playing of "Onward Christian Soldiers" and that other officers remain seated. When all rose either on their own initiative or at the chaplain's urging, it was thought that members of other faiths and, indeed, agnostics might be placed in an unfair position or that the observance of a proud moment might lose its meaning. It was considered to be customary and acceptable for the hymn to be sung by those present.

While it was recognized that only the commander of the formation or base could control the practice to be followed at his unit, to the extent that chaplains have influence in the matter, it was requested that the chaplain general's recommendation be implemented. The custom of chaplains and other attached officers standing for the marches of all the corps or classifications with which they have previously served was also discussed. It was noted that this routine varied from place to place. It was decided that those serving in the military as officers before becoming a chaplain should stand with the group to which they belonged.

There are traditional military graces which may be used and are sometimes requested at formal dinners. The chaplain general supported the right of the individual chaplain to choose the grace which he will offer.

By and large, this effort on the part of the old guard to advise the young chaplains on the importance of their dress and manners, a view which arose from their own experience, was met with suspicion and cynicism. The younger chaplains understood that the military was a conservative element in Canadian culture. But the times had changed.

STAN PARKHOUSE: SENSITIVITY AND INTEGRITY

Padre S.M. Parkhouse succeeded Nickerson as chaplain general, serving from 1978 to 1981. He was the first Royal Canadian Air Force chaplain general in the new era. Parkhouse, a minister of the United Church of Canada, came from Pembroke, Ontario, and was educated at Emmanuel Theological College in Toronto. The son of a minister, he had served during World War II as a navigator in the RCAF. Parkhouse successfully completed the course at the Canadian Forces Staff College in Toronto in 1968 and 1969 and had become director of pastoral activities in July 1973. He was a capable leader who could carry any weight of responsibility.

During his time as chaplain general, Parkhouse was pleased to report that he had accomplished three objectives. He had replaced the branch manual, he had re-established the Reserve Entry Scheme Officers (RESO) program that would aid in the recruiting of new chaplains, and he had prepared the *Divine Service Book* for reprinting.[20] Perhaps of greater significance, it was in Parkhouse's time that the first woman chaplain was hired. Under Parkhouse there was also continuing discussion on the role of the chaplain in the 1980s.

Conference On The Role Of The Chaplaincy 1980

During the seventies, civilian liberal theological seminaries went through an extraordinary period of change. In the effort to keep the Gospel alive and meaningful in the hearts and souls of Canadians, every tradition and value was subject to examination. The traditional curriculum with its Greek and Hebrew was set aside in the name of relevance. Older clergy and lay people felt that some of the most sacred traditions of the Church were being threatened. Little wonder, then, that the senior chaplains asked a command chaplain, Padre F.P. DeLong, who was noted for his pastoral ability, to introduce a discussion of pastoral ministry at their 1980 conference. DeLong's reflections and those of others at that conference,[21] while not subscribed to by every chaplain, did offer a general picture of the way in which chaplains were expected to work in the 1980s.

Reflecting on his own role as a pastor, DeLong remarked: As a padre, true to my vocation, I demonstrate a concern for people through the

193

following relevant and specific activities: visiting, counselling, providing special interest groups, responding quickly and showing stability in crisis situations, supporting life-quality groups, and meticulous observing of confidentiality." DeLong saw the chaplain as an ordained clergyman who, having been successful within his own denominational structure, then commits himself to go beyond parochial limitations. In this capacity the chaplain became not just the representative but almost the embodiment of the Church itself. For this reason it was necessary for every padre to have a clear understanding of the place of the Church in society.

"The Church," said DeLong, "is the body of Christ, and as such she owes her very existence to God and is accountable to God alone. Much of the padres' task is to build new relationships of God to people, people to God, people to people." DeLong was concerned that the chaplains were too intent on becoming counsellors or specialists of some kind and so were losing sight of their true vocation. The chaplain was not a physician, a professional psychological counsellor, or a lawyer; he was a theologian and a pastoral minister.

> The job of the chaplain was to clarify and to articulate the Word of God into the values and the devalues[sic] of human life; to assist people to use freedom with responsibility and accountability and to aid in the formation of conscience.
>
> To this end the chaplain must identify with the military community and get to know personally the people whom he serves. His goals and objectives being to portray God's love to mankind, to let people know they are accepted where they are and to help them move a little closer to achieving their Creator's purpose."

DeLong reported that in spite of civilian welfare agencies, regional social welfare officers, drug education officers, preventive work by medical people, addiction clinics, and all the rest, military people still reacted to personal stressful situations in the same way: "Soldier, you've got a problem, go see the padre." And the padres would respond. They would listen. They would comfort. If indicated, they would refer. They would take a load onto their own shoulders, and they would see an individual leave with a lighter step because he knew that someone cared. The padre offered the same help for the wives and children of military personnel. Frequently, the most effective ministry for the chaplain was to serve the spouse and children and sometimes even the parents of military members.

DeLong concluded his presentation with an appeal for Bible-centred counselling as opposed to personal counselling based on behaviouralist principles. In the Bible, the process of helping is everywhere associated with the restoration of broken relationships not with pretending to be a psychiatrist. Translated into practice for the chaplains, DeLong took this to mean that the appropriate response of the padre should not be to exhort or to instruct, but to say in effect: "I understand what you are talking about; I know what you are going through." And to continue in the same fashion, saying in effect: "You don't have to be afraid; I am your friend; I want to help; I will do what I can; I am here; I love you; I am for you."

The chapel ministry was the subject of another presentation at the 1980 conference.[22] Padre A.G. Reid observed that the "lostness" and "loneliness" of military parishioners testified to the fundamental human need for community and meaning in life. These notions of human need, of the Church, and of its mission were the framework for the ministry of chapel congregations to the Canadian Forces. Chaplains did minister to troops who were engaged in surveillance or peacekeeping operations and who maintained, through continuous training, a high level of operational preparedness. However, these activities did not present the daily threat to life of a wartime situation, and these soldiers in fact spent a good part of their careers with their families in permanent military communities. Personnel could plan to have a complete career and to raise their families in a military community. In peacetime, therefore, it was surely the Church's responsibility to minister to the whole military family, to involve them in the Christian community, and in every possible way to help prepare personnel and families for their eventual move to civilian denominational church life. The challenge for the chaplains was to bring these parishioners the living, vibrant, and life-giving society of a community in Christ—a community in which the gospel phrases such as "deliverance," "salvation," "freedom," "forgiveness," "life," "eternal life," and "life that is really worth living" would come to be the wellsprings of its daily life and the interpersonal relationships of its members. The chapel communities were the instrument that Christ would use to continue his work.

The chaplain was a professionally trained, ordained, and officially appointed resource for chapel congregations. His style of leadership should be a non-directive one. By his pastoral ministry, by his personal faith and life style, by the clarity of his own visions of what the local church should be and could be, by his knowledge of things administrative and otherwise, he would enable the chapel community to be what it should be. If he was lacking in any of these areas, he could prevent or frustrate the life and work of the Church in his military parish. Certainly, the chaplain who was content to keep busy with administrative matters, with ministry to persons and families in crisis situations, and with doing only what was obviously expected of him by the military community would never provide the kind of pastoral leadership which budding congregations required. The chaplain must have some vision of the role of the Church and the ministry in peacetime if he was not to succumb to the pressures within the military to domesticate him: "to turn him into an ecclesiastical mascot which is dragged out as required for special occasions." The chaplain would have to be sure of where he was going theologically or else he would drift into a situation wherein the military community, which usually did not envisage congregational ministry, would set the parameters for his ministry and cause his officer status to begin to take precedence over his real vocation.

In that members of chapel congregations were representatives of various civilian churches, a mosaic approach to ecumenical involvement was the only appropriate one and certainly the most productive one for chaplains and chapels alike. The denominational differences that had little importance in wartime combat situations or in peacetime with troops at sea or in United Nations stations overseas had an unavoidable significance in all other peacetime ministry situations. Every effort should thus be made to place chaplains of differing denominations on multi-chaplain bases. The Church on that base then had a better chance of fulfilling its ministry to a multi-denominational parish. Chaplains were counselled to be quick to offer the denominational services of another chaplain when their own tradition did not match that of parishioners. No chaplain should dare presume that he is the best one to minister to parishioners of denominations other than his own.

In the area of outreach and stewardship, it was suggested that chapel congregations should be concerned about people near and far. Only as the parishioners live to serve do they gain eternal life. The chaplain should encourage parishioners to identify human need both in the military community and in faraway places; to check out their resources of people, talents, time, opportunities, and money and other materials to determine congregational goals; and then to apply the resources to these goals in the most practical way.

It was suggested that Chapel congregations, which took the business of being the Church where they were seriously, would be looking first at the human need within their own parish—in single barracks and in PMQs. The need for healthy interpersonal relationships within and around families and for a sense of meaning and purpose in everyday life meant that congregations should look for practical ways to meet those needs. Chapel groups such as Sunday Schools, choirs, chapel committees, ladies' guilds, altar committees, servers' guilds, youth groups, and adult Bible study and prayer groups could provide people with a sense of community and purpose to an extent that no other groups could match.

Chapel groups were seen to have a threefold function. They were the chapel's way of organizing its people resources to fulfil a specific ministry goal; they allowed a practical outlet for lay ministry; and they provided a structure for Christian "community" and fellowship.

To people outside the church the activities of these groups might be perceived as no more than a busy round of teas and bazaars and other social events centred on an "irrelevant" religious belief. Such people with such opinions would never be attracted to the chapel as a place where they might find concern for their needs and acceptance as individuals unless they saw that the church was doing things that made sense to the average man. Chapel efforts to raise funds for Vietnamese boat people, to enrich family life, to promote personal growth and development, to collect furniture for a burned-out family, to run programs that help rehabilitate people with alcohol or other social problems, or to provide facilities and programs to meet the needs of the kin of the seriously ill were all activities to which the average person could relate and respond. And when, if ever, such a person was moved to check out the chapel, he must discover that he is treated in ways which respect his personal privacy and intelligence and value him just as he is. Bishop Robinson's notion of the church as the "Gracious Neighbour" depicts, graphically, the kind of public relations that is appropriate to the Church.

Christian education was another facet of chapel life. Sunday Schools were expected to have a curriculum of studies but the aim was not to teach the Christian way. The aim of the Sunday School was to make the children the object of adult love and concern and to bring them into and keep them in the Christian community where they can experience the Christian life and way and grow in communion with others and with Christ.

Other Christian education activities also attempted to draw people into the community. Most chaplains provided pre-baptism and pre-marriage instruction. On these occasions every effort should have been made to strengthen the ties of couples and children with the local Christian community. Confirmation classes should aim not only to impart factual information but to build and strengthen membership in the Christian community and to prepare military parishioners for taking their rightful place in a civilian church setting after retirement.

On a more practical level, a teachers' workshop held in Penhold in October 1979 made it clear that at least some Sunday School teachers were prepared to give military children a quality Sunday School course, provided they had the padre's support. Chaplain General Parkhouse indicated that he, the command chaplains, and the Chaplaincy Committee had thrown their support behind the Joint Educational Development curriculum. Plans were under way for workshops on the new curriculum and all chaplains were encouraged to become familiar with it.

At the Penhold conference Padre D.A. Hatfield[23] suggested that Christian education, Christian nurture, and guarding the faith was often the last thing on the chaplain's agenda, whereas it should have a higher priority. He realized that any discussion of teaching ministry made clergy feel uneasy and suggested that this was a result of the failure of theological colleges to provide proper training. Once in the pastorate, clergy never seemed to have the time to learn how to teach. He argued that teaching skills should be sought out and mastered, and he praised the charismatic renewal for raising the profile of Bible study and the work of the Holy Spirit in small groups. Hatfield went on to point out that no new method or teaching material was good enough to do the job all by itself. Current fads like transactional analysis were not the answer:

> Rather, the truths will be found—as they have been in former "revitalization" of the Faith—when we immerse ourselves in the study and practice of the Scriptures; when we allow for the effective functioning and interaction of the living fellowship of believers through worship, prayer, and sacraments; and when we hold ourselves in open expectancy to the guidance and the power of the Holy Spirit. If our teaching ministry is to be about God's will it has to begin with the Bible and then continue through every other facet of God's continuing revelation to mankind.

At the 1980 conference,[24] the chaplain was counselled to assume that each of his parishioners was a child of God as important to God as any other and a fellow pilgrim. Each parishioner had a vocation to contribute of his life and talents to the life and functioning of the local Christian community; each had a ministry to fulfil; and each had a need of Christian community to combat his loneliness and lostness. The chaplain must accept that each of his parishioners is intelligent and fully capable of making decisions. In consequence, a non-directive and participative style of leadership was the appropriate one. Any other approach showed disrespect for persons and frustrated the formation of the Christian community and the achievement of congregational goals.

Chapel committees were normally the executive committees of chapel congregations. The committees bore the responsibility for co-ordinating the Church's being and work in the military parish. Chaplains must allow the committees freedom to assume and fulfil their responsibilities. The good chaplain was not a director or supervisor of the committee, though he might be its chairman, but rather a resource for it,—an enabler and an adviser. The chaplain who wanted to provide positive leadership to a congregation must himself have some well-defined notions of what the Church is and what it should be and be doing at the local level. In fact, the chaplain must be a dreamer with visions of what the local church should be while retaining a realistic assessment of what it is at the moment. He should be more interested in discovering what is possible than in the reasons why things cannot be done. He will not permit the past or traditional ways of doing things to limit the scope of his visions for the Church. History can tell us how we got to be where we are now: it can inform the present, but it should never be allowed to dictate the future. In short, the pastoral leader will know where he is going and he will find practical ways to get there.

Of course, the chaplain's primary responsibility was to conduct worship. In so doing he must always remember his responsibility to minister to people of various denominational liturgical customs using traditional worship modes which range from the very informal to the very formal: the one with a tendency to focus on the "otherness" of God, the "numinous," and the other upon the congregation and God's immediate presence; the one upon the individual worshipper and the other upon the congregation's common action in worship. The previous decade's experiments with worship forms had not resulted in a form better designed to meet the needs of an ecumenical congregation than that of the *Divine Service Book*. It provided an acceptable form that could be inflected with each chaplain's own denominational traditions. Base chaplains were told to take care to provide for the sacramental traditions of all parishioners and never to allow their own denominational inclinations to interfere with that responsibility. Care would have to be taken to ensure both the regularity and the suitability of the hours of Holy Communion. Where officiating clergy are used for the sacraments, occasions were to be made for the clergy and the parishioners to get to know one another. Using a visiting pastor who celebrates an Anglican Eucharist at 8:00 a.m. on a Sunday morning but who has to leave the base at 8:30 a.m. is not a satisfactory way to fulfil this commitment.

Sermons should be well prepared and delivered. The sermon should begin where parishioners are and show sensitivity to their faith and life and spiritual longings. Private study, meditation, and prayers were prerequisites for good sermons. But all of this would be of no effect if the principle "The Medium is the Message" was ignored. It was pointed out that parishioners would interpret what the chaplain says in the pulpit in terms of what he is and of what he has been to his parishioners during the previous week. The person speaking, and his relationship with his parishioners and with God,

BGen J. Cardy, MC
Sixth chaplain general
October 1968 - November 1973

BGen R.G.C. Cunningham
Seventh chaplain general
November 1973 - July 1976

BGen C.D. Nickerson, MC
Eighth chaplain general
July 1976 - September 1978

BGen S.M. Parkhouse, OSJ
Ninth chaplain general
September 1978 - August 1981

Padre O.A. Hopkins welcomes Padre G.L. Kling, the first ordained woman to serve as a peacetime padre, 1981.
(Photo Features Ltd.)

First woman in the chaplain branch: chaplain assistant Wilna Thomas, 1944.
(UCC Archives)

Padres at Cold Lake during Operation Dismantle: G.D. Prowse, P.B. Mullin and D.C. Kettle.

Padres H.I. Hare and A.I. Wakeling at the alcohol clinic in Halifax.

BGen O.A. Hopkins, OMM, OSJ
Tenth chaplain general
August 1981 - September 1984

BGen C.E. MacCara, OSJ
Eleventh chaplain general
September 1984 - September 1987

BGen S.H. Clarke, OSJ
Twelfth chaplain general
September 1987 - September 1990

BGen D.C. Estey, OSJ
Thirteenth chaplain general
September 1990 - August 1995

203

are more important in terms of Christ's reconciling love than are the content of sermons and the manner of their delivery.

Overall, chaplains were to see their congregations as the local expression of the whole Christian community and the obvious instrument which Christ would use for his ministry of reconciliation to military parishioners. The congregation could minister to an individual and to the whole parish in ways and to a degree that an individual chaplain could not.

Military Christian Fellowship

One of the ways that the more evangelical military parishioners could minister was through the Military Christian Fellowship(MCF) which had emerged from the charismatic movement of the 1970s. The constitution of the MCF described the organization as "a body of believing military personnel whose commitment to Jesus Christ included both concern for and expression within the military society." The organization had its roots in the Officers' Christian Union which was formed in 1948 with the support of the British Officers' Christian Union and the American Officers' Christian Fellowship. The Canadian organization became the Military Christian Fellowship in 1975 and opened its membership to all ranks.

The MCF constitution stated[25] that its "primary concern" was to encourage fellow servicemen/women to walk faithfully with the Lord and to grow in Him. Members were encouraged to:

a. stimulate interest in fellowship and witness;
b. seek out others to engage in study and prayer together;
c. pray for those in their area of contact;
d. keep other members informed of regional and national MCF activities;
e. encourage occasional activities in addition to Bible Study and Prayer (eg. retreats, social and recreational activities, tours, etc.)
f. encourage others to bring interested persons into MCF fellowship; and
g. Share regional/base/station successes/problems with other MCF gatherings for mutual prayer.

In 1977 representatives were encouraged to keep in contact with chaplains and commanding officers, seeking to ascertain the chaplain's views regarding all plans and operations.

By 1983 the objectives of the MCF of Canada[26] had evolved to be:

a. to build up the individual member to spiritual maturity in his walk with God, his family and his associates; and

    b. to be an instrument through which the individual member is
      helped to lead men and women in the military society to:
      (1)commit their lives to Jesus Christ;
      (2)grow in spiritual maturity in Him; and
      (3)use their individual and spiritual gifts towards these same ends
      in the lives of others; and
    c. to offer support to the chaplain and the chapel program.

Prayer for the chaplain and the chapel program, co-operation with the chaplain and the chapel committee, and participation in the chapel program were seen to be essential elements of the MCF.

As the organization grew, an MCF national office was established to co-ordinate activities and to produce a monthly newsletter and prayer reminder. It supplied a link between members on postings and held periodic conferences and seminars. The national office loaned books and tapes and was a resource for bumper stickers, lapel pins, evangelism aids, and material for Bible study and other small group study.

The MCF is totally separate from the Chaplain Branch of the Canadian Forces, although some chaplains have been members of the MCF and many MCF members attend chapels. Membership is open to all present and past Regular and Reserve members of the military, to civilians working for the Department of National Defence and to the spouses of all members. In 1983, the MCF mailing list included 1000 people spread throughout the forces and in various other endeavours, but only about 100 to 150 were actively involved in MCF activities.[27]

All members of the MCF had to subscribe to the belief of the MCF: "I accept the Holy Scriptures as the Word of God, and I hold the Apostles' Creed as the simple and universally accepted statement of evangelical faith." The organization has been assisted at times by other Christian ministries such as Campus Crusade for Christ, the Navigators, and the American and British sister fellowships. The MCF has given assistance in return to such organizations as World Vision, New Tribes Mission, and the Association for Christian Conferences, Teaching and Service.

While the chaplains had the official responsibility for the spiritual care of members on bases, it is possible that these small groups were able to reach persons who had not responded to the chaplain's ministry. The chaplains were directed to co-operate with MCF members so long as they respected the Chaplain Branch's view that proselytizing in the multi-denominational atmosphere was unwelcome and divisive. MCF groups were invited to take an active part in chapel worship and organizations. Should they refuse, then the chaplains were not encouraged to support them because the Chaplain Branch was not interested in any type of "exclusive" Christianity which might be divisive.

In some cases, such as at Work Point Barracks in Victoria and at the Uplands Chapel in Ottawa, the support of MCF members proved to be a great benefit to congregational life. At Work Point, services opened with gospel choruses and MCFr Bob Burns was at times chapel committee chairman or leader of the Sunday School. In Ottawa, the prayer editor of the MCF magazine, Rod Cook, was the chapel treasurer and the leader of many inspirational songs.

WOMEN CHAPLAINS

While senior chaplains talked about reform within the limitations of tradition and the Military Christian Fellowship could pray and praise, the new recognition of the role of women in the chapels and in the chaplaincy led to a more radical change: in 1981 the first woman chaplain in the Canadian Forces was appointed by Chaplain General Parkhouse. Georgina Kling was a native of Ottawa. Growing up in a military family, she attended DND schools in five of Canada's provinces. She obtained her Bachelor of Arts degree from the University of Winnipeg and her Master of Divinity from the Vancouver School of Theology. Following ordination she served for three years as minister of the Sicamous-Malakwa pastoral charge of the United Church of Canada.

Women had been interested in entering the Chaplain Service for some time. In response to an article in the *Ottawa Journal* in 1975,[28] some correspondence had been received by the chaplain general about women chaplains. At that time, Padre Cunningham did not see the need for a woman chaplain and believed that someone was just trying on the chaplaincy for size, but it was recognized that before long there would indeed be a female chaplain. During the next few years a couple of women were called to serve in a part-time or term capacity but there is little information on these experiments. In one case, Padre H.T. Cox appealed to the United Church of Canada for a qualified student with camp experience to work at the cadet camp at CFB Gagetown. The church supplied not a first-year theology student but a first-year university student whose call to the ministry, according to Padre Bill MacLennan, still required some clarification. The student served her term but did not advance the cause for female padres.

Padre Kling was not, in fact, the first woman to serve in the Chaplain Service. As early as 1942, women's organizations had expressed an interest in the appointment of women to work amongst CWAC personnel in Canada. Similar work had been done by the non-uniformed members of the

Christian Work for Women group in the British Auxiliary Territorial Service since the beginning of the war. Unfortunately the value of this service was not immediately recognized, and it was not until the summer of 1944, following earnest representations to the adjutant general, that a decision was made to appoint two CWAC ancillary officers as assistants to Protestant chaplains, on an experimental basis.

The request went to the churches through the Inter-Church Chaplaincy Committee and the names of two women were put forward. Wilna Thomas was twenty-eight years old and an honours graduate in mathematics and economics from the University of Saskatchewan. She had then trained as a deaconess at the United Church Training School in Toronto, had served for two years at All Peoples Church in Hamilton, and had travelled from coast to coast organizing the younger groups of the Women's Missionary Society. In the latter role, she was a popular preacher across the country. Madeline Hawkins was ten years older and also trained as a deaconess. She had seven years' experience working with troubled young women and an additional two years' experience as a member of the Royal Canadian Air Force Women's Division. Her brother, a navigator with a Pathfinder squadron, had been lost overseas.

The two women took eight weeks of basic officer training at Ste. Anne de Bellevue, and then had a few days' special instruction in Brockville and at Ottawa. Second Lieutenant Hawkins commenced her duties at the CWAC barracks, No. 3 CWAC Kitchener, in December 1944, and Thomas was posted to work in the Ottawa area under Major B.D. Armstrong.

At the very beginning it was clearly established that the women would not be replacements for padres and that they would not be permitted to administer the sacraments or conduct public worship. In a letter on the subject,[29] the principal chaplain noted: "The duties of the women assistants, CCS, are primarily to seek the spiritual and moral welfare of the women of the formation to which they are posted. The methods adopted will vary according to existing conditions and must at all times conform to the requirements of the military authorities." Weekly reports would be required. In the end, the principal chaplain declared: "it is the life that is led, as well as the creed professed, that will count." These women conducted brief devotions, Bible study, church membership classes, and padre's hours. They offered Christian counselling to the women and advised commanding officers of the women's personal problems. They maintained a high standard of ethics and behaviour and fostered a strong esprit *de* corps and high morale among the CWACs. They ministered to the sick and suffering, visited the jails, and sought the support of local churches to help foster morale.

The reports on the work of these two young women were most satisfactory, and early in 1945 authority was sought to extend this service. Reflecting the increase in the number of females serving, three additional pastoral assistants were appointed in May 1945. This would mean that there was one chaplain's assistant per 1000 CWACs. It was estimated a total of nine assistants could actually be justified, but only five were appointed. At the end of the war, they were serving, respectively, in Military Districts 1, 2, and 3, at Pacific Command, and in Ottawa.

Eldon MacCara, who was DCA at the time of the Kling appointment, thought that women chaplains were an inevitable development and would hire others during his term as chaplain general. As MacCara reported: "We simply proceeded to advertise and an endless number of enquiries came in to the office."[30]

An early challenge for the women chaplains was the definition of their role. Some people were of the view that it would be all right for them to serve on training bases such as Camp Borden or Cornwallis—and perhaps on an air base. To such remarks, MacCara would be quick to respond that these women were chaplains like all other chaplains and would serve when and where required: "If women are going to be in combat then presumably women chaplains will be in combat." The branch has been very fortunate in the women who have been attracted to it. Chaplain Leslie Potts (later Dawson), for example, has carried out her duties with the Navy in Halifax and with the Army in Petawawa, including a short tour in Cambodia. In the fifteen years since Kling became a chaplain, six women have served as Regular Force chaplains and five in the Reserves.

On retirement, General Stan Parkhouse was praised for his patient, competent style, and it was observed that he had lent a stability to the whole chaplain organization. He was also remembered for his hospitality, but most of all he was remembered for his integrity: "It has been the quality of your integrity that has made our association a particularly amiable and joyous one, and we are all most grateful for the complete trust and communication which you have been zealous to maintain with the Chaplaincy committee."[31]

ORMOND HOPKINS–A MAN OF PRAYER, AND A MAN OF GOD

Ormond Hopkins succeeded Parkhouse as chaplain general in 1981. An Anglican, Padre Hopkins was born in Perth, Ontario, and had served as assistant rector at St. Matthias Church, (Ottawa) from 1949 to 1953. He joined the Chaplain Branch of the Canadian Army in April 1953 and, after a brief stay in Wainwright, proceeded to Korea. Of his time in Korea, it is said that Padre Hopkins "was never one of the boys in the popular sense, but was always with them." He was a highly respected young chaplain. Hopkins went on to serve at several bases, including Lahr from 1972 to 1976. He was made Anglican archdeacon to the Forces in 1973 and he served as Director of Chaplaincy Administration before eventually becoming chaplain general.

During his term, Padre Hopkins dealt with many of the same issues that had faced his predecessors. He developed a special interest in the peace movement, and he excelled in his understanding of the military ethos. Hopkins fully identified with the military and was aware of the moral and ethical ambiguities inherent in the role of the armed forces in the event of war.

When he was DCA, Hopkins had found a certain amount of job dissatisfaction among the chaplains. He believed that every reasonable effort should be made to give chaplains the posting of their choice within the aim of the posting plot, which was to promote the highest possible standard of Christian nurture and pastoral care in the Forces. Still, there were limitations on the number of moves that the branch could make in any one posting season and on the amount of money allowed for the moves. Chaplains reaching compulsory retirement age or the end of a fixed tour and those who were promoted would have to be moved "off the top", as would any who resigned or became casualties. Then there were padres with medical or compassionate problems to be considered as well as those who had to be moved because of professional limitations or inadequacies. The age of a chaplain's children and the availability of suitable schools were also factors. To facilitate a smoother working organization, the DCA was given charge over policy matters and the chaplains' career manager, a dentist, was tasked with the administrative details and budgets for postings, course loadings, and service courses.

While Hopkins was DCA the command chaplains were addressed by Major General Vance, chief of personnel careers and senior appointments. Vance told them that people were the military's most important resource but that manning shortfalls were a severe problem. Attrition was too high, and the pool of young people of the right age (17 to 24) was drying up. New restraints were being placed upon the military by changes in legislation and by changes in life style. He stressed that members of the military "belonged to a paternalistic hierarchy and as a result they tended toward ultra-conservatism." Vance reported "great cause for concern over the increasingly civilianized approach to military problems." He went on to explain: "The problem is not the large number of civilians involved in military business. Rather it is the imposition of civilian standards and values in managing the Forces and in assessing their needs and goals. Thus the basic fibre of Canadian military society is being eroded ... we face a crisis in the understanding of the military ethos ... there is a need to research the ethos and to write it down."[32]

The chaplains' experience reflected the general's. Many civilian clergy had reservations about a career in the military. They would admit to the validity of the ministry but would say that it was not for them. Various reasons were offered. Some were uncomfortable with the restraints and limitations they perceived to be inherent in the chaplaincy's ecumenical approach. Some were unwilling to face the rigorous physical demands of basic officer training. Some wives would not even consider short-term separations. The financial incentive of the early 1970s when a new chaplain would receive three times the pay of his civilian equivalent had disappeared by 1980. There seemed to be little appetite for adventure among the theological students and ordinands of the 1970s.

The inability of the branch to enrol new chaplains led to the call out of six reservists. This solution was in harmony with the increased stress on a greater role for the militia. These chaplains were contracted to serve for a specific period of time at a specific place and at a rank deemed appropriate by the chaplain general. While employed, all the benefits and the responsibilities of the Regular Force applied, except that there would be no postings. Either the chaplain or the military could terminate the employment on thirty days' notice. This proved to be a satisfactory short-term solution to the manning problem while waiting for new chaplains to join the Regular Force.

Having resolved their manning problem, the senior chaplains turned their thoughts to the evolving military ethos. A statement on ethos, issued by the chief of defence staff in July 1981, had made a convincing case for the necessity of a strong military community.[33] Hopkins and his chaplains enthusiastically supported that view but were concerned that the final version of any such statement should acknowledge the Canadian heritage which was rooted in the Hebrew/Christian religious tradition.[34] The chaplains realized that it was difficult for military officers to get beyond their corporate self-image to understand the spiritual essence of their calling. Yet the chaplains perceived the military chapels as "symbols of the moral and spiritual values inherent in our military heritage as well as nurturing an all-important dimension of our ethos."[35]

The chaplains proposed that the ethos statement should not treat war as inevitable but should take into consideration how the military had contributed to the security of Canada, how it had deterred war, and how it had supported the country's allies. The service person's will to serve and, if need be, to sacrifice his or her life in the line of duty must be seen to be fuelled not just by loyalty and devotion to unit but by the ideal of service before self, of discipline and honour holding up the leader as the living rule whose example will instruct and inspire those whom he or she leads. Considering the way in which the mores of the permissive society had infiltrated the military leadership, Padre Hopkins felt that if a statement on the military ethos was to be more than high-sounding rhetoric, then aspirations must be nurtured by the practice of religion and by a healthy life style as reflected in the Canadian Forces' socialization program and the quality of life program, then being developed by the Directorate of Preventative Medicine. He argued that the moral and spiritual dimensions of military leadership should be developed in the broadest sense and could be developed by chaplains if they were given the time and the opportunity.

When a paper on the Canadian military ethos by Lieutenant Colonel C.A. Cotton was published in December 1982,[36] it was heralded by Hopkins as "a monumental contribution to the ongoing undertaking of formulating a statement of the Canadian Military ethos."[37] Cotton pointed out the historical truth that the spiritual dimensions of military systems were more important than the physical ones, and he quoted James Fallows, who had concluded a major review of the American defence system in this way:

> The most important task in Defence is the one most likely to be overlooked, since it lies in the realm of values and character rather than in quantities that can be represented on charts. Before anything else, we must recognize that a functioning military requires bonds of trust, sacrifice, and respect within its ranks, and similar bonds of support and respect between an army and the nation it represents.

Cotton argued that the need for a short ethical code setting out how members of the military ought to behave and stating their basic beliefs was more important than any institutional model of the ethos. A statement on ethos should be clearly understood at all levels, from general to recruit, and should be easy to put into practice. Cotton proposed a brief statement of the ethos centering it on pride, concern, and commitment.

As he approached retirement, Padre Hopkins observed that he was leaving the branch with a group of young command chaplains. They would be able to build strong and productive working relationships which would give the branch a much needed stability for the ensuing years. He believed that chaplains general should encourage the greatest degree of collegiality

211

possible within the limitations of the military system because this was the best approach to doing the chaplain's job at all levels of chaplain work. He encouraged the chaplains to make the best use of all knowledge, advice, and recommendations. Above all, he stressed the need to respect the normal channels of communications.

After his retirement, it was said of Padre Hopkins that "his influence for good as a Chaplain was rooted in the conscious fulfilment, in that role, of his priesthood as a minister of Christ and a steward of the mysteries of God."[38] Hopkins was recognized as a man of prayer and a man of God.

ELDON MACCARA–CONCERN FOR THE CHURCH AND FOR THE INDIVIDUAL

When Padre C.E. MacCara took over from General Hopkins in 1984, one of his major challenges was dealing with the peace movement especially within his own denomination, the United Church of Canada. Eldon MacCara was born in Pictou County, Nova Scotia, and was a graduate of Dalhousie University and Pine Hill Divinity Hall. He had served as command chaplain of Training Command in Winnipeg in 1973, as director of pastoral activities in 1976, and, following a time as Air Command chaplain in Winnipeg, as DCA from 1981 until he became chaplain general.

The peace movement and anti-military sentiment was not a new strand in the traditions of the United Church. There was a large Methodist peace movement before the First World War which seemed to vaporize as the first shots were fired; certainly it was not in evidence during the war when Methodist churches were used as recruiting centres. Between the wars, a good many United Church clergy became pacifists, but, once again, the strength of this view disappeared during World War II. From 1946 to 1959, the United Church took a conservative approach to Cold War politics but as the years went by the peace movement revived and grew.

In the late 1950s, a small but vocal secular group based in Montreal had protested the presence of nuclear weapons on Canadian soil, but by the mid-1960s only two members of that group's successor, the Student Union for Peace Action, could be found demonstrating over the Gulf of Tonkin incident in front of the American consulate in Toronto. When these two protesters approached the head office of the United Church of Canada for support they ran headlong into the ecclesiastical bureaucracy and were politely asked to leave the building. That was also a summer of marches in Chicago and in the southern United States, and in Canada the social problems of blacks in Nova Scotia and Native poverty on the prairies and in the north became more prominent. In consequence, the national peace movement began to evolve into a more general, locally directed, social action movement. By the end of the summer of 1965 little more than one hundred assorted Quakers and non-violent peacemakers could be rallied to demonstrate at the La Macaza Bomarc missile base north of Montreal. By the following summer such protests had become popular happenings within the youth sub-culture, and many of the dedicated members of the peace movement began to look for other ways of making their point.

While the two Student Union protesters had received a cool reception at church headquarters, the United Church still had some outspoken critics of the Vietnam War and the military among its members. In an exchange of letters with Chaplain W.L. Howie in 1968, the Reverend C.P. Beaton asked: "How do you feel about being a Christian minister and part of the 'war machine?' " Padre Howie replied:

> I don't have any difficulty with the ethical questions in regard to the "war machine" any more than a rural minister would worry about the growing of rye and barley and the likelihood of their being used for booze. I minister to people who have the burdens of mankind—my people sometimes might have the burden of the necessity of "war guilt" but they are people with problems and that is why I am here. I minister to people, not to a policy or a machine. Military people need a ministry as does anyone else. In effect we are trained specialists dealing with a special group. Most chaplains are really pacifists at heart—I know I am—and I know of no war-mongering servicemen.[39]

During the 1970s and the early 1980s, the peace movement became more active, and a few of the youthful protesters of the late sixties had become the young ministers of the 1970s. In a speech at the United Nations in May 1978, Prime Minister Trudeau predicted the suffocation of the nuclear arms race, but it was not long before that hope vanished. The Doomsday clock moved closer to midnight and the fear of nuclear catastrophe, whether accidental or planned, was always present.

In 1979 the Soviet intervention in Afghanistan and troubles in Poland precipitated yet another arms build-up. To counter the perceived Soviet threat, the United States gave a higher priority to the development of its air-launched cruise missile. An agreement permitted the Americans to use Canadian airspace during test flights of the missile, and these tests led to considerable outcry both from the New Democratic party in parliament and from peace groups outside parliament. When a formidable protest took place at CFB Cold Lake during the winter of 1982-3, it was the base chaplain, David Prowse, who liaised between the protesters and the military and was able to defuse a difficult situation.

The peace movement of the 1980s consisted of many organizations which, although independent, were prepared to come together for the common cause. There were organizations specifically targeted to disarmament such as Dismantle and the Christian Movement for Peace as well as women's organizations, particularly those with feminist goals, and youth groups for whom this was one interest among many. At this particular time the actual leadership of the Protestant churches seemed to be strongly disposed towards pacifism, even though the average person in the pews seemed to be more conservative or at least more cautious and deliberate than the leaders. One of the larger groups was Project Ploughshares. Funded by several Protestant churches, Ploughshares tended to speak out on peace issues for the largest Protestant denominations. Two members of Project Ploughshares prepared a brief pressing for disarmament which was presented to the prime minister on behalf of the leaders of the major religious denominations, including the Roman Catholics, in December 1982. The well-intentioned efforts of Project Ploughshares were always a kind of heartbreak for the chaplains because of the tendency to paint everyone in uniform as a member of some war-mongering horde. The chaplains were only too aware that no one in the Canadian military wanted a nuclear or even a non-nuclear war.

Perhaps MacCara's greatest pacifist challenge came in 1982 when there was a move at the Manitoba Conference of the United Church of Canada to have all the United Church chaplains removed from the military. A memorial by the conference was not approved but it did spark considerable concern within the chaplaincy. At the annual meeting of the United Church chaplains, held during the next chaplains retreat,[40] the chairman of the Canadian Council of Churches Chaplaincy Committee, the Reverend Stan Parkhouse, outlined some of the main points prepared by Eldon MacCara for presentation to the General Council of the United Church.

a. Chaplains are ordained clergy persons who fulfil their ministry within the Canadian Armed Forces.

b. Chaplains do not exercise command, are non-combatant and serve under the provisions of the Geneva Convention.

c. No specific theology of Chaplaincy (military) exists and none is required.

d. Chaplains are, in brief, clergy who are sent by the United Church to become members of the Canadian Forces to join with Chaplains of other denominations in providing a full range of

pastoral services to the military community including dependents, and in some instances civilians who work for D.N.D.
e. The Chaplaincy does not serve the cause, but the people. Chaplains are in the military for reasons of faith and calling.

In a move to broaden the civilian church's knowledge of the chaplaincy and its work, MacCara encouraged greater participation by the United Church chaplains in the courts of their church and chaplains began to appear on committees throughout the system of church government. In 1987 Colonel David Estey became chairman of Ottawa presbytery. One result of this increased participation by chaplains in the courts of the church appeared when the Statement on Sexuality was being hotly discussed in the United Church. Because of their counselling experience, arm's distance from the regular work of the church, flexibility, and ready access to means of communication, the chaplains were extremely good at giving pastoral care and support to individuals on both sides of the argument.

So long as he was chaplain general, Eldon MacCara continued to be deeply involved in the peace issue. On one occasion he even locked horns at Queen's University with the theologian Gregory Baum. The question was: "Is the Civilian Church against the Chaplaincy?" From the debate it appeared that the opposition was more against the government than the chaplaincy. As MacCara explained:

A great deal of the tension caused is due to the lack of full understanding of the place the Canadian Forces and the military generally holds in Canadian society. It's shaped a lot by the media. In other countries the military has a political lobby. That is not our way. In Canada the military is a function of the people, it is entirely governed by the people ... by Parliament. It does not carry out any action other than what it is directed to carry out by the Government. The term "militarism" is not a part of our society. A lot [of misunderstanding] is due to a lack of understanding of these relationships."[41]

On another occasion, in 1985, the chaplains were challenged by a professor from the Atlantic School of Theology. Martin Rumscheidt wondered if chaplains, under the dual authority of church and state, were free to express themselves in public on issues of faith, theology, and ethics. "To what extent," he asked, "can the Churches' authorized declarations on peace and disarmament, on alternatives to nuclear deterrence as Canada's declared policy, etc. have an impact on their work and, especially, their public statements?"[42] Clearly Rumscheidt, like the churches, was not very well acquainted with the chaplains and their work. At the annual meeting of United Church chaplains later that year, it was decided that an even greater effort would have to be made to explain their position and their ministry to the church.

In November 1984, building on MacCara's work, a paper on the issue of United Church ministers serving as chaplains in the Canadian Forces had been prepared by Padres J.F. Coutts, G.A. Milne, and D.H. MacLean and presented to the General Council of the United Church by Stan Parkhouse. When the Reverend Hallett E. Llewellyn brought greetings to the chaplains from the General Council in 1986, he referred to the paper and commended the chaplains for the way in which their ecumenism worked at a time when across the church a great many shared ministries were in trouble. Llewellyn recognized the importance of the chaplain's role, especially within the context of military peacekeeping duties. He nevertheless observed that the ministry of the chaplains seemed to be isolated from the civilian church and encouraged the chaplains to keep the channels of communication open with the civilian church.

In response to criticism from the pacifist elements of their church, United Church chaplains have always seen themselves as being part of the Canadian Forces, but in some ways able to stand outside of the military organization. Chaplains would not have their jobs if they did not support the existence of the Forces. Often, they have been called upon to explain the Church to the military and the military to the churches, because of the way in which each group has been caught up in misjudging the other. The chaplains felt that they had to be objective in these respects, carrying out the functions required by their military and political masters, while being careful to guard their own thinking and viewpoints as United Church ministers.

During MacCara's time as chaplain general the stress and strain on individual chaplains seemed to increase as it had for clergy in every church outside the military. As a response to the impact of these increasing levels of stress, Padre A.M. Flath was asked to assess clergy burnout. His paper[43] stated that it was generally agreed that any chaplain could allow the pressure of his job to become a cause of stress and that the support of fellow chaplains was essential. Chaplains were counselled to take all of their annual leave entitlements and a stress management workshop was held in Ottawa. In keeping with the move towards greater sensitivity, it was suggested that the program at the annual retreat should provide some refreshment and rest rather than being strictly dedicated to business.

Around the time of MacCara's retirement, Brian Brown wrote about him in an article in the *United Church Observer*:

The General is perhaps the most gentle and humble clergyman you might ever hope to meet, as is indicated by the low key manner in which he offers his considerable talents and experience to the Church ... [these] do nothing to lessen the General's high expectations [of chaplains]in terms of pastoral effectiveness and spiritual nurture of Christians and others under their care in situations of high stress. He is equally noted for his encouragement of and insistence upon a self-disciplined personal devotional life on the part of ministers under his authority. The retirement of Brigadier-General C.E. MacCara, CD, may be an appropriate occasion for fellow Christians to make a more charitable and unbiased examination of each other's efforts toward peace.[44]

STEWART CLARKE: DEDICATED PROFESSIONAL

In 1987 Padre S.H. Clarke succeeded General MacCara. Stewart Clarke was a native of Pembroke, Ontario, and a graduate of Bishop's University. After his ordination as a priest in the Anglican Church of Canada in 1959, he joined the Royal Canadian Army Chaplain Corps. At a time when only the best chaplains had an opportunity to serve in Germany, Clarke was fortunate to serve two tours: once with the 4th Canadian Infantry Brigade in the 1960s and then as senior brigade chaplain in Lahr from 1976 to 1980. After three years as command chaplain of Training Systems in Trenton and a year studying the French language, he moved to Ottawa to serve as director of pastoral activities and, subsequently, as DCA and then chaplain general.

When MacCara retired, he said: "I've never felt better about the Chaplain Branch than I do right now."[45] Clarke reiterated the same sentiment at successive command chaplains meetings. Everything in the Chaplain Branch seemed to be going reasonably well. The chaplains even acquired a tailor-made retirement plan, the Officer Career Development Plan (Specialist Officers). The only fly in the ointment, besides the ever increasing push to have a totally bilingual officer corps, came in the form of the defence white paper of 1987. The wind of change was starting to be felt at National Defence Headquarters.

The white paper assigned specific wartime taskings to the Reserve Forces as well as setting out a plan to improve Reserve training and operational effectiveness. By the year 2002, the Reserves were to be as well equipped as, and interchangeable with, the Regular Forces. Perhaps only the chaplains at headquarters really understood what this could eventually mean to the Chaplain Branch. Military planners were looking for ways to restructure for leaner times and, specifically, for ways to reduce the total manpower.

On the international scene, the ability of the major powers to control the many potential flashpoints for conflict was beginning to weaken. Not wanting to be caught without properly trained chaplains, it was decided in 1987 to hold a battlefield ministry course. This course, "The Chaplain in Combat Operations", covered a wide range of subjects that would be relevant for the chaplain on the modern battlefield. Padre F.W. Love reported that "battle shock was examined from both an historical and a modern point of view and the treatment of this condition from a psychological perspective."[46] Among those who provided first-hand information was Colonel Ed Mechinbier, a United States Air Force pilot who spent six years as a prisoner of war in North Vietnam, and the Reverend Angus Smith, the senior chaplain of the Royal Army in Scotland, who spoke of his duties during the Falklands conflict (May to August 1982). The chaplains who took the course naturally wondered if Canada would ever be drawn into a war zone on such short notice as Smith had been. It didn't take that long for them to find out.

Operation Vagabond

In 1988, Padre P.C. Morley had just moved to Petawawa and had taken the paratroop refresher course when he was ordered to Baghdad, Iraq, to serve with the 88th Signals Regiment in United Nations blue. Because of the number of soldiers, there would be no Roman Catholic padre: only one chaplain was required.

The operation was a masterpiece of rapid deployment. Morley had been given a warning order a few days in advance but then at 1:30 a.m. on April 12, 1989, he received the order to move out six hours later. The trip, a direct flight from Trenton to Baghdad, was made on a huge American C-5 Galaxy transport. Inside each aircraft were fourteen heavy, loaded, vehicles and seventy soldiers, with room to spare. Morley described the flight as a rather "awesome" experience.

The reality of entering a war zone set in as the aircraft neared Baghdad. Morley reported that a warrant officer shouted orders to the soldiers just before landing: "On landing you will be in full combats, wearing your issued bulletproof vest, carrying full NBCW kit with live atropine, in your right leg pocket will be an intravenous with saline solution for rectum insertion if you get shot and are losing bodily fluid. Every man will carry his personal weapon with two magazines of live ammunition."[47] The tense atmosphere as the aircraft touched down soon dissipated when the soldiers marched into the air-conditioned terminal and were treated to ice-cold Coke. The red carpet treatment continued through to the United Nations work area, which was in a modern building, and even to the furnished apartments in which the men would live until they moved to the front.

At the troop level, a certain degree of stress was reflected in requests for information, welfare, and spiritual needs. The men wanted more information on the local currency, language, religion, and news. They wanted to know about writing and phoning home. Because this was the first time that reservists had been a part of an initial Canadian deployment in a United Nations operation, attached reservists needed reassurance about their place in the unit. There were the usual personal counselling problems and requests for church services, Bibles, and St. Michael medallions.

While in Baghdad, Phil Morley kept in constant touch with the chaplains and support groups at the home bases of the men. His many adventures were set down in "The Padre's Mesopotamian Chronicles."[48] The complete operation lasted only six months, and Morley returned to Canada with the soldiers aboard Soviet Aeroflot jets via Moscow.

Namibia

The next group of chaplains to serve under the blue flag of the United Nations did so in Namibia in 1989-90. The purpose of the United Nations Transition Assistance Group (UNTAG) was to oversee the birth of the country of Namibia as it finally gained its independence from South Africa. The largest element in the Canadian contingent of two hundred and three personnel was the 89th Canadian Logistics Unit. The Canadian contingent set up at a former Mercedes showroom in Windhoek and had detachments in Keetmanshoop and southern Namibia. The group included thirty-one women and nineteen reservists. They returned to Canada in January 1990.

Padre W.R. MacLennan arrived by Boeing 707 at Windhoek, the capital of Namibia, on April 13, 1989. Bill MacLennan found Namibia a land of intense contrasts: tremendous wealth and prosperity against the backdrop of poverty and injustice; miles of beautiful sandy beach with the most beautiful birds and animals that he had ever seen as well as the most venomous snakes and scorpions, lions, and other predators. MacLennan described himself and his situation in a report to the chaplain's newsletter, *Dialogue*: "I am a Cape Bretoner in Namibia, a political 'hotbed' eagerly awaiting the birth of independence of this land. But to me the real excitement is in being a chaplain with our Canadian men and women on any of our active United Nations postings."[49]

Padre Stewart Clarke was an excellent chaplain and a capable commander. It was his blessing to serve as chaplain general with a good team of chaplains who knew their jobs and did them well. As 1990 approached, there was an air of optimism in the Chaplain Branch and life did not look that bad. Administratively, the carefully laid plans of the chaplaincy fathers in the early 1970s were coming to fruition with the promise of strength and stability. Padre David Estey, a talented, traditional leader with a flytrap mind for detail, brought extremely broad experience of all areas of chaplaincy work to the position of chaplain general. Estey knew that the 1990s would be challenging and that finances would be tight, but neither he nor anyone else had the slightest idea of what the future really held for the Chaplain Branch of the Canadian Forces.

ON THE FRONT LINES WITH THE CHAPLAINS

While senior chaplains administered and looked on, at times with real concern, the chaplains working in the field were sometimes too busy to be worried about what was happening at the national level in Ottawa. They were content to let the leaders lead without challenge or comment, providing that they led supportively and did nothing to interfere with the work in the parish or in the field. In the "front lines" in the eighties, chaplains were dealing with cases of sexual deviance, attempted suicide, welfare fraud, family breakdown, and downright skulduggery. Increasingly, they referred cases to those professional counsellors who could help, but it was usually the padre who was first on the scene when a crisis broke. And for certain problems it was the padres in the field who instigated the necessary long-term responses.

Halifax Lodge, Ottawa

The Halifax Lodge in Ottawa was one such initiative. In the early seventies, all seriously ill military personnel would be brought, if it was possible, to the National Defence Medical Centre in Ottawa. Padre D.H.T. Fuller saw the need for some type of safe and inexpensive accommodation for close relatives of the patients near the hospital. Base authorities at CFB Rockcliffe consented to providing a small house and the rest was up to the padre. With the help of his Ladies Guild, through Jean Fendick and Pat Couvrette, a loan was obtained to buy furniture and major appliances. A request was put out to the bases across Canada for small articles to make the house a home and the response was tremendous. In 1972, preparations were speeded up for its first occupants, a family from Lahr in which the husband was dying of cancer at the medical centre. From then on through the next fifteen years, the house was occupied almost constantly. It was maintained by the Protestant and Roman Catholic ladies groups at Rockcliffe and remained in use until the late 1980s when military doctors began to use more civilian hospitals for their more critical patients.

Halifax Alcohol Treatment Clinic

The finest example of the way in which padres cared for the men could be found in the alcohol treatment clinic in Halifax. Throughout the years chaplains had led the way in concern for those in the Forces who had serious drinking problems. However, it was not until 1967 that the first recognized treatment facility for members with alcohol problems was established by the base chaplain at Halifax. The chaplains were the moving spirits behind the project, especially Padres E.G. Leslie and T. Fenske. Counsellors worked on an on-call or as-needed basis, and there were many growing pains for the program in terms of personnel, type of program, and treatment process.

Responding to the need for something to be done about drinking problems, Ted Fenske had teamed up with a psychiatrist and Navy Chief Petty Officer Wildsmith from HMCS *Bonaventure* to give some hard-hitting lectures. They travelled from ship to ship and even made several trips to the training base at Cornwallis. The program was based on the principles of Alcoholics Anonymous.

In recognition of the chaplain's efforts, the base commander in Halifax found an offset position from the staff of the base personnel services officer and so made a senior non-commissioned officer available to work at the clinic on a full-time basis. Then, in 1974, in a move to put the program on a more formal footing, the base chaplain appointed one of his staff, Major A.I. (Alex) Wakeling, as director. Another non-commissioned officer, whose duty was restricted for medical reasons, was also made available to work at the clinic as a counsellor.

The first full-time program began in 1975. In that year twenty-nine patients were treated on a full-time basis in a twenty-day Monday-to-Friday program spread over four weeks. They then attended weekly follow-up counselling sessions for the next twelve months. The patients came from Canadian Forces bases coast to coast. Across the country interest in the problem was reinvigorated and a number of bases expanded their own counselling services, relying heavily on the experience that chaplains had gained from their pastoral work. The Chaplain Service contributed to these efforts by training more chaplains in group therapy and marriage counselling, and at the Donwood Clinic in Toronto. More courses were offered by the Canadian Forces drug education program and a serious revision of the Canadian Forces administrative order on alcohol abuse was undertaken. Increasingly, support came from the medical officers and some of them started to attend the Donwood training course. Plans were made to establish regional treatment centres.

In 1976 it was decided to offer a training course for chaplains, one at a time, at the clinic. The first chaplain arrived on January 10, 1977, and was fitted into a newly arrived treatment group. Since those participating in the program were normally in residence for a month, the chaplain's course lasted the same period of time to allow him to observe the procedure from admission through departure.

Chaplains took part in all activities as members of the staff. In the initial week they served as a co-therapist in the group therapy sessions and in time took over as a group leader. The chaplain was involved in patient assessments and one-on-one counselling with each patient, in marriage counselling, and with the married couples' group. Two hours each day was spent on studies relating to alcohol counselling, scientific papers on all aspects of the subject, and the various modalities of treatment, with specific reference to the Halifax philosophy of treatment. To focus the experience, a paper on some aspect of alcohol addiction was to be written for discussion with staff during the final week. Time was also spent visiting other staff persons who participated in the program such as the personnel selection officer and many people on the staff of the hospital. One of the course requirements was to spend two hours a day on the administration process that is required to bring a patient into the program, the building of a patient profile, the gathering of patient data and its uses, and the writing of suitable patient reports. Visits to local AA groups, physical exercise, daily meditation, and private prayer were also encouraged. It was hoped that the course would help chaplains to be more effective resource persons in support of the many preventive, educational, and treatment programs that were coming into existence.

In December 1978, Padres R.A. MacLean and G.E. Tonks established a family therapy session at the clinic in Halifax to encourage wives to become involved in the rehabilitation of their husbands. These sessions were designed to reawaken old and new interests and resolve non-productive family tensions and to produce glimpses of a potentially better future life as a family. MacLean had studied at Rutgers and the clinic was based on the ideas of Vernon Johnson, an Episcopalian minister.

By 1979, the average number of patients on full-time active treatment at any one time had grown from eight to twenty-four. The clinic processed two hundred and thirty-seven patients in 1979 and 270 in 1980; the follow-up patient list grew from zero in 1975 to one hundred and eighty in 1979. In response to the heavier work load, a third counsellor was scrounged from a ship, because he was unfit for sea duty, but the patients still lacked the quality of treatment they needed and deserved.

As the program developed and gained recognition, the counsellors were requested to do outside lectures, educational programs, and seminars. The clinic began to provide a training ground and facility in basic addictions counselling for chaplains and follow-up counsellors of other bases and commands. However, with this workload and the small staff, only the most glaring cases of abuse got any attention. Some personnel who needed attention were denied it because of the lack of facilities and staff. The problem was simple: not enough staff for the demand, not enough space to work in, and lack of training for the counsellors.

In 1980, the clinic became a formal entity in the Canadian Forces under the Directorate of Preventative Medicine. Padre Ted Fenske retired from the chaplaincy and was rehired as a medical officer to go to CFB Borden and help set up five additional clinics across the country and one in Lahr. Fenske also lectured at the Medical School in Borden. While the purpose of Fenske's work was to provide an opportunity for service personnel addicted to alcohol to effect a personal rehabilitation and, through the clinic program and subsequent follow-up, a return to active duty, he continued to push the greater importance of preventive work over treatment.

Field Duties

While the main emphasis of the chaplain's work during the 1970s and 1980s seemed to be the chapel life, there was no mistaking that the real and more interesting duties of the chaplain were those which involved him more directly with the soldiers, sailors, and airmen in their workplaces. It was here that the chaplain was meant to serve and here that he was often at his best.

In the Air Force, chaplains were an important part of the leadership team. The maintenance of good morale among flight crews was essential to their safety and that of the aircraft. The officers and men needed to know that, even in their absence, their families were secure and cared for. When things went wrong in the air, the crews needed to know that the chaplain would be on the ground waiting for their safe return. For years, RCAF chaplains were required to live on constant alert and within ten minutes of the runway.

In the Navy, the chaplain reached his peak effectiveness when he was at sea. On a destroyer on the North Atlantic, the chaplain soon learned to put aside any feelings of discomfort and to get on with his job. He would do his rounds daily, making quiet visits to the places where the men worked and stopping to socialize when invited. In port, at home or abroad, the good chaplain soon learned that he was neither the first off the ship at the dock or the last aboard before sailing.

In the Army, the chaplains participated in a tremendous variety of activities. One chaplain, whose career spanned this period, served from coast to coast in Canada and completed a tour of Cyprus. He served with armour, infantry, and artillery units as well as at the combat arms school in Gagetown. His travels with soldiers involved living in a tent in the Arctic, bobbing around off the Pacific Coast in a landing craft, and training exercises with the Jamaican Defence Force. He attended formal mess dinners in the field at Wainwright and in the Gagetown training areas. He was at Fort Lewis, Washington, with soldiers learning to fight in built-up areas, in the northern interior of British Columbia, and along the Alaska Highway. He learned to live comfortably in Canada's west coast rain forest. On one occasion, having been mistaken for a chaplain with a civilian flying licence, he was invited to fly in a military helicopter as copilot. He reneged on the take-off, letting the craft's pilot do the job, but managed to get the machine through the air with considerable dexterity. It was only after landing that the he was able to clarify to the pilot that his only previous flying experience had been "behind the wheel" of an Expediter aircraft during basic officer training with the RCAF.

It was in situations such as these that the true value of the chaplain could be seen. It was behind the machinery in the hangar, at a quiet moment on the mess deck, or sitting in a jeep looking out over the hills of Alberta that the chaplain built a rapport with his parishioners. It was in the field, beyond the reach of kith and kin, that men's lives were changed in ways that sergeant majors never thought possible.

Chapter 8

STEWARDSHIP AND OUTREACH

POLICY ON STEWARDSHIP

OVER THE YEARS the chapel congregations have used their offerings to contribute to outreach activities in much the same way as the churches of the civilian community. As early as 1948, the chaplain of the fleet, the Army director of chaplain services, and the RCAF director of religious administration recognized the need for a policy regarding the use of the offerings received at chapel services. Many of a chapel congregation's financial needs were already met in that the place of worship and a great deal of the infrastructure were provided by the military. The director of religious administration therefore recommended that twenty-five percent of a chapel's offerings should be spent on local needs and the remaining seventy-five percent should be sent to Chaplain Service headquarters in Ottawa. Two-thirds of the Ottawa amount would be divided among the five churches that supplied chaplains to the military, based on the percentage of adherents a denomination could claim in the forces. These funds would be administered and disbursed by the appropriate committees within the churches. The remaining third of the Ottawa amount would be split among the Canadian Council of Churches, the RCAF theological bursary scheme, and other approved funds and projects. This plan was accepted, and most of the chapel congregations responded by remitting annual contributions of more than the required seventy-five percent.

As more chapels were established over the next few years, there were some questions about the proper use of the local portion of weekly offerings. Everyone agreed that the funds retained by the chapel should cover small items not routinely provided by the military such as flowers for the altar but it was not always clear where to draw the line. In 1953, for example, one chaplain asked the military to supply appropriate carpets for his chapel. The Principal Supply Officer's Committee agreed to purchase carpets for all the chapels,[1] but suggested that a policy should be established on which chapel refinements were the responsibility of the military and which were to be paid for by the congregation. The Personnel Members Committee came to the chaplains' support, noting that a policy already existed. Nonetheless the committee did remind chaplains that "additions or improvements that might be termed 'luxuries' should be covered by the offering plate."[2]

With the partial integration of the Chaplain Service in 1958, the general policy for the collection and division of chapel offerings did not change. However, with the consolidation of the three separate service committees under a single Directorate of Religious Administration, decisions on disbursements were now made by a Stewardship Committee composed of the chaplain general, the directors of the three services, and the command chaplains. This committee met annually and gathered for the first time in 1960. Each of the current mission projects was reviewed and individuals wishing to establish a new project were given the opportunity to make their case for inclusion.

In 1965, as part of the overall unification of the services, it was announced that the chapel money at all levels of the military bureaucracy would now be looked after under the Non-Public Funds (NPF) system. The advantages of the new system were "the use of professional bookkeeping and accounting facilities, greater security, more frequent reports and the payment of interest on money accruing to the central fund."[3] Chaplains were told that their money would be banked quickly, recorded separately, and spent only in accordance with military administrative rules. Chapel committees were allowed to retain the calendar fiscal year but were to count and bank the weekly offerings with the base accounting officer. The money would be forwarded from units quarterly to the central account in Ottawa, which would help to maximize the interest earned. Unit chaplains would receive regular reports on the health of the central fund. Command chaplains were asked to write letters to acknowledge all contributions from the chapels and to produce financial reports.

In 1972 the chaplain general decided that the stewardship policy needed to be revamped. Responding to the growing lay participation in chapel management and activities, Padre Cardy decided that the inclusion of lay members on the Stewardship Committee would make it more effective. In June of that year, therefore, a new Canadian Forces Protestant Chapel Stewardship Committee was formed and the distribution of chapel funds was reorganized to involve more participation by the chapel lay people. The new committee was chaired by the director of pastoral activity and its members were the command chaplains, two lay delegates chosen by the command chaplains from each of Maritime, Mobile, and Air Commands, and one lay delegate from each of Training Command and Canadian Forces Europe. Other members of the Chaplain General's Division who attended meetings were present solely in an advisory capacity. The committee was to meet annually and to be responsible for reviewing and appraising all current and proposed Wider Missions Fund projects, for recommending overall monetary objectives for Wider Missions projects, and for ensuring proper disbursement of all monies allocated to Wider Missions projects.

At the first meeting of the new committee, it was decided that each chapel should operate on a locally planned budget and that each congregation should establish a target for its contribution to the Wider Missions Fund rather than merely remitting a percentage of the monies collected. Funds for the current Sunday School mission project and for the Vellore/Ludhiana medical centres would be raised separately and be kept separate as in the past. The new stewardship policy was a great venture of faith and those attending the inaugural meeting of the committee were confident of the leadership of the Holy Spirit in this important area of the life of the chapel congregations.

At its second meeting in June 1973, the recommendations of the Stewardship Committee were again directed towards encouraging the individual chapels to be more active participants in this area of the Church's work. The committee decided that it would not provide recommended fund-raising objectives for 1974 but that each congregation would be asked to set its own objectives for its contribution to each official project and to the overall Wider Missions Fund. It was hoped that allowing the congregations increased scope for decision-making on these issues would result in even greater support for the worldwide mission work of the churches. In that this procedure brought the projects to the attention of the chapel congregations a small increase in weekly offerings was experienced.

In 1977, in assessing the current state of stewardship, Padre MacCara described the Stewardship Committee as "an essential part" of the administration of the Wider Missions projects.[4] He went on to comment favourably on various changes that had been made under the committee's leadership. It was essential for each chapel congregation to "recognize and exercise its freedom to set its own objectives for the official projects and also to forward recommendations and opinions regarding these to the Stewardship Committee." He added: "The wisdom of this new approach, which encourages self-determination and participation in Stewardship matters, has been vindicated by subsequent events." MacCara also praised the removal of another obstacle to the program's work: a lack of information. "We desperately needed information being fed out on a continuing basis. Stewardship has become a more common subject in chapel circles and contributions to the Wider Missions projects have increased since this new approach was taken." In 1979, there were four representatives from Air Command on the Stewardship Committee, three from Mobile Command, and two from Europe.

The administrative end of the stewardship activity ran much the same way through the 1980s and into the early 1990s. In 1994 the annual stewardship conference changed under the guidance of Padre W. Fairlie, director of pastoral activities, to a week-long event for lay people at the new Chaplain's School at Camp Borden. All decisions made at the conference would have to be ratified by the command chaplains at a later meeting, but the lay delegates felt that they had been empowered and took that feeling back to the chapels with them.

WIDER MISSIONS PROJECTS

Detailed records on the use of chapel givings in the pre-unification years are difficult to find, but the major mission projects of the Chaplain Service in those early years have been documented. Some, such as assistance to the Vellore/Ludhiana medical complexes, continue to this day. Others, as was the case with Project Pipeline or the military contribution to World Refugee Year in 1960, were responses to a particular need, emergency, or disaster at a particular time: sometimes responding to the specific experience or perception of an individual chaplain or lay person. Since the early 1960s records are more complete but it would not be possible to describe the multifarious international, national, and local projects of the Chaplain Service and individual chapels over the past half-century. Those sketched here offer a mere sample of the breadth and depth of the concerns of the chaplains and their congregations.

THEOLOGICAL COLLEGE ASSISTANCE FUND

Many of the serving chaplains in the 1950s were soldiers, sailors, and airmen who had served as combatants during World War II and had then studied theology prior to their re-entry into the military. It was, in any case, not surprising that the Chaplain Service would be interested in assisting theological education through bursaries and scholarship. The RCAF chapels had supported bursaries for theological education as their own special project ever since the war. In 1957 the Theological College Assistance Fund was created to formalize for the three services the support formerly provided by the RCAF chapels. Many of the chaplains of the 1970s and 1980s, including Padres A.G. Fowler and D.C. Estey who were sons of RCAF personnel, received bursaries from this fund in support of their theological education before entering the chaplain service.

The fund provided bursaries and scholarships for attendance at every theological college in Canada whose denomination was a member of the

Canadian Council of Churches. It was also used to assist the theological colleges directly in a variety of ways. In the fund's early years, several theological colleges were given a $2500 donation to be invested so that the annual interest could be used to assist students, whether service connected or not, in training for the ministry. As well, several bursaries were awarded to certain colleges in memory of deceased chaplains. Outright gifts up to the amount of $2500 were given to some colleges for the purchase of theological books for their libraries. In 1964, for example, the RCAF Protestant Chapel Book Collection was established in the theological library at Union College in Vancouver. The amounts of these direct grants to colleges were based on the denominational census of the forces.

Between 1957 and 1971 a total of $157,000 was disbursed from this fund. The awards for 1963 and 1964 to Queen's Theological College were combined to create the $5000 James Gordon Brown scholarship. Padre Brown was a wartime RCAF chaplain killed instantly by a German rocket only a few days after the Normandy landing. In 1969 the Canadian Council of Supervised Pastoral Education received $1000 from the interest portion of the Wider Missions Funds in Ottawa and a further $2000 from the Theological College Assistance Fund. By 1972 the chapels had fewer people in them and very few, if any, student ministers coming out of them. The project was dropped.

CANADIAN BIBLE SOCIETY

For years it has been the mission of the Canadian Bible Society to supply Bibles and New Testaments in the quantities and languages that are required by all churches. These scriptures are distributed in over 1200 languages. Many people around the world cannot afford to pay the full cost of a Bible or even of a New Testament, so the Bible Society has attempted to provide the scriptures either below cost or free of charge. For a number of years in Canada, every person who has enrolled in the military has been given an attractive and readable New Testament, courtesy of the Canadian Bible Society. The Bible Society has received monies drawn from chapel offerings to support their work for many years. In the early postwar years, in addition to regular offerings, a special Sunday service was designated as Bible Sunday by the RCAF chapels. As time went on, Bible Sunday was observed in most of the chapels. In 1995, $15,652.60 was sent from the chapels to the Canadian Bible Society.

VELLORE/LUDHIANA MEDICAL CENTRES IN INDIA

Among the earliest and most long-lasting mission projects of the Chaplain Service were the Christian medical centres at Vellore and

Ludhiana in India. The idea of raising funds to support these hospitals came from an Army chaplain, Colonel J.P. Browne in the early 1950s. Right from the start he envisaged this mission project as a specific undertaking for the chapel branches of the Women's Missionary Society (later the Chapel Guild) and sent the wife of Padre Carson from Camp Borden down to Toronto to check out the possibilities. The Vellore/Ludhiana project was readily accepted because four of the five churches involved in the chaplaincy were long-time supporters of the hospitals.

The Christian Medical College and Hospital at Vellore grew out of the vision of a remarkable Christian medical doctor. In 1900 Dr. Ida S. Scudder began the practice of medicine in one room in Vellore. Out of that beginning grew a great modern 1200-bed hospital with 600 nurses and 400 doctors on staff. In addition there is a 900-student medical college, a school of nursing, and a training centre for medical auxiliaries such as pharmacists and physiotherapists. Vellore also has a mobile eye unit which visits the villages enabling thousands of villagers to have their sight restored. Following a visit to Vellore, the Canadian high commissioner to India, J.R. Maybee, wrote:

> We were greatly impressed with the College and the Hospital as well as the associated units dealing with mental health, rehabilitation and rural medical services. More impressive than the facilities was the remarkable spirit of service which was apparent at every level of personnel we encountered, which obviously had a great deal to do with the fine reputation which the College and the Hospital enjoy. The staff at Vellore emphasize their service to the whole man—body, mind and spirit.[5]

The story of Ludhiana goes back even further than that of Vellore. It was on May 4, 1881, that Miss Rose Greenfield opened a small dispensary in the Ludhiana bazaar. Then, in 1888, Miss Kitty Greenfield founded a college of nursing. According to Padre Eldon MacCara:

> It was at Ludhiana that Dr. (Dame) Edith Brown pioneered medical education for Indian women and inspired interdenominational and international cooperation at a time when this was quite new. She would be amazed to see how the work has expanded. There is now a co-educational Christian medical college and College of Nursing affiliated to the Punjab university. There are 300 medical students, 200 nurses, 14 post-graduate specialties and various para-medical training. There is also a 700 bed Brown Memorial Hospital providing clinical experience for students and

medical care annually to 18,000 inpatients and 300,000 outpatients. There is a newly built health centre in a downtown area of the city and three satellite rural hospitals from which comprehensive medical care including preventative medicine, maternal and child welfare, family planning, etc. is ministered to a further 100,000 in the city and surrounding villages. Surely a vision of community medicine in the tradition established by Dame Edith Brown.[6]

These hospitals continued to be a special concern of the guilds and the chapel congregations. In 1967 representatives from Vellore visited the chapels in Germany in support of a special project for Canada's centennial. The guilds and chapels committed themselves to raising $30,000 to build and equip a paediatric centre at Vellore. In the event, over $50,000 was raised. Then in May 1971 Dr. Constance Jackson, a retired missionary from India, visited the chaplain general to seek his support for a major project. Padre Stan Parkhouse remembers Dr. Jackson as an old and tired, but fascinating, lady who made frequent visits to Canadian chapels after 1960 to talk about the hospitals.

Jackson explained that the source units for the cobalt bombs used in the treatment for tuberculosis at Vellore and Ludhiana were both nearly worn out. The one at Vellore could be replaced through funds from the Canadian International Development Agency, but Ludhiana did not have enough money for its replacement. Even the cheapest supplier, Atomic Energy of Canada, was asking for $48,000. Since all of the funds raised in centennial year had gone to Vellore, Dr. Jackson requested that for the next several years the guild funds go to Ludhiana. The chapel guilds were pleased to take on this project and soon raised the money that was needed.

Later that year Jackson died and the Vellore-Ludhiana Committee of the Canadian Council of Churches was formed in Toronto. The first chapel representative on this committee was Padre J.H. McAvany. Since that time, a number of chaplains' wives have served on it. In 1973, the Protestant chapels raised over $16,000 to help build a pipeline to provide fresh water to the college at Vellore.

Beginning in 1974, the Vellore/Ludhiana centres were included in the projects of the Wider Missions Fund. In previous years monies for this project had always been raised by the guilds alone, although that money had often been supplemented by chapel offerings. As a regular chapel project, the Vellore/Ludhiana fund would not suffer and now each chapel could properly budget for its share made up of the funds raised by its guild plus a bit extra.

In 1979, the Rev. A.C. Dommen wrote that the possibilities of Vellore remained great: "If the students who go out are inspired with Christ, they could be beacons of light in every part of India. If the patients who come return to the remote places of the country not only with physical well-being, but also with meaning and purpose, then light will be spread. If our staff in our life together can give a living example of a Christian community in the body of Christ, then we will be able to demonstrate Christ's love. We need your help. Above all, we need your prayers."[7]

In 1981 Dr. K.N. Nambudripad, director of the Christian Medical Centre and of the Brown Memorial Hospital, visited the Camp Borden Chapel Guild to speak about the work at Ludhiana. He outlined the centre's aims in this way: "To contribute effectively to India's real health needs by the training of health workers, by providing total health service, both preventative and curative, in the hospital and the community, to be carried out by Christians serving in Christ's name, along side those other faiths who identify with these goals."[8]

In 1986 chapel congregations and guilds donated $45,448.28 to the work of these two Christian medical centres.

SUNDAY SCHOOL MISSION PROJECTS

From the earliest days of the chapels, the Sunday Schools raised money to support their own mission projects. For example, there is a record from 1957 of the Army Sunday Schools using their annual collections to give grants to the Anglican church at Watson Lake for an organ, to St. Paul's Church at Albany, Saskatchewan, for a lighting plant, and to the work of the Sunday School by Radio in Canada. Beginning in 1960, they were asked to participate in an across-the-services project offered by one of the participating denominations. Between 1969 and 1970 over $65,000 was raised by the children of chapel Sunday Schools to help other children in many parts of the world. Children in Africa, Asia, and South America, and in the Canadian North have benefited from this act of Christian concern.

The Sunday School mission projects gave chaplains and their congregations opportunities for creativity in the effort to make the projects real to the children. When art work depicting life at the Kei Oi centre in Hong Kong was circulated to the chapels, one chaplain had his Sunday School draw pictures of their homes and activities and send their art work back to Hong Kong. Return correspondence left everyone with the feeling that these were real people who were being helped with the offerings. Another chaplain, stationed at CFB Gagetown, arranged for a phone call with the Baptist minister in Inuvik. The conversation was taped and when it was discovered that the minister in question had served as a nurse in the

Gagetown area before ordination, it was not long before the civilian churches in the Gagetown area were involved. The community involvement spread as boxes of local crafts and games were exchanged by Girl Guides.

SUNDAY SCHOOL MISSION PROJECTS, 1968-1995

1968-9 School for the Blind, Jerusalem
1969-70 Microbus for kindergarten in Shimonoseki and
　　furnishings for orphanage in Kobe, Japan
1970-1 Operation Cedeco, Congo
1971-2 Kei Oi Welfare Centre, Hong Kong
1972-3 North Preston and Cornwallis Street Baptist Churches,
　　Halifax
1973-4 Lutheran Seaman Centre
1974-5 The Four Seas, Port Harcourt, Nigeria
1975-6 Sleeping Children Around the World
1976-7 St. Christopher's Home, Fiji
1977-8 Inuvik Baptist Church
1978-9 Lutheran Association of Missionary Pilots
1979-80 Orphanage support for Korean children in Japan
1980-1 "God is Love" refugee hospital in Zaire
1981-2 Children of the rain forest in Ecuador
1982-3 Camp Hermon
1983-4 Project Calcutta
1984-5 Project Cameroons
1985-6 Thomas Crosby mission boat
1986-7 Project Mampong Babies' Home in Ghana
1987-8 Project Reach for Bolivia
1988-9 Labrador Christian Youth Camp
1989-90 Learning for Life
1990-1 Children's homes in Central America
1991-2 Brazil's street kids
1992-3 Making a difference for the world
1993-4 Grain Power–bring hope to the children of the city
1994-5 Water Gives Life

AFRICAN STUDENTS' FUND

During a meeting at Knox Presbyterian Church in Ottawa, just after integration, Padre John Goforth made the acquaintance of Jackson Gomani and Elijah Mkhupela. These students had been brought to Canada by one of the churches and by November 1960 were in danger of running out of funds. Goforth took an interest in them and established the African Students' Fund. In December 1960 the chaplains made plans to entertain the students over the Christmas break.[9] At the end of April 1961 arrangements were made for Mkhupela to work on a farm for the summer while Gomani would work in a local garage.

The chaplains decided to support the two for one more year using money from tri-service funds. Plans were also made to get in touch with the Church of Scotland in Nyasaland to arrange for Mkhupela's return at the end of the next academic year. In June 1961, the students were asked to write letters of thanks for their support and efforts were made to find better programs for them. It was decided, if at all possible, to send Mkhupela to Tuskegee Institute in Alabama for further study.

A progress report in September 1962 noted that Gomani had completed grade 9 at Ottawa Technical School in 1961 and, having the second highest marks in the class, had been put straight into grade 11. Mkhupela had been enrolled at Tuskegee for a four-year degree course and was securely accommodated and registered in the first semester. It was suggested that accounts of the students' progress should be produced for all to see and that it was now time to turn responsibility for them back to the United Church of Canada Board of World Missions.

By January 1963 Elijah Mkhupela had returned to Northern Rhodesia and no further word had been heard. In March 1963 it was noted that Gomani had gone on to the Ontario Institute of Technology and a decision was made to sponsor him for another three years. Unfortunately, by January 1964, the tide had turned for Gomani. He had failed his Christmas exams badly, and there was little hope that he would pass his first year. Gomani returned to Africa.

After all the attention that they received, it was as though the two disappeared into thin air. After the death of her husband in 1961, Mrs. Goforth went to Africa to visit them, but no further reports have been found.

ASSISTANCE TO NOVA SCOTIA'S BLACK COMMUNITY

On March 18, 1965, a chaplain representative attended an executive meeting of the Nova Scotia Association for the Advancement of Coloured People and heard an appeal from this organization for financial help to assist the education of worthy Negro students. The Central Chapel Fund had $908.46 in trust as a balance from the African Students' Fund, and it was decided to donate this money to the Nova Scotia association. For the next few years assistance continued to be provided to the association in money and in services under the direction of the chapel committees of CFB Cornwallis and CFB Greenwood. The monies were divided between the educational fund and a community centre at North Preston.[10]

In 1970 $1,132 was given to the Nova Scotia association for the higher education of black students in the Maritimes. Two typical students were a girl who was doing postgraduate work in community nutrition and a medical student. Both were capable, of sound character, in need of financial assistance, and had plans to return to their community when they completed their studies. In 1986 $16,935 was donated to this project and seventy-seven college/university level students received an average bursary of $350.

ASSISTANCE TO NATIVE PEOPLES

The Canadian Indian Assistance Fund was started in 1962 to provide financial help for Indian and Métis students, either male or female, who did not qualify for assistance from the educational division of the Indian Affairs Branch of the federal government. The money was for further education at the high school or university level and could be used to help cover the cost of tuition, books, room and board, even clothing.

The standard of scholarship and selection of the student was to be decided by some competent church authority, such as the principal of a day or residential school, or by some qualified person who was aware of the academic interest and capacity of a possible candidate. After a student was selected it was requested that all pertinent information concerning the candidate, including school chosen and the cost, be forwarded to National Defence Headquarters so that direct liaison might be maintained with the student and chapel organizations could be informed of his or her progress.

After 1962 grants were also made to several Indian fellowship centres from coast to coast in Canada. Their objective was to provide cultural, educational, and recreational programs of a constructive nature. These centres also assisted Indian people in finding work and provided other counselling activities. By 1971 the provinces had started to give more generous support to these centres, and the chaplains decided to review the future of the fund.

In 1972 the name of the fund was changed to the Canadian Native Peoples' Fund. In 1977, contributions were being directed to the Canadian Association for the Support of Native Peoples to be used in its curriculum development project: an effort through public education to rectify some of the prejudices that exist against native people. The association also conducted training for native people in management and communication skills to supplement the political and organizational skills they have acquired. Chapel supporters seemed to lose interest in this particular project as government funding took over and particular activist groups from the United States seemed to be gaining power in the Canadian organization.

PROJECT PIPELINE

While visiting with Padres P. DeLong and K.D. Benner at CFB Cornwallis in 1970, Captain Donald C. Denison, a personnel selection officer from Halifax, shared some coloured slides of a school building project in the village of Mpeseduadze, Ghana, and outlined a subsequent development project which he had kept in touch with over the years. Small amounts of money had already been received from United Churches in the Halifax area and from the Halifax Rotary Club. Following further discussion of the project, DeLong encouraged him to contact the chaplain general for additional support.

Denison's involvement with the people of Mpeseduadze had begun in 1963 when he was sent to Ghana as a member of a training team at the Ghanian Military Academy. He served in Ghana until 1965. In his spare time Denison worked with the villagers of Mpeseduadze and neighbouring communities on an Operation Crossroads Africa self-help project to build a three-room junior high school. He gave his time and talent so unstintingly that, in appreciation, the villagers made him an honorary chief.

During the building of the school, Captain Denison noted that water for mortar and the construction of concrete blocks had to be carried by the men, women, and children of the village more than half a mile. Often the villagers told him of their dream that one day fresh water would flow in Mpeseduadze. The problem was that the nearest source of fresh water was at Krofu, some two miles distant, and the cost of a pipeline would be from $25,000 to $30,000. As an honorary chief and as a dedicated Christian layman, and after consultation with officials in the Ghanaian department of Social Welfare and Community Development, Denison decided to do what he could to bring water to Mpeseduadze.

In the spring of 1971, Denison visited the Protestant and Roman Catholic chaplains general to seek the chaplaincy's financial support of a "walk for water" that he had planned for August 1971. During the previous six years the villagers had earned $1200 and had contributed a considerable amount of voluntary labour to clear the jungle and do other preparatory work. Captain Denison, through his own efforts in Canada, had been able to raise $2700 towards the project. Now, Denison's plan was to travel to Ghana during his annual leave and to walk from Accra, the capital, to Mpeseduadze, a distance of seventy-five miles. If he could get sponsorship

236

at a level of $400 per mile, the cost of the pipeline would be covered and the village would have its water. A mark of this man's character was the fact that he was prepared to sponsor himself at a rate of $1.00 per mile.

The chaplains liked Denison's idea but believed that there was not enough lead time to ensure the required sponsorships would be gathered. They suggested a much broader fund-raising drive that would incorporate Denison's walk as one of its features. Initially, this drive was conceived of merely as a joint ecumenical venture of the chaplaincy, but subsequently it received the approval of the chief of defence staff and the minister of national defence. As the snowball started to roll, a central committee was formed with the chaplains general—Padres J. Cardy and J.A. MacLean—as co-chairmen and Captain Denison as project officer. Padre C.D. Nickerson, the Protestant director of pastoral activities, served as the committee's secretary and Major P.A. Roggeveen, comptroller of Personnel Support Programs 3, as treasurer. Project Pipeline became a diverse forces-wide, "one-shot" project with a goal of $25,000. Local Project Pipeline committees were set up on most bases and many imaginative ideas were used to publicize the project. Local events were planned and support was encouraged but every effort was made to ensure that the offerings were given on a strictly voluntary basis. Some bases sponsored their own Project Pipeline walks while others sold pipeline at $3.00 per foot.

During the campaign over $42,000 was raised. Then an extra bonus turned up when it was discovered that the project could qualify for help from the Canadian International Development Agency. In August 1972, Captain Denison and a civilian engineer from the Department of National Defence, E.G. Taylor, were sent to Ghana with almost $60,000. Contracts were negotiated with the Ghana Water and Sewage Corporation which would supervise the building of the pipeline using the volunteer labour of the villagers. Because of lower than expected estimates the pipeline was extended one and one-half miles farther to the village of Asafuna.

The project was completed when water began to flow on April 21, 1973—the Saturday prior to Easter, with much being made of the religious symbolism. Padre Parkhouse reported that "Don Denison was on hand for the official 'tap turning.'"[11] By February 7, 1974, a water storage tank was completed and all bills had been paid. Not one but two villages that once relied on contaminated water from stagnant ponds now had pure water.

There was still some money left and to keep within the intent of the donors, it was decided that it would be directed to the Crippled Children's Centre at Nsawam, Ghana. A total of $32,784.14 was given to provide that centre with desperately needed facilities to expand its orthopaedic work with polio victims, spastic children, and amputees.

During his time in Ghana in 1972, the indefatigable Denison also managed to raise an additional $2000 towards creating a library for the Mpeseduadze school. For Captain Denison's concern and work in Ghana, a school in Accra was named the Donald International School.

ECUMENICAL MINISTRY OF THE DEAF

The Ecumenical Ministry of the Deaf (EMD) received its charter as a religious organization in 1972 for the purpose of working with deaf persons in the Maritime provinces. It was largely the result of the work of the Rev. Gordon Simons, Catherine Mercer, and others in the Halifax area. The EMD was administered by 15 deaf directors. An advisory and support committee was composed of representatives from the Anglican, Baptist, Lutheran, and United churches. Ex officio members were also invited from the Presbyterian and Roman Catholic churches and the Wesleyan Friends in the Halifax area.

In February 1976, the EMD became an officially sponsored Wider Missions project of the Canadian Forces Protestant Chapels. In 1975, the organization had a budget of $22,500 and one full-time chaplain who covered the four Atlantic provinces and worked with seven Christian denominations. By 1986 the budget had grown to $69,428 and there was one full-time chaplain/director and pastoral workers were employed in Halifax, Truro, and Amherst. The services offered to the deaf included regular church services in Halifax, Truro, and Amherst, a summer camp near Pugwash, and sign-language instruction at the Atlantic School of Theology. There was an extension of services to deaf members of the Pentecostal Assemblies. Confirmation classes, hospital visitation, Bible studies, and Sunday School classes were conducted or interpreted. Also, the EMD helped young people to develop programs for social contact and fellowship. There were opportunities for self-expression and guidance counselling. Interpreter services were provided for deaf people who needed help with doctors, hospitals, lawyers, courts, banks, and social agencies. Requests for assistance came to the EMD from all over the Maritimes and over the years a core of dedicated volunteers, both deaf and hearing, developed. In 1995, $9,316.31 was given to this charity by the Canadian Forces Protestant Chapels.

THE EMERGENCY RELIEF FUND

This is the most direct and straightforward of all the Wider Missions projects. In 1973, the Stewardship Committee agreed that the monies be handled as a cumulative fund with disbursements to be made by the chaplain general on the advice of the Canadian Council of Churches in

238

response to emergency situations. Thousands of dollars have been sent to central Africa for famine relief (1973-5), to Guatemala for relief (1976), to Angola for a rehabilitation program, and to Turkey for earthquake relief. In 1978 and 1979 money was sent to assist the work with the Vietnamese boat people.

In 1986, a total of $39,898.62 was donated by the chapels for this purpose and money was sent to Greece to support an earthquake medical team, to El Salvador in response to an earthquake appeal, to the Cameroons where people had been struck down by toxic gas, and to Bolivia, Peru, and Argentina in response to flood appeals. On April 9, 1987, $10,000 was sent to Ecuador for earthquake and landslide relief and on September 25, 1987, $20,000 was sent to Bangladesh in response to an appeal for food, shelter, and medical supplies in the wake of devastating floods. In 1995, $20,000 was sent in response to an appeal from Chechnya and $40,000 went to the Church World Action project in Yugoslavia.

OPERATION EYESIGHT UNIVERSAL

Operation Eyesight Universal became an official Wider Missions project in 1979. The program had been started in 1963 by a group of Christian businessmen in Calgary in response to an address given by Dr. Ben Gullison, superintendent of a small hospital in India. He spoke about the service that his hospital was rendering in an area in which 200,000 needy curable blind persons lived. These Calgary businessmen pledged that they would pay for cataract surgery each year. In 1963 the cost of surgery for two eyes and glasses was only $25 per operation and that included a ten-day stay in the hospital. The idea spread and Operation Eyesight Universal became an international organization. In 1963 it was responsible for 148 operations; in 1977 over 19,000 blind eyes were opened.

In the early stages of the project, Op Eyesight was supported through the Baptist portion of the chapel missionary givings, but in 1972 the Baptists ceased to support individual missions and started to put their money into their church's general mission funds. Some chapels continued to support Op Eyesight on their own and then, in 1978, the chapel committee at Trinity Chapel, CFB Kingston, under the guidance of Padre D.A. Hatfield, recommended to the Stewardship Committee that Operation Eyesight Universal become a Wider Missions project. The congregation in Kingston argued that not only did the project give sight to the blind but that it did so in the name of Christ. The specifically Christian approach of Op Eyesight was in no way denominational, it was not limited to one small sector of the world, and it was something with which every Canadian family could easily identify. A very positive aspect of the project was that excellent promotional material was available at no cost and that the project's founder, Dr. Gullison, and its president, Art Jenkyns, both dedicated Christian laymen and dynamic speakers, travelled across Canada on other business and were available to speak to the chapels.

This project gained widespread support across the Canadian Forces. On one occasion, members of St. Barbara's Chapel in Victoria were challenged to wrap their Christmas presents in newspaper and to give the money saved to Op Eyesight. Around 1980, recruits at CFB Cornwallis were inspired, largely by Padres Bill MacLellan and Mike Wellwood, to engage in friendly competition as Op Eyesight became the "Recruit Mission Project." The donation of each group of recruits was fixed to the wall of the chapel fellowship hall. At one point a mess hall cake was raffled off for a tidy sum and immediately eaten by the purchasers. Always a popular project, Operation Eyesight Universal received $17,026.79 from the chapels in 1995.

GRENFELL MISSION PROJECT

In the spring of 1978 Padre G.N. Ward and the Stewardship Committee from the Goose Bay Protestant Chapel received approval from the chaplain general to raise $10,000 to purchase a heavy-duty twelve-passenger van for the International Grenfell Association (IGA) in Labrador, which had been established in the late 1800s to support the work of Sir Wilfred Grenfell, a pioneer medical missionary in Labrador. By 1979 the role of the IGA was to maintain and staff all of the health service delivery systems in northern Newfoundland and Labrador. This included a hospital and three dormitories in North West River for children who, for various reasons, could not enjoy the care of their natural parents. For several years the United States Air Force had provided buses to the mission to transport children over the seventy-seven-mile gravel road to the many recreational facilities at Goose Bay, but when the USAF reduced its strength at the air base in 1976 this service could not be continued. There was no public transport and the only vehicle owned by the IGA was an ambulance. The new van would be used to transport small groups on outings from the mission to Goose Bay for recreation, picnics, and school events.

Padre R.H. White reported to the 1979 meeting of the Stewardship Committee that funds for the project had started to trickle in slowly during the fall but by December money had been received from bases across Canada, from Germany, and even from as far away as Cyprus. In January 1979 the chaplain general, Brigadier General Stan Parkhouse, was able to present the van to the mission.

CHRISTIAN DEVELOPMENT FUND

The Christian Development Fund was one of Padre Eric Porrior's ideas and during the Stewardship Committee meeting in Halifax in 1981, it was adopted as one of the Wider Missions projects for 1982. In 1981, it had been recognized that some bases were working under a handicap because they were located at some distance from national chaplain activities and available forces airlift. In these situations the military would assist its members with travel but it could not help their dependents or their invited guests. Civilian speakers could not be easily brought to isolated bases; nor could non-military lay persons easily attend such events as the National Guild Conference. The purpose of the Christian Development Fund was to help congregations on bases and stations that were off the beaten track to transport and to train their people. The director of pastoral activities was to consider it a working fund within his directorate to support resource persons, workshops, and seminars which would contribute to the development and promotion of congregational leadership and programming. In practice, this took the form of bringing in leaders to the local chapel or sending out congregational members for training.

In 1987 new guidelines stated that the purpose of the fund was to help develop congregational leadership and programming where such training was too expensive for the congregation to handle alone. These terms of reference were interpreted in a broad fashion and in 1987 the fund supported a variety of activities.

SAMPLE CHRISTIAN DEVELOPMENT FUND PROJECTS, 1982-1995

1. The distribution of *House of Many Windows*, a book on modern India, to bases and stations in response to suggestions from the Vellore/Ludhiana committee.
2. Support for a west coast chapel to run a vacation Bible school during the months of July and August.
3. Various levels of support to eleven different chapels to help send their guild representatives to the National Guild Conference.
4. Purchase of a VCR tape to be used on one of the training bases for padre's hours.
5. The cost of sending a chapel guild speaker to various bases to promote the work of Vellore/Ludhiana.
6. Sending five women from a semi-isolated base to a weekend "Word of Life" camp at Schrom Lake, New York.

As the "perks" of military life dwindle with budget cuts in 1995, the Christian Development Fund remains as a source of reliable funding for the chapels' pastoral activities.

CHURCHES' MISSIONS

In 1948 it had been decided that two-thirds of the money remitted by the chapels to Ottawa would be distributed to the five churches which provided the Protestant chaplains to the Canadian Forces. Later, when the basic chapel furnishings were all in place, this guideline was dropped and chapels began to remit the bulk of their weekly offering to Ottawa. The monies allocated to each church were determined according to the percentage of its adherents in the military and that has remained the case to this day. At first it was left up to the individual churches to decide how they would distribute the money and that usually meant that it was incorporated into the general funds of the church rather than being spent on a discrete activity. However in later years—often after some lobbying by the chaplains—these monies were directed to particular projects. This change gave the chaplains and the chapel congregations a greater sense of involvement in the way in which their offerings were used to assist those in need.

Anglican Church

From 1968 to 1970, with encouragement from the chaplains, the Anglican Church of Canada used its portion of the offerings to assist the church's work in construction at Hay River, NWT, towards purchase of a motor launch on the Niger Delta, Africa, for a dispensing van in Amritsar, India, in Bogota, Colombia, for Sudanese clergy relief and settlement, to repair Ogoki Church in Moosonee, towards an Indian friendship centre in Victoria, and to assist in the publication of the Hendry Report concerning native people in Canada. Bishop Ivor Norris bursaries totalling $5000 went to assist theological students with their seminary expenses, preference being given to those who had some relationship with the Forces, and another $1000 bursary was also awarded.

The distribution of the Anglican share of chapel offerings was decided by a committee made up of the Anglican bishop ordinary, who was chairman, two chaplains, two lay persons, and the general secretary and treasurer of General Synod. In 1977 the Anglican money went to support the Reverend John Wesley, a fully bilingual (Cree-English) priest who was serving at Rupert's House on the east coast of James Bay, to support the church community at Coppermine, NWT, probably one of the most northern Christian communities in the world, and to fight drought with agricultural assistance in Sudan. A missionary, the Reverend John Rye, was able to purchase a pickup truck with an additional grant which enabled him to visit, teach, and lead in worship as well as to transport agricultural supplies in Ghana. As in all years, the Ivor Norris bursary was awarded and other bursary money was sent to the Pacific Theological College, Fiji, where a member of the faculty was the Reverend John Fife, a graduate of Emmanuel College, Saskatoon, and a Second World War Army chaplain.[12]

United Church Of Canada

From 1972 it was the chaplains' understanding that the United Church used its portion of the chapel offerings to support four churches that had missions to the underprivileged. One was Brunswick Street United Church in Halifax which had a heavy involvement in the surrounding low-income community. Located in an older part of the city, near the waterfront, Brunswick Street was noted in the mid-1970s for its street corner recreation program. The second was a church near Regent Park, Toronto, which reached out to those in public low rental housing. The Central Winnipeg Mission, later called People Acting on Concerns Together (PACT), was really in the north end of Winnipeg. It was located in what had been J.S. Woodworth's Methodist church, now known as All Peoples' Mission. PACT sought to improve the self-help and leadership skills in the community, particularly among the native people and the Métis. When PACT ceased, it was replaced by the North End Community Ministry (NECM). Lastly, support was given to First Church Vancouver, the "Church of the Open Door," which stated its mission to be "a Christian presence in the inner-city and through worship, counselling, community programs and projects, social services and social action, to express the Good News of the Christian faith and to enable the people of the downtown-east-side community to hear and appropriate this Good News and to experience human love relationships."[13] More recently, money given to the United Church has found its way into the wider mission funds of the church.

Baptist Church

As mentioned above, the Baptist portion of the funds went to Operation Eyesight Universal until the late 1960s. Since then it has gone to the general missionary funds of the church.

LUTHERAN COUNCIL OF CANADA

In 1986 there were 1479 Lutherans registered as members of the Canadian Forces, representing only 4.63 percent of the total strength of the Protestants in the Forces. This meant that the Lutheran Council received only $2,942 as its share of the chapel offerings. Some money was used to cover the cost of sixty copies of the *Canadian Lutheran*, which was sent to the chapels, and the remainder was divided between the Pax Natura Society for Rehabilitation of the Deaf in Edmonton, the Saskatchewan Ministry to the Deaf, and the work of a pastor at the Sir James Whitney School for the Deaf in Belleville, Ontario. In 1987, a committee of the Lutheran Council decided to spend the chapel money to help build churches destroyed by earthquakes in Indonesia.

Presbyterian Church In Canada

In 1977 Presbyterian Church assigned its money to two projects. One was the Kenora Fellowship Centre, a meeting place recognized as an independent institution dedicated to justice and reconciliation. The other was sent to Baring Union Christian College in Batala, India. From Baring, students go out into the villages where they help to overcome illiteracy, establish libraries, and give advice and assistance regarding such services as sanitation.

Canadian Council Of Churches

The money which came to the Canadian Council of Churches from chapel offerings was placed in the general funds of the council. Each year, the activities of the council included: inter-church consultations, conferences, studies, training schools, and workshops on Bible study. In the area of national and international concerns, the council studied, spoke out, and acted on matters which involved the moral and spiritual principles inherent in the Christian Gospel, with particular emphasis on the areas of justice, liberty, peace and war, and human rights and relationships. Also, the council sought to bring member churches into a living encounter with other Christian Church bodies and to advance the development of ecumenism in Canada through assistance to local and regional ecumenical groups. Considering the breadth of the council's concerns, the impact of chapel money would not go very far, but the offerings certainly offset any expenses that might have been incurred in the administration of the Chaplain Service by the general secretary on the Council, Dr. Gallagher. In 1956, the chapels donated $10,000 to the general funds of the Canadian Council of Churches. During the 1950s and 1960s money given by the chapel for refugees usually went to the council for its programs.

After integration, the work of the Canadian Council of Churches Chaplaincy Committee seemed to be less important to the chaplains and financial support for the Canadian Council of Churches declined. This prompted Dr. D.W. Anderson to make a special appeal to the Stewardship

Committee in 1979. In 1995, $9,610 was given to the Canadian Council of Churches.

Over the years chapel congregations and military personnel have given generously to those in need. Projects have been carefully chosen to represent the concerns of military people and the denominations from which the chaplains have come. Many people in Canada and abroad are better off today because of the stewardship program in the Canadian Forces chapels.

Chapter 9

MOVING INTO THE TWENTY-FIRST CENTURY

THE POST– COLD WAR ERA

THE DISINTEGRATION of the Soviet Union and the collapse of its empire ushered in a new era in world history and a new era in the history of Canadian military chaplains. The demise of the Soviet threat meant that Western nations, which faced severe financial restraints, would be able to reconfigure their military forces and in the case of Canada bring them home after forty years on the central front in Europe. With the threat of global nuclear war seemingly behind them, the West could cease research, development, and production of arms. Armies, navies, and air forces could be reduced in size, and many of their units could be disbanded. Military management policies became more business-oriented and less paternalistic.

In Canada, various force reduction plans came into effect, although these did not affect the chaplains before 1995 because the branch was already manned at the minimum level of positions necessary to do the job. As bases in Canada and in Germany closed and the overall number of personnel was reduced, a sufficient number of chaplains reached retirement age so that the number of personnel and the number of active chaplains remained in balance. Nevertheless there was pressure from their military superiors to slim down the size of the chaplain establishment.

The objective of the defence review in 1987 was to find ways for the Canadian Forces to make better use of its dwindling resources. The adoption of the Total Force Concept meant that the Militia would be upgraded and equipped to Regular Force standards. Militia area headquarters would be increased in size and would be responsible for all of the soldiers, Regular and Militia, within their geographical areas. This new force structure was to be in place by the year 2002.

In the wake of this broad change, the need to bring the Army chaplains in line with the new concept was evident. Prior to 1987 there were a few good Militia padres but many more who were untrained and often ineffective. Some found themselves in the Militia only because they were a good friend of the local commanding officer. Others were unable to go into the field or lacked the desire and the willpower to do so. Some thought that the chaplain's only job was to be present at parades and, afterwards, in the officers mess. The time was right for change and the Army command chaplain, Lieutenant Colonel W.J. Fairlie, was given Padre W.C. MacLellan to help make the Total Force Concept happen.

MacLellan was posted to Army headquarters at St. Hubert and immediately embarked on a massive recruiting job. Prior to his time many good applicants for positions as Militia padres would give up after waiting as much as three years to hear if they had been accepted. It was a credit to the hard work of MacLellan, of his successor, Padre F.A. Walker, and of Lieutenant Colonel Fairlie that within five years, three-quarters of the Militia positions had been filled with the right men.

In 1990, the traditional command chaplains conferences ceased and all Regular and Militia chaplains were required to join together at area conferences. These were largely organized by the militia area chaplains, with a tremendous amount of help from the assistant command chaplain in St. Hubert.

By 1993, the way was clear and Regular Force and Militia chaplains were moving forward as equals. All of the Army chaplain manuals were brought up to date, and *Chaplains in Battle*, a bilingual guide for chaplains on active service, was produced in co-operation with the Roman Catholic chaplains. An increasing number of Militia padres began to appear on temporary assignment on the bases and on United Nations deployments. They were competent and keen young men. Indeed, some were better trained for what they were doing than some of the Regular Force chaplains.

In the meantime, while these administrative changes were under way, it had become clear that frictions at home and growing instability abroad following the collapse of the bipolar Cold War world would continue to place the Forces and their chaplains in harm's way.

OKA

During the summer of 1990, a land dispute erupted between the local native Canadians and residents of the town at Oka, just south of Montreal. Soldiers from CFB Valcartier were called out for a short period of time in support of the civil power. Once again, a padre found himself playing a unique role.

Behind the native lines, sympathetic with their cause and working in the food bank and community centre, were two workers from the United Church of Canada. Prior to the arrival of the Protestant padre from Valcartier, it was determined by the chaplain general, talking with the head office of the United Church, that he would liaise with these two church workers.[1]

For the short duration of the conflict, in addition to his normal duties as the brigade's Protestant chaplain, Padre D.C. Kettle therefore performed humanitarian acts such as taking medical prescriptions into no man's land and leaving them for the native warriors to pick up. Initially, after the warriors were in detention, it was also Kettle's job to verify that the many people who wanted to visit them were either members of their families or shamans.[2] Padre Kettle found the whole experience very meaningful.

THE GULF WAR—OPERATION FRICTION

Charging that Kuwait had cheated on its oil production levels and therefore lowered the world price of oil, thus depriving Iraq of some of its oil revenues, President Saddam Hussein invaded his neighbour, Kuwait, on August 2, 1990. The United Nations Security Council responded by ordering a worldwide economic embargo against Iraq. Countries and organizations around the world joined in the condemnation. Canada immediately announced that it would "contribute to the defence of the integrity of nations" by sending the destroyers, HMCS *Athabascan* and HMCS *Terra Nova,* and the supply ship HMCS *Protecteur* to help maintain the embargo. The naval contingent consisted of nine hundred and thirty-four personnel and would be supported by eighteen CF-18 jet fighters with a support crew of four hundred and fifty and a field hospital. On both coasts and across Canada, military and civilian crews worked around the clock to get the people, the equipment, and the ships ready for deployment.

On August 24, 1990, *Athabascan, Terra Nova* and *Protecteur* left Halifax for the Gulf. Their mission was to help enforce an economic blockade against Iraq in support of United Nations resolutions 661 and 665 which called upon Iraq to withdraw from Kuwait which it had now annexed.

Sailing on HMCS *Protecteur* was a young chaplain with just over a year's experience in the military. Being the serving chaplain with the 1st Canadian Destroyer Squadron, Padre B.D. Park was the first to go with the fleet to the Gulf. Park spent the few days before deployment visiting the ships and getting to know the men. Ashore, he had to deal with others who had shore postings but who wanted to join the trip.

The Roman Catholic chaplain on the trip was Lieutenant Commander Ron MacFarland who sailed on HMCS *Terra Nova.* On Sundays the chaplains would transfer between ships by helicopter. In the event that neither chaplain could reach the *Athabascan,* as was the case after the ships entered the Gulf, the ship's commander, Captain(N) Dusty Miller, would conduct services of worship on his ship.

Before he left Canada, Baxter Park told reporter Pam Sword of the *Halifax Chronicle-Herald* that his main role was "one of celebrating the Eucharist,'to give people a chance to worship God'."[3] When interviewed by a reporter from Corner Brook's *Western Star* on his return, Park described the ships as "a floating parish ... "I travel from ship to ship doing the normal things clergy do in a parish: visitations, counselling, services, death and sickness notifications." Park reported "my message as a priest was that God is still in charge and though sometimes it's difficult to understand how we humans can mess up our world, in the end we have a promise that the Prince of Peace is going to take charge."[4]

In his formal report, Park praised the work of the team of chaplains who had been left behind in Halifax to look after the families of those who were at sea. Because there had been little cause to exercise the wartime system of dealing with multiple casualties, some felt it necessary during Operation Friction to review the procedures surrounding the notification of next of kin and the release of casualty information to the press. Messages were sent that reiterated the "normal" procedure which was that next of kin would be notified by the chaplains.[5]

The trip to the area of operations was very much a part of the whole experience. At the Port of Gibraltar the Canadians were reminded of the long line of young men who had given their lives as a sacrifice for the cause of freedom. In Sicily they were reminded of some of the fiercest fighting of the Second World War. As the group passed through the Suez Canal, lined with the wreckage of the Arab-Israel wars, the reality of the situation started to sink in.

The greatest fear for Park and the all others on the trip was being caught in a nuclear, biological, or chemical attack. The most rewarding aspect of the trip for Park was being able to move freely among the sailors and talk with them about their fears, their concerns, and their good and bad news from home. Many questions were asked about the long history of violent conflict in the area. A small number of fundamentalist Christians were concerned that they might be heading into the battle of Armageddon. Park was thankful for the reading he had done before the trip on the Book of Revelation and on Arab culture and customs.

The task force proceeded into the Gulf of Oman, through the Straits of Hormuz, and into the Gulf. Their first stop was at Manama in the island-nation of Bahrain. This would be their permanent supply base. Each ship then went out to patrol a section of the Gulf. Vessels passing through the section were hailed by the Canadians and asked their port of origin and their destination, their flag of registry, and what cargo they were carrying. When the information received was questionable, a boarding party was detached from the ships to conduct a search.[6] Because HMCS *Protecteur* was the only supply ship in the northern part of the Gulf, she also spent a lot of time replenishing American, British, Australian, Dutch, and other ships which were at sea enforcing the blockade.

During the tour there were moments of tension when the crew didn't know if a drill was the real thing or not. Bad news and sometimes even good news from home could bring on bouts of loneliness and homesickness. There were occasions when men had to be reminded that being in a war zone meant that it was not always possible to be repatriated if someone at home was seriously ill or died. There were times when the routine was busy and yet boring because of its repetitive nature. Nonetheless, Park reported that the men and women on duty "found the inner strength and the personal stamina to rise to the occasion."[7] The chaplain found that his main job was often just to listen and to give the person a chance to work through their feelings.

Park's fondest memories of the trip related to Christmas. In a "sundown" service on *Terra Nova* and a "midnight" service on *Protecteur*, practically everyone who could come was there. Park saw the way in which the men were drawn closer to the Christmas experience than ever before. Geographically and climatically closer, but also in the sense that the Christmas story was about a displaced family, about the slaughter of innocents because a king became threatened by the arrival of the Wise Men, and about Jesus and his parents having to flee their native land. Later, Park discovered that a sailor who attended services wrote home to his wife: "I was in the worst possible place having the best possible time."[8]

In the effort to keep its crews fresh but to control costs, the Navy decided to rotate the crews on its ships. Park returned to Canada with the crew of the *Protecteur* in January 1991. *Athabascan's* crew was to be replaced in February and *Terra Nova's* in March. Unfortunately, the war against Iraq started six days after *Protecteur's* crew rotated, and the rotation of the crews of *Athabascan* and *Terra Nova* never did take place. The three ships returned home on April 7, 1991, with Park's replacement, Captain R.J. Waye.

Captain R.P. Brinn had a different experience of the Gulf War. Bob Brinn deployed with 1st Canadian Field Hospital to Al Jubayl and Al Hyasumah in Saudi Arabia, on what was described as Operation Scalpel. The operation started with three intensive weeks of training that included everything from combat first aid to how to handle prisoners of war and what to do if captured by the enemy. The hospital departed for the Gulf in January 1991, prepared for a mass of casualties, but in the event the nature of the battle left it with little work. This in itself was a problem, and the

250

padres were called upon to help the senior officers come up with ideas such as a sports day and a desert recreational walk similar to the German Volksmarch to keep everyone busy. Worship services were held on Sunday mornings and on Wednesday evenings in the mess hall. Attendance was about the same as it would be for soldiers on exercise in Canada. Brinn prepared for worship with service books and a tape of hymn tunes supplied by his organist at his home base, CFB Petawawa. Support for the chaplains in the field and back in Petawawa, the home of 1st Canadian Field Hospital, was extremely good.

Serving in succussion as chaplains with the CF-18s were Captain D.K. Friesen, Major R.M. Gardner, and Major B.L. Yager. These aircraft flew out of an airfield at Bahrain, first over the northern end of the Gulf and then over southern Iraq. Lieutenant Colonel Donald Matthews, commanding officer of the largest combat squadron the Canadian Forces had put together since the Second World War, said: "It was very intense out there because people were trying to kill us."[9] He remembered Scud missile alerts and putting on his gas mask and chemical suit. Every time one of his aircraft took off, Matthews commented: "I said a little prayer and every one of them that came back I said a little prayer. And that happened every time they took off and returned."[10] The air force chaplains had their work cut out for them.

Back on the home front, the Canadian Council of Churches, which had a delegation visiting Cyprus and Lebanon when the war broke out, delivered a firm public commitment to a pacifist stance. Without any consultation with chaplains in the Forces, the Canadian Council joined with the Middle East Council of Churches to call for "an immediate cessation of hostilities," "the withdrawal of all troops from the region," and a peace conference to solve the real problems of the area.[11]

The moderator of the United Church of Canada, the Right Reverend Dr. Walter Farquharson, followed with a complementary statement[12]: "We deplore the bombing of Baghdad and the claim that it was a success. It is, in fact, a tragic failure, even as the invasion of Kuwait by the Iraqi forces was a failure." Rejecting the claims of leaders that there were no alternatives, he continued: "We remain committed to the principles of a just world order and to the United Nations, but in the light of modern warfare and the technological changes in weaponry, we are convinced that ultimately world order is only effectively pursued by non-military means." The United Church's Division of Mission in Canada, with representatives from the executive of the Division of World Outreach, commended the moderator's statement and called on the government of Canada to use all of its diplomatic resources to achieve a ceasefire and to restore Canadian military personnel and resources to peacekeeping duties.[13]

The one ray of light for United Church chaplains came in the same mailing from church headquarters as the moderator's message. This was a resolution from Peterborough Presbytery proposing that initiatives be undertaken to assist the victims of war and to encourage reconciliation and peace. Also, church members were called upon "to offer spiritual support to those in the Armed Forces through letter writing, continual prayer, and assuring them of consistent outreach to their families; and to assist families of Armed Forces personnel through the formation of support groups, pastoral counselling for those affected by stress and grief, financial help, and through other appropriate means."[14]

In the light of reactions, such as the one from Peterborough, and with a sober second thought, the moderator of the United Church of Canada wrote to the chaplain general assuring him of the prayerful support of the church for all persons in the services without regard to their religious beliefs. Farquharson wrote:

> While deploring war and calling on our members to speak out about the political, economic and, most importantly, the human costs of war, we honour the decision you made to serve your country in the armed services. We pray for a quick resolution of the conflict, for your safety and well-being, and for the establishment of a new day of peace and justice for all the peoples of the world.
>
> Members and officers of The United Church of Canada remember you and your families in prayer. We acknowledge the dilemmas and hard choices that confront us all in the name of justice, peace and freedom. We will not forget you and promise to offer you, your families and friends, all the pastoral and spiritual support we can. As Moderator, I write this knowing that every service person's prayer must be for peace and for a world where armed conflict is rendered obsolete.[15]

Farquharson requested the widest possible distribution of the letter to United Church members and adherents serving in the Canadian Forces.

Messages came in to the chaplain general from other individuals and churches who wished the service persons and their families well. The Lake of Bays pastoral charge of the United Church sent a simple but meaningful message to the families left behind through the chaplains: "Our thoughts and prayers are very much with the families of all members of the Canadian Armed Forces at this time. You are remembered each Sunday at our

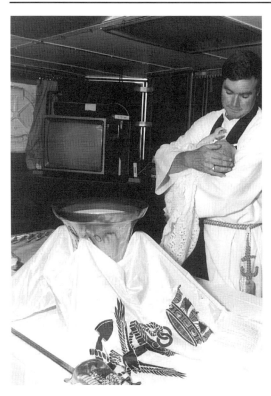

Chaplain R.C. Humble conducts a baptism in the ward room of HMCS *Qu'Appelle*, Esquimalt Harbour, BC

Padre B.D. Park does his daily rounds on the deck of HMCS *Protecteur*, Gulf of Oman, December 1990

Padre G.D. Fillmore conducts a communion service, Doha, Kuwait.

Padre Fillmore's staff car in the deserts of Kuwait.

Worship. We pray that your faith may comfort and strengthen you and that your loved ones may quickly return home."[16]

Softening the earlier statements of the United Church, the Division of Ministry, Personnel and Education recognized the difficult role of chaplains in ministering to the military personnel involved in the conflict. At the end of February the general secretary of the division was requested to write personally to each United Church chaplain with the following resolution: "That the Division express its prayerful concern and support to the United Church Chaplains in the Canadian Forces as they exercise their ministry in this difficult time and that we convey this motion of support from the Division to the Executive Secretaries of the Conferences, asking that this action be conveyed to the Presbyteries within their bounds where Chaplains exercise their ministry."[17] Of course, by the time this message was circulated, the war was over.

Fortunately, the Gulf War did not last very long. A tense world was still breathing a sigh of relief when the Reverend Lawrence R. Likeness, Lutheran chairman of the Council of Churches Chaplaincy Committee, sent an Armed Forces Day message to the men and women of the Canadian Forces.

> The Canadian Armed Forces played their assigned role in the conflict and we rejoice that no Canadian lives were lost in combat. However, the carnage wreaked on the Persian Gulf area will take years to repair, both environmentally and economically, not to mention the cost in human misery and tragedy, and for that we are indeed sorry. But perhaps there is renewed hope in recognizing the possibilities of peace for this troubled area.
>
> It is the hope of many Canadians that we may now resume our task as peacekeepers in troubled spots around the world, and we look to our Armed Forces to carry out new assignments under the United Nations.
>
> The Canadian Council of Churches Committee on Chaplaincy in the Armed Forces is thankful that we have been able to supply chaplains for the ministry of Word and Sacrament, as well as for spiritual counselling and moral support, to our military personnel wherever they may be serving. It is our privilege to continue to do so, thanks to the cooperation of the churches participating in the committee. We encourage members of the Armed Forces to use the many services our chaplains offer.[18]

UNITED NATIONS IRAQ-KUWAIT OBSERVER MISSION

Long after the news media forgot about the Gulf, Canadian soldiers were still there and the chaplain with them was G.D. Fillmore. The United Nations Iraq-Kuwait Observer Mission (UNIKOM) was composed of 300 observers from 33 nations plus a headquarters, an aviation element, a logistic support unit, a medical group, and engineers totalling 1440 personnel. They were stationed in the demilitarized zone along the border to ensure that there were no military personnel or installations belonging to either side in the zone. The force was also tasked with the removal of mines and unspent munitions. Fillmore served with UNIKOM until the end of its mandate in October 1991.

THE CHAPLAINS SCHOOL

In keeping with the need for the proper training of all chaplains for active service and in the light of the ever shrinking size of the Chaplain Service, the increased co-operation with the Roman Catholics, and the increasing number of United Nations taskings, it was decided to reactivate the case for a chaplains school. The idea of a school for Canadian chaplains was first raised during discussions concerning integration in 1957. It would provide courses for new entrant chaplains, chaplains with a minimum of five years, service, staff and hospital chaplains, Reserve or Militia chaplains, and lay persons from Sunday Schools, Guilds, and men's and young people's organizations. Military chaplains' schools had proven their worth in the United States since just after the Civil War and in Britain since the turn of the century, but Canadian chaplains had never had a "school" of their own.

The chaplains soon discovered that they were not about to have their own school in 1957. All that was on offer was a chaplain qualifying course, to be held at the Royal Canadian Army Medical Corps School at Camp Borden. This course would be given after completion of the regular direct entry officers basic training. An additional three-week course would be given to chaplains if they were going to be sent to the Navy. It was decided that the chaplain needed a basic understanding of the framework in which he would function and that there was a need to give integrated information to all chaplains. This was especially important with respect to personnel counselling: chaplains needed a thorough understanding of the conditions of service and of the regulations of the organization in which the man served. Any additional training would have to be done out of service or in conjunction with an existing school.

However, in 1992 all of this changed. The Protestant and Roman Catholic base chaplains in Camp Borden, Padres W.C. MacLellan and Ron Bourque, visited chaplain training centres in the United States with a view to learning from their experiences and examining possible resources that could be adapted to the Canadian situation. Early in 1993, the two Training Command chaplains, Padre G.E. Peddle and Roman Catholic Padre Julien Rheault, brought twelve Protestant and Roman Catholic, Regular and Reserve chaplains to Trenton. With the assistance of a training development officer, these chaplains "hammered out" the basic specifications for chaplain training. As a direct result of this planning process, it was discovered that ninety to ninety-five percent of chaplain training could be conducted "in common" (Protestant and Roman Catholic combined) and that the remaining ten to fifteen percent covering, for example, sacramental preparation and unique ecclesiastical requirements, could be conducted in separate denominational groupings. The march towards an integrated approach to chaplain training had begun.

After the initial meetings the organization developed quickly. Boards met to develop a basic chaplain course and to design standards and training plans for a senior chaplain course and a chaplain in peacekeeping operations course. On the evening of the first basic chaplain course to be offered at the Canadian Forces Chaplain School and Centre (CFChSC) on April 12, 1994, formal chaplaincy training was inaugurated at CFB Borden with a religious celebration held in Trinity Protestant Chapel.

The first basic chaplain course received very positive comments from the course candidates. The twinning of Roman Catholic and Protestant, Regular and Reserve chaplains was seen as a positive contribution. The daily routine of each course began with morning worship (alternating "common" worship periods with denominationally specific celebrations) and then a full day of lectures and discussions as well as practical exercises in ministry in a military setting. Topics for the basic course, to name only a few, included: military ethics and professionalism; the "nuts and bolts" of advising the commanding officer on matters of an ethical, moral, and spiritual nature; the law of war and the applicability of the Geneva Conventions to chaplains; military-specific religious celebrations (weddings, funerals, commemorative services, and the consecration of colours); serving in a pluralistic environment; duty chaplaincy; padre's hours; introduction to battlefield ministry; pastoral care in abusive, suicidal, and compassionate situations; operational updates involving Canadian troops; how to design a chaplain support plan during the pre-deployment, deployment, and post-deployment phases of an operation; designing mission and vision statements to assist in the integration of ministry for the benefit of the unit(s) served and the military community as a whole; how to integrate civilian ministry into a military environment; dealing with critical incident stress and combat stress reaction. The basic course ended with a practical phase during which chaplain-candidates deployed to a training area and were afforded the opportunity to put into practice their "holy" battlefield crafts.

Shortly after the first basic chaplain course, Padre Peddle handed over command to Bill MacLellan, who had been recently promoted to the rank of lieutenant colonel. His staff at the school included: Roman Catholic Padre L.D. MacIsaac, as chief instructor; Padre J.A. Alexander, as director of the CFChSC resource centre; Padre E.T. Reynolds as an instructor, and Sgt. Yves Tétreault as chief clerk. Militia Padre Rick Ruggle rounded out the contingent as the Reserve training officer and instructor.

OPERATION LANCE—RWANDA

On July 27, 1994, 1 Canadian Headquarters and Signals Regiment and 3 Airborne, augmented by specialists from different bases in Canada left for Kigali, Rwanda. Their mission was to establish communications between the various United Nations forces sent to stabilize the country in the aftermath of a very bloody civil war. With them was Chaplain D.C. Melanson. Before leaving Canada, the group had undergone combat training at CFB Petawawa, and David Melanson had taken a specifically designed course at the Chaplain School, but nothing prepared the padre or his soldiers for the experiences they were about to have. Melanson later described it this way:

> When we first arrived the city of Kigali was very sparse in population. The majority of people here were RPA [Rwanda People's Army] soldiers carrying AK47's (Soviet made rifles) and looking very nervous. The villages in the countryside, set in a beautiful landscape, were all but vacant of life.
>
> There were those of us who had experienced the death of others before, but for many young soldiers it would be their first encounter with it. Our jobs took us into areas of the country that the troops called, for lack of better words, "killing fields." The majority of these places that I saw were local community parishes and churches. Around the church grounds and in the sanctuaries we found the remains of thousands of human beings; children, women, and men slaughtered without mercy. The scenes, the smell and the horror of it all was beyond any words that could be uttered. Silence was the only language understood at these sights. In the darkness of night these "killing fields" were often revisited in our dreams.
>
> Many thousands of people had fled to the refugee camps in Zaire, Burundi and Tanzania, only to find that their nemesis had followed

them into the camps. There, the beatings and killings continued. Our medical unit worked overtime, day after day, treating the inflictions caused by machetes, bullets and mortars. Many people lost limbs from the detonation of mines, especially children.[19]

Indelible pictures were etched into the hearts and minds of the soldiers and, like the great stream of chaplains in war zones before him, Padre Melanson found himself listening to an endless flow of stories and emotional outpourings: in 1990s jargon, critical incident stress experiences.

After being in the country for a short time, the soldiers discovered an orphanage which housed about five hundred displaced children of all ages. Most were sick, with diseases ranging from scabies to cholera. The soldiers, especially those who had children at home, were deeply moved and spent a lot of their off-duty time trying to help the orphans. Eventually, the regiment was supporting 2300 children in six orphanages, and a steady stream of medicine, blankets, school supplies, and clothes, dubbed Operation Skylink, was coming to Rwanda from all parts of Canada. In recognition of his excellent work in Rwanda, sometimes in the company of hostile forces, Melanson was awarded the meritorious service medal.

WAR IN THE FORMER YUGOSLAVIA

While Rwanda held its own special kind of horror, other appalling events were happening in the former Yugoslavia. Christopher Ryan, a United Church minister serving at Maitland pastoral charge near Truro, Nova Scotia, and a reservist with 33 Service Battalion, had a typical peacekeeping experience.

After four years in the Militia Ryan was sent to the former Yugoslavia to serve with the seven hundred and fifty-man strong Strathcona battle group at CANBAT 2 in Bosnia. Ryan lived in a tent erected on the third floor of an old industrial building in Visoko, a city that continually smelled of sewage just as Sarajevo smelled of burnt garbage.[20] The grey foreboding group of buildings was surrounded with razor wire and sandbags. Everywhere the soldiers went they had to go in threes and one person always had to be armed. Remembering the unpleasant smells of Bacovici hospital, a sombre Ryan commented on how important it was to retain a positive attitude. He worked in close co-operation with the Roman Catholic padre.

Among the responsibilities of the padres were re-deployment briefings. Often they amounted to a forty-five-minute talk led by soldiers who had been on previous United Nations tours. They were mandatory and were well received. As well, Ryan was called upon to conduct a critical incident stress debriefing after one of the soldiers was shot in the chest. For Ryan, this work with the members of the soldier's troop mirrored what good ministers have always done as a part of their calling.

After his return, Ryan reported:

I walked a Muslim and Croat trench line. These 'soldiers' are farmers, some of them old men. Friendly sorts, as are the Serbs. Much more grizzled looking than the average Padre, but seem to be good sorts none the less.

I do not understand this kind of war. Our guide on the Muslim lines is a forestry engineer. A pleasant man in his fifties who carries a gun and is prepared to kill.

How does one respond to finding an eight year old boy in a dumpster gathering food for his family?

I also spent a few nights at OP Romeo 4. This is on the Serb lines. We visited the Serbians in the afternoon. These people are exceptionally hospitable. They shared their Vivo and one of their women made supper for us. It is difficult to understand how they can be so kind to strangers and cruel to neighbours. Again, this is true of each of the warring factions.

I went on an overnight to checkpoint Papa. This is the checkpoint where the thirteen Canadians were held in December 93. In fact, one of the Serbs manning the checkpoint was involved in the incident. Again, he was a pleasant sort. I was shown their array of anti-tank mines, automatic weapons, rocket propelled grenades and 82 mm recoilless anti-tank weapons. The Serbian who showed me the rocket propelled grenade told me that it was good for tanks and cougars. He was joking. Although he was correct. They have no intention of using them against us."[21]

Ryan described his ministry as "a rare opportunity to share Christ's basic message free of denominational restrictions. What's important is what we are doing in this world as individuals. What happens in the next world is up to God."[22] And he was quoted in the September 1994 edition of the *United Church Observer*: "I believe we are fulfilling more than a mandate of a nation or United Nations, but of one who taught us, 'Greater love hath no man than this, that one lay down their life for their friends.' I could not be more proud of these ordinary men and women doing extraordinary work."[23]

Back when Padre Ryan had left for training at CFB Calgary, he wondered how his experiences overseas would be relevant to his pulpit in Canada. As he was preparing to return to Canada, he wrote: "Issues here are much more intense, so much so it is impossible to comprehend. If I am unable to grasp [their meaning] while I am here, how do I communicate this to my congregation? I have come to the conclusion that what I will take back from this place will not be knowledge or insight to educate minds but a new attitude, a new awareness of our blessing and God's Grace. Christ's Gospel is to be cherished and lived with joy."[24]

Later, Chaplain Barclay Mayo went to Bosnia with the Royal Canadian Dragoons, but was returned to Canada for medical reasons. The conflict continues at this time of writing, and chaplains continue to serve in support of Canadian soldiers.

1995 AND BEYOND

At the time of writing, in 1995, the Chaplain Service of the Canadian Forces is in the midst of change. In response to pressure from the military to downsize, senior Protestant and Roman Catholic chaplains have met to develope a strategic plan for the future. It was decided that when the two current chaplains general, the Protestant D.C. Estey and the Roman Catholic Roger Bazin, retired in 1995, they would be replaced by a single chaplain general, the Roman Catholic Jean Pelletier. The deputy chaplain general, and head of the Protestant chaplains would be Captain(N) G.R. Ives. This union at the very top will certainly establish a new way of "doing business" for the chaplains and would be the next chapter in the history of the organization.

As always, and quite apart from the activities in Ottawa, the chaplains, work continues at the "pit face." Canadian chaplains are still on duty in the former Yugoslavia and now in Haiti. Service persons, at home and abroad, continue to face loneliness, uncertainty, and danger. Families worry about the well-being of their loved ones serving in the conflict zones of the world. As much now as ever before, good chaplains and the services that they offer are needed and appreciated by Canadian Forces personnel and their families.

APPENDIX I
ON BEING A PADRE WITH 27th BRIGADE: EXCERPT
J.A. Davidson

After appropriate salutations and personal references, Davidson wrote:

We very definitely are priests and ministers actively engaged in our vocation. A lot of people, including some who should know better, have rather silly ideas about what a padre is and what a padre does. They tend to think of him as merely a miscellaneous welfare worker who wears a funny collar and goes about being jolly at people ...

We aren't looked upon as welfare odd-job men.[1] Most of the welfare jobs we are called upon to do are those which generally we can do better than anyone else simply because we are priests and ministers. And the army isn't trying to make soldiers of us either. Although we do wear badges of military rank on our shoulders, the badge which indicates our real place in the scheme of things is found around our necks. We have no power of command, and one of the *Queen's Regulations for the Canadian Army* states that, "No chaplain shall be required to perform duties other than those pertaining to his calling." Of course, the pattern of our ministry in the army necessarily differs in many details from that of the normal parish ministry, but it is the same in most of the essentials.

I generally spend the first part of every morning in study and sermon preparation. Then I take advantage of the mid-morning coffee break. I am a sort of poor-man's Duncan Hines, and I have tried during the year to visit all the private coffee dives in the garrison ...

After coffee I go to my office for interviews. Most of the interviews are in the morning, but I do have them all hours. One morning a week I keep office hours with the 194 Infantry Workshop of the Royal Canadian Electrical and Mechanical Engineers, the unit which shares Chatham Barracks with the Highland Battalion.

Many of the interviews are with soldiers wishing to marry.[2] Most of the prospective wives are German girls, but a number are British girls the lads have met while on leave in the United Kingdom. A soldier must have official permission to marry a girl who is not a Canadian citizen. Ordinarily there is a five month waiting period from the date of application until the marriage can take place. During that period the prospective wife is examined by the Canadian Immigration Mission, and she must be certified as eligible for entry to Canada on a permanent basis before official permission to marry is given.

Every soldier making application for permission to marry must be interviewed by his chaplain. Frequently the fiancees are interviewed too. The chaplain's position here is in loco parentis ... I am occasionally reminded of Stephen Leacock's quip: "Many a man in love with a dimple makes the mistake of marrying the whole girl." But most of the lads are quite sensible in their approach to marriage, and some splendid young brides will be going to Canada shortly.

Some of the interviews are with married soldiers who have problems peculiar to the married. There are a few cases of estrangement and separation ... Some of the problems are financial, such as unexpected expenses because of family sickness—I know a bit about that myself.

There have been days when I had so many interviews with single men wishing to be married and with married men with problems that I feel that I could have done at college with less Palestinian Archaeology and play-by-play accounts of the Reformation and with more on Christian Marriage and Marriage Counselling. This is a field in which the chaplain can make one of his most significant pastoral contributions.

I think that a minister has no task more important than the leading of his people in the public worship of God. Almost once a month we have a Church parade at which attendance is compulsory, but most of the services are "voluntary."[3]

The service normally lasts the best part of an hour—and no one has yet complained that it is too long. We follow the order of service in the *Divine Service Book*, the book used by Protestants in all three services. The order of service is simple and reasonably flexible, and it seems to me most suitable for use in a congregation consisting of people from a number of denominations. The service is very definitely "church." One Sunday a young soldier, after attending a service for the first time, said to me, "Padre, I liked that. It was just like going to church." I knew what he was trying to say, so I smiled and asked him to come again. He did.

For music we have an "Organ, Field, Portable," a small folding harmonium of outrageously defiant character. On most Sundays the commanding officer, Lieutenant Colonel Harry Parker, plays it. Somehow,—perhaps it is intimidated by rank—he manages to dominate the thing and get good music out of it. It means something to the lads that "the old man" plays the organ for them, and they do sing ...

Some Sundays we have a few wives and children at the service.[4] When children are present I tell them a story. One Sunday I told a simple little story about tongues—the frog's tongue, the giraffe's tongue, the kitten's tongue, the little-boy's-and-girl's tongues—you know the kind of thing. I finished by saying, "And God would like you to know just what kind of tongue you have." Immediately four year old Lynn MacAlpine said in that clear, shrill, serious, penetrating voice of all small girls, "And I'd like to know just what kind of tongue God has, too." ...

As I preach I can look out a chapel window and see big trucks rumbling by on the Ruhr-Berlin Autobahn which skirts Hanover right past our barracks. Less than forty miles along that great highway is the Iron Curtain. It is not easy to preach here; it is like preaching on the edge of a volcano. So much of what I might say from a pulpit back home seems utterly irrelevant here. This is not the place for be-happy-though-human pep talks, nor for what in Scotland they call "a cauld clatter o' morality," nor for the practice of the fine art of calling spades by more genteel names. We have to dig deep, and get right down to the fundamental simplicities. We have all found that the lads can make a surprising response to the deep things of the faith.

Occasionally at Sunday lunch some of the officer members of the congregation will dissect the sermon with alarming skill. They merciously [sic]lay bare all my fallacies and sentimentalities. And they tear me to shreds if I am the least bit pompous in my preaching. The men in the canteens don't spare me either, and they can ask the most searching questions. The whole thing was a humbling discipline for me, but an instructive one ...

During the year a number of the men of the brigade have attended short courses at a British Army Church House at Verden, about fifty miles from here. In October we took over the Church House for four days, and ran an all-Canadian confirmation and communicants course on behalf of several of the Canadian Churches. We had about thirty students, ranging in rank from private up to major. They were a keen, enthusiastic lot, and it was a joy to work with them. There is nothing spectacular to report, but as a result of the courses the names of some very fine young men will be added to the Church roles in Canada. A few of the lads here have even been considering offering themselves as candidates for ministry.

Much of our pastoral ministry falls into the traditional pattern. Sometimes we are called upon to break the news of the death or serious illness of a loved one to a soldier, and then do what we can to comfort him in his sorrow and worry. Occasionally we have to minister to the dangerously ill and the dying. And we have our regular ministry by visitation with Canadian patients in the hospitals.

Source: CGA, Davidson file, September 28,1953. By permission of the author.

---

1. Men's problems were first of all the concern of the regimental officer and the padre was only called in when his experience or judgement was needed. This meant that many of the routine matters were not seen by the chaplains. Dealing with the more severe cases and the problems which would come to them via the padre net from Canada left the chaplains feeling that they were doing more social work than a civilian pastor would expect to do.

2. The actual solemnization of the marriage in Germany was a civil ceremony in an office known as the Standesampt. This would be followed by a religious ceremony, normally held in the girl's home church. It was very rare for a Canadian chaplain to perform such a service.

3. At three garrison locations voluntary services were held at locations designated as chapel spaces. One chapel was in a former German cavalry stable, but the chaplain was quick to point out that a very important man in Christianity was born in a stable. Another chapel was in a barrack block which had an enormous bomb crater in the middle. In two other centres there were British chapels which Canadian chaplains were permitted to use: at Hanover detachments stationed with British troops in the Rhineland visited the British chapels as did movement control people in Hamburg and the Hook of Holland.

4. Some of the soldiers had brought families with them, but these were constantly on the move because of housing problems.

APPENDIX II
THE CHAPLAIN IN THE THEATRE OF ACTIVE OPERATIONS
R.C.G. Cunningham

A certain young man left his Parish in Nov 1950 to answer the call for chaplains to serve with 25 Cdn Inf Bde in Korea. The Army was new to him, and after being documented and outfitted, he was posted to 2 Bn RCR. In my mind, his reception to that battalion was historic. His CO said, "George, you are my spiritual Staff Officer," and went on to request that he make a point of seeing him at least once a day. "If you have anything on your mind concerning the unit," he said, "bring it up. If you haven't, come and see me anyway." I doubt if this would have happened in 1939. But this is our heritage from our brethren who served from 1939-1945, and who left their mark indelibly on the Canadian Army.

The Royal Canadian Army Chaplain Corps has an important part to play in our Army of today, and its vital importance to the life of the Army is readily recognized and acknowledged.

Today let us consider something of the Army Chaplain's role in the Theatre of Active Operations. The ideal situation is of course to have a chaplain serving one unit, which becomes his "home". But our Army has in it many small units which must be served, and consequently the average chaplain may find that he has a widely scattered "flock". It is inevitable that most of his time will be spent with the largest formation, but the others must not be forgotten. This frequently involves a great deal of travel simply to carry out normal Sunday Services.

No doubt many a Padre has felt at times that somewhere in the motto of the Corps should be included the word "UBIQUE".

But now let us consider the role of the chaplain around this framework—The Padre—Priest, Prophet and Person.

PRIEST

1. CHURCH SERVICES AND SACRAMENTS
Perhaps the primary task of any Chaplain, even as that of a civilian Clergyman, is the providing of an opportunity for organized worship, where the great truths of the gospel are presented in an atmosphere of reverence and worship. Equally important is his responsibility to see that the sacraments of the Church are administered.
(a) Opportunities for Services
    (i) In training areas, concentration areas or rest areas, the Sunday Service should be an event of real importance. The time and place being decided upon, the administrative details should be left to the Adjutant, and his staff. Whenever possible organize a choir. Every chaplain is now equipped with a portable organ, and every unit has talent. Men love to sing, and if you are fortunate enough to have someone in your unit who plays well, and most units have, leave the choir in his hands. Any effort along this line is indeed rewarding. The atmosphere of worship, such as comes in the quiet beauty and dignity of our churches, is often hard to attain in the humdrum of a military

encampment, but the touch of music created by men's voices, more than anything I know, can, in these circumstances, provide a fit setting for worship. So make your Sunday Service the big event of the week.

(ii) As services are now largely voluntary, the good will of commanders is most helpful for good attendance. One Company Commander was quite convinced that all his men needed a Church Service. So lining up his Company, he informed them that services were entirely voluntary—"You can either attend RC Service, Protestant Service or pick up rocks." That Sunday there was a full turnout from his Company. And even though the Commanding Officer took the Company Commander to task for the slightly irregular methods he employed, in subsequent services his Company was well represented because he concerned himself with the services, he attended himself, and he expected his officers to set the example with their attendance. In Church attendance as in all else, men follow good leaders. It seemed only fitting that this Company which consistently provided the best turnout for Sunday services should also prove itself outstanding in action.

(iii) It is a good idea never to lose sight of the injunction "where one or two are gathered together in my name there will I be also." In the small group the Padre is on his mettle. He is not preaching to a congregation, he is talking very intimately to individuals. I suppose all of us know how good it feels to have someone compliment us on a well preached sermon, but one soon learns it is a shallow feeling compared to the one following a soldier's, "Thank you, Sir."

These Services with small groups mean much on the rare occasion when the men themselves request the service. One Sunday I was walking among the men of a Company which had just been drawn back into the shelter of a hill after hard fighting and several casualties. They were sitting around drying out socks and boots, cleaning up, and heating "C" rations. One of them asked,

"What day is it, Sir?"

"Sunday"

"Are we going to have a Service?"

"Do you want one?"

"Yes, Sir"

In a few minutes about thirty-five were gathered in a tight group. Our cathedral was the great outdoors, our choir the noises of battle, our altar the sod, but the spirit of worship was upon us.

(iv) And then again the days of the week mean little. A Sunday Service is missed because of the uncertainty of making plans during action. But every day is Sunday and you pick up your services when and where you can.

(v) When you have services, and the soldiers of other nations are in the area, send them the invitation to worship with you. Particularly in the case of United States soldiers, the response to the invitations we extended was excellent, and those who attended seemed sincerely appreciative for the opportunity to worship.

(b) Preaching Material

Here I can only speak from personal experience. At first I approached this task of preaching with the attitude that I should seize upon the many lessons of soldiering and war which can be applied to the equally important Christian warfare we are continually waging. Certainly there is no lack of material here. But it wasn't long before I felt strongly that this was not what was needed. There was too much soldiering every day. What the men wanted, I felt, was the oasis in the wilderness, the cool shade in the heat of the day, the words of comfort and hope. And so my sermons became the stories of God's love revealed in Christ and the challenge to better living in the light of this love. What the overall effect of this was I'll never know, but this was the preaching that felt right to me. In any event several weeks ago a Corporal who had served with us came to me and said, "Sir, do you remember a service you held in Korea last spring in a tent on the side of the road?" I couldn't recall it, but he continued, "the things you said bothered me for a long time, but they helped me, and I wanted you to know they helped."

2. CASUALTIES AND FUNERALS

(a) Wounded

During action the chaplain should try to make the R[egimental] A[id] P[ost] his headquarters, where he can see the casualties as they pass through. This is probably the place where he can be the greatest help. While there will no doubt be occasions when he will take the end of a stretcher and help bring out the wounded, let him remember that a chaplain is not always easily replaced, and his responsibility is to the whole battalion. In addition to his attendance on casualties in the RAP, wherever possible the chaplain should seize every opportunity to visit the various components of the Field Ambulance, and any Hospitals which might be within easy access.

(b) Burials

(i) Canadian Way—Most of you are fairly familiar with this method, and briefly it is this: The Divisional Chaplain will recce a spot for his Divisional Cemetery and all chaplains will be notified of its location. Bodies will be collected and buried there. The chaplain sees that personal effects are removed from the body, identity carefully checked, part of identification tag removed, body wrapped in a blanket and necessary forms completed. The battalion will provide a burial party and, whenever feasible, a firing party, and the casualty will be buried in the Divisional Cemetery by the chaplain. The Engineers or Pioneer Platoon will provide a grave marker in the form of a cross, which bears the number, rank, name, unit and date and cause of death. In the event it is impossible to evacuate the casualty to the Divisional Cemetery, and he must be buried where he fell, the same procedure is carried out as far as possible. However, in addition a very careful map reference of the spot is taken and a careful sketch of the location is made in order that later the body may be recovered and re-buried in a permanent cemetery.

(ii) American Way—As we were fighting under American Command in Korea, it was necessary to conform to their methods in the matter of burials. According to their instructions nothing was to be removed from the body.

267

Identification was very careful, then the body was wrapped in a blanket and tagged with all particulars. The Graves Registration Unit set up casualty points, and our dead were evacuated to these points. From there they were removed to the United Nations Cemetery at Tanggok near Pusan where they were given burial by RC, and Protestant or Jewish chaplain as their religion required. Unit Chaplains did no burying, but could if desired, hold short services over the casualties before they were evacuated. We made one change in procedure on advice of the Casualty Collecting Point Staff. We removed all personal effects from the bodies. It was the unfortunate experience that with the bodies receiving so much handling, anything of value rarely reached Pusan. These personal effects we turned in to our Orderly Room, which in turn passed them to the Quartermaster for parcelling and forwarding to the next-of-kin. On occasions when no Casualty Collecting Point was in the immediate area, bodies were evacuated to the Ration Point. It was the consensus of opinion among the chaplains of the British Commonwealth Brigade, with whom I had occasion to confer on this matter, that it was a cold, impersonal method, and one which would not be voluntarily chosen. However we were under direct command of the US 8th Army, and this was the method they laid down.

(c) Letters of Condolence

This is one of the most difficult yet most important aspects of the chaplain's work. Perhaps one or two points on this matter will suffice.

(i) Try to avoid the stereotyped letter. It is so easy to be lazy and grind out all the letters on the same pattern with the same trite phrases, changing only the name. If you are not too familiar with the casualty, before you write, talk to his Company Commander, his Platoon Commander, his friends, and form a picture of the boy. Don't delay in these letters but turn them in to your Orderly Room at once.

(ii) Give an accurate account of the death, i.e., how and where he died, if death was from wounds, where he was treated, and finally, where he was buried. Very often the Padre's letter is the only detailed account the next-of-kin ever have.

(iii) Tell the exact circumstances of the death, even if you feel that a little change might soften the blow. If you don't conflicting reports may reach the next-of-kin, and much confusion and heartache result. We had a few tragic deaths in our battalion as a result of drinking "canned heat". The two letters which it became my task to write were extremely difficult, but I told exactly the circumstances of each death. One of the wives sent me a note of thanks. It was the first accurate account she had received. The official notification had been very vague, and beyond this she had only rumours. Once she knew the truth she could face the future and not be thrown off balance by some disconcerting turn of events, such as the refusal of the government to grant pension.

(iv) Finally, if at all possible, include a personal touch, for these letters become the treasured possessions of wives, mothers and families.

3. PADRE'S HOURS

(a) Padre's Hours are the rare privilege of the Unit Chaplain. In them he has the opportunity for an hour of purely religious instruction. On active operations, the greatest difficulty is trying to fit in these periods. Ideally one such hour is made available to every man weekly, but invariably, because of the exigencies of the service, this is impossible. So the chaplain must seize opportunities for these hours when and where they present themselves. When the unit is employed in a tactical role, Padre's Hours as a formal thing must of necessity be forgotten. Then, however, visits among the troops provide an acceptable substitute.

(b) Material for use in such Hours as are possible is not difficult to find. Topics come up as the result of troops visitation and frequently are suggested by religious problems encountered in personal contacts with the men.

4. CHURCH MEMBERSHIP CLASSES AND RETREATS

Usually these are arranged on at least a Brigade basis in order that chaplains from as many different denominations as possible may take part. This means that a man may receive instruction from a Minister of his own church and either confirmation, reception into full membership, or baptism, as the case may be made available to him. Last summer arrangements were made in Korea for a Retreat to be held for any soldiers of 25 Cdn Inf Bde, who wished to take instruction leading to Church Membership, or who wished simply to enjoy the fellowship of a week spent in study, worship and recreation. [Private Jim MacIntosh, later Padre MacIntosh, was one of the young men who attended the church membership instruction.] It was proposed that a camp lasting roughly a week be organized, where the men interested could live together in an atmosphere conducive to worship and spiritual refreshment. But once again the demands of war interposed themselves, and the plans for the retreat were temporarily set aside. But I understand that at a later date these plans were revived and put into action, a very successful Retreat being the result.

PROPHET

There are occasions when the need arises in every battalion for an Amos or a Nathan. The chaplain must be the voice of conscience for his battalion. Often it seems that he stands quite alone even as Elisha when he said, "And I, even I only am left," but he must speak out.

1. MORAL ISSUES

(a) Profanity—Profanity is often the first indication we have of a relaxation on the part of the individual of his moral alertness. In many quarters it is argued that profanity is merely a habit and means nothing, or else it is a safety valve through which the individual releases the built up pressures of emotion and thereby safeguards himself against hasty or ill-advised action. Be that as it may, profanity that takes the form of vile, rotten filth, all too often coupled with the blasphemous use of our Saviour's name, is a cancerous sore in the soul of any man. The person who gives expression habitually to such profanity cannot by any stretch of the imagination be considered to possess a healthy soul. During war, when a man does not come immediately under the restraining influence of our social conventions, the voice of conscience is often faint and the profane tongue is heard all too loudly

269

and frequently. Then it is that the Padre must speak plainly and unmistakably against this threat to man's moral integrity.

(b) Drunkenness—All the arguments against drunkenness, with which you are quite familiar, hold equally true in the case of the soldier on active service. The statement of LCol J.R. Stone, DSO, MC, of 2 Princess Patricia Canadian Light Infantry in Korea, that, "while he enjoyed his drink as well as the next man, if he had his way no liquor would be allowed the troops in Korea," is worthy of note. Anyone who has had lengthy connection with the Army knows that drink is at the bottom of an extremely high percentage of all the trouble into which soldiers seem prone to stumble. Let it suffice to say that anything which continually leads soldiers into trouble and often tragedy must necessarily be classed as evil, and must be actively opposed. Here again the Padre must speak out.

(c) Venereal Disease—This, like the poor, we seem to have with us always. There is no question but that every chaplain does speak out against this evil. But let the Padre remember—it is the Medical Officer who approaches this question from the standpoint of health, and who speaks of precautions to be taken; it is the Regimental Officer who approaches this question from the standpoint of impaired efficiency and lost man hours; but it is the Padre who must approach this question from the standpoint of morality. For this is a question which ultimately resolves itself into one of right and wrong, of marriage vows, of moral laws, of spiritual values.

2. INTOLERANCE

Fortunately Canadians are not prone to racial prejudice, yet on occasion there is evidenced marked racial intolerance and national vanity. However this is largely the result of a distorted sense of values which would equate civilization with refrigerators, chesterfields, cars, washing machines and indoor plumbing, but fails to recognize that possession of such luxuries must always be secondary to personality and strength of character as the yardstick for human appraisal. Jesus asked His hearers "Why beholdest thou the mote that is in thy brother's eye, but considerest not the beam that is in thine own eye?" Again it is necessary for the Padre to speak out, but let it be with kindness and understanding, for these faults are largely the results of the "sins of omission", not of the soldier himself, but of the society which has produced him.

3. MAN MANAGEMENT

The Padre stands in a peculiar position in a unit, as he is accepted by all ranks more or less equally. Perhaps no one has the opportunity of observing the Unit quite so impartially. Certainly no one else is in the position where he shares the confidences of both officers and men. It is not unusual for him to discover causes of friction between men and NCOs or officers. On occasion a word spoken in private can indicate where a change might be made for better man-management and leadership. As advice is not always readily accepted, it may be that the Padre must have recourse to plain and pointed language.

PERSON

The Padre stands in a unique position within a unit on active operations. Nowhere is the burden of the Church heavier on a minister's shoulders and heart. He is the lone representative of the church among some eight hundred men. To the soldier he is Church, Minister, Session, Sunday School, Young People's Society or whatever aspect of Church life may have touched him. He stands alone with his tremendous responsibility. But not quite alone—there is another—and he needs to call on those infinite resources of strength and courage made available to him in Christ.

How he stands in the eyes of his men will largely determine the attitude of many towards church and religion in later years. Here in the most real sense his sermons are not his words, but his day by day living—his attitudes, his conduct, his understanding, his example of Christian living.

We all realize that there is an attitude among many soldiers, more marked in some cases than others, that conditions of warfare ease the restraining force of our conventions. In a lesser degree there may be times when a Padre feels that being away from his Women's Associations and other seemingly confining and restricting agencies in the Pastorate, he may relax his guard. But he must not, for it is absolutely essential that he continue to "produce" as a Minister.

He is in an envied position in-so-far as his opportunity of access to the hearts of men is concerned. But it lies in his own person—how he stands in the eyes of his men—whether he is able to seize this opportunity. He must carry in his person unswerving loyalty to Jesus Christ.

(a) The Padre's Relationship with Officers

May he never forget that not only men but officers are equally in need of a Padre. His ministry is not a cloak to be worn with the man and thrown aside within the Officers' Mess. What a tragedy on a Sunday Morning the chaplain has preached a particularly poor and uninspiring sermon, to hear officers remarking, "Padre's hangover must be too much for him today".

Let the Padre never lose sight of the fact that his first enlistment is in the service of Christ—a service which demands that he be "On Parade" at all times.

(b) The Padre's Relationship with Men

(i) It is well for the Padre to remember that he is not a welfare officer, he is not an economic or social expert, he is not a second paymaster. His first concern is the spiritual welfare of the unit.

(ii) He should seek to be a good fellow, but with reservations. This attempt to be a good fellow should not over-reach itself to the extent that it jeopardizes his position with the men. For example, he will be invited on occasion to attend Company or Platoon parties. Perhaps the temptation to be "one of the boys" will be strong—to take just a small drink—perhaps to tell an off colour story. Should he let down, he may receive a momentary acclaim, and enjoy a fleeting sense of easy natural relations with the men—but in the long run his effectiveness has been impaired and the task of succeeding chaplains to that unit made more difficult.

A soldier wants to look up to the Padre. Certainly the Padre is given more than ordinary opportunity to touch the inner life of men. As has been pointed out before, in the Padre's Hour he has an enviable opportunity for talk of the most intimate nature. These are moments too precious to be held lightly. A common meeting ground must be sought, but not by the Padre compromising his position. The man must come into his territory. He must be met on the Padre's terms. If these terms, by virtue of making too great demands on the soldier's spiritual resources, render the way impassable for him, then the immediate problem is to find a way into the Padre's territory over which, with the Padre's help, he is able to travel. Perhaps a natural impulse is to go down to the man's level of spiritual perception. But what damage has been done the cause of the Church on the rare occasion which a chaplain has compromised his position, will never be known. Certainly the soldier who told of a Padre's talk on the subject of a soldier's relationship with women—a talk full of suggestive innuendo and double talk—made no effort to conceal his disgust for the Padre, or his obvious concern over the completely unacceptable way in which the Padre represented his Church. Because of a momentary lapse, much of this chaplain's future ministry was rendered ineffective.

Finally the Padre should not try to be a good fellow if it throws him out of character. Never forget that everyone is not a hail fellow well met, and he will be accepted and loved for his own qualities.

(iii) The Padre should make a definite effort to familiarize himself with every possible aspect of his unit's life. Let him learn its make-up, its task, the way the men must think, act and live. To be an effective minister, the Padre must identify himself with his men—their problems, their fears, their hopes, their joys. But let him do this naturally and not consider it an event every time he does something with the men, e.g., go on a march with them, eat a meal with them. There comes to mind the Padre who, not having concerned himself particularly with the training of his unit, picked up the persistent rumour that the battalion was soon to see action. At this time the battalion was taking part, in a driving rain, in an exercise which made harsh physical demands on the men. Late in the evening orders came for the battalion to bed down. Exhausted after a long arduous march, the men curled up in the wet to sleep with such protection and comfort as a gas-cape provided. Into this situation arrived the Padre in his truck, complete with batman, tent, sleeping bag, bed and various other comforts. The batman set up the gear and in a loud voice the Padre announced to all and sundry that he thought he should get used to "roughing it", crawled into his warm sleeping bag, which, to the wet shivering soldiers represented warmth and comfort to an undreamed of degree, and proceeded to enjoy the same hardships he would have endured had he remained in his billets. The ensuing remarks are unfit for publication.

(iv) Let the Padre never forget that he is concerned with the whole life of a unit. With this in mind, he should studiously avoid becoming deeply involved in minor aspects of the work at the expense of the whole work, e.g., sport, canteens, relief among refugees, and many other good causes. It is a true saying "The good is often the enemy of the best."

(v) Finally let the Padre love his men and above all be kind. Let him care for them. Let him not become like the Padre who was known in his unit as "Burying Sam". Daily he visited each Company with the stock question, "Anyone to be buried today?" This seemed to be the extent of his ministry.

But a Padre needs to be careful. He is only flesh and blood. He cannot suffer each wound vicariously, or break his heart with each death. It is a harsh saying but true "let the dead bury the dead", his task is with the living.

But so much for advice, this paper has contained too much of it. In the final analysis the Padre will not go far wrong in any aspect of his work if he but humbly say to himself, "I stand before these men as the personal representative of Jesus Christ, and with God's help I will be true to my calling."

Source: CGA, Cunningham file.

APPENDIX III
Canadian Council of Churches Chaplaincy Committee Members, 1946-1995

ANGLICAN
1946-1953	Canon C.J. Stuart (represented by Canon W.W. Judd in 1946 and 1949)
1951-1968	Bishop I.A. Norris (chair 1961-1963 and 1966-1968)
1969-1970	Bishop J.O. Anderson
1970	Archbishop H.H. Clark (also at a meeting in 1977)
1970-1977	Bishop H.F. Appleyard (chair 1975-1976)
1977-1980	Archbishop G.F. Jackson
1980-1986	Archbishop R.L. Seaborn (chair 1985)
1986-1990	Bishop J. Clarke
1990-	Bishop R. Hatton (chair 1992-1995)

BAPTIST
1946-1950	Dr. H.H.Bingham (chair 1946-1949)
	temporarily replaced by Dr. T.B. McDormand in 1950
1950-1982	Dr. R.F. Sneyd (chair 1959-1961; secretary 1967-1982)
1966-1976	Dr. E.J. Bailey (chair 1968-1971)
1976-1983	Dr. H.A. MacLeod (chair 1980-1982)
1984-1990	Dr. W.C. Harvey (chair 1986-1988)
1992-	The Rev. J. Mills (chair 1995-)

LUTHERAN
1953-1977	The Rev. P.W.H. Eydt (chair 1971-1973)
1978-1986	The Rev. L.C. Gilbertson (chair 1984)
1987-1992	The Rev. L. Likeness (chair 1991-1992)
1992-	The Rev. J. Von Schmeling

PRESBYTERIAN
1946-1947	Dr. W. Barclay
1948-1954	The Rev. C.K. Nicoll
1954-1960	Dr. J.G. Murdock
1960-1964	Dr. D.P. Rowland (chair 1965, died before appointment)
1965-1970	Dr. J. Logan-Vencta
1971-1974	Dr. E.G.B. Foote
1975-1978	Dr. R. Cameron
1979-1984	Dr. C.H. MacLean (chair 1982-1984)
1986-1990	The Rev. L. Sams (Chair 1989-1990)
1990-	The Rev. J.P. Jones

UNITED CHURCH OF CANADA
1946-1959	Dr. W. Harold Young (chair 1950-1959)
1959	Dr. E.E. Long
1959-1968	Dr. T.R. Davies (chair 1963-1965)

1968-1975	Dr. W. Rodger (chair 1973-1975)
1975-1980	Dr. J.A. Davidson (chair 1976-1980)
1980-1983	Dr. J.A.O. McKennitt
1983-1987	The Rev. S.M. Parkhouse
1988-1990	The Rev. C.E. MacCara
1992-	The Rev. J. Barr

CANADIAN COUNCIL OF CHURCHES REPRESENTATIVE

1947-1964	Dr. W.J. Gallagher
1964-1967	Dr. W.F. Butcher
1969-1975	Dr. F. Honey
1976-1989	Dr. D.W. Anderson
1989-1992	Dr. S. Brown
1994-	Dr. D. Oliver

APPENDIX IV - THE SENIOR CHAPLAINS TEAM 1945-1995

1945-54	R.M. Frayne	E.G.B. Foote	C. Stone	
1954-55	E.G.B. Foote	C. Stone	F.W. MacLean	
1955-59	E.G.B. Foote	J.W. Forth	F.W. MacLean	
1959-60	J.W. Forth	F.W. MacLean	E.G.B. Foote	J.P. Browne
1960-61	F.W. MacLean	E.G.B. Foote	J.P. Browne	E.S. Light
1961-62	F.W. MacLean	E.G.B. Foote	E.S. Light	H.A. Merklinger
1962-63	F.W. MacLean	E.G.B. Foote	E.S. Light	J.P. Browne
1963-64	E.G.B. Foote	H. Ploughman	J.P. Browne	E.S. Light
1964	E.G.B. Foote	H. Ploughman	J.R. Millar	E.S. Light
1964-65	E.S. Light	J.R. Millar	E.G.B. Foote	
1965-66	E.S. Light	J.R. Millar	E.G.B. Foote	C.H. MacLean
1966-67	E.S. Light	J.R. Millar	C.H. MacLean	H.A. Merklinger
1967	E.S. Light	J.R. Millar	C.H. MacLean	W. Rodger
1967-68	E.S. Light	J. Cardy	P.D. Ross	
1968	E.S. Light	J. Cardy	P.D. Ross	E. Sigston
1968-69	J. Cardy	P.D. Ross	E. Sigston	R.G.C. Cunningham
1969-70	J. Cardy	P.D. Ross	R.G.C. Cunningham	J.N. Bracher
1970-71	J. Cardy	R.G.C. Cunningham	C.D. Nickerson	J.N. Bracher
1971-72	J. Cardy	C.D. Nickerson	J.N. Bracher	
1972-73	J. Cardy	R.G.C. Cunningham	C.D. Nickerson	
1973-74	J. Cardy	R.G.C. Cunningham	C.D. Nickerson	S.M. Parkhouse
1974-76	R.G.C. Cunningham	C.D. Nickerson	S.M. Parkhouse	
1976-78	C.D. Nickerson	S.M. Parkhouse	O.A. Hopkins	C.E. MacCara
1978-81	S.M. Parkhouse	O.A. Hopkins	C.E. MacCara	E.V. Porrior
1981-83	O.A. Hopkins	C.E. MacCara	E.V. Porrior	J. MacIntosh
1983-84	O.A. Hopkins	C.E. MacCara	E.V. Porrior	R.S. Wood
1984-87	C.E. MacCara	S.H. Clarke	D.C. Estey	G.D. Prowse
1987-88	S.H. Clarke	D.C. Estey	G.D. Prowse	F.W. Love
1988-90	S.H. Clarke	D.C. Estey	G.R. Ives	F.W. Love
1990-92	D.C. Estey	G.R. Ives	G.G. Davidson	G.E. Peddle
1992-94	D.C. Estey	G.R. Ives	G.G. Davidson	W.J. Fairlie
1994-95	D.C. Estey	G.R. Ives	W.J. Fairlie	
1995	G.R. Ives	G.E. Peddle	W.J. Fairlie	

APPENDIX V
Regular Force Protestant Chaplains, 1945-1995

Name	Rank	Denom	Service Term		Remarks*
Adams J.B.	Maj	UCC	Army	1953-68	
Alcock R.N.	Capt	ACC	CF	1981-85	Class C call out
Alexander J.A.	Maj	Bapt	CF	1977-96	
Alfred A.J.	Maj	UCC	Army	1952-65	British army 1939-41; RCA 1941-45
Alston H.J.	Capt	UCC	CF	1983-87	
Anderson D.R.	Maj	UCC	Army	1948-62	RCA chaplain 1942-46
Anderson J.M.	LCol	Pres	Army	1948-68	MC and Bar; RCA chaplain 1942-47
Archer W.	Maj	UCC	RCAF	1953-79	
Baker R.E.	Maj	Pres	CF	1977-	
Barclay L.T.	Maj	Pres	RCAF	1962-81	British Home Guard 1942-44; RAF 1944-47
Barnett J.	LCol	ACC	Army	1940-61	
Bartlett H.M.	Capt	UCC	CF	1981-85	Class C call out
Bartlett R.M.	Maj	UCC	RCAF	1959-74	RCAF 1942-45
Barwise D.	Maj	UCC	CF	1985-92	
Batty W.K.R.	S/L	Bapt	RCAF	1942-58	
Bell G.R.	LCdr	Bapt	RCN	1954-71	
Bell J.C.	Capt	Bapt	RCAF	1965-70	
Benner K.D.	LCol	UCC	CF	1966-87	OMM; RCN Reserve 1952-66
Beveridge J.M.W.	Maj	UCC	RCAF	1951-70	
Bezanson L.H.L.	Capt	ACC	CF	1984-	break in service 1991-93
Bickley G.F.	LCol	UCC	Army	1950-68	
Bill H.	Capt	UCC	RCAF	1957-71	
Bingham M.M.	F/L	ACC	RCAF	1955-64	RCA 1941-43; RCAF 1943-45
Bingham W.J.	LCdr	Bapt	RCN	1957-72	
Blaber K.R.J.	Capt	ACC	CF	1981-83	Class C call out
Black C.S.	LCdr	ACC	RCN	1966-87	
Blair D.R.	Maj	UCC	Army	1967-87	
Blizzard T.W.	Capt	ACC	CF	1984-88	
Bokovay W.K.	Capt	Bapt	CF	1995-	
Bonham J.S.	S/L	UCC	RCA	1952-65	RCAF chaplain WWII
Bonney G.E.	F/L	Bapt	RCAF	1962-65	
Bracher J.N.	Col	ACC	RCAF	1949-73	
Brinn R.P.	Capt	UCC	CF	1987-	
Brown J.H.	Capt	ACC	CF	1985-90	reclassified to RC

Brown R.H.	Capt	UCC	RCAF	1963-80	
Browne J.P.	Col	UCC	Army	1940-63	MC
Bryce C.W.	F/L	ACC	RCAF	1956-67	
Butler M.G.	Maj	UCC	Army	1948-62	RCN 1944-46; RCNVR 1946-48
Butt F.C.	Capt	ACC	CF	1991-91	
Buxton W.W.	LCol	ACC	Army	1952-73	
Callaghan L.D.S.	Capt	UCC	CF	1988-	
Campbell C.A.	Capt	ACC	Army	1965-68	
Canning M.J.B.	Lt(N)	ACC	CF	1987-95	RESO 1982-83
Cardy J.	BGen	ACC	Army	1942-73	MC; 6th chaplain general
Carlson D.G.	F/L	Bapt	RCAF	1951-62	RCAF Chaplain 1941-45
Carney D.A.	Capt	ACC	CF	1984-87	British army chaplain 1981-84
Carson M.J.D.	LCol	UCC	Army	1940-63	
Chapman R.E.	LCdr	UCC	CF	1976-96	
Chapman W.G.	Maj	ACC	RCAF	1955-72	
Christie E.A.	F/L	UCC	RCAF	1955-68	
Christmas E.H.	LCol	ACC	RCAF	1954-73	
Clarke S.H.	B.Gen	ACC	Army	1960-90	OSJ; 12th chaplain general
Clifton L.E.M.	Maj	Pres	CF	1978-	
Coffin P.D.	Capt	ACC	CF	1988-92	
Cole M.G.	Capt	ACC	CF	1972-78	RAF 1953-57; RAF Reserve chaplain 1957-63; RAF chaplain 1963-68
Coleman H.R.	Maj	ACC	Army	1957-68	RCN 1942-45
Coleman L.R.	LCol	ACC	Army	1959-84	
Colley S.J.	Capt	ACC	RCAF	1957-68	
Collins P.A.Q.	Capt	Bapt	CF	1985-86	
Collison K.M.	F/L	ACC	RCAF	1953-56	
Condon R.P.	S/L	UCC	RCAF	1944-68	
Cook J.M.	Maj	UCC	Army	1965-85	
Cope R.B.	Capt	ACC	RCAF	1954-83	
Cosman D.I.	LCol	UCC	RCAF	1965-91	
Coutts J.F.	LCdr	UCC	RCN	1965-89	
Cox H.T.	LCol	UCC	RCAF	1954-77	RCAF 1940-45
Craig J.E.	Capt	Bapt	CF	1981-	
Crawley A.A.	Capt	Bapt	CF	1988-	
Croft A.M.	Capt	UCC	Army	1964-69	Reserve 1936-38, 1945-51; RCA 1940-45, 1951-64

Cudmore R.I.	LCdr	UCC	CF	1979-	
Cunningham R.G.C.	BGen	UCC	Army	1950-76	RCA 1940-44; 7th chaplain general
Currie R.A.F.	Maj	ACC	RCAF	1950-71	RCA 1940-46
Curties C.G.	Maj	UCC	CF	1967-81	
Daisley J.C.	Maj	ACC	Army	1952-64	RCA chaplain 1942-46
Dalton W.L.	Cl.2	UCC	RCN	1957-67	RCA 1943-46; RCA chaplain 1944-46
Darrach G.E.	LCol	UCC	Army	1950-66	Croix de guerre; RCA 1942-44; RCA chaplain 1944-46
Davidson D.D.	Capt	UCC	Army	1960-78	
Davidson G.G.	Col	UCC	Army	1966-95	
Davidson J.A.	Capt	UCC	Army	1952-61	RCA
Dawson L.A.	Capt	UCC	CF	1989-	RESO 1984-85; née Potts
Day P.G.	Capt	Bapt	CF	1987-96	
Dean D.G.L.	Capt	ACC	CF	1987-95	Reserve 1982-87
Dean J.H.	W/C	UCC	RCAF	1950-68	
DeLong F.P.	LCol	ACC	RCAF	1954-82	
Deobald R.K.	Capt	Luth	CF	1985-96	
De Wolfe White C.	Cl.2	ACC	RCN	1940-50	
Dickey D.K.	LCdr	UCC	RCN	1962-84	
Dignan L.A.	Capt	ACC	Army	1952-63	RCA 1939-45
Dingwell T.K.	Maj	UCC	CF	1984-	
Dobson R.H.	Maj	UCC	Army	1951-68	RCA 1942-45
Doig H.A.	Maj	Pres	Army	1950-64	RCA chaplain 1942-46
Docksey K.G.	Capt	ACC	Army	1953-57	
Dossett E.J.	Maj	ACC	Army	1951-63	RCA
Duncan J.W.D.	LCol	Bapt	Army	1940-61	MBE
Dunbar F.J.	Capt	Pres	Army	1954-57	
Dunn J.	W/C	Pres	RCAF	1942-63	Croix de guerre (palm);
Durnford R.C.H.	Maj	ACC	Army	1948-58	DSO; RCA chaplain, 1940-45
Durrett R.M.	Lt(N)	ACC	CF	1990-	Reserve 1987-90
Edwards I.R.	Cl.4	UCC	RCN	1942-63	
Eglisson E.	F/L	UCC	RCAF	1951-53	
Estey D.C.	BGen	UCC	RCAF	1965-95	OSJ; 13th chaplain general
Evans E.M.	Capt	ACC	Army	1951-52	
Fairlie W.J.	LCol	ACC	CF	1971-96	
Faraday A.G.	Cdr	Pres	RCN	1952-69	
Farmer J.F.	Maj	ACC	Army	1960-81	

Fee G.B.	LCol	ACC	RCAF	1942-68	
Fenske T.	Maj	UCC	RCN	1960-77	
Fillmore G.D.	Capt	Bapt	CF	1986-	
Filshie J.A.	Capt	UCC	Army	1951-57	MBE; RCA
Flath A.M.	LCol	Luth	RCAF	1965-89	
Fletcher J.M.	Capt	ACC	CF	1989-	ROTP
Foote E.G.B.	Cl.6	Pres	RCN	1941-66	OBE; 3rd chaplain general
Foote J.W.	Maj	Pres	Army	1939-48	VC
Ford J.F.S.	Maj	ACC	Army	1951-62	
Foreman S.R.	F/L	ACC	RCAF	1952-55	
Forth J.W.	BGen	ACC	Army	1940-59	MBE; 1st chaplain general
Fowke S.C.	Capt	UCC	CF	1971-85	
Fowler A.G.	Maj	UCC	CF	1971-96	OMM
Fralick A.J.	LCol	ACC	Army	1958-80	RCAF 1939-45; RCAF Reserve 1945-57
Fraser G.S.	Maj	UCC	Army	1948-59	RCA chaplain 1942-45
Frayne R.M.	G/C	UCC	RCAF	1940-53	
Friesen D.K.	Capt	ACC	CF	1985-	
Fry W.N.C.	LCdr	UCC	CF	1982-96	
Fuller D.H.T	Lt(N)	ACC	RCN	1956-73	RCNVR 1941-45
Funnell D.V.	Maj	UCC	CF	1978-	
Galbraith M.	S/L	UCC	RCAF	1952-64	RCAF 1941-45
Gans A.E.	Maj	ACC	CF	1978-92	US Army chaplain
Gardner R.M.	Maj	UCC	CF	1979-96	
Garrett B.	F/L	UCC	RCAF	1951-57	
Garrity K.J.	Capt	ACC	CF	1983-86	Reserve 1959-83
Gaudin G.A.	Lt(N)	UCC	CF	1985-89	
Gilbert E.W.S.	W/C	ACC	RCAF	1943-63	
Gilbert R.E.	Maj	ACC	CF	1982-89	
Gillard B.R.	Lt(N)	ACC	CF	1982-88	
Gillard G.L.	Cl.4	UCC	RCN	1941-57	MBE
Gillard R.P.T.	Capt	ACC	Army	1965-67	
Godfrey F.H.	Cl.4	ACC	RCN	1942-64	
Goforth J.F.	LCol	Pres	Army	1940-61	MC
Goldie J.K.	S/L	UCC	RCAF	1953-69	DFC; RCAF 1940-45
Gordon J.D.	Capt	Pres	Army	1956-58	
Gordon J.P.	Capt	Bapt	Army	1951-61	RCA chaplain 1940-45
Graham W.J.	Maj	Pres	RCAF	1962-79	RCAF Reserve 1943-45, 1950-53; RCAF Auxiliary 1953-62
Greatrex W.R.	Cl.2	ACC	RCN	1963-66	
Guntley V.C.	Capt	ACC	CF	1984-95	
Guzzwell D.E.	Lt(N)	UCC	CF	1983-92	

Hall J.B.	F/L	ACC	RCAF	1957-59	
Hanna, S.J.	Capt	ACC	Army	1963-67	
Hansen D.C.	Capt	Luth	CF	1989-92	
Harding C.L.	S/L	ACC	RCAF	1948-58	RCAF chaplain 1943-46
Hare H.I.	LCdr	UCC	RCN	1955-79	
Harkness B.A.	Capt	Bapt	CF	1991-92	
Harvey F.J.	Capt	ACC	CF	1993-	
Hatfield D.A.	LCol	ACC	RCN	1964-83	Class C call out 1983-85
Hatton G.A.	Maj	ACC	Army	1950-61	RCA chaplain 1942-46
Hedley-Smith G.	LCol	ACC	Army	1950-73	
Henstock R.C.	S/L	ACC	RCAF	1949-49	RCAF chaplain 1942-46
Hewitt W.C.	S/L	ACC	RCAF	1951-63	RCAF 1940-46
Hicks B.C.A.	Capt	ACC	CF	1991-	CF Reserve 1987-91
Hobbs W.E.	Capt	ACC	Army	1953-56	
Holobow M.M.	Maj	Luth	RCAF	1957-81	RCAF 1944-45; RCAF Reserve 1947-49; RCAF Auxiliary 1949-54
Hongisto H.O.	Capt	UCC	RCAF	1958-70	
Hopkins O.A.	BGen	ACC	Army	1953-84	OMM, OSJ; 10th chaplain general
Hopkins S.G.	Maj	Bapt	CF	1973-	
Horne S.G.	Maj	ACC	Army	1956-80	Class C call out 1984-5
House K.W.	S/L	Pres	RCAF	1948-62	RCAF chaplain 1941-45
Howie W.L.	LCdr	UCC	RCN	1962-82	
Howson J.D.L.	Maj	Pres	Army	1951-58	RCN chaplain 1944-45
Howson R.H.	S/L	ACC	RCAF	1954-69	
Humble R.C.	Lt(N)	UCC	CF	1987-	
Irwin E.C.	Capt	ACC	RCAF	1962-83	
Irwin J.T.	F/L	UCC	RCAF	1956-59	Cdn loan officer 1942-46
Irwin M.M.	Capt	UCC	Army	1953-55	
Isaac W.J.O.	Capt	Pres	Army	1960-76	
Ives G.R.	Capt(N)	ACC	RCN	1967-	OMM, OSJ
Jackson J.H.	Maj	ACC	Army	1955-75	RCA 1945-46
Jackson R.N.	Maj	UCC	Army	1965-84	
Jackson T.L.	Cdr	UCC	RCN	1951-60	
Jenkins F.B.	LCol	UCC	Army	1967-92	
Jensen C.H.	Maj	ACC	RCAF	1951-77	
Johnson F.R.L.K.	Capt	UCC	RCAF	1960-73	British army 1945-47
Johnson H.W.	LCol	ACC	Army	1952-69	MBE; RCA chaplain 1943-46
Johnson V.H.	Maj	UCC	Army	1952-67	RCAF 1941-45; RCAF Reserve 1945-51
Johnston D.G.	Capt	ACC	CF	1987-90	
Johnston H.H.	Maj	Bapt	Army	1953-76	

Johnstone D.C.	Capt	UCC	Army	1957-63	
Johnstone S.G.	Maj	Luth	CF	1980-	
Jolliffe J.G.	Capt	ACC	CF	1985-89	reclassified to RC
Jones E.H.	F/L	ACC	RCAF	1958-64	
Jones R.A.	Maj	Bapt	RCAF	1967-86	previously RCAF NCO
Jones T.D.	F/L	ACC	RCAF	1942-49	
Kearley B.S.	Capt	UCC	CF	1990-90	
Kettle D.C.	Maj	Pres	CF	1981-	
Kling G.L.	Lt(N)	UCC	CF	1981-	
Klingbeil J.A.	Maj	Luth	Army	1966-88	
Knipfel D.O.	Maj	Bapt	Army	1951-88	RCA, 1942-46
Lake E.L.	Capt	ACC	Army	1953-57	
Lanctôt G.W.	Maj	Bapt	CF	1978-93	
Lark G.A.W.	Capt	ACC	Army	1949-51	
Latimer A.W.	F/L	UCC	RCAF	1953-53	RCA chaplain 1943-46
Lauder R.A.	Capt	ACC	CF	1984-	
Lawton D.J.W.	Lt(N)	ACC	CF	1981-96	
Lee A.D.	Capt	ACC	CF	1973-77	
Leslie E.G.	Maj	UCC	RCN	1960-82	break in service 1963-65
Levatte W.W.	Cl.2	ACC	RCN	1955-62	
Lewis A.W.	F/L	UCC	RCAF	1954-55	
Light E.S.	BGen	ACC	RCAF	1948-68	RCAF chaplain 1942-46; 5th chaplain general
Littlewood A.T.	S/L	UCC	RCAF	1941-54	
Logan D.L.	Cl.2	UCC	RCN	1963-66	
Lord W.J.	Maj	ACC	RCAF	1954-73	
Love F.W.	LCol	UCC	CF	1969-90	
Lynch F.W.	Capt	ACC	CF	1965-81	Class C call out 1981-83
Lynn G.J.	Lt(N)	ACC	CF	1979-96	break in service 1985-87
McAvany J.H.	LCol	UCC	RCAF	1952-75	RCAF 1942-45
MacCara C.E.	BGen	UCC	Army	1958-87	OSJ; 11th chaplain general
McClintock J.D.	Capt	ACC	Army	1963-67	
McConnell D.	Capt	UCC	Army	1960-64	
McGregor F.A.	Capt	ACC	Army	1962-65	
MacIntosh J.H.	LCol	UCC	Army	1962-84	RCA 1951-52
MacIsaac L.D.	Capt	UCC	CF	1987-90	reclassified to RC
MacIver A.R.	W/C	UCC	RCAF	1949-63	RCAF chaplain 1941-45
MacKay J.F.	Maj	UCC	RCAF	1954-69	RCAF 1944-45
MacKenzie B.A.	Lt(N)	UCC	CF	1991-	
MacKenzie N.W.	Maj	Bapt	Army	1951-67	
McLaren C.A.	F/L	UCC	RCAF	1951-63	RCAF chaplain 1942-45

MacLean A.C.	Capt	UCC	Army	1962-67	RCAF 1944-46
Maclean C.H.	Cl.5	Pres	RCN	1951-67	RCA chaplain 1942-46
MacLean C.I.	Lt(N)	Pres	CF	1983-90	
MacLean D.A.	Capt	ACC	RCAF	1963-73	RCAF 1941-45
MacLean D.H.	Maj	UCC	CF	1979-	
MacLean F.W.	A/C	UCC	RCAF	1941-62	2nd chaplain general
MacLean J.P.	Maj	UCC	RCAF	1956-81	RCA 1944-45; RCA Reserve chaplain 1954-56
McLean K.R.	Capt	ACC	CF	1987-	
MacLean R.A.	Maj	UCC	CF	1970-83	
MacLean R.A.B.	LCdr	Pres	RCN	1964-87	
McLeish D.B.	Capt	ACC	CF	1982-86	
MacLellan W.C.	LCol	Pres	CF	1976-	
MacLennan W.R.	Capt	UCC	CF	1974-94	break in service 1981-87
MacLeod H.A.	Maj	Bapt	RCAF	1959-72	RCAF 1939-45
MacQuarrie E.W.	Maj	UCC	Army	1951-65	RCA chaplain 1941-46
Madill D.G.	LCol	ACC	RCAF	1951-73	
Maindonald T.A.	Cdr	ACC	CF	1975-	OMM
Martin D.L.	Maj	Bapt	Army	1958-77	
Martin E.	S/L	UCC	RCAF	1951-66	
Massey C.J.E.K.	Maj	UCC	CF	1981-96	
Mayo B.A.	Lt(N)	ACC	CF	1990-96	
Melanson D.C.	Capt	UCC	CF	1990-	
Mercer G.G.	Maj	ACC	Army	1951-72	
Merklinger H.A.	Col	Luth	Army	1942-67	
Merriman S.M.	Lt(N)	FM	CF	1991-	
Millar J.R.	BGen	UCC	Army	1941-66	4th chaplain general
Miller K.K.	F/L	Bapt	RCAF	1955-67	
Mills J.I.	Maj	Bapt	Army	1961-84	
Mills L.L.	Capt	UCC	CF	1979-84	
Millson B.D.	Capt	ACC	CF	1989-	
Milne G.A.	Maj	UCC	CF	1969-89	
Minchin K.A.	LCol	ACC	Army	1960-80	RCAF 1943-45; RCAF Reserve chaplain 1957-58; Reserve Arty 1958-60
Moeller T.C.	Capt	Luth	CF	1987-96	
Montgomery J.A.	Capt	ACC	CF	1977-91	USMC Reserve 1954-62; CF Reserve 1976-77
Moore E.G.	F/L	Pres	RCAF	1951-61	
Moore D.S.	Capt	Pres	CF	1967-70	
Moore S.K.	Capt	UCC	CF	1990-	
Moorhead J.F.	Capt	ACC	Army	1951-55	
Morley P.C.	Capt	ACC	CF	1983-96	
Mortimer H.A.	LCdr	ACC	RCN	1952-73	RCNVR 1951-52
Mould L.W.	Maj	UCC	RCAF	1951-69	

Mowatt A.J.	Cl.4	UCC	RCN	1951-66	Chevalier, Order of Leopold (palm), Croix de Guerre (palm); RCA chaplain 1942-46
Mullin P.B.	Capt	UCC	CF	1982-89	
Mundy W.B.	Capt	ACC	Army	1958-59	
Munroe J.A.	Capt	ACC	Army	1953-58	
Murphy K.S.	Lt(N)	UCC	CF	1995-	
Murray R.R.	LCol	UCC	CF	1974-	
Mury C.	LCdr	ACC	CF	1984-	
Needham T.P.R.	Maj	ACC	CF	1981-96	CF 1964-74; CF Reserve 1976-78
Neff J.S.	S/L	Luth	RCAF	1951-64	RCA 1944-46
Newton-Hilton D.	Capt	UCC	RCAF	1963-77	
Nickels J.A.	Cl.2	ACC	RCN	1959-62	RN chaplain 1939-45
Nickerson C.D.	BGen	UCC	Army	1951-78	MC; RCA 1941-45; 8th chaplain general
Norcross N.J.	Capt	ACC	CF	1967-68	
Nunn R.C.	Maj	UCC	Army	1950-65	
Nurse E.M.	Capt	ACC	CF	1973-74	
Oakes L.C	Capt	Bapt	Army	1967-83	
O'Driscoll T.H.	Cl.2	ACC	RCN	1957-60	
Ohs D.F.	LCdr	ACC	CF	1987-	
Organ J.	Capt	ACC	CF	1992-	
Otke A.F.	Maj	Luth	Army	1952-66	RCA chaplain 1943-46
Park B.D.	Capt	ACC	CF	1989-	
Parkhouse S.M.	BGen	UCC	RCAF	1953-81	OSJ; RCAF Reserve 1942-45; RCAF 1945-53; 9th chaplain general
Patey C.V.	Capt	UCC	CF	1977-78	
Peddle G.E.	LCol	ACC	CF	1975-	OMM
Peebles D.G.	LCdr	UCC	RCN	1950-74	RCNVR 1943-45
Peglar B.A.	Cl.4	ACC	RCN	1946-64	RCA chaplain 1943-46
Pierce R.W.	Maj	ACC	Army	1952-62	
Phillips W.J.	Capt	ACC	Army	1951-61	RCA chaplain 1940-46
Pike H.R.	Cl.4	Bapt	RCN	1942-58	
Pippy M.G.	Maj	UCC	RCAF	1954-78	
Ploughman H.	Cl.5	ACC	RCN	1948-64	RCN chaplain 1941-45
Pocock L.R.	Maj	ACC	RCAF	1955-74	RCAF 1937-46
Porrior E.V.	Col	ACC	Army	1956-84	
Potvin J.J.M.	Capt	Bapt	CF	1988-	ROTP 1978-83
Powell J.A.	Capt	ACC	CF	1976-87	break in service 1979-84

Pritchard A.	Capt	UCC	CF	1985-96	
Prowse G.D.	Col	ACC	CF	1973-95	
Pudwell A.D.D.	F/L	ACC	RCAF	1952-54	RCAF 1941-46
Quigg D.M.	F/L	Bapt	RCAF	1954-59	
Radcliffe E.S.	Cl.2	ACC	RCN	1957-63	
Raeburn-Gibson I.	Capt	Pres	RCAF	1963-75	RCAF 1940-51
Rand J.L.	LCol	ACC	Army	1948-65	RCA chaplain 1942-47
Randall B.G.	Capt	ACC	CF	1977-82	
Rathbone B.A.	F/L	ACC	RCAF	1961-65	
Regal E.	F/L	Luth	RCAF	1952-57	
Reid A.G.	LCol	UCC	Army	1955-81	
Rennie R.A.	Maj	UCC	CF	1980-96	
Reynolds E.T.	Capt	ACC	CF	1988-	
Risch R.E.	Maj	UCC	CF	1970-92	
Ritchie R.J.G.	Maj	Pres	RCAF	1953-74	RCN 1939-44
Robbins H.J.	Maj	UCC	Army	1954-70	RCAF 1942-45
Roberts M.K.	Maj	ACC	Army	1951-67	
Robinson R.C.	Capt	Bapt	CF	1985-86	
Rock R.E.	Capt	Luth	RCN	1960-63	
Rodger W.	G/C	UCC	RCAF	1942-67	
Rose E.J.	Capt	ACC	CF	1967-70	
Rose H.S.	Capt	ACC	CF	1973-76	
Ross P.D.	Col	UCC	RCAF	1950-70	RCAF 1942-45
Sams P.L.	Maj	Pres	Army	1957-79	RCA Reserve 1942-43; RCAF 1943-46
Saunders D.R.	Maj	ACC	CF	1970-	
Sawatzky P.R.	Capt	UCC	Army	1954-65	RCA 1942-46
Scharf G.W.	Maj	ACC	CF	1980-	
Schaus G.N.	LCdr	Luth	RCN	1955-73	break in service 1959-63
Schooley S.A.	Capt	UCC	CF	1989-92	CF Reserve 1986-89
Schurman W.G.E.	Maj	UCC	CF	1977-96	
Scott L.C.	W/C	ACC	RCAF	1940-58	
Self A.H.	Capt	Pres	CF	1987-96	
Self S.D.	Maj	Pres	Army	1963-83	
Semple S.W.	F/L	ACC	RCAF	1953-58	
Shannon R.	Cl.3	ACC	RCN	1954-65	
Sharkey N.F.	Capt	Pres	Army	1951-53	RCA chaplain 1940-45
Shaw N.	Capt	ACC	CF	1986-	
Shields W.G.	Maj	ACC	CF	1973-95	
Sigston E.	Capt	ACC	RCN	1950-69	RCA chaplain 1943-46
Sim G.A.	Capt	ACC	CF	1983-94	
Simmons M.R.	Capt	Bapt	Army	1961-74	

Simons W.J.	Lt(N)	ACC	CF	1987-92	
Sinyard B.G.	F/L	ACC	RCAF	1952-53	
Soutar G.	Cl.2	UCC	RCN	1952-55	
Sparks R.H.	Capt	Pres	CF	1988	
Sprung A.P.	Lt(N)	Luth	CF	1986-	RESO 1982-83
Stannard D.R.O.	Cl.2	ACC	RCN	1963-67	British Army, 1939-46
Stenson A.G.	Lt(N)	UCC	RCN	1967-85	
Stibbards B.G.	S/L	Bapt	RCAF	1942-54	
Stone G.A.	Cl.3	ACC	RCN	1948-57	
Stone C.G.F.	Col	ACC	Army	1939-54	MBE
Stringer W.R.	Lt(N)	Pent	CF	1991-92	
Stuart E.D.	W/C	UCC	RCAF	1949-66	RCA chaplain 1941-46
Sutton R.H.	Capt	UCC	RCAF	1967-76	
Swaren O.S.	Maj	Bapt	RCAF	1958-78	RCAF 1942-45
Sweet B.E.	Maj	UCC	CF	1979-	
Tarrant J.E.S.	Lt(N)	UCC	RCN	1966-69	
Tassinari F.L.	Maj	ACC	CF	1978-94	OSJ; USMC Reserve 1957- 59, 1960-65; USMC 1959-60
Taylor E.W.	Capt	ACC	CF	1978-83	
Taylor G.E.	Capt	ACC	CF	1981-86	Class C call out
Taylor W.B.	Cdr	UCC	RCN	1956-73	RCN 1940-45
Thompson C.	Cl.2	UCC	RCN	1953-55	RCA chaplain 1942-46
Thompson D.R.	Maj	ACC	RCAF	1952-69	
Thompson W.H.	Cl.2	UCC	RCN	1955-58	RCN WWII
Timmons E.P.A.	Lt(N)	ACC	RCN	1962-80	
Tipping M.J.R.	Capt	ACC	Army	1963-82	
Titus J.G.	Lt(N)	ACC	RCN	1962-69	
Todd H.	Cl.3	UCC	RCN	1948-62	RCN chaplain 1943-46
Tonks G.E.	Maj	Bapt	CF	1974-96	OSJ
Turnbull A.D.	Maj	ACC	CF	1969-84	CF 1956-63
Tyrrell J.J.A.	Maj	ACC	CF	1974-87	
Vaillancourt J.D.	Capt	ACC	CF	1990-	
Van Gorder J.W.T.	S/L	UCC	RCAF	1942-50	
Vines H.H.	Maj	ACC	Army	1952-71	
Von Schmeling J.W.	Maj	Luth	CF	1967-87	
Waite C.F.	Cl.2	UCC	RCN	1963-65	DFC; RCAF 1941-5
Wakeling A.I.	Maj	ACC	CF	1968-87	RCA chaplain 1962-65
Walker F.A.	Maj	UCC	CF	1975-95	COTC 1961-63; RCA 1963-68
Walsh J.H.	Capt	ACC	RCAF	1963-75	
Walter W.J.	Cl.2	ACC	RCN	1959-65	
Ward G.N.	Maj	UCC	CF	1974-87	

Warne K.S.	Capt	UCC	CF	1981-85	Class C call out
Warnock R.E.	Capt	ACC	CF	1985-93	
Watson N.L.	F/L	UCC	RCAF	1952-60	
Waye R.J.	Capt	ACC	CF	1989-93	
Webb R.F.	Capt	ACC	Army	1952-62	
Webber R.G.	Capt	UCC	Army	1955-58	
Wellwood M.F.	Maj	ACC	CF	1977-96	
Wentzell B.E.	Lt(N)	UCC	CF	1982-90	
White C.H.	LCol	ACC	RCAF	1953-77	
White R.H.	Maj	UCC	CF	1970-91	
Whyte R.E.	Capt	ACC	Army	1965-68	
Wilcox J.W.	Lt(N)	ACC	CF	1986-	RESO 1982-83
Wiley J.E.R.	Capt	Pres	CF	1985-	RESO 1981-82
Wilkes R.O.	LCol	ACC	Army	1940-60	MC
Wilkinson J.W.W.	F/L	UCC	RCAF	1951-53	
Williams J.E.	LCdr	ACC	RCN	1952-70	
Williams M.W.	S/L	UCC	RCAF	1948-58	RCAF chaplain 1942-46
Wilson D.S.	Capt	UCC	Army	1964-66	
Wilson J.	Cl.2	Pres	RCN	1952-57	
Wood R.S.	LCol	ACC	Army	1964-84	
Woods K.M.	Lt(N)	UCC	CF	1986-	
Wright D.A.	Capt	UCC	CF	1984-94	
Wright L.K.	Capt	UCC	CF	1987-	
Yates G.W.	Maj	UCC	RCAF	1957-81	
Yager B.L.	Maj	Bapt	CF	1978-	
Yerburgh R.E.M.	Capt	ACC	Army	1951-52	
Yeung P.K.	Capt	ACC	CF	1978-84	
Youmatoff G.	Maj	ACC	Army	1958-71	RCA 1939-45, 1946-56
Zimmerman G.L.	LCdr	Pres	CF	1980-	

*Note: Many chaplains have received the Canadian Forces Decoration (CD) but this has not been listed in the table. The CD is awarded for twelve years of good conduct and efficient service. A clasp is awarded for each additional 10 years of service.

Chapter Notes

ABBREVIATIONS

ACOA   Anglican Church, Ottawa Diocese, Archives
CGA   Archives of the Chaplain General
CGOHP Chaplain General's Oral History Project
DHist   Directorate of History, DND
JSCC   Joint Services Chaplaincy Committee, DND
NAC   National Archives of Canada
PMC   Personnel Members Committee, DND
QUA   Queen's University Archives
UCMCA United Church, Maritime Conference, Archives

CHAPTER ONE

1. The context of Hepburn's remarks: "The fighting during October, as we concentrated on canals, dykes, etc., was marked by extreme difficulty in handling the wounded and the dead. To hear Chaplains tell how they would 'cat walk' across canals and dykes, made one feel that every last Padre should be awarded a medal." DHist, *Annual Report of the Principal Chaplain of the Army 1945-1946*, prepared by Brigadier C.G. Hepburn.

2. Aseltine, "Sky-Pilots of the RCAF," 1.

3. During the First World War the Catholics had been forced to serve under the same organization as the Protestants. There were some benefits but it was not always a happy situation. Poor leadership on both sides at the beginning of the war and the ecclesiastical exclusiveness of both the Church of England and the Roman Catholic Church led to separate conferences, poor communication, and many misunderstandings. Towards the end of the war the Roman Catholics were worshipping in the churches of France, while the Protestants were not permitted to enter them. When the chaplains met to prepare *A Message to the Churches*, the chaplains' impressions of what lessons the war should have taught Canadians, the Roman Catholics were not included in the meeting. This lack of religious sensitivity had not been forgotten.

4. QUA, Power papers, box 84. Power, who was then postmaster general and whose seat was in Quebec City, was requesting Villeneuve's permission to use the large churches of Quebec as possible air raid shelters.

5. J.F. Ryan, Roman Catholic bishop of Hamilton, to the prime minister, W.L. Mackenzie King, September 16, 1939, quoted in Castonguay, *Unsung Mission*, 17. Castonguay's book is a history of the Roman Catholic chaplaincy in the RCAF during World War II.

6. NAC, mf C3751, 238195, King papers, September 26, 1939.

7. Castonguay, *Unsung Mission*, 18.

8. In his declining years, Wells dictated his memoirs to his daughter, Jean Carden Wells. They were published in 1971 in a volume entitled *The Fighting Bishop*.

9. H.H. Matthews to Archbishop Owen, October 7, 1939, in ibid., 394.

10. It was commonly believed that, upon enrolment, if a soldier hesitated when asked his religion, he would be recorded either as Church of England or Roman Catholic.

11. Despite their equal status as individual clergy, the Anglicans did receive some special considerations in terms of numbers. When there were four chaplains in a brigade, one would have to be from the Church of England. Similarly, of the three chaplains assigned to each hospital, one would always be an Anglican.

12. This is not to suggest that there were no problems arising from differing practices. Salvation Army Officers were not ordained ministers in the ordinary sense and did not practice the sacraments of Baptism or Holy Communion and this made some co-operative

work difficult. On the whole it was felt that the Salvation Army fitted more naturally into the Auxiliary Services in which many of its officers played a unique and valuable role. The Jewish rabbis in the armed forces came under the Protestant Chaplain Service for administrative purposes though obviously their co-operative work with the other denominations was limited by the rules of their faith. The only real denominational difficulty arose because of the internal splits in the Orthodox communion. The Ukrainian Greek Orthodox Church, the Russo-Greek Catholic Orthodox Church, and the Ukrainian Orthodox Church of North America all wanted representation in the service. A man was eventually selected from the Ukrainian Greek Orthodox Church because it was the largest and best organized. The others found this arrangement unsatisfactory and it was agreed that someone would be taken from the Russian-Greek Orthodox Church, but this body was not able to provide a suitable candidate. The rules of the Orthodox communion also imposed certain restraints on co-operative work but the chaplains from the Ukrainian Greek Orthodox Church were a real asset to the service.

13. DHist, *Annual Report of the Principal Chaplain of the Army 1945-1946.*

14. The Inter-Church Advisory Committee was sometimes known as the Protestant Advisory Committee and at other times as the Inter-denominational Advisory Committee. The basic concept of the committee was not unique to Canada or to World War II. The concept had come into being in 1911 with the Royal Australian Navy.

15. NAC, RG 24, acc. 83-84/167, box 6582, Wells to the Reverend Harold Young, June 24, 1941.

16. Chaplain Leonard Outerbridge edited a book on HMC *Puncher.*

17. QUA, Power papers, box 60, file D1052, Power to the Reverend H.H. Bingham, January 22, 1944.

18. Ibid., Bingham to Power, January 30, 1944.

19. Wells, *The Fighting Bishop,* 531.

20. Wells retired to Toronto and died there on April 10, 1964. He was buried in St. James Cemetery, Toronto, and a window was dedicated to his memory in the Cathedral Church of St. John's, Winnipeg.

21. Aseltine, "Sky-Pilots of the RCAF," 12.

22. Ibid., 5.

23. *The Happy Warrior,* 10.

24. QUA, Power papers, box 60, file D1051.

25. Aseltine, "Sky-Pilots of the RCAF," 90.

26. Ibid., 47.

27. CGOHP, Rogers tape.

28. I have drawn the story of Foote largely from the following sources: Baldwin, "Stayed Behind after Dieppe"; Cragg, "Chaplain Who Won VC"; Jones, "Dieppe"; Roy, "#1282: The Gallant Padre"; and Stevens, *In This Sign.*

29. Baldwin, "Stayed Behind after Dieppe."

30. Ibid.

31. Cragg, "Chaplain Who Won VC."

32. Jones, "Dieppe."

33. Cragg, "Chaplain Who Won VC."

34. Ibid.

35. Jones, "Dieppe."

36. Vic Sparrow, president of the Toronto and Western chapter of the Dieppe Veterans and Prisoners of War Association, quoted in *Legion,* July/August 1988, 31.

37. Spoken to the assembled chaplains at the chaplains' annual retreat, Royal Military College, Kingston, 1988.

38. Baldwin, "Stayed Behind after Dieppe."

39. *Legion*, July/August 1988.

40. The story of the chaplains in Hong Kong is based largely on the diaries of James Barnett, Uriah Laite, and F.J. Deloughery held at NDHQ in the CGA.

41. CGA, Laite diary.

42. Ibid., Barnett diary.

43. Barnett's green frontals are now on display in the Chaplain General's Office in Ottawa.

44. CGA, personnel files, U. Laite.

45. Aseltine, "Sky-Pilots of the RCAF," 126.

46. Extract from a chaplain's final report, December 18, 1945, quoted in Johnston and Porter, "Sky Pilots in Blue," 138.

47. Aseltine, "Sky-Pilots of the RCAF," 127.

CHAPTER TWO

1. David Marshall, "Methodism Embattled: A Reconsideration of the Methodist Church and World War I," *Canadian Historical Review* 66(1985), 48-64.

2. NAC, H.W.E. Cdn./1939/11/Chap/1.

3. NAC, RG 2, PC 100/5928, vol. 1911, September 8, 1945.

4. NAC, H.W.E. Cdn. V/575/1.

5. CGA, personnel files, C.G.F. Stone.

6. CGOHP, Howie tape.

7. *The Happy Warrior*, 1.

8. *Ottawa Citizen*, November 12, 1945.

9. NAC, RG 24, acc. 83-84/167, box 7737, memo from MacKlin to adjutant general, July 5, 1946.

10. Ibid., King's Regulation for the British Army 1605-1608, September 4, 1945.

11. Ibid., Personnel Members Committee (PMC) minutes, November 8, 1946.

12. Ibid., Gallagher to Claxton, September 22, 1947, and Claxton to Gallagher, June 10, 1948.

13. Ibid., PMC meeting, May 26, 1949.

14. CGA, Technical Narrative and Report of the Chaplain General, 1945.

15. Pennington, "The Ministry of Our Chaplains."

16. NAC, finding aid 24-111.

17. NAC, RG 24, acc. 83-84/167, box 7737, notes of the personal views of Weeks on a number of matters raised by the Inter-Church Advisory Committee on the Chaplaincy, item (e), December 20, 1946.

18. Ibid., Gallagher to Mackenzie King, August 8, 1945.

19. Ibid., PMC 86, July 19, 1946.

20. Ibid., Weeks to Inter-Church Committee, December 20, 1946.

21. Ibid.

22. NAC, RG 24, acc. 83-84/167, box 7737, Defence Committee of Cabinet, minutes, March 7, 1947.

23. Ibid., Inter-Service Combined Functions Committee (ICFC) report, March 2, 1947.

24. Ibid., memo, chair of ICFC to the PMC, March 14, 1947.

25. Ibid., report of the PMC to the ICFC, June 10, 1947.

26. Ibid.

27. NAC, RG 24, acc. 83-84/167, box 7737, memo from Weeks to PMC, January 31, 1947.

28. Ibid., memo from A.B. Conly to Weeks, June 5, 1947.

29. Ibid., memo from PMC to Defence Committee of Cabinet, May 23, 1947.

30. Ibid., memo from Defence Committee of Cabinet to PMC, May 29, 1947.

31. NAC, RG 24, acc. 83-84/167, box 6581, Gallagher to chairman, Defence Committee of Cabinet, September 22, 1947.

32. Ibid., minister of national defence to Gallagher, October 9, 1947.

33. Ibid., Gallagher to minister of national defence, November 24, 1947.

34. Ibid., Gallagher to minister of national defence, January 28, 1948.

35. NAC, RG 24, acc. 83-84/167, box 7737, Weeks to PMC, February 25, 1948.

36. Ibid., Defence Committee of Cabinet minutes, March 18, 1948.

37. Roman Catholic chaplains had been dealing with the same issues in parallel but there is very little documentary evidence of their side of the struggle beyond the impressive letters of Archbishop Roy. Canadian politicians were always sensitive to the wishes of the French Catholic Church because of the effectiveness with which it could control and direct the mass voting of its parishioners at that time. See Presthus, *Elite Accommodation in Canadian Politics.*

38. NAC, RG 24, acc. 83-84/167, box 7737, Roy to Claxton, March 22, 1948.

39. NAC, MG 32, B5, notes of a meeting between Roy, Gallagher, and Claxton, May 28, 1948.

40. NAC, RG 24, acc. 83-84/167, box 6582, Claxton to Gallagher, June 10, 1948.

41. Ibid., box 6581, Gallagher to Claxton, August 15, 1948, and Claxton to Gallagher, September 20, 1948.

42. CGA, Gallagher to Claxton, December 13, 1948.

43. NAC, RG 24, acc. 83-84/167, box 6581, Roy to Claxton, December 30, 1948.

44. Ibid., box 7737, meeting of senior officers, minutes, March 15, 1949.

45. Ibid., box 6581, Claxton to Gallagher, April 12, 1949.

46. Ibid., Gallagher to Claxton, May 17, 1949.

47. Ibid., Roy to Claxton, October 3, 1949.

48. The JSCC minutes (RG 24, acc. 83-84/167, box 6582, are cluttered with extraneous material but do reflect the chaplains' points of view. File 2-70-57-1, pts. 1-3, contains the material relating to the Protestant subcommittee but is more a duplication of than a supplement to the files of the full committee. The Roman Catholic subcommittee's documents are in file 2-70-57-2.

49. CGA, Gallagher to McCann, July 3, 1950.

50. Ibid., McCann to Gallagher, December 15, 1950.

51. Ibid., Gallagher to McCann, January 3, 1951, and McCann to Gallagher, January 15, 1951.

52. Ibid., Gallagher to St. Laurent, February 8, 1951.

53. Ibid., Claxton to Gallagher, March 6, 1951.

54. Ibid., briefing notes, Gallagher's visit to Claxton, May 22, 1952.

55. In permanent married quarters the chaplain paid $74.00 per month for rent, light, and heat, and $26.56 per month income tax. If he must find his own living quarters, he must almost inevitably pay a higher charge for rent, light and heat, and for some reason he becomes liable for a higher income tax on his allowances, of $36.46 per month.

56. CGA, Littlewood to Frayne, June 15, 1951.

57. Ibid.

58. CGA, Littlewood to Frayne, March 5, 1952.

59. Grostenquin was composed completely of prefabricated metal huts and so earned the Canadian nickname "big tin can." In 1958 it was the scene of a tragic accident when two CF-100 fighters collided and one crashed into the station hospital. The base chaplain was away at the time and had left a student, David Estey, in charge of chaplain activities. It was an experience that left an indelible impression on young Estey's mind. CGOHP, Estey tape.

60. CGOHP, Parkhouse tape.

61. CGA, Rand to C.G.F. Stone, August 25, 1953.

62. Rand, "The Chaplain in the 27th Brigade," *Canadian Army Journal*, January, 1954, 52-6.

63. The "padre's hour" was a technique introduced during the Second World War to bolster morals and morale during the long wait in England for the invasion of the continent. An innovation of Sir Frederick Browning, commander of a British airborne division and husband of novelist Daphne du Maurier, the concept spread through the Commonwealth armies. It received official authorization in Canadian Overseas Training manuals in December 1942. For one training hour each week the chaplain would meet with the troops to discuss religious and moral problems. As chaplains became more adept at its use, the padre's hour became very popular with men, quite apart from religious background. After the war, the retiring chaplain general described the padre's hour as "one of the most important developments of the Canadian Service during the war": Stevens, *In This Sign*, 39.

64. *Kilt and Sporran*, July 18, 1953.

CHAPTER THREE

1. NAC, RG 24, acc. 83-84/167, box 6582, Stone to primate, Anglican Church of Canada, October 27, 1950.

2. In *The Navy Chaplain and his Parish*, Waldo Smith discusses the problem of venereal disease in Korea at some length: see p. 216 ff.

3. A standard joke of the day was that Padre Cunningham was going to Korea to replace an R.C. Nunn.

4. CGA, Durnford file. Durnford was a gallant padre who spent his days, in his own words, "working to beat Hell." Interview, Vancouver *Province*, January 22, 1971. Yet one more Durnford story was of the padre showing up with six German prisoners at the point of a swagger stick. In another version the swagger stick was a rifle from which the bolt had been removed, so it would not be a weapon

5. Fred Love, "Out of Our Past," *Dialogue*, no. 1 (1987).

6. For an in-depth examination of the manner in which the Japanese treated prisoners of war, see Michael A. Zarate, "American Prisoners of Japan: Did Rank Have Its Privilege?" Master's thesis, Cameron University, 1983. Available on microfiche from US Army Command and Staff College, Fort Leavenworth, KS.

7. Originally the Canadians were to serve with the 29th Brigade (British) on the line beside the Gloucestershires but Belgium took that position. Later the Gloucestershires were hit hard and the Belgians also suffered many casualties. Not being where they were initially slotted to be created envy among some Canadians and relief among others.

8. NAC, RG 24, vol. 18, 317-320.

9. CGOHP, Cunningham tape.

10. Ibid.

11. Ibid. No Canadian chaplain has ever been given permission to carry a weapon of any kind. Under the Geneva Convention chaplains are non-combatants. There have been occasions when commanding officers have insisted that a chaplain carry a weapon and

the chaplain has quite rightly refused to comply. The chaplain policy has always been that, while deployed, no chaplain will bear arms.

12. Ibid.

13. CGA, Johnson file, Stone to Johnson, April 21, 1952, and Merklinger to Stone, May 5, 1952.

14. The full citation is in ibid., Johnson file.

15. CGOHP, Cardy tape.

16. Ibid.

17. CGA, "Military Chaplain Experiences," by R.H. Dobson.

18. Ibid., Dobson Diaries.

19. NAC, RG 24, acc. 83-84/167, box 6581, report on the Chaplain Services (Army), March 31, 1954.

20. CGOHP, Cardy tape.

21. As a result of the pestering of a cousin, Dobson managed to send some grass seeds from the Korean roadside back to Canada. The seeds were distributed to several research stations in western Canada. On one occasion, Dobson was stopped by the provost as he was about to enter a minefield in order to get a photo and seeds from an exotic bloom. On returning to Canada, Dobson discovered that a plant, hitherto unknown, had been given the name *Koreansis Dobsonsis*. CGOHP, Dobson tape.

22. CGA, first letter from Dobson in Korea to his wife in Canada, April 12, 1952.

23. CGOHP, MacIntosh tape.

24. Dobson, who was missing some of the fingers on his right hand, was well known for his ability to play the saxophone.

25. CGA, Dobson to Stone, May 16, 1952.

26. Gordon Shields, "The Life of a Padre in Korea," *Dialogue*, no. 2(1988).

27. Ibid.

28. CGA, memo CB 6-6-1(P), Butler to Stone, July 30, 1952.

29. As a student, Hopkins worked at St. Matthias Church in Ottawa, where Padre Stone was a close friend of the rector. Seeing a bright young man like Hopkins about to be sent to the rural parishes for five or six years was too much for Stone who so desperately needed Anglican chaplains. Arrangements were made and Hopkins found himself being welcomed into the military and soon en route to Korea.

30. Filshie suffered from an intestinal injury sustained in the Second World War.

31. CGOHP, MacIntosh tape.While in Korea, MacIntosh was attempting to study a course in chemistry. Filshie was of great assistance to him.

32. CGA, citation for MBE to Filshie.

33. CGOHP, Cardy tape.

34. Ibid.

35. The whole story of Willy Royal appeared in the *Reader's Digest* of April 1988.

36. The story of the British Gloucestershire Regiment is told in S.J. Davies, *In Spite of Dungeons* (London: Hodder and Stoughton, 1954).

37. NAC, RG 24, acc. 83-84/167, box 6581, Gallagher to Claxton, February 3, 1950.

38. Ibid., box 6582, memorandum, Stone to PMC, May 25, 1951.

39. Ibid., box 6581, JSCC minutes, January 16, 1952.

40. Ibid., box 7737, PMC to JSCC, January 28, 1952.

41. Ibid., box 6581, JSCC minutes, February 4, 1953.

42. Ibid., Claxton to Gallagher, March 13, 1952; PMC to JSCC, March 27, 1952; PMC to JSCC, April 2, 1952.

43. Rodger R. Venzke, *Confidence in Battle, Inspiration in Peace*, (Washington 1977), vol.5, 42ff.

44. The Right Reverend C.M. Nicholson, moderator of the United Church of Canada, was accompanied by the Anglican primate, Bishop W.F. Barfoot, the moderator of the Presbyterian Church of Canada, the Right Reverend N.D. Kennedy, and the three principal chaplains: Stone, Frayne, and Foote.

45. UCMCA, Nicholson papers, telegram from United Church Headquarters in Toronto to Nicholson with Canadian soldiers in Korea, no date.

46. Ibid., sermon notes, "Our Korean Interest," no date.

47. Ibid.

48. NAC, MG 32, B5, table 2 to Appendix "A" of memorandum to Defence Committee of Cabinet, June 11, 1952.

49. CGA, Korea file.

CHAPTER FOUR

1. Fred Love, "After the 2nd World War," *Dialogue*, no. 2, (1989), 8.

2. The following description of Cardy's experience at Camp Borden is drawn from the Cardy tape in CGOHP.

3. CGOHP, Light tape.

4. ACOA, file 9, W12, 1, items 11-15. A typical criticism was the concern expressed by Church of England clergymen in the Ottawa area about Bishop Wells's apparent disregard for canon law: specifically the canon on discipline which forbade priests to officiate in any ecclesiastical body not in communion with the Church of England. On one specific occasion Wells was taken to task by Bishop Jefferson of Ottawa, prompted by the Reverend R.H. Steacy, for preaching in a local Presbyterian church without first gaining his approval. The letter was only contemptuously polite, for it was soon followed by a letter of complaint from Jefferson to the primate.

5. When new suburbs were being built in the early 1950s each denomination sought the best location for itself. The new suburbanites found themselves selecting "religious outlets just as they did supermarkets." Grant, *The Church in the Canadian Era*, 169.

6. The most helpful and best organized of the Anglican archives is the one in Ottawa. Files on Canon C.G. Hepburn, Bishop Clarke, and Bishop Wells provided valuable insight into the ecclesiastical jurisdiction issue. Most Anglican archives retain correspondence files and some newspaper clippings on all of the clergymen who have served in that diocese. Of some interest was the file of material on Bishop Luxton that was forwarded from the archives in London, Ontario. The information so obtained reflected a positive attitude towards the military and contained no indication of any conflict over jurisdiction.

7. NAC, RG 24, acc. 83-84/167, box 6581, bishop of Huron to the minister of national defence, December 7, 1949.

8. Ibid.

9. Ibid., minister of national defence to bishop of Huron, January 9, 1950, and bishop of Huron to minister of national defence, January 16, 1950.

10. Ibid., bishop of Algoma to the minister of national defence, enclosing petition of Anglican chaplaincy committee, April 18, 1950.

11. ACOA, file of Canon Hepburn, letter from Gallagher to Luxton, May 15, 1950.

12. Ibid., Luxton to Gallagher, June 5, 1950.

13. Ibid., Minutes of the General Synod of the Anglican Church of Canada, 1950.

14. For details, see above page 73.

15. RG 24, acc. 83-84/167, boxes 5539-5540, file block 5100. One file is on the construction of various chapels. It contains several lists describing the conditions of chapels in use and the need for additional buildings. Blueprints of several chapels are included, although they are not controversial plans or reflective of the struggle for a specific plan or chapel. These are simple technical files and do not include debates on related issues.

16. One example was the chapel at Gordon Head. By far the best chapel of this era was built by the engineers in Chilliwack. The chapel in Goose Bay, Labrador, was constructed of logs.

17. Wells, *The Fighting Bishop*, 498.

18. CGA, CFB Cornwallis, historical records file 5111-1. The chapel at Cornwallis, built during the war, was in good repair and was used in 1950 by Roman Catholics and Protestants. It seated 100 people at a time when the base trained all of the sailors for the Canadian Navy on the east coast. In 1992 it was still in use as the CFB Cornwallis Roman Catholic Chapel.

19. NAC, RG 24, acc. 83-84/167, box 6581.This took place on February 14, 1951.

20. Ibid., director of construction engineering (DCED) to Marani and Morris, Architects, June 19, 1951.

21. Ibid., Marani and Morris to DCED, August 14, 1951.

22. Ibid., JSAC minutes, October 12, 1951.

23. NAC, RG 24, acc. 83-84/167, box 7737, PMC minutes, May 28, 1952.

24. Ibid., box 5539, Survey of Military Chapels, June 5, 1952.

25. Ibid.

26. NAC, MG 32, B5, appendix B of the memo of the minister of national defence to the defence secretary, June 11, 1952.

27. NAC, RG 24, acc. 83-84/167, box 6581, JSCC(P) memo to the minister of national defence, June 23, 1952.

28. Ibid., box 6582, JSCC(P) minutes, August 2, 1952.

29. Ibid., deputy minister to the chaplain of the fleet, August 22, 1952, referred to in a copy of a memorandum for Claxton from W.J. Gallagher, October 14, 1952. On the letter had been added a note that truly reflected the thought of the uncaring bureaucratic attitude of the day: "the government does not assume responsibility for the welfare of dependants, either spiritual or physical."

30. Ibid., JSCC(P) minutes, May 8, 1950.

31. Maritime Museum Archives, CFB Halifax, Shannon Park history file.

32. DND, Queen's Regulations and Orders, volume I, para. 33.01 and 33.03.

33. NAC, RG 24, acc. 83-84/167, box 6582, notes on Dr. Gallagher's private interview with the minister of national defence, October 14, 1952.

34. Ibid., box 6582, Gallagher to Claxton, December 13, 1952.

35. Ibid., box 6581, JSCC(P) memo to PMC, December 29, 1952.

36. CGOHP, Pike tape.

37. NAC, MG 32, B5, George R. Pearkes to Brooke Claxton, February 20, 1953.

38. NAC, RG 24, acc. 83-84/167, box 7737, PMC minutes, April 14, 1953.

39. Ibid., PMC meeting, April 23, 1953.

40. Maritime Museum Archives, CFB Halifax, Shannon Park history file.

41. DHist, 1-6-0, vol. II, J.W. Duncan to C.G. Stone, May 15, 1954.

42. Ibid., J.W. Duncan to J.W. Forth, August 3, 1954.

43. Ibid.

44. CGOHP, Hopkins tape.

CHAPTER FIVE

1. Byers, "Reorganization of the Canadian Armed Forces," and Kronenberg, *All Together Now*, 10.

2. NAC, RG 24, acc. 83-84/167, box 7738, PMC minutes, August 8, 1957.

3. NAC, RG 24, vol. 21502, file CSC 2150:1, part 1, contains the minutes of the Ad Hoc Committee on the integration of the Chaplain Service.

4. NAC, RG 24, acc. 83-84/167, box 7738, PMC minutes, August 27, 1957.

5. Cited in ibid, box 6582, chairman, JSCC(P) to each member of Council of Churches Chaplaincy Committee, August 30, 1957.

6. See above, 2000-0.

7. NAC, RG 24, acc. 83-84/167, box 6582, minutes, Chiefs of Staff Committee, September 6, 1957.

8. Ibid., minister of national defence to Dr. W.J. Gallagher and to Archbishop Roy, August 16, 1957.

9. Ibid., chairman, JSCC(P) to each member of the Council of Churches Chaplaincy Committee, August 30, 1957.

10. Ibid., memo from the Council of Churches Chaplaincy Committee to the minister of national defence, September 24, 1957.

11. Ibid., Forth to Council of Churches Chaplaincy Committee, October 7, 1957.

12. NAC, RG 24, acc. 83-84/167, box 7738, memo from Plomer to PMC, November 14, 1957.

13. Ibid., memo from PMC to Chiefs of Staff, November 22, 1957.

14. Ibid., PMC minutes, December 19, 1957.

15. NAC, MG 32, Pearkes papers, memo from the PMC to the Chiefs of Staff, December 23, 1957.

16. Ibid., memo from Pearkes to Chief of Staff, January 8, 1958.

17. NAC, RG 24, acc. 83-84/167, box 6582, minister of national defence to chairman, Chaplaincy Committee, January 28, 1958.

18. Ibid., box 7738, memo from PMC to chairman of the Chiefs of Staff, file HQ 2-177-2, February 7, 1958.

19. Ibid., memo from CDS to chairman, PMC, February 12, 1958.

20. *Ottawa Journal*, September 29, 1958.

21. NAC, MG 32, Harkness papers, vol 7, file 6-1, vol 1, F.J. Tonkin to minister of national defence, George Pearkes, September 24, 1958, and minister of national defence to F.J. Tonkin, October 9, 1958. (This exchange is misfiled in Harkness papers.)

22. NAC, RG 24, acc. 83-84/167, box 6582, chaplain general (P) to all chaplains, September 23, 1958.

23. Ibid., chairman of the Chiefs of Staff to chaplain general, September 24, 1958.

24. NAC, RG 24, acc. 83-84/167, box 7738, PMC minutes, September 25, 1958.

25. Ibid., box 6846, Roy to minister of national defence, January 4, 1960.

26. Ibid., box 7738, memo from chaplain general (P) to PMC, July 21, 1960.

27. Ibid., PMC minutes, November 3, 1960.

28. Ibid., PMC minutes, December 10, 1962.

29. Ibid., memo from chaplain general(P) to PMC, December 10, 1962.

30. Ibid., background paper presented by the PMC, dated June 10, 1963.

31. Fowler, "The Growth of the Protestant Chaplain's Service in the Canadian Military 1945-1968."

32. NAC, RG 24, acc. 83-84/167, box 7737, Harold Young to chairman, PMC, April 18, 1957.

33. Ibid., box 7738, PMC minutes, May 2, 1957; and box 7737, letter from staff officer, JSC London to PMC, June 27, 1957.

34. Ibid., PMC minutes, June 27, 1957.

35. Ibid., PMC minutes, November 7, 1957.

36. Ibid., PMC minutes, July 14, 1960. The Roman Catholic chaplain general had been made a prelate of the Roman Catholic Church: an honour bestowed by the Pope which entitled Roman Catholic chaplain generals to be called "Monsignor."

37. Ibid., PMC minutes, March 2, 1961.

38. Ibid., PMC minutes, February 13, 1964.

39. CGOHP, Cardy tape.

40. The first chaplains promoted by the PER system were Padres R.S. Wood, S.H. Clarke, K.D. Benner, and G.G. Davidson. One year later Padre D.C. Estey was promoted.

41. DHist., P 5225-28-1 (CP), chief of personnel to commander, air command, October 10, 1969.

42. Ibid., P 1180-4385/10 (DCP(P)), Cardy to all command chaplains, March 28, 1969.

43. Ibid., P 1180-4385/10 (DCP(P)), Cunningham to command chaplains, November 9, 1970.

44. Ibid.

45. CGA, survey of promotions by service, annex B to 5111-0 (CG(P)), November 29, 1976. Each service demanded its share of the promotions.

46. Academy of Parish Clergy Incorporated (1972) and (1975), *Evaluation of Christian Ministry* and "Measuring Ministries, Resources for Evaluation," an article in *The Christian Ministry.*

47. CGA, minutes of command chaplains conference, October 5, 1977.

48. Ibid., 5111-26-2 (DCA(P)), chaplain general (P) to all chaplains, April 28, 1976.

49. Ibid., "Education of Children - Europe," Adjutant General Instruction No. 58/2, January 9, 1958.

50. Ibid., minutes, JSCC meeting, May 20, 1958.

51. NAC, RG 24, acc. 83-84/167, box 7738, PMC minutes, June 19, 1958.

52. CGOHP, Hopkins tape.

53. For example, the fine depiction of the Last Supper in the window above the communion table at Marville was removed and taken to Lahr. Then in 1970-1 it was moved to the chapel at Moose Jaw.

CHAPTER SIX

1. The general picture of chaplains' activities as well as the various specific incidents in this chapter have been drawn to a large extent from taped interviews with the chaplains who served in the theatres concerned. Specific sources have been cited only for actual quotations.

2. Buxton, "Out of Our Past," *Dialogue*, no. 1 (1987).

3. Ibid.

4. CGA, Congo file, J.P. Browne to D.L. Martin, November 7, 1960.

5. Davidson, "Canadian Chaplain in Cyprus."

6. CGA, L. Coleman report, September 1972.

7. CGA, personnel files, L. Coleman, "In Retrospect - Cyprus 1972."

8. *Dialogue*, February 1977, 15.

9. CGA, Middle East file, H.R. Coleman report, June 6, 1963.

297

10. CGA, H.R. Coleman to J.P. Browne, June 25, 1963.

11. CGA, Middle East file, report of Major Les Barclay, December 1979.

12. *Dialogue*, no. 3 (1989), 3.

13. CGA, personnel files, G.A. Milne, electronic communication, United Church Users Group - Milne #3, July 30, 1989.

14. Later Domotor returned to Canada and joined the Roman Catholic Chaplain Service.

15. Because of the nature of the operation, some chaplains had problems getting a vehicle and driver. On the war establishment the chaplains were entitled to a vehicle, but there was no such provision during peacetime.

16. CGA, Vietnam file, Estey to C. Nickerson, May 5, 1973.

17. Ibid.

CHAPTER SEVEN

1. During World War II Cunningham served with the Carleton and York Regiment in New Brunswick, then with the West Nova Scotia Regiment in the south of England, at battle in Sicily and Italy as a platoon commander and then as a company commander. He experienced a great deal of death and destruction, serving with distinction until he was invalided home in 1944.

2. Nickerson, "The Chaplain General," *Dialogue*, July 1976.

3. CGA, Council of Churches Chaplaincy Committee, minutes, January 23, 1973, annex B.

4. CGOHP, Cunningham tape.

5. CGA, 5111-0 Chap Gen (P), April 25, 1974.

6. Ibid., Cunningham to all chaplains, April 25, 1974.

7. When word leaked back to Ottawa that a certain chaplain's marriage had fallen apart and he had been seen at a church function with another woman, the chaplain was called to Ottawa for an immediate interview with Cunningham. Back at his base the next morning, the chaplain commenced release proceedings. The popular rumour was that he had been given a choice: to apply for a release or to be reported to his civilian ecclesiastical authority for immoral behaviour.

8. CGOHP, Cunningham tape.

9. CGA, Purple Net letter, Cunningham to all chaplains, February 1975.

10. CGOHP, Cunningham tape.

11. CGA, pastoral letter, Cunningham to all chaplains, June 5, 1976.

12. CGA, Purple Net letter, Nickerson to all chaplains, August, 1976. "I have always counted myself among those who hold that anyone who aspires to high office is like the baboon, in that the higher he climbs the more he exposes his objectionable features."

13. Cunningham, "Change Worketh Wonders," *Dialogue*, July 1976.

14. *Dialogue*, September 1978.

15. CGA, Purple Net letter #7, Nickerson to all chaplains, September 30, 1976.

16. Ibid.

17. Ibid.

18. CGA, Purple Net letter #8, Nickerson to all chaplains, October 26, 1977.

19. CGA, 4591-2 (DCA(P)), Nickerson to all chaplains, October 26, 1977

20. CGOHP, Parkhouse tape. In the 1950s, Parkhouse had worked for the principal chaplain of the RCAF, Bob Frayne. In that office he chose many of the hymns that went into the first edition of the *Divine Service Book* and proofread the text. Unfortunately, the Council

of Churches Committee were not ready to support the revision and, in any case, insufficient funds were available to produce it.

21. CGA, Comman, Chaplains Conference, minutes, January 7, 1980, annex A.

22. Ibid.

23. Reported in CGA, Command Chaplains Conference, minutes, December 4, 1979, annex C. Don Hatfield and his wife, Sylvia, travelled extensively, during his tour as assistant command chaplain of Air Command, taking the Gospel and good Christian education methods to most if not all of the chapels on the Canadian radar chain.

24. Ibid., Command Chaplains Conference, minutes, January 7, 1980.

25. Ibid., Constitution of the Military Christian Fellowship, November 17, 1977.

26. Ibid., Constitution of the Military Christian Fellowship, November 6, 1983.

27. Ibid., Military Christian Fellowship Operation Order No. 1, no date.

28. *Ottawa Journal*, February 11, 1975.

29. NAC, RG 24/15.632, letter from the principal chaplain, #80/1944.

30. CGOHP, MacCara tape.

31. CGA, Council of Churches Chaplaincy Committee, minutes, June 8, 1981, item 9.

32. CGA, Command Chaplains, minutes, October 27, 1980, 4.

33. Ibid., Chief of Defence Staff letter, July 23, 1981.

34. Ibid., memorandum to CPCSA from Hopkins, October 16, 1981.

35. Ibid., 5111-2 Chap Gen (P), Hopkins to all chaplains, February 25, 1983.

36. Cotton, "A Canadian Military Ethos."

37. CGA, 5111-2 Chap Gen (P), Hopkins to all chaplains, February 25, 1983.

38. Ibid., Hopkins file, note to file by Bishop Robert L. Seaborn, October 8, 1986.

39. CGA, Beaton to Howie, February 15, 1968, and Howie to Beaton, March 3, 1968.

40. Ibid., Minutes of United Church Chaplains Conference, 4 June 1983.
    At every annual retreat provision has been made for meetings of denominational groups of chaplains. This is an opportunity for the denominationally like-minded to compare notes, do business, air problems, and receive guidance from the more experienced and the senior members of their church. Being a gathering of old friends which often includes former classmates and team members, there is normally a joyous air of frivolity. In the United Church of Canada meeting, the chairperson, elected at the previous retreat, opens with prayer and welcomes new members. After acceptance of the previous minutes, the United Church membership roll, which is held at NDHQ, is reported. Other business follows and before the nominating committee reports, the visiting representatives of the United Church on the Canadian Council of Churches Chaplaincy Committee and of the General Council of the United Church are invited to speak.

41. CGOHP, MacCara tape.

42. CGA, Martin Rumscheidt, "Questions for AST-Chaplains Discussion," February 13, 1985.

43. CGA, file 5111-16-10 (DCA(P)(2), annex A, 25 February 1985

44. Brown, "Blessed are the Peacemakers."

45. *Dialogue*, no. 3 (1987).

46. *Dialogue*, no. 1 (1988), 11.

47. Morley, "Iran-Iraq: Operation Vagabond," *Dialogue*, no. 3 (1989).

48. CGA, Phil Morley, "The Padre's Mesopotamian Chronicles."

49. *Dialogue*, no. 4, (1989).

CHAPTER EIGHT

1. The contractor called the rich red colouring of these carpets "playboy red."
2. NAC, RG 24, acc. 83-84/167, box 7737, PMC minutes November 5, 1953.
3. CGA, tri-service Command Chaplains Conference, November 15-17, 1965, minutes. 11.
4. Ibid, MacCara, *Stewardship Projects of the Canadian Forces Chapels (P)*, 1977. This pamphlet, which updated chaplain stewardship publications from 1973, was used as a guide in the writing of this chapter.
5. Ibid., 8.
6. Ibid.
7. *Dialogue*, no. 3 (1979), 12.
8. Ibid., no. 2 (1981), 23.
9. NAC, RG 24, acc. 83-84/167, box 6582, Chaplain General's Committee, minutes, November 14, 1960, item 18.1.
10. A small community has been encouraged and assisted in a self-help project: a community centre and recreation facilities.
11. CGOHP, Parkhouse tape.
12. In 1976, Lieutenant Colonel Clary White was tasked to collect $2000 for the library at the Pacific College in Fiji. Within the year, White received 20 donations which totalled $2900 and forwarded the amount to the college.
13. CGA, MacCara, *Stewardship Projects*, 7.

CHAPTER NINE

1. Interview with D.C. Estey.
2. Interview with D.C. Kettle.
3. Sword, "HMCS *Protecteur* Floating Parish for Gulf-Bound Anglican Minister," *Halifax Chronicle-Herald*, August 26, 1990.
4. Crossley, "Minister Back from Gulf," Corner Brook *Western Star*, January 22, 1991.
5. CGA, Unclass PER 015 221315Z, January 1991.
6. Park, "Operation Friction: A Chaplain's View of Canada's Naval Response."
7. Ibid.
8. Ibid.
9. Kennedy, "Leader's Prayers Guarded CF-18 Pilots," Victoria *Times-Colonist*, March 3, 1991.
10. Ibid.
11. Ross, "CCC Representatives Visit Cyprus and Lebanon as Gulf War Breaks Out," 9.
12. The United Church of Canada Statement on the Gulf War, circa January 1991, quoted from the minutes of a meeting of Victoria Presbytery of the United Church of Canada, February 1991.
13. The Division of Mission in Canada with representatives of the executive of the Division of World Outreach, United Church of Canada, January 20, 1991, quoted from the minutes of a meeting of Victoria Presbytery of the United Church of Canada, February 1991.
14. From the minutes of a meeting of Victoria Presbytery of the United Church of Canada, February 1991.
15. CGA, moderator of the United Church of Canada to the chaplain general, January 21, 1991.

16. Ibid., Lake of Bays pastoral charge note to chaplains, circa January 1991.
17. Ibid., Division of Ministry, Personnel and Education to all United Church chaplains in the Canadian Forces, February 26, 1991.
18. Ibid., 5111-5 (DPA(P)), G.E. Peddle to all chaplains, May 6, 1991.
19. *Dialogue*, 1 (1991), 28.
20. Dunlop, "Canadian Soldiers Fulfil Christ's Work," Halifax *Chronicle-Herald*, July 18, 1994.
21. Lockhart, "Conforms with What Christ Preached," Fredericton *Daily Gleaner*, September 12, 1994.
22. CGA, Ryan to Chaplain General (P) Division, October 11, 1994.
23. "People," *United Church Observer*, September 1994.
24. Ibid.

Bibliography

NOTE ON SOURCES

The main repository of archival material on Canada's chaplains is the National Archives in Ottawa, backed up by the resources of the Directorate of History in the Department of National Defence. From 1944 until unification in 1967, the chaplains reported to their immediate military commanders and, at the highest levels, to the Personnel Members Committee. All the major administrative decisions of the chaplains had to be approved by the PMC. There are fifteen volumes of PMC files in the National Archives relating to the affairs of the chaplains, and they are of particular value because of their quality. They appear to be fairly complete and often contain summaries or collations of other relevant documents.

The PMC soon devolved more mundane matters relating to the administration of the Chaplain Branch to the Joint Services Chaplaincy Committee. At its initial meeting the JSCC decided to break into two sub-committees in line with the organizational division of the branch. The JSCC (Protestant) was very active but the JSCC (Roman Catholic) was more private and left limited records. The minutes of the JSCC are cluttered with much extraneous material but do reflect the chaplains' point of view on particular issues. Following integration of the chaplains in 1957, the JSCC became the Chaplain General's Committee (later the Chaplain General's Advisory Committee) and the two sub-committees were replaced by the CGAC(P) and the CGAC(RC).

At the time of integration a single office was established in Ottawa as the headquarters of the integrated chaplains. With this change a considerable amount of house cleaning was done, and many records were lost. Some files were retained by the principal chaplains (especially those of the Navy tradition) in their own homes and these files, too, were subsequently and most unfortunately lost. For example, E.G.B. Foote, the chaplain of the fleet, had kept his files at home. Both he and his wife died shortly after he retired and his files and memorabilia were sold to an antique dealer and all trace has been lost. Indeed, until 1989 it was thought that virtually all records of the pre-integration period had been lost, but in fact many original documents had routinely found their way through the Directorate of History to the National Archives.

Ecclesiastical decisions concerning the chaplains were made outside the military bureaucracy. The chaplains were individually responsible to their own church courts on matters of moral and spiritual significance. Collectively, they were responsible to their parent churches through the particular representatives of their church. During the Second World War the war committees of the churches had appointed representatives to the Inter-Church Advisory Committee. Records of the war committees are to be found in the archives of the respective national churches; the records of the ICAC are in the Archives of the Chaplain General. After the war the churches decided that the oversight body for the Protestant chaplaincy should be a committee of the Canadian Council of Churches and in 1947 the Council's committee on the chaplaincy was created to "exercise a general oversight of religion in the forces" and to be the link between the chaplains and the churches and between the churches and the government. All major ecclesiastical decisions made by the chaplains needed the approval of this committee. The files of the Canadian Council of Churches were in process and thus inaccessible at the time of writing. However, the minutes of the Council of Churches Chaplaincy Committee are in the Archives of the Chaplain General.

Other documents of interest in the National Archives include a largely technical file on the construction of chapels and the chaplain files of the ministers of national defence. The value of the latter lies in the notations on documents that offer "the other point of view."

The chaplain files at the Directorate of History in the Department of National Defence are diverse. Some documents may not be of lasting significance aside from the personal interest of the Chaplain Branch itself: the returns of a 1938 survey of militia chaplains on changes to the chaplain's mess kit, for example. Other materials, such as the annual reports of wartime activities, are of considerable importance. Some information on chaplain activities is also found in the records of specific battles and operations.

The Archives of the Chaplain General contain a variety of materials: administrative files, books, manuals, diaries, and general memorabilia. The various unpublished manuscripts of use for this book are listed below. Perhaps the most significant documents for this book were the minutes of the Council of Churches Chaplaincy Committee and the minutes of the Command Chaplains Conferences which began in 1958. As well, these archives now include the taped interviews with retired and serving chaplains which were collected under the Chaplain General's Oral History Project.

The archives of the various churches which have clergy serving as chaplains vary considerably in both size and quality. The national archives of the major churches contain records of the war committees as well as the papers of some chaplains or members of the chaplaincy committees. The papers of the latter—who often had significant careers outside the military setting—seldom include records or even references to the chaplaincy. The national archives of the United Church of Canada hold an extensive collection of the papers of W.J. Gallagher, who was deeply involved with the Council of Churches Chaplaincy Committee for many years and wrote many important letters on behalf of the chaplains to the minister of defence and the prime minister. Yet if you go through these papers, you would think he had no more than a patriotic interest in the military.

The more valuable records for the postwar years are to be found in the regional archives of the churches. The archives of most dioceses of the Anglican Church of Canada possess correspondence files and some newspaper clippings on the clergy who have served in that diocese. Those in Victoria and Halifax offered interesting but limited material for this book. The most helpful and best organized of the diocesan archives is that of Ottawa. Files on Canon Hepburn, Bishop Clarke, and Bishop Wells provided valuable insight into the ecclesiastical jurisdiction issue. Material from London on Bishop Luxton reflected a positive attitude towards the military in contrast to material in Luxton files from other sources.

Local archives of the United Church of Canada are often limited to local church records, but some have yielded useful material. The Maritime Conference Archives in Halifax were of particular value, especially the recently acquired memorabilia of Dr. C.M. Nicholson. Indeed some of his correspondence from his time as moderator was discovered by this researcher in an old box in the basement of the Atlantic School of Theology where it had been placed when Nicholson retired as president of that institution. This cache included critical papers relating to issues raised as a result of his visit to servicemen in the Far East during the Korean crisis.

The current thrust of the chaplains' History Project is to track down and study in a systematic fashion the personal records and memorabilia of clergy who were chaplains.

ARCHIVAL SOURCES

Anglican Church Of Canada, General Synod Archives, Toronto
    Biographical files
    Files of Bishop Ordinary to the Canadian Forces

Anglican Church Of Canada, Diocese Of Nova Scotia, Archives, Halifax
    Biographical files
    The Portsmouth Cross file

Anglican Church of Canada, Diocese of Ottawa, Ottawa
    Biographical files
    H.H. Clarke papers
    C.G. Hepburn papers
    G.A. Wells papers

Anglican Church of Canada, Diocese of Victoria, Victoria
    G.A. Wells papers
    Anglican Church of Canada, Diocese of Huron, London ON
    H. Luxton papers

Archives of the Chaplain General (CGA), Canadian Forces Headquarters, Ottawa
    Command Chaplains Conferences, Minutes, 1958-
    Council of Churches Chaplaincy Committee, Minutes, 1947-
    Correspondence files
    Diaries and other memorabilia
    Manuals and other books
    Personnel files
    Tapes, Oral History Project

Canadian Baptist Archives, McMaster Divinity School, Hamilton ON
    Biographical files

Department of National Defence, Directorate of History (DHist), Ottawa
    Biographical files
    Chaplain files
    War diaries

National Archives of Canada (NAC)
    Manuscript Group (MG) 32, Minister of National Defence files, 1945-1963
    Brooke Claxton papers
    Douglas Harkness papers
    George R. Pearkes papers
    Record Group (RG) 24, Department of National Defence Chapels, technical files,
     boxes 5539-5540
    Joint Services Chaplaincy Committee, boxes 6581-6582
    Personnel Members Committee, boxes 7737-7738

Presbyterian Church in Canada, Archives, Toronto
    Biographical files

Public Archives of Nova Scotia
    Biographical files
    Chaplains files

Queen's University Archives (QUA)
    W. Gordon papers
    C.G. Power papers

United Church of Canada, Archives, Toronto
    Biographical files
    Gallagher papers

United Church of Canada, Maritime Conference Archives, Halifax
    Nicholson papers

SECONDARY SOURCES

Adams, Harold J. "In This Sign Conquer." Notes for an article on the chaplain's hat badge prepared for *Sentinel* magazine in 1981. Chaplain General's Archives, Ottawa.

Aseltine, M.E. "Sky-Pilots of the Royal Canadian Air Force." Unpublished thesis, bachelor of divinity, McMaster University, 1952. Copy in Chaplain General's Archives, Ottawa.

Baldwin, Warren. "Stayed Behind to Aid Injured after Dieppe." Toronto *Globe and Mail*, February 12, 1946.

Brodsky, G.W. Stephen. *God's Dodger*. Sidney BC: Elysium Publishing, 1993.

Brown, Brian. "Blessed Are the Peacemakers." *United Church Observer*, September 1987.

Buxton, W.W. "Out of Our Past." *Dialogue*, no. 1 (1987).

Byers, R.B. "Reorganization of the Canadian Armed Forces." Unpublished doctoral dissertation, Carleton University, 1970.

Card, B.Y. *Trends and Change in Canadian Society*. Toronto: Macmillan, 1968.

Carlson, Don. *R.C.A.F. Padre–With Spitfire Squadrons*. Red Deer AB: Skytone Graphics, n.d.

Castonguay, Jacques. *Unsung Mission*. Montreal: Institut de Pastorale, 1968. A history of the Roman Catholic chaplaincy in the RCAF during the Second World War.

"Chaplain's Handbook." Unpublished manuscript from about 1958, updated in part in 1977. Chaplain General's Archives, Ottawa.

Colling, J.M. "The Canadian Chaplain Service." *The Legionary*, December, 1946.

Cotton, C.A. "A Canadian Military Ethos." *Canadian Defence Quarterly*, December, 1982.

Cragg, Kenneth C. "Chaplain Who Won VC Describes His Mission to Nazi Prison Camps." Toronto *Globe and Mail*, February 12, 1946.

Crerar, Duff. *Padres in No Man's Land*. Kingston & Montreal: McGill-Queen's University Press 1995.

Crossley, Connie. "Minister Back from the Gulf." *Corner Brook Western Star*, January 22, 1991.

Cunningham, R. "Change Worketh Wonders." *Dialogue*, July 1976.

Daisley, J.C. *Bits, Pieces and Papers*. Taber AB: Taber Times, 1980.

Davidson, G.G. "Canadian Chaplain in Cyprus." *The Chaplain*, April 1968.

Davidson, J.A. "Padre's Patter." *Kilt and Sporran*, February-July 1953.

Davis, Eldon S. *An Awesome Silence*. Carp ON: Creative Bound, 1991.

Dialogue. Publication of the Chaplain Branch. On October 1, 1970, the first limited edition of a monthly newsletter was published by the Protestant chaplain general. Renamed *Dialogue* in September 1971 and occasionally included a detachable section "for chaplain eyes only" called *The Purple Net*. In March 1981 the magazine became a quarterly and took on a more professional appearance. In 1990 only three issues appeared because of financial constraints and in 1991 the quarterly became an annual. Complete runs of *Dialogue* are available at the National Library in Ottawa and in the Chaplain General's Archives.

Divine Service Book for the Armed Forces. Toronto: Ryerson, 1950.

Dunlop, Malcolm. "Canadian Soldiers Fulfil Christ's Work." *Halifax Chronicle-Herald*, July 18, 1994.

Dunn, James. "The Chaplains of the Royal Canadian Air Force." Unpublished thesis, bachelor of divinity, McMaster University, 1952.

Fallis, George. *A Padre's Pilgrimage*. Toronto: Ryerson, 1953.

Fowler, A.G. "The Growth of the Protestant Chaplain's Service in the Canadian Military 1945-1968: The Pursuit of Assumed Status." Unpublished master's thesis, Carleton University, 1990.

Gauvreau, Michael. "War, Culture and the Problem of Religious Certainty: Methodist and Presbyterian Church Colleges, 1914-1930." *Journal of the Canadian Church Historical Society*, 29 (April 1987): 11-31.

Gordon, Charles W. *Postscript to Adventure*. New York: Farrar and Rinehart, 1938.

——. The Sky Pilot in No Man's Land. New York: G.H. Doran, 1919.

Grant, John Webster. *The Church in the Canadian Era*. Toronto: Welch Publishing, 1972.

The Happy Warrior: In Memory of the Life and Work of Group Captain R.M. Frayne, C.D., D.D. Edited by a group of his associates. Toronto: United Church Publishing House, 1953.

Hickey, R.M. *The Scarlet Dawn*. Campbellton NB: Tribune Press, 1949.

Honeywell, R.J. *Chaplains of the United States Army*. Washington DC: Department of the Army 1959.

Johnston, M.C., and Gordon H. Porter. "Sky Pilots in Blue: A Presentation of the Organization and Work of the Protestant Chaplaincy Service of the Royal Canadian Air Force, 1939-1945." Unpublished manuscript, Chaplain General's Archives, Ottawa, no date.

Jones, Lyndon. "Dieppe." *Kingston Whig-Standard*, June 15, 1984.

Kennedy, Brian. "Leader's Prayers Guarded CF-18 Pilots." *Victoria Times-Colonist*, March 3, 1991.

Kronenberg, Vernon J. *All Together Now: The Organization of the Department of National Defence in Canada 1964-1972*. Toronto: Canadian Institute of International Affairs, 1973.

Lockhart, Bob. "Conforms with What Christ Preached." *Fredericton Daily Gleaner*, September 12, 1994.

Love, Fred. "After the 2nd World War." *Dialogue*, no. 2 (1989).

——. "Out of Our Past." *Dialogue*, no. 1 (1987).

MacCara, C.E. *Stewardship Projects of the Canadian Forces Chapels (P), 1973*. Chaplain General's Archives, Ottawa.

MacKinnon, Clarence. *The Life of Principal Oliver*. Toronto: Ryerson, 1937.

——. *Reminiscences*. Toronto: Ryerson, 1938.

Marshall, David B. "Methodism Embattled: A Reconsideration of the Methodist Church and World War I." *Canadian Historical Review*, 66 (March 1985): 48-64.

——. "Secularization in the Church." Unpublished doctoral dissertation, University of Toronto, 1986.

"Measuring Ministries, Resources for Evaluation." *The Christian Ministry* 4 (no. 1, 1973).

Mersereau, Charles J. *A Navy Chaplain Speaks to the Fleet*. Ottawa: Queen's Printer, 1968.

Morley, P.C. "Iran-Iraq: Operation Vagabond." *Dialogue*, no. 3 (1989).

Murdoch, B.J. *The Red Vineyard*. Toronto: Hunter Rose, 1928.

Nickerson, C. "The Chaplain General [R.G.C. Cunningham]." *Dialogue*, July 1976.

Ogle, Robert. *The Faculties of Canadian Military Chaplains*. Ottawa: Queen's Printer, 1956.

Park, Baxter D. "Operation Friction: A Chaplain's View of Canada's Naval Response." *Military Chaplain's Review*, summer 1991.

Pennington, Chester A. "The Ministry of Our Chaplains." *The Chaplain*, March/April 1971.

"People." *United Church Observer*, September 1994.

Presthus, Robert. *Elite Accommodation in Canadian Politics*. Toronto: Macmillan, 1973.

Protestant Chaplain's Manual, R.C.N. Edited by Ivan R. Edwards. Ottawa: Department of Naval Service, 1951.

Rand, John L. "The Development of the Army Chaplain in Great Britain." *The Chaplain*, June 1968.

———. "The Development of the Military Chaplain in Great Britain." *The Chaplain*, June 1968.

———. "The Origin of the Military Chaplain." *The Chaplain*, April 1968.

Rand, L.R. "The Chaplain in the 27th Brigade." *Canadian Army Journal*, January 1954,52-6.

Ross, Marjorie. "CCC Representatives Visit Cyprus and Lebanon as Gulf War Breaks Out." *Entre-Nous*, 2 (March 1991).

Rowland, Barry D. *The Padre*. Scarborough ON: Consolidated Amethyst Communications, 1982.

Roy, Allan. "#1282: The Gallant Padre." *Military Collectors Club of Canada Journal*, December 1982.

Scott, F.G. *The Great War as I Saw It*. Toronto: F.D. Goodchild, 1922.

Shields, Gordon. "The Life of a Padre in Korea." *Dialogue*, no. 2 (1988).

Smith, Waldo E.L. *The Navy Chaplain and His Parish*. Ottawa: Queen's Printer, 1967.

———. *The Navy Chaplain in Days of Sail*. Toronto: Ryerson, 1961.

———. *What Time the Tempest*. Toronto: Ryerson, 1953.

Smythe, Sir John. *In This Sign Conquer*. London: A.R. Mowbray, 1968.

Stevens, Walter. *In This Sign*. Toronto: Ryerson, 1948.

Swan, Canon Minto. *Props, Bars and Pulpits; Or, Minto's Minutes*. Kingston ON: Hanson and Edgar, 1965.

Sword, Pam. "HMCS *Protecteur* Floating Parish for Gulf-Bound Anglican Minister." *Halifax Chronicle-Herald*, August 26, 1990.

Thornton, Francis B. *Sea of Glory*. New York: Prentice-Hall, 1953.

Wells, George Anderson. *The Fighting Bishop*. Toronto: Carwell House, 1971.

Index

310